Living Standards in Southeast Asia

Transforming Asia

Asia is often viewed through a fog of superlatives: the most populous countries, lowest fertility rates, fastest growing economies, greatest number of billionaires, most avid consumers, and greatest threat to the world's environment. This recounting of superlatives obscures Asia's sheer diversity, uneven experience, and mixed inheritance.

Amsterdam University Press's Transforming Asia series publishes books that explore, describe, interpret, understand and, where appropriate, problematize and critique contemporary processes of transformation and their outcomes. The core aim of the series is to finesse 'Asia', both as a geographical category and to ask what Asia's 'rise' means globally and regionally, from conceptual models to policy lessons.

Living Standards in Southeast Asia

Changes over the Long Twentieth Century, 1900-2015

Anne Booth

Amsterdam University Press

Cover illustration: Women working on the rice fields. Java, 1946. Photo collection Van de Poll

Cover design: Coördesign, Leiden
Lay-out: Crius Group, Hulshout

ISBN	978 94 6372 981 9
e-ISBN	978 90 4855 023 4
DOI	10.5117/9789463729819
NUR	740

Printed and bound by CPI Group (UK) Ltd, Croydon, CR0 4YY

Table of Contents

Preface

This book has resulted from many years of thinking and writing about issues relating to poverty and inequality in Southeast Asia. I am very grateful to the many economists and statisticians, both in the region and elsewhere, who have shared with me their research findings, as well as their doubts and frustrations, over the years. The lengthy bibliography testifies to the extent of the work which has been carried out since the 1960s, and which is ongoing across Southeast Asia. In addition, I have benefited from my own and other work on the history of Southeast Asia in the last phase of European and American colonialism, and the on the often difficult transition to independence across what are now ten independent nations. I have always felt that an understanding of the legacies from the decades from 1900 to 1960 is essential if we are to grasp the complexities of more recent economic developments across Southeast Asia. Nowhere is this more true than when we address the issues tackled in this book.

I am especially grateful to the Lee Kong Chian Foundation, which granted me a fellowship to visit the Walter H. Shorenstein Asia-Pacific Research Center at Stanford University in 2015, and the National University of Singapore in 2016. In Singapore I was able to use the libraries of both the National University of Singapore and the Institute of Southeast Asian Studies-Yusof Ishak Institute. In London I have benefited greatly from access to the collections of both the School of Oriental and African Studies and the London School of Economics. I have also benefited from interaction with colleagues in London and elsewhere who work on issues relating to poverty and inequality in other parts of Asia, as well as in the Middle East and Africa. Their work has helped me to understand both the similarities and the differences between Southeast Asia and other parts of the world.

I am also grateful to two referees from Amsterdam University Press whose comments persuaded me to undertake a revision of the manuscript, which I hope has improved the final version. Lastly, thanks to Vicki Blud for her careful copy-editing.

Anne Booth
London, April 2019

List of Tables

1 Assessing Changes in Living Standards in Southeast Asia in the Twentieth and Early Twenty-first Centuries

What Indicators Should We Look At?

Poverty and Development Indicators in Southeast Asia: An Overview

This book studies changing living standards in the ten Southeast Asian countries which are now members of the Association of Southeast Asian Nations (ASEAN), from the early years of the twentieth century to the early years of the twenty-first century. We know that in the second decade of the new millennium, these ten nations differed widely in terms of per capita gross domestic product (GDP). There was also considerable variation between them in other widely used development indicators such as adult literacy and life expectancy (Table 1.1). The Human Development Index (HDI), computed by the United Nations, is a weighted average of per capita GDP, life expectancy, adult literacy and years of schooling. This index ranked Singapore fifth in the world in 2015, while at the other end of the scale, Myanmar was ranked 145 (Table 1.1). In spite of these differences, most countries in Southeast Asia have experienced some improvement in their HDI score since the 1980s, and several have improved their ranking. All now fall into what is termed the medium human development group, or higher.

But indicators such as per capita GDP, and composite indicators such as the Human Development Index are based on averages, and they tell us little about the distributional impact of economic growth. They cannot by themselves answer what is, for many students of human development, a crucial question: For any given rate of economic growth, or any given improvement in average life expectancy or educational attainment, who has benefited the most? Who has benefited the least? In order to answer these questions, we need evidence on the distribution of incomes and household expenditures. We also need evidence on the distribution of other indicators such as life expectancy and educational attainment by income or expenditure group, as well as by region and gender, and by social class. By the early twenty-first century, most ASEAN countries were collecting and publishing household survey data which allowed the calculation of a

Table 1.1:   GDP and other social indicators: Selected Asian countries

Country	HDI rank	Life expectancy		MYS*	GNI per capita** ($PPP 2015)
	2015	1970/75	2015	2015	
ASEAN-10					
Singapore	5	69.5	83.2	11.6	78,162
Brunei	30	68.3	79.0	9.0	72,843
Malaysia	59	63.0	74.9	10.1	24,620
Thailand	87	61.0	74.6	7.9	14,519
Indonesia	113	49.2	69.1	7.9	10,053
Vietnam	115	50.3	75.9	8.0	5,335
Philippines	116	58.1	68.3	9.3	8,395
Lao PDR	138	40.4	66.6	5.2	5,049
Cambodia	143	40.3	68.8	4.7	3,095
Myanmar	145	49.3	66.1	4.7	4,943
Other Asia					
Hong Kong	12	72.0	84.2	11.6	54,265
Japan	17	73.3	83.7	12.5	37.268
Korea (Rep)	18	62.6	82.1	12.5	34,541
China	90	63.2	76.0	7.6	13,455
India	131	50.3	68.3	6.3	5,663

* Mean years of schooling for the population over 15 years.
** PPP data from the 2011 revisions; see World Bank (2014a).
Note: 188 countries are ranked according to a composite index; countries ranked from 52 to 105 are considered 'high human development' and those ranked from 107 to 147 are considered 'medium human development'. In the ASEAN group, no country is in the low human development group.
Source: 2015 rankings from UNDP (2016); Life expectancies: UNDP (2003: 262-5); UNDP (2016); MYS: UNDP (2016). Per capita GDP in current international dollars: UNDP (2016).

range of poverty and distributional indicators. National and regional poverty lines were estimated and used to calculate the proportion of the population below these lines, a measure usually referred to as the headcount measure of poverty. The estimates of the headcount measure prepared by national governments for early twenty-first centuries also showed, as would be expected, wide variation.

It was not always the case that the poorest countries in the region in terms of per capita GDP had the highest proportion of the population in poverty, using the poverty lines computed by their governments. In the Philippines, the official figures showed that 25 per cent of the population was poor in 2012, compared with 20.4 per cent in Cambodia in 2014, although per capita GDP was over twice as high in the Philippines (Tables 1.1 and 1.2). In Thailand, the government estimated that 12.6 per cent of the population was below the official poverty line in 2012, which was higher than in Indonesia and Vietnam, although per capita GDP was considerably higher in Thailand than in either Indonesia or Vietnam. What explains these differences? It appeared that different countries across Southeast Asia were using different methods to estimate their national poverty lines, with the result that the poverty line was set higher relative to GDP in Thailand than in Indonesia or Vietnam. In addition, it was possible that the distribution of income was more skewed in Thailand and the Philippines than in some other parts of Southeast Asia, so that there were more people in the very poor segments of the population, and fewer in the middle.

Table 1.2:   **Estimates of the headcount measure of poverty using national and international poverty lines, 2010 and 2012**

Country	National poverty lines		International poverty lines	
	2010	2012	A	B
Malaysia	3.8 (2009)	1.7	0.4	2.3 (2009)
Thailand	16.4	12.6	1.1	3.5 (2010)
Indonesia	13.3	12.0	28.0	43.3 (2011)
Philippines	26.3 (2009)	25.2	26.9	41.7 (2012)
Vietnam	14.2	11.1	22.4	12.5 (2012)
Laos	33.9	26.0	38.1	62.0 (2012)
Cambodia	21.1	18.9	25.4	41.3 (2011)

Note: International poverty lines: A refers to the poverty line of $1.51 per day, converted using PPP-adjusted exchange rates. This was used by the Asian Development Bank in their estimates for 2010 (Asian Development Bank 2014c: 11). B refers to the poverty line of $2 per day, converted using PPP-adjusted exchange rates, as reported in Asian Development Bank (2015: 211). Countries are ranked according to actual individual consumption expenditures per capita.
Sources: National poverty lines: Thailand: National Statistical Office (2015), Table 8.12; Indonesia: Central Board of Statistics (2015b: 175); Philippines: Philippine Statistics Authority (2016); Vietnam: General Statistics Office (2013: 739): 9. National headcount measures for Laos and Malaysia are taken from Asian Development Bank (2014a). Malaysian figures refer to 2009 and 2012; for Cambodia they are taken from Asian Development Bank (2014b: 4).

Because national poverty lines often reflect the economic, social and political concerns of national governments and are not comparable across countries, or even over time in the same country, efforts have been made by international agencies to establish 'international poverty lines' which are supposedly more comparable, both across national boundaries, and over time. The best known in recent decades are the dollar-based poverty lines, which have been published by the World Bank from the 1990s onwards, and are very widely quoted in the literature. These are estimated simply by converting a poverty line set in American dollars into the currency of the particular country and then adjusting the resulting number for differences in the purchasing power of the national currency, relative to the American dollar. The World Bank used the 'dollar a day' line for some years; this was raised to $1.25, and more recently to $1.90. Higher poverty thresholds of $2, raised to $3.10, have also been used. These dollar-denominated poverty lines are converted into national currencies using the data on the purchasing power of the national currency relative to the dollar. These 'PPP adjustments' are derived from the International Comparison Project (ICP), carried out by the World Bank (Ravallion, Chen and Sangraula 2009: 168). The ICP estimates of purchasing power parities have in turn been subject to several revisions, the most recent in 2011. These revisions have in turn led to significant changes in the headcount measure of poverty in many Asian countries.

In the Asian context, the Asian Development Bank (ADB) has also carried out estimates of poverty levels which have produced rather different results from those of the World Bank. An important study published in 2008 used a different methodology for estimating the purchasing power of individual currencies, which relied on data on the prices paid by the poor. These were used to construct poverty lines and headcount measures of poverty (Asian Development Bank 2008). But this study was not repeated, and the estimates have not been updated. More recently, the ADB put forward a poverty line of $1.51, again converted into local currencies using exchange rates adjusted for differences in the purchasing power of currencies but using the World Bank PPP data. The estimates of the headcount measure of poverty using national poverty lines were often lower than the ADB results using the $1.51 poverty line (Table 1.2). This was especially the case for Laos, Indonesia and Vietnam. But in Thailand and Malaysia, the ADB estimate was much lower. The results for Indonesia were especially striking; according to the ADB estimates, 28 per cent of the population in 2010 was below the $1.51 poverty line, which was a higher figure than in the Philippines, Cambodia, or Vietnam in spite of the fact that per capita GDP in Indonesia was higher than in these three countries, at least according to the PPP data. Do these disparities reflect the fact that the cost of basic needs, especially foodgrains, was much higher in Indonesia than in these other countries? It is also possible that household expenditures were a much lower proportion of total GDP, or that the distribution of consumption expenditures were more skewed towards richer groups in Indonesia than elsewhere. Or do the data reflect problems in the household surveys on which the estimates were based? These questions are obviously important and will be taken up again in subsequent chapters.

Conceptual and Measurement Issues

Before embarking on an analysis of trends in poverty and living standards over time in Southeast Asia, it is necessary to say something more about both conceptual and measurement problems, which have been extensively discussed in the literature. In recent years there has been much debate over how economic progress should be measured, and especially how changes in the standard of living should be captured in quantitative terms. It has already been noted that in recent years, development banks have published estimates of poverty based on income and expenditure data derived from household surveys. But other studies have cautioned against too much reliance on income-based measures. In a number of influential writings, Sen argued against using income data as the principal way of estimating changes in poverty. He put forward the alternative concept of capabilities. His argument can be summarized as follows (Sen 1999: 87-88; italics in the original):

1. Poverty can be sensibly identified in terms of capability deprivation; the approach concentrates on deprivations that are *intrinsically* important (unlike low income, which is only *instrumentally* significant).
2. There are influences on capability deprivation – and thus on real poverty – *other* than lowness of income (income is not the only instrument in generating capabilities).
3. The instrumental relation between low income and low capability is *variable* between different communities and even between different families and different individuals (the impact of income on capabilities is contingent and conditional).

Sen's work was very influential in the construction of the Human Development Index (HDI), the results of which for countries in Asia were reported in Table 1.1. The HDI has been used since the 1990s, both internationally and also in regional studies in a number of countries in Southeast Asia. More recently it has been argued that it should be possible to create new, and much broader composite indicators which include more non-monetary data. Ranis, Stewart and Samman (2006) suggested new composite indicators which include up to 40 quantitative measure on mental well-being, gender empowerment, political freedom, social relations, community well-being, inequality, work and leisure conditions, economic stability, political security and environmental conditions. Many of these indicators have been incorporated in the Multidimensional Poverty Index, which is discussed

further below. By incorporating a broader range of non-monetary indictors.
it is argued that more satisfactory ranking of countries in terms of human
development can be achieved. Critics of the HDI point out that the non-
monetary components of the index (life expectancy, literacy, educational
attainment) are highly correlated with per capita gross domestic product
(GDP), and so the composite index produces a ranking of countries at a
point in time which is little different from that which would be obtained
by using per capita GDP alone. This may be true, although the correlation,
while high, is not perfect.[1] One of the advantages of the HDI is that it does
make clear which countries, and regions within countries, have done well
in terms of the non-monetary indicators in spite of relatively low incomes,
and which have done badly in spite of relatively high incomes.[2]

Another argument in support of composite indicators such as the HDI is
that they tend to give a different, and indeed a more optimistic picture of
human progress over time than national income figures alone. As is well
known, the historical national income figures compiled by Maddison (2003,
2007) show growing disparities between countries over the nineteenth and
twentieth centuries, a trend which Pritchett (1997) referred to as 'divergence
big time'. But because there has been a rapid decline in mortality and
considerable improvements in access to education in almost all parts of
the world over the last 50 years, especially in Asia and Africa, composite
indicators such as the HDI show a greater degree of catch-up than do the
national income data (Crafts 2002: 404). A more recent survey of well-being
indicators confirms the finding that inequality in health and education
indicators declined over the the twentieth century, and argues that this
'challenges the idea that per capita income provides a good predictor of
welfare trends' (Escosura 2018: 24).

A further argument in support of composite indicators as a measure
of change over time is that historical national income series can, when
extrapolated across decades and even across centuries, give rather misleading
results. Inevitably measurement errors are cumulated over time, and the
imposition of modern price structures on historical economies, which were
producing very different goods and services from contemporary ones, is

1   Ranis, Stewart and Samman (2006) have argued that many of the indicators they suggest
are not highly correlated with per capita GDP.
2   Although it is often thought that composite indicators are a relatively recent innovation,
some economists were estimating them as early as the 1950s. Bennett (1951) ranked 31 countries
according to a range of non-monetary indicators in 1934-1938. He included calorie consumption,
infant mortality, doctors per capita, household energy consumption, transport facilities and
school attendance. His results will be discussed in more detail in Chapter 2.

highly problematic (Allen, Bengtsson and Dribe 2005: 9). Indeed, even over relatively short periods of two or three decades, indicators of growth of GDP can be misleading. Both the World Bank and other development agencies have published very high estimates of Chinese economic growth since the reforms of the late 1970s and early 1980s. And yet in the early twenty-first century, per capita GDP in China was lower than in Malaysia, and lower than Thailand if PPP data are used. If the growth estimates are broadly correct, China must have had a very low per capita GDP in the 1970s, not just relative to Thailand and Malaysia but also relative to India. As Sen (1987: 34) pointed out, that is at odds with other evidence on Chinese GDP in the pre-reform era.

It can of course be argued that the non-monetary indicators of capabilities favoured by Sen, such as life expectancy, infant and child mortality rates, literacy and educational enrolments are also subject to measurement error, and in many parts of the world cannot easily be extrapolated backwards over time. Usually they are prepared by national statistical offices, which in turn rely on population censuses, and a range of household surveys, or registration of births and deaths. All these estimates contain inaccuracies, and in some cases it is possible that governments have put pressure on statistical agencies to manipulate the figures. Furthermore, like the GDP data, they refer only to national averages and often disguise very substantial variations by region, gender and social class. This point has been made by Therborn (2013: 48-49), who argued that inequalities in health-related indicators by region and social class are often considerable even in the European welfare states, let alone other parts of the world. It is important for countries to prepare more disaggregated indicators of infant mortality or literacy broken down according to region, gender, income class or ethnic group. Such data have become more abundant for many parts of Southeast Asia over the past three decades, and are now being analysed by several scholars. Their results are discussed in Chapter 7.

The poverty estimates shown in Table 1.2 are prepared not from national income statistics but from household income and expenditure surveys which by the 1990s were being conducted in all the ASEAN countries with varying degrees of regularity. These estimates do try to capture distributional aspects of changes in household income and expenditure over time. But the surveys from which poverty measures are derived have been the target of considerable critical scrutiny, in Southeast Asia as in other parts of the world, which are examined further below. However reliable the figures might be, it is difficult to estimate similar indicators for most parts of the region further back than the late 1960s. Only the Philippines conducted national household income and expenditure surveys in the 1950s, and the few surveys which were carried out before 1940 by colonial statistical authorities used small samples, and were often restricted to particular localities. To explore trends in poverty and indeed other measures of living standards during the colonial era, we have to use other, perhaps less reliable, indicators.[3]

If historical national income series are unreliable guides to changing living standards, and poverty estimates can only be estimated for the past four or five decades in many parts of the world, what other indicators are available? One indicator which has been widely used in a number of studies is the real wage. It has been argued that the real wage is a 'distributionally sensitive' indicator in that it measures the purchasing power of incomes accruing to the less well-off (Allen, Bengtsson and Dribe 2005: 9). To what extent is this really the case, especially in pre-industrial economies? The next section examines the problems associated with using real wage data to monitor living standards in Britain in the nineteenth century, and the lessons which the British debate offers more recent studies.

Another important source is demographic evidence. As we have seen, life expectancy at birth is one component of the HDI, and together with infant and child mortality, this indicator has been widely used in comparative studies of living standards across regions and countries. But such indicators can only be estimated with any degree of accuracy if reasonably comprehensive population census or survey data are available, or if accurate registration procedures are in place for births and deaths. This has not been the case everywhere in Southeast Asia over the twentieth century. Similar problems emerge with data on literacy and educational attainment. Some recent researchers who advocate including a measure of educational attainment in a composite indicator of human development base their arguments not just on efficiency or 'human capital' grounds. They also point out that education endows people with a greatly enhanced capacity to participate in, and enjoy, leisure, cultural and community activities as well as making them more productive workers (Sen 1999: 128-129). But as with demographic data, figures on literacy and school attendance are only available from official records on school attendance, or from censuses and surveys. These are not always very reliable, even for recent decades.

It has also been argued that the proportion of total consumption expenditures devoted to basic commodities with low-income elasticities of demand, such as foodgrains or cotton cloth, are also good indicators of living

---

3   Leigh and Van der Eng (2009) used income tax data to estimate trends in inequality in Indonesia in both the colonial and postcolonial eras, paying particular attention to the income share accruing to the top 1 and 5 per cent of the population.

standards of the poorer classes of society in many societies. This reasoning is based on Engel's law, originally put forward in the mid-nineteenth century on the basis of German consumption data, although analysis of data from several European and Asian countries in the 1930s showed that a fall in the proportion of consumption expenditures devoted to food only occurs at quite high levels of household expenditure (Zimmerman 1936: 99-107). When people are struggling to survive at a very basic level of subsistence, it is likely that a large part of any increment in income will be spent on more food, clothing and shelter.[4] Once a certain threshold level of income is reached, increments in income are more likely to be spent on better quality food and clothing, and semi-luxuries such as more household furniture and utensils, consumer durables, or improvements to housing. Thus an increase in per capita availability of basic foodgrains is likely to indicate a fairly broad-based improvement in income among the lower groups in the overall distribution, while a fall may signal the onset of serious stress. On the other hand, some economists also consider a decline in the proportion of total household income spent on food as a sign of improvement in living standards, especially if it is sustained over long periods of time.

It is also important to bear in mind that in many parts of the world severe distress has been caused to large numbers of people by sudden increases in prices, especially of basic foods. Sen's work on famines has demonstrated that it is possible to have a rapid, indeed catastrophic, increase in mortality without there being any evidence of a decline in per capita food availability for the country or region as a whole. This was the case in Bengal in 1943, and could have also been the case in parts of Southeast Asia, both in the 1940s and in earlier times. During the Japanese occupation, inflation accelerated in many parts of Southeast Asia with serious consequences for food consumption and mortality, especially in poorer regions, and among poorer households. In more recent times, there is evidence from Southeast Asia that sharp increases in food prices have caused an increase in the headcount measure of poverty.[5]

---

4   Shammas (1983) has argued that Engel's law, and the theory that has been built up around it, was developed at a time when the proportion of household income devoted to food was falling in Europe and elsewhere. She pointed out that it does not hold for all time periods; her time series for English households suggests little change until well into the twentieth century.

5   Bengtsson (2004: 49) produced a table based on his research on villages in southern Sweden in the nineteenth century; he argued that high food prices affect different socio-economic groups in very different ways. The worst affected were those who depend on wages paid in cash for part or all of their income; those most likely to benefit were freeholders who paid a fixed money tax and sold part of their output.

Given both the problems of defining living standards, and those of measuring changes over time, I would argue that any study must draw on a range of indicators, both monetary and non-monetary. In the context of Southeast Asia in the twentieth century, there is a wide range of material to draw on, although inevitably both the quantity and the quality diminishes in the early part of the century compared with the decades from 1970 to 2000 and beyond. If it can be demonstrated that a particular country or region has experienced falling infant mortality rates, improved school attendance, and increased consumption of basic foodstuffs, sustained over a period of years, or decades, can we say that living standards have improved, even if there is little evidence of growing per capita GDP, or increases in real wages? The answer is probably yes, although the case for an improvement in living standards would be stronger if these indicators were supplemented with evidence that real GDP and per capita consumption expenditures had increased, that inequality had not worsened, and that the headcount measure of poverty had also declined. Such evidence can only be obtained from national income statistics and household expenditure surveys, although in Southeast Asia, as in other parts of the world, such data have been subject to considerable critical scrutiny over the years.

Standard of Living Debates in Economic History: The British Debate

Anyone embarking on a study of changing living standards in any part of the world over the last century would do well to study some of the debates among economic historians about the consequences of accelerated economic growth and structural change on living standards in other parts of the world economy. The most famous, and longest running, of these debates concerns the impact of the Industrial Revolution on living standards in Britain over the nineteenth century. Controversies about the impact of economic change in Britain on living standards extend well back into the nineteenth century, but the modern debate was started by exchanges between Hobsbawm and Hartwell in the 1950s and 1960s. Both these authors re-stated their views in Taylor (1975). Subsequently important contributions have been made by Lindert and Williamson (1983), Crafts (1997), Mokyr (1988), Huck (1995), Szreter and Mooney (1998) and Feinstein (1998). In essence, the empirical part of the debate has revolved around which indicators are the most appropriate for estimating changes in the standard of living in an industrializing society, and how these indicators can best be estimated. In addition to the empirical discussion there was also some discussion about the theoretical underpinnings, especially of the pessimist case that there was in fact little improvement until the second part of the nineteenth century. It is useful to evaluate both these strands separately.

As far as the empirical part of the debate was concerned, the evidence reviewed dealt specifically 'with real incomes or consumption, such as information about wage-rates, earnings, prices, household expenditure, actual consumption and other relevant data such as unemployment etc.' (Hobsbawm 1975: 179). Inevitably some of these data were easier to obtain than others, but most participants in the debate did try to review more than one indicator. The 'super-optimist' case put forward by Lindert and Williamson (1983) was based on a new series for the real wages of adult males which, according to the authors, nearly doubled between 1820 and 1850. It was argued that this implied substantial gains in real household incomes. Critics such as Mokyr (1988) pointed out that it was difficult to reconcile this result with evidence that per capita consumption of commodities such as sugar, tea and tobacco grew little over these decades. In his review of the controversy, Feinstein (1998) produced new estimates of nominal full-employment earnings, and also a new deflator. His results showed only a 'very moderate rate of improvement' in real earnings adjusted for changes in employment (Feinstein 1998: 642).

Other participants in the debate have looked at demographic evidence, in addition to that on incomes and expenditures. Huck (1995: 546) found that 'the biological evidence of life expectancy and average height provide evidence of stagnation in living standards after 1820, although they show improvement earlier'.[6] Szreter and Mooney (1998: 110) found the super-optimist case difficult to reconcile with the 'serious deterioration in the standard of living of the growing proportion of the population recruited into the urban industrial workforce'. This deterioration, according to their analysis, was reflected in low and in some cases declining life expectancies in most industrial cities. According to their estimates, while the average life expectancy for England and Wales was 41 in the 1850s, it was only 32 in Manchester and 31 in Liverpool. The low life expectancy figures in the large industrial cities reflected the very unhealthy conditions under which most people lived and worked, compared with smaller towns and rural areas; these conditions persisted until the end of the nineteenth century,

6   Huck (1995: 536-537) used parish records to support his argument that levels of infant mortality were higher in cities than in rural districts. He suggested that infant feeding practices were often better in rural areas, in part because women worked less outside the home.

and beyond. To the extent that the populations of large cities were growing faster than those in more healthy rural and small town environments, it could be argued that living standards for many were declining.

Other studies using demographic and educational data have not confirmed the pessimists' case. Crafts found a considerable improvement in the Human Development Index for Britain from 1760 through to 1850, due to increases in per capita GDP, life expectancies, literacy and years of schooling. Admittedly, there was little improvement in life expectancy after 1820, but on balance he argued that the HDI estimates were consistent with 'a fairly optimistic assessment of aggregate trends in well-being during the industrial revolution' (Crafts 1997: 625). Indeed, the main lesson from the long-running British debate would seem to be that different indicators produce different results. Certainly it is rash to draw strong conclusions on the basis of one indicator alone.

There has also been controversy about reliance on wage rates. Critics have argued that estimating trends in annual real incomes on the basis of daily or weekly wage rates is fraught with problems, as data on hours worked per year tend to be scarce or unreliable, even for industrial workers, let alone those in less stable employment in agriculture, construction, trade and transport (Feinstein 1998: 649). Simply multiplying daily or weekly wage rates by some arbitrary number produces unreliable results about annual household incomes. In addition, wage and earnings trends can differ markedly by region, as can prices. Much care needs to be taken in estimating deflators for wage earnings, especially where consumption patterns may be changing over time because of changing relative prices, or changing tastes.

A further criticism of studies which rely largely or solely on wage rates has been made by Horrell and Humphries. They compared trends in male wage rates with trends in household incomes and found that in the first part of the nineteenth century, family incomes grew less rapidly and were subject to more fluctuations than male wage rates, so 'welfare gains imputed from the latter may overstate actual improvements' (Horrell and Humphries 1992: 872). They also found that the family income data showed that industrialization brought with it greater inequality than was shown just by wage series alone. Their evidence indicated that in periods when nominal wages for males fell, such as the 1840s, the earnings of women and children also fell, and their ability to contribute to family incomes never recovered. In a further study, these authors also found that from the mid-nineteenth century onwards, participation rates and relative earnings for women in many parts of England tended to decline, leading to the rise of the male breadwinner family (Horrell and Humphries 1995).

Recent work on the impact of industrialization on household budgets has confirmed the argument advanced by Thompson (1968: 347) that the 'controversy as to living standards during the Industrial Revolution has perhaps been of most value when it has passed from the somewhat unreal pursuit of the wage-rates of hypothetical average workers and directed attention to articles of consumption: food, clothing, homes: and beyond these, health and mortality'. This advice should be borne in mind when we turn to other debates on differences in historical living standards across countries and continents.

The Debate over the Great Divergence

Over the past decade there has been much discussion among economic historians as to when, and why, the 'great divergence' between 'the West and the rest' occurred. As with the debate on living standards in nineteenth-century Britain, an assortment of indicators have been used by participants in this debate, although several studies have relied heavily on wage evidence. One of the main participants in this debate has compared indicators of living standards between China and Europe, and argued that there is 'little reason to think that most Europeans – even northwestern Europeans – were uniquely well-off, even as late as 1750' (Pomeranz 2000: 42). He bases this assertion mainly on calorie consumption and demographic indictors. Elsewhere he has argued that in the lower Yangtze Delta calorie consumption could have been as high as 2,400 per adult equivalent per day (Pomeranz 2005: 24). This is lower than estimates for Sweden during the eighteenth century and roughly comparable with estimates for England. It is certainly higher than the estimates for France by Toutain in the nineteenth century, and higher than estimates for parts of Italy, Germany and Belgium (Das Gupta 1979: 37). Pomeranz (2005: 25) has also suggested that the supply of foodgrains in the Yangtze Delta was relatively stable, although this might not have been the case in other parts of China.

Other scholars have relied more on real wage data to compare trends in living standards across countries and continents. This 'real wage revivialism', to use Maddison's (2005: 24) not entirely complimentary term, is due mainly to the increasing scholarly awareness of data on both wages and prices for many parts of Europe, the Mediterranean lands and also parts of Asia, not just for the twentieth century but for earlier periods as well. Several researchers have used their results to support often quite strong claims about trends in output and living standards in, for example, Europe and parts of Asia prior to the nineteenth century (e.g. Parthasarathi 1998; Allen 2005; Allen et al., 2005).[7] Williamson (1998, 2000) has used a large data set to answer a broad set of questions regarding the emergence of disparities in income and living standards within Asia in the years from 1870 to 1940. Ozmucur and Pamuk (2002) have used their evidence on wages in various cities in the Ottoman Empire to make comparisons in living standards not just within the Ottoman economy but also between it and the economies of other parts of Europe. De Zwart and Van Zanden (2015) estimated a series on real wages from 1680 to 1914 for urban free workers in Java, which they used to compare with wage trends in other parts of Asia and Europe. They found that over the eighteenth century, real wages of 'free coolies' in urban Java were high in comparison with Bengal and Beijing and even cities such as Leipzig, although over the nineteenth century they declined.

While this work is certainly producing interesting and provocative results, it sometimes appears to rest on rather fragile foundations. Several key issues relating to the reliability of the data, and the extent to which meaningful comparisons can be made across countries and continents over long periods of time, are either not addressed at all by many authors or only in an ad hoc fashion. Some authors using wage data make no attempt to examine the underlying dynamics of the labour markets from which the wage data are extracted. There seems to be an assumption that markets for various types of labour operate in accordance with the simple supply-and-demand model, that they clear quickly and efficiently and that wages equal the marginal product of the workers participating in that particular labour market. It is also assumed that workers have good information about the availability of jobs, and are free to move from their home regions to where wages are higher, or where more jobs are available. Problems such as nominal wage rigidity in the face of severe price shocks, or ethnic and regional segmentation of labour markets, are often ignored. So are issues relating to the role of markets for wage labour in the wider economy. The valuable insights of Horrell and Humphries on the divergence between trends in male wage rates and household expenditures are also often ignored.

In addition, many studies of living standards outside Europe have ignored, or underestimated the role of women in household production. Pomeranz (2000: 98-106; 2003: 132-141) discussed the role of women in household

---

7   A more cautious analysis of wage data in England, India and China is given in Broadberry and Gupta (2006). They conclude that the most prosperous parts of Asia between 1500 and 1800 look similar to the stagnating southern, central and eastern parts of Europe, rather than the developing northwestern parts.

production in China. He argued that although Chinese women were important in home production of textiles, they rarely organized or marketed their production by themselves, but were usually supervised by husbands or mothers-in-law. Most were expected to stay at home; there were no markets for the labour of single women as there were for men. This contrasts with historical evidence from parts of Southeast Asia which shows that women not only produced goods within the home but were actively involved in trading and other activities outside the home (Reid 1988: 162-172). Bearing in mind the important role which women have played in both production and marketing of goods in parts of Southeast Asia, it could be argued that trends in male wages by themselves are not a wholly reliable indicator of trends in living standards of the population as a whole. Certainly claims by authors such as Williamson (2000: 19) that 'living standards of ordinary workers as captured by real wages are a better indicator of the economic well-being of the vast majority in any society' than per capita GDP in Asia in the early part of the twentieth century need to be treated with caution.

In most parts of Southeast Asia, data on sources of household income only became available in the 1960s, or later. But other evidence can be collected which gives important insights into how household members reacted to the challenges presented by growing domestic and global demand for tropical products in different parts of Southeast Asia in the nineteenth and twentieth centuries. By the 1930s, population censuses were gathering information on labour force participation by both men and women in British Malaya, Burma, the Philippines and Indonesia. These data together with other evidence show that some of the arguments about the divergence between the West and the rest put forward in the recent literature do not always apply in Southeast Asia. Female labour force participation rates were high in some parts of Southeast Asia in the 1930s; in Thailand the census carried out in 1937 found that women accounted for around 47 per cent of the total labour force. The percentage was lower in other parts of the region, although in parts of Java the 1930 census found high female labour force participation rates, with women employed in a range of non-agricultural occupations (Booth 2016: 171-174).

Theories of Immiserizing Growth

Having examined the various indicators which have been used in debates over trends in living standards in both Europe and Asia, it is useful to look at some of the theoretical approaches which have been used to explain why economic growth, to the extent that it occurred, did not always result in improved living standards for large segments of the population. Inevitably in the Southeast Asian case, analyses of 'immiserizing growth' have become intertwined with debates over the impact of Western colonialism. For around a century, from the middle decades of the nineteenth century to the decade after 1946, most parts of Southeast Asia were under the control of foreign powers. The Dutch had occupied Java and some parts of Eastern Indonesia since the sixteenth century, and over the nineteenth century they consolidated their control over Sumatra, Kalimantan and Sulawesi, often by co-opting local rulers.

The British also kept local rulers in place in much of peninsular Malaya although the Straits Settlements (Singapore, Malaka, the island of Penang and the adjoining hinterland) were directly governed, with the island of Singapore being transformed into a major port and naval base which served as an entrepôt not just for British Malaya but also for western Indonesia. From the mid-nineteenth century the French gained control over Vietnam, Cambodia and Laos, which they governed as Indochina. The Spanish had had a presence in the Philippines since the sixteenth century; after the defeat of Spain by the USA at the end of the nineteenth century, the Philippines became an American colony. Burma was also under the control of the British, but ruled until 1937 as part of British India. Only Thailand remained an independent kingdom, but its economic policies were influenced by pressures from both Britain and France, especially by resident British financial advisers.

Given these diverse experiences, it might be expected that economic policies and outcomes across Southeast Asia diverged considerably in the century up to 1940. To some extent this was the case, but for many indigenous people who participated in the struggle for national independence across the region in the first part of the twentieth century, it was widely believed that the economic policies of the colonial regimes had a number of common features. The main goal of colonial governments, in the eyes of many nationalists, was to extract profits from the exploitation of the region's abundant agricultural and mineral resources, which were then remitted abroad. It was further argued that the various colonial regimes had little interest in providing education or public health facilities for the indigenous populations they controlled; neither did they promote the growth of modern industry, except for a limited amount of agricultural and mineral processing. These concerns were shared by some colonial officials who, especially after 1900, were worried that the policies pursued by their governments were not leading to improved 'native welfare'.

One consequence of colonial rule in Southeast Asia was clear by the early twentieth century. Indigenous populations across the Southeast Asian region were growing fast in comparison with most other parts of Asia. The population of Southeast Asia was probably no more than 35 million in 1800, and grew by around 1 per cent per annum through the nineteenth century (Boomgaard 2014: 133). By 1931, when reliable census data became available for most parts of the region, the population was estimated to be around 134 million. The growth rates through the nineteenth and into the early twentieth century were thus much faster than in China or the Indian subcontinent. By 1931 the population of Southeast Asia was around 40 per cent of British India (excluding Burma) and 27 per cent of that of China. After 1950, population growth rates in Southeast Asia were about the same as in the Indian subcontinent, but faster than in China, with the result that by 2018 the population of Southeast Asia was almost 47 per cent of that in China (Table 1.3).

Table 1.3: Population of Southeast Asia as a percentage of China, and the Indian Subcontinent, 1881-2018

Year	China	India+
1881	21.2	30.4
1931	27.2	39.6
2018	46.5	37.3

Note: 1881 and 1931 population data refer to British India excluding Burma; in 2018 data refer to India, Pakistan and Bangladesh.
Sources: British India, 1881 and 1931: Visaria and Visaria (1983: Table 5.7), Davis estimates; China: Maddison (2003: 160-162); Southeast Asia: Boomgaard (2014: 133). Data for 2018 from Population Reference Bureau (2018).

The evidence of rapid population growth, combined with slow improvements, or even declines in food availability, was by the early twentieth century causing concern on the part of colonial officials in the more densely settled parts of Southeast Asia, about the possibility of 'Malthusian traps'. It was argued that increasing populations on limited supplies of agricultural land were leading to diminishing returns to agricultural production, and a growing number of people living at bare subsistence. In addition, the influx of cheap manufactures from Europe, and after 1920 from Japan, was thought to be destroying traditional handicrafts which in earlier times had provided many households with extra sources of income. Paradoxically, these worries were often combined with the conviction that in the less densely settled regions, the development of agricultural and mineral resources was being held back by small populations, most of whom had access to land under some form of traditional tenure, and did not wish to become involved in wage labour markets, where wages were considered low and the conditions of employment humiliating.

One solution was to encourage in-migration from the huge population reservoirs of China and India; another was to encourage migration of workers from densely settled areas within the colonies to regions where local populations were sparse. The latter option was particularly appealing to Dutch officials, who by the early twentieth century were worried about what they viewed as the problem of overpopulation in Java. They sought to promote both agricultural intensification in Java and out-migration, especially to the rapidly developing estate regions in northeast Sumatra. The French, worried about population pressures in Northern Vietnam, also encouraged people to move southwards. Over the 1930s, both French and Dutch officials also became more preoccupied with policies to promote non-agricultural employment, especially through industrial development.

A second argument concerning 'immiserizing growth' which has been advanced in the literature, both in the colonial era and more recently, concerns the impact of growing involvement in international trade on living standards in Asia and Africa. That exports from Southeast Asia grew rapidly in the century from 1830 to 1930 has been well documented; as with the population data, a comparison with both China and India is instructive. Between 1830 and 1937, the value of exports from Southeast Asia increased from only 9 per cent of the Asian total to 37 per cent (Table 1.4). The percentage share of both China and India declined; by 1937 exports from China comprised only 9 per cent of the Asian total. Southeast Asian exports as a percentage of total exports from the tropical world also increased rapidly between 1883 and 1937 (Booth 2004: Table 3). Over much of the nineteenth century, it has also been estimated that the net barter terms of trade improved for several countries in the region (Williamson 2011: 37).

The impact of increased participation in global trade on living standards among the indigenous populations of Southeast Asia was, and remains, a contested issue. Williamson (2011: 231-234) has argued that three factors reduced the benefits of trade for the poorer countries in Asia and Africa through the nineteenth century and up until 1914, and led to the widening gap in incomes between the West and the rest. They were deindustrialization, rising inequality and volatility of primary product prices. To what extent did these factors affect living standards in the economies of Southeast Asia? Is there persuasive evidence of an absolute decline in living standards in

Table 1.4: Asian and third world exports, 1830 to 1937

Year	Asia as a % of third world
1830	44.0
1860	47.4
1900	47.8
1912	47.9
1928	49.9
1937	44.5

Percentage of the Asian total

China	India	Southeast Asia
20.6	43.8	9.8
19.1	47.9	16.9
15.1	46.8	21.8
15.0	44.0	30.2
16.5	32.3	35.4
7.3	29.3	37.0

Note: Asia includes the Middle East, as well as China, Korea, Hong Kong and Southeast and South Asia. India includes Ceylon, Burma, and other parts of British India. Southeast Asia includes French Indochina, British Malaya, Indonesia and the Philippines. Data refer to three-year averages centred on the years shown.
Source: Booth (2004: Table 2).

Southeast Asia, as distinct from a growing gap between the region and other parts of the global economy, both before and after 1945? Was there indeed a growing gap, or was there some catch-up, especially with the leading industrial economies? These questions are complex, and the answers vary both across colonies and within colonies over time. They will be investigated in more detail in subsequent chapters, but a few preliminary points can be made.

The first concerns deindustrialization, where the evidence is mixed, but increasingly many historians are casting doubt on the idea that deindustrialization occurred, if the term is defined as a decline in output of mining, manufacturing, construction and utilities as a percentage of total output. In fact, the evidence from national income accounts shows that the industrial sector at least maintained its share of national output in most parts of Southeast Asia in the years from 1913 to the late 1930s, and in some colonies it increased (Booth and Deng 2017: Table 3). The evidence for the nineteenth century is mixed but several scholars have challenged the view that indigenous textile industries declined over the nineteenth century; Meerkerk (2017) has examined the evidence for Java. Other industries in

sectors such as agricultural processing grew rapidly, while the construction sector developed as a result of both public and private investment
in infrastructure and buildings. While it is true that no government in
Southeast Asia actively promoted industrial growth until the 1930s through
protectionist policies or other means, and exchange rate policies were often
harmful to traded good producers, that does not mean that the industrial
sector stagnated or declined.

It is possible that inequality rose in some parts of Southeast Asia from
1870 to 1940, although the evidence is not very robust. Williamson (2011:
Table 9.1) provides estimates of the Gini coefficient for Java in 1880 and
1924 which shows a decline, although it is not clear how the estimates
were derived. Williamson (2011: Table 9.4) also gives estimates of the ratio
of wages to rents in Burma and Siam from the 1870s to the 1930s; in both
countries there was a steep decline. But the mechanisms through which
such a decline could have led to a rise in income inequality are not made
clear, and, in addition, the wage data which he used are problematic. I
return to this issue in Chapter 2. Williamson (2011: Chapter 10) also argues
that volatility in the terms of trade was also a drag on growth in many
Asian, African and Latin American countries between the 1860s and the
1930s. While it true that the terms of trade were more volatile over these
decades in the periphery than in the core industrial economies, it is not
clear that this necessarily affected either economic growth or income
distribution. For many producers across Southeast Asia of crops such as
rice, timber, rubber, vegetable oils, sugar, coffee, tea, spices and minerals,
the net barter terms of trade improved until 1913, and the income terms
of trade in many cases increased until the depression of the early 1930s.
Volume increases more than compensated for falling prices. While it is true
that higher prices would have led to higher incomes for most producers,
whether large companies or smallholders, the evidence does not support
the argument that volatility in the terms of trade led to absolute falls in
output of traded goods, or to lower incomes for producers, at least until
the 1930s.

Indeed, it is difficult in the Southeast Asian context to reconcile the
Williamson arguments with the evidence that in several Southeast Asian
colonies, per capita GDP grew more or less in step with that in the metropolitan power from the late nineteenth century to 1940. In Indonesia, per
capita GDP was around 27 per cent of that in the Netherlands in 1870: it fell
to 23 per cent in 1913 and then increased until by 1939 the ratio was little
different from 1870 (Table 1.5). A sharp fall in per capita GDP relative to the
metropolitan powers only occurred after 1950. This was also the case in the

Philippines and Vietnam. The only colonies in Southeast Asia to experience a significant degree of catch-up with the former colonial power after 1960 were Malaysia and Singapore. The reasons for this are complex and will be investigated in more depth in subsequent chapters, but it is clear that, in several parts of Southeast Asia, economic policies were pursued after 1950 which proved more damaging to economic growth than those imposed by the colonial powers from 1870 to 1940.

Table 1.5:   Per capita GDP in Indonesia, Philippines, Vietnam, Singapore and Malaysia as a percentage of the metropolitan power, 1870 to 2016

Year	Indonesia/ Netherlands	Philippines/ USA	Vietnam/ France	Singapore/ UK	Malaysia/ UK
1870	26.7	12.2 (1902)	28.7	25.2	29.5
1913	23.1	14.9	19.0	19.3	24.1
1929	28.1	16.4	n/a	30.7	39.0
1939	25.2	17.6	n/a	31.6	32.5
1960	13.7	9.9	13.0 (1950)	19.7	20.7
1990	12.6	10.0	4.9	64.5	35.3
2016	21.3	13.6	15.6	171.5	57.9

Source: Bolt et al. (2018).

The Argument in Brief

It seems clear from Table 1.2 that, at the end of the first decade of the new millennium, poverty was still a serious problem in several ASEAN countries, according to estimates produced by both national governments and international agencies. According to the Asian Development Bank estimates published in 2014, well over 100 million people in Southeast Asia in 2010 fell below the $1.51 poverty line. Many of these people were located in three countries: Indonesia, the Philippines and Vietnam. The more recent estimates produced by the World Bank using the 2011 PPP data, and a poverty line of $1.90 also show that Indonesia and the Philippines have the highest number of poor people, around 26 million people in 2015/16 (Table 1.6). But the total number of poor, using the $1.90 poverty line, was much lower than 2010, in spite of the fact that the estimates used an aparently higher poverty line. Is it really the case that such a large fall in poverty occurred over five or six years? Or is the apparent fall the result of different estimation procedures? These questions are addressed in Chapter 7.

Table 1.6: Headcount measures of poverty in Southeast Asia using the $1.90 poverty line and national poverty line

Country	$1.90	National	Numbers of poor (millions)	
			2015/16*	2010**
Malaysia (2016)	0	0.4	0.0	0.1
Thailand (2016)	0	8.6	0.0	0.8
Indonesia (2016)	6.8	10.9	17.6	67.2
Philippines (2015)	8.3	21.6	8.4	25.1
Vietnam (2016)	2.0	7.0	1.8	19.4
Laos (2012)	22.7	23.2	1.5	2.4
Myanmar (2015)	6.4	32.1	3.4	n/a
Cambodia (2014)	n/a	14.0	n/a	3.6
China (2014)	1.4	(4.5)***	19.2	n/a
India (2011)	21.2	21.9	256.6	n/a

* Using the $1.90 threshold
** Using the $1.51 threshold
*** The national poverty line may not include the whole country
Sources: Asian Development Bank (2018); Asian Development Bank (2014c).

Given the problems which surround estimates of poverty and inequality based on monetary data, there have been renewed attempts to produce estimates based on non-monetary data, including attempts to measure poverty using a method which 'shows whether people satisfy a set of specified basic needs, rights, or – in line with Sen's capability approach – functionings' (Alkire and Santos 2014: 251). As with the Human Development Index, the Multidimensional Poverty Index (MPI) has been used to rank low- and middle-income countries according to a composite index. But the MPI excludes monetary indicators. The rankings for seven Southeast Asian countries together with China and India are given in Table 1.7. The rankings differ in several respects from those derived from the headcount measures of poverty produced by the World Bank and the Asian Development Bank. Cambodia, which had a lower headcount measure of poverty compared to Indonesia and the Philippines in 2010, according to the ADB data, ranks below all the other countries in the table except Laos and India according to the MPI index. The Philippines ranks above Indonesia according to the MPI index, although its headcount measure of poverty was above Indonesia's according to the World Bank's $1.90 measure (Table 1.7).

The divergence between the headcount measures of poverty, and the rankings according to the Multi-dimensional Index (MDI) suggests that

Table 1.7: **Countries ranked according to Multidimensional Poverty Index (MPI) and headcount measure of population in multidimensional poverty**

Country	Index	Headcount	Data source/year
Thailand (21)	0.003	0.9	MICS 2012
China (37)	0.017	4.0	CFPS 2014
Vietnam (46)	0.029	7.1	MICS 2013/14
Philippines (52)	0.052	11.0	DHS 2013
Indonesia (55)	0.066	15.5	DHS 2012
Myanmar (66)	0.134	30.1	DHS 2015/16
Cambodia (69)	0.146	33.0	DHS 2014
Laos (73)	0.174	34.1	n/a
India (76)	0.191	41.3	IHDS

Note: Figures in brackets give rankings: 113 countries were ranked. A score closer to zero means that the country was ranked higher. For full details on how the rankings were compiled, see Alkire and Robles (2017a)
Source: Alkire and Robles (2017b: Table 1.1 [Main MPI Results]).

some countries in Asia appear to be doing worse on a range of non-monetary indicators than their poverty estimates, and indeed their GDP numbers, would suggest. Indonesia stands out as the country where its score on the Multi-dimensional Index is low given its relatively high per capita GDP. Does the low Indonesian result for the MDI reflect low levels of government spending per capita on health and education over several decades? By contrast, Vietnam scores well on both the headcount measure of poverty and the MDI, given its relatively low per capita GDP. The use of multi-dimensional indexes remains controversial, although these indexes were given somewhat grudging approval in the report of the Commission on Global Poverty, published by the World Bank in 2017. But they do serve to strengthen the argument that countries should track progress on a range of both monetary and non-monetary indicators rather than relying simply on headcount measures of poverty, derived from social survey data which may not be very accurate.

If particular countries have performed badly on estimates of poverty based on either monetary or non-monetary indicators, what are the reasons for their failures? Does the poor performance of Indonesia, for example, result from an unfavourable colonial legacy, or from the inability of post-colonial governments to tackle deep-seated problems of deprivation and inequality? Chapters 2 and 3 review the evidence on poverty and changing living standards in the various colonial territories of Southeast Asia, and comparisons are made with colonies in other parts of Asia. Particular attention is paid to the question of how growing populations found employment, both in agriculture and in other sectors of the economy, in the context of both the land-scarce and land-abundant regions in Southeast Asia, and the consequences of these employment patterns for the living standards of the indigenous populations. Chapter 4 examines the consequences for living standards of the Pacific War, and the difficult transition to independence in many parts of Southeast Asia after 1945. Evidence is presented that most countries in Southeast Asia in 1960 were, in terms of per capita GDP, behind many countries in Africa and the Middle East. Chapter 5 examines the research on poverty and inequality which was carried out in Southeast Asia in the years from the 1950s to around 1980, including work by international agencies including the World Bank and the International Labour Organization.

The period from the mid-1960s to the mid-1990s is often seen as a golden era of accelerated economic growth in Southeast Asia, although the rapid growth was confined to Singapore, Malaysia, Thailand and Indonesia, while others stagnated or struggled to overcome the legacies of prolonged conflict. Chapter 6 addresses the sometimes contentious evidence concerning the impact of growth on poverty decline and improved living standards in the countries which achieved rapid growth. It also examines the evidence in those countries which were falling behind. In the latter part of 1997, several currencies in the ASEAN region including the Thai baht, the Malaysian ringgit and the Indonesian rupiah all underwent substantial devaluations relative to the dollar and other major currencies. These devaluations were the result of massive capital outflows which in turn caused not just a slowdown in economic growth in the affected economies, but actual declines in national product in 1998. The impact of these declines on poverty and living standards is also discussed in Chapter 6.

Chapter 7 examines the sometimes contentious evidence on trends in poverty and income distribution after 2000. Has the return to economic growth led to a sustained reduction in poverty across the region, and an improvement in non-monetary indicators, including health and education, in all regions and for all social classes? What was the impact of the financial crisis which erupted in the USA and parts of Europe in 2008? Did the Southeast Asian countries escape this crisis without serious effects on living standards, and if so why? Chapter 7 also reviews recent controversies on the measurement of poverty which have intensified, especially after the release of new poverty measures from the World Bank, based on new estimates of purchasing power parities (PPP) data prepared in 2011. The new PPP data was used to estimate new headcount measures of poverty, shown in Table 1.6. These estimates caused considerable surprise among the development community, and in 2017 the World Bank published a substantial report, prepared by a committee chaired by Professor A. Atkinson of Oxford University, which reviewed the methodology used by the World Bank to estimates poverty across countries and over time, and made recommendations for change. The implications for poverty measurement in Southeast Asia of these recommendations are discussed in Chapter 7.

In most parts of Southeast Asia since the 1950s, governments have been implementing a range of policies designed to reduce poverty. Chapter 8 examines the impact of a number of policy interventions, which began in the 1950s, including, land reform and land settlement policies, employment creation through public works, government intervention in food markets, and, more recently, targeted cash transfers. Most of these policies have been adopted by several countries in Southeast Asia. What impact have they had on the incomes and living standards of the poorest groups in society? Is there a case for using budgetary funds to expand these programmes in the future?

One question which has been raised repeatedly in the literature on economic growth since the 1970s concerns the relationship between economic growth, poverty reduction and inequality. An influential school of thought, in both Southeast Asia and other parts of the world, argues that economic growth is not just a necessary condition for poverty decline but also a sufficient one. Policies which promote growth should focus on open trade and investment policies, infrastructure development and human resource development. It has been argued that the countries in Southeast Asia which have followed such policies, such as Singapore, Malaysia and Thailand and, more recently, Vietnam, have all had improvements in living standards, shared by the great majority of their populations. An implication is that targeted government policies intended to reduce poverty are probably unnecessary, and can even be counterproductive. Chapter 9 reviews the evidence for these arguments.

Chapter 9 also draws together the various arguments made in the book by addressing three questions. First, can we say with confidence that the evidence supports the view that living standards have improved across Southeast Asia, not just in the past three or four decades but over the past century? Second, to the extent that some countries and regions have been left behind, what are the reasons? Is it possible to sort out the contributions made by agricultural and rural development on the one hand, and urban-industrial development on the other? What has been the role of demographic change? Third, to the extent that governments across the region have been implementing policies which are intended to reduce poverty, and bring about broad-based improvements in living standards, which policy interventions have been most successful and why? Answers to these three questions should help both national governments and international agencies to frame more effective policies for egalitarian growth in future decades.

2 The Colonial Period: Population and Output Growth in Agricultural and Non-agricultural Sectors

Changing Official Attitudes to Welfare Policies

The previous chapter described the gradual assertion of control over Southeast Asia by the European colonial powers in the latter part of the nineteenth century, and the American occupation of the Philippines after 1900. But what did colonial governments do with the often large territories they had acquired? There is much evidence that by the early twentieth century, governments in several parts of Southeast Asia were adopting a more activist approach to promoting economic development in the territories they controlled, even if they did not define economic development in the way it came to be understood after 1945. This was at least partly motivated by a growing awareness among private businesses in the metropolitan countries that Southeast Asia had land and other resources which could be used to produce valuable agricultural and mineral commodities in increasing demand in the industrializing countries in Europe and North America.

The private companies which were formed to exploit both agricultural and mineral resources often operated in more than one colony. They had considerable influence with governments in London, Paris, the Hague and Washington and lobbied to get them to adopt policies which favoured their enterprises. But at the same time, non-governmental groups and some politicians began to realize that in developing the resources of their colonies, they had an obligation to improve the welfare of the indigenous populations. Such concerns were motivated not just by feelings of moral responsibility, but also by more hard-headed calculations about the importance of colonial markets for home industries. If the growing indigenous populations in Southeast Asia and elsewhere were getting richer, they would buy more products from the metropolitan countries, which in turn would benefit industries such as textiles, which were under growing competitive pressure in their domestic markets.

Reflecting these various pressures, the Calvinist-Catholic coalition which had come to power in the Netherlands announced in 1901 that a 'new approach would be taken in colonial management' (Penders 1977: 61). The emphasis was on enhancing the economic welfare of the indigenous population in Indonesia by increasing agricultural output through irrigation and the dissemination of new technologies, by expanding education in vernacular languages, particularly at the primary level, and by moving people from the densely settled parts of Java and Bali to other parts of the huge Indonesian archipelago, where it was widely believed that economic development was held back by low population densities. Government expenditures on irrigation, education, transport infrastructure and land settlement all increased substantially over the first two decades of the twentieth century. In addition, the Dutch developed a rural credit system, established village rice banks and reformed the network of pawnshops, which were the most important source of credit for many indigenous Indonesians (Van Laanen 1990). These policies were intended to improve the incomes of the indigenous population, in part by improving their productivity in agriculture, and in part by encouraging them to diversify into non-agricultural activities.

These policies attracted considerable attention from officials in other Asian colonies, who felt that Dutch policies offered them valuable lessons. To more modern eyes, they can be seen as fairly standard state-sponsored attempts to promote faster economic growth through education, infra-structure and building institutions, especially in the financial sector, which would support a more diversified market economy. Indeed, many of the programmes initiated by the Dutch in Indonesia between 1900 and 1930 were adopted again in the 1970s, in the development plans implemented by the Suharto government. But by the 1920s, criticism was mounting both in the Netherlands and in the colony. To some of the more conservative Dutch colonial officials and businessmen, the policies which became known as the Ethical Policy (Ethische Politiek) were simply extravagant 'welfare handouts' to the indigenous population, who showed their gratitude by making ever more strident demands not just for better economic opportunities, but also for greater political participation in the governance of the colony. At least part of the growing expenditures were financed by borrowing, and the mounting debt worried both officials and business groups in the colony and in the Netherlands (Booth 1998: 144-146).

The debates over the Ethical Policy in the Netherlands reflected a serious dilemma which confronted governments not just in the Netherlands but in also Britain and France in the early twentieth century. Colonies were seen as essential if European countries were to maintain their status as major players in global politics, and respond to the challenge of rising powers, including the USA and Japan. But at the same time it was becoming clear that the living standards of populations in Asia and Africa were, on average, lower than those in Europe, and that impoverished colonial populations would not just be of little benefit to the metropolitan power, but could become a serious liability. In the early decades of the twentieth century, the metropolitan populations were making increased demands for economic security, as well as a stronger voice in political affairs. Lindert (2004: Table 1.2) showed that expenditures on social transfers (including unemployment benefits, pensions, health and housing subsidies) in France and the United Kingdom at least doubled, relative to GDP, between 1890 and 1930; in the Netherlands they tripled. Given these growing demands on the public finances from their own populations, the main European colonial powers were very reluctant to undertake policies in their colonies which might lead to further charges on the home budgets. If public expenditures were to increase in the colonies, the money would have to come from revenues raised by the colonial governments. And increased revenues would be easier to mobilize if colonial economies were dynamic and growing, rather than stagnating. The policy challenge was to accelerate economic growth in the colonies, without adding to the fiscal obligations of the metropolitan power.

Another reason why the policies of not just the Dutch but also the British and French colonial regimes in Southeast Asia were being rethought after 1900 was that two important new colonial powers had emerged in the region, the USA and Japan. After the defeat of Spain by American forces in 1898, President McKinley decided to impose an American administration on the Philippine Islands. A bloody struggle with nationalist forces ensued, and after their defeat William Howard Taft was dispatched in 1900 to form a civilian government. McKinley instructed Taft to promote the 'happiness, peace and prosperity of the people of the Philippine Islands' (Hutchcroft 2000: 277). This reflected the strongly moralistic view that the administration took of its colonial mission, which both McKinley and Taft realized was deeply unpopular with large sections of American public opinion.

Although Taft and other supporters of the American colonial project in the Philippines thought that the Americans could learn from both British and Dutch colonial policies in Asia, especially as they related to the development of infrastructure and commerce, by the 1920s the idea of the 'exceptionalism' of American colonialism was widely held (Adas 1998: 46-50). Unlike the Europeans, who, according to many Americans, viewed their colonies as economic assets to be exploited mainly for the benefit of the metropolitan power, American policy in the Philippines was dominated by the need to prepare the population of the Philippines for self-government, and ultimate independence. Crucial to this strategy was mass education.

In 1935, substantial self-government was granted to the Philippines, with a promise of complete independence after a further ten years.

The other new colonial power in Asia in 1900 was Japan. As the only Asian country to acquire colonial possessions in the early twentieth century, Japan was an 'anomaly' in the history of colonial Asia (Peattie 1984: 6). Japan's empire in East Asia was created between 1895 and 1913, largely as a result of military victories over two decaying imperial states, China, and Tsarist Russia. The island of Taiwan (or Formosa, as it was known during the Japanese period) was annexed from China under the Treaty of Shimonoseki, and an administration was established under a Japanese governor-general in March 1896. The military pacification of the island in the latter part of the 1890s was not unlike similar exercises carried out by the French in Tonkin, the Americans in the Philippines, or the Dutch in northern Sumatra at about the same time, and was probably no more ruthless than these other military campaigns (Peattie 1984: 19). By 1900 the island was largely under Japanese control. The Treaty of Portsmouth, signed in the wake of the Russo-Japanese conflict, gave Japan control over the Liaotung Peninsula, which became known as the Kwantung Leased Territory. Finally in 1910, Japanese control over the Korean peninsula was consolidated in its formal annexation. Unlike in Taiwan, colonial status was fiercely resented, and resisted, by Korean nationalists, but their opposition was put down by massive and often brutal police and military force.

Japanese military strength in the first decade of the twentieth century was based on the growth of its non-agricultural sectors, including manufacturing industry and financial services. But Japan at that time was still very much a developing economy. Its per capita national income was well below that of the European colonial powers in Asia, and little more than a quarter of that of the USA (Table 2.1). This relative backwardness was both an advantage and a disadvantage for its colonies. The main advantage was that with its own 'superbly successful modernization efforts' in the decades after the Meiji Restoration still fresh in their minds, Japanese colonial administrators could implement similar development policies in both Korea and Taiwan, especially in the agricultural sector (Peattie 1984: 23). The disadvantage was that the Japanese inevitably tended to view their colonial territories as assets to be exploited in their own race to catch up with the top industrial powers. This attitude to their colonial possessions became more pronounced over the 1930s, as the Japanese economy shifted to a war footing, and the colonial possessions became more tightly integrated into a rapidly growing military-industrial complex centered on metropolitan Japan.

Table 2.1: Per capita GDP in Japan and Southeast Asia as a percentage of per capita GDP in the USA, 1870-1960

Year	Philippines	Thailand	Burma	Singapore
1870	20.4	19.7	18.9	26.0
1913	14.9	12.6	11.9	15.3
1929	16.4	9.1	n/a	21.5
1939*	17.6	10.2	10.6	25.5
1960	9.9	7.6	4.4	13.1

Year	Indonesia	Malaysia	Vietnam	Japan
1870	20.5	30.3	18.3	26.4
1913	15.6	19.0	12.1	22.9
1929	14.9	27.2	n/a	25.7
1939	14.4	26.3	n/a	35.8
1960	8.2	13.7	6.0	28.7

* Thailand and Burma figures refer to 1938.
Source: Bolt et al. (2018).

In spite of the different attitudes to their colonial possessions between the European powers, the USA and Japan, the issue of living standards attracted considerable attention across Asia, especially after 1920. At several conferences of the Institute of Pacific Relations (IPR), an independent research organization funded mainly by American foundations, to which the principal colonial powers in the Asia-Pacific region were affiliated, the difficulties inherent in making cross-country comparisons of living standards were discussed. In the 1930 conference, a Japanese paper argued that the decline in consumption of grains other than rice in Japan between 1916 and 1929 indicated an improvement in living standards of rural people, as did the increased consumption of legumes, fruits and animal foods (Morimoto 1931: 47). The emphasis on changing household consumption patterns as indicators of changing living standards was taken up by other contributors to the conference panel on living standards. A Chinese paper compared data from household surveys on calorie consumption among working families in Shanghai and Peiping (Beijing), and also compared the percentage of total food expenditure devoted to cereals in Japan, Bombay, Shanghai and Peiping. It was much higher in Peiping than in the other locations (Tao 1931: 56). While the author was careful to stress the possible inaccuracies in the survey data, this paper argued that careful comparisons of family budget surveys could give important information on living standards across regions and countries.

In the 1933 meeting of the IPR in Banff, Canada, there was more discussion of ways of measuring living standards. A representative of the International Labour Office (ILO) argued that:

> In the vocabulary of many specialists, the term 'standard of living' implies principally the totality of goods and services consumed and utilized by a family or a category of people during a stated period and in a specified place. Large quantities and superior qualities of these goods and services indicate a high standard. Comparisons have proved feasible and even easy within the same region. The difficulties multiply when different regions or unlike countries become the object of investigation.

However, the ILO delegate went on to suggest that

> For everyday purposes, useful approximations may be arrived at chiefly by the judicious and critical use of two methods. The first consists in measuring the purchasing power of income in a certain aggregate of commodities and services. Between regions and countries with somewhat similar tastes, habits, and social conditions, real incomes usually indicate the prevailing standard of living with sufficient accuracy to be of practical service to statesmen and social scientists.
>
> The second method consists in a minute comparison, item by item, of the elements entering into the daily consumption of the groups under investigation. The material may be found in the various national budget inquiries which supply the necessary figures for cost-of-living indices and give us the most reliable picture we possess at present of the actual needs and manner of living among working-class populations. (Lasker and Holland 1934: 87-88)

Both the IPR and the ILO carried out a number of studies of living standards and labour conditions in various parts of Asia in the 1920s and 1930s, often in conjunction with the various colonial authorities. The results of some of these studies in Southeast Asia will be examined below. But first, it will be useful to summarize the available data on changes in population and national output across the region between 1870 and 1940.

Growth of Population and Output

In 1939, the population of Southeast Asia was around 150 million people. Over the first four decades of the twentieth century, rates of population growth varied from a little more than 1 per cent per annum in the more densely settled regions such as Java and Vietnam to well over 2 per cent per annum in British Malaya, the Philippines, and Thailand. In the faster-growing parts of Southeast Asia, especially British Malaya, high rates of in-migration contributed to the growth of total populations; elsewhere it is probable that falling mortality accounted for at least part of the growth in population. The evidence for this is reviewed below. In British Malaya, sustained in-migration from China and India meant that, by 1930, over half the population originated from these two countries (Table 2.2). Elsewhere the proportions were much lower; indeed, by the early part of the twentieth century, several colonial powers, including the Americans and the Dutch, had placed restrictions on further in-migration from China. Dutch official opinion was that, if more labour was needed to exploit agricultural and mineral resources outside Java, the Javanese should move.

Table 2.2:   Population and population growth in Southeast Asia, 1913-1939

Colony	Population: 1939 (millions)	Indigenous population as a percentage of total	Population growth (c. 1913-1939)
Java	47.0	98	1.1
Outer Islands	21.4	96	1.5
Indonesia	68.4	98	1.3
Tonkin	10.4	99	1.4
Annam	8.0	100	0.7
Cochinchina	6.1	96	1.1
Vietnam	24.5	99	1.1
Cambodia	3.4	96	1.4
Laos	1.0	100	1.3
Thailand	15.2	87	2.2
Burma	16.4	90	1.2
Philippines	16.2	99	2.4
British Malaya	5.4	45	2.5
North Borneo	0.3	24	1.3
Sarawak	0.5	26	1.4

Sources: Indonesia: Central Bureau of Statistics (1947: 6), with additional data from Boomgaard and Gooszen (1991); Vietnam: Banens (2000: 33); Cambodia and Laos: Slocomb (2010: 46) with additional data from Direction des Services Economiques (1947: 271); Thailand: Manurungsan (1989: 32); Burma: Saito and Lee (1999: 7); Philippines: National Statistical Coordination Board (2000); British Malaya: Department of Statistics (1939: 36). North Borneo and Sarawak: Jones (1966: 39).

In spite of, or to some extent because of, quite rapid population growth, output growth was also rapid in many parts of the region after 1900, sometimes exceeding population growth by a considerable margin. It was argued in Chapter 1 that per capita GDP in Indonesia, the Philippines and British Malaya grew at about the same rate, or even more rapidly than in the metropolitan powers between 1870 and 1939 (Table 1.5). The available estimates of gross domestic product (GDP) between 1900 and 1938 suggest that growth was fastest in per capita terms in British Malaya, Indonesia, and the Philippines, at least until the latter part of the 1920s (Table 2.3). Over the early part of the 1930s, per capita GDP fell in most colonies; the steep decline in Burma and Indonesia reflected the contraction in output of export-oriented agriculture and the processing of primary commodities. The colonies were unable to devalue their currencies; the problem was particularly severe for Indonesia, where the colonial guilder was tied to the Dutch guilder, and the Dutch government decided to stay on the gold standard when other countries left. Indonesia underwent a severe deflation between 1929 and 1935. The wholesale price index fell more sharply than in any other part of Asia (Touzet 1939: 220). The deflation in turn adversely affected both consumption and investment expenditures. Responding to evidence of output declines, colonial officials in both Indonesia and Indochina began in the mid-1930s to promote economic diversification, especially industrial development, by imposing import controls on manufactures, and in the case of Indonesia, by a devaluation of the colonial guilder, in line with the metropolitan guilder.

Table 2.3:   Index of growth of real per capita GDP for selected years between 1902 and 1940 (1938 = 100)

Year	Burma	Malaya	Indonesia	Philippines	Thailand	North-Vietnam	South-Vietnam
1902	94	40	59	46		85	89
1911	82	45	79	68		83	91
1913		51	82	73	102	81	99
1916	111	55	81	72		78	91
1918		71	82	90		80	90
1926	110	87	94	95		89	101
1929		128	103	98	96	96	91
1931	122	122	95	94		84	79
1936	113	115	93	95		96	95
1938	100	100	100	100	100	100	100
1940		102	107	104			

Note: Data for Burma refer to net domestic product; Malaya refers to British Malaya excluding Singapore; the final estimate for Malaya refers to 1939.
Sources: Burma: Saito and Lee (1999: 7, 214); Indonesia: Van der Eng (2013a); Thailand: Manurung-san (1989: 251); Philippines: Hooley (2005); Vietnam: Bassino, unpublished estimates supplied by J.-P. Bassino; Malaya: Shah (2017: 197).

Agricultural production, for both domestic and international markets, together with the processing of agricultural products, were the main drivers of economic growth everywhere in Southeast Asia over the first part of the twentieth century. However, in those countries for which we have national product data by sector, the share of agriculture tended to fall after 1913, although the decline only appears to have been substantial in Burma (Table 2.4). Even so, agriculture was the largest single sector of the economy in all parts of the region except the Straits Settlements, and by far the most important source of employment. In Thailand almost 90 per cent of the labour force was estimated to be employed in agriculture, falling to 61 per cent in British Malaya (Table 2.4). Of course, many of those employed in agriculture were also engaged in various forms of non-agricultural 'by-employment'. The implications of this for incomes and living standards are examined further below. But first, it is important to review the ways in which an expanding population was absorbed in agriculture.

Table 2.4: Agriculture as a percentage of GDP, agricultural workers as a percentage of total labour force, and agricultural productivity ratios

Country	Agriculture output as percentage of GDP		Agricultural workers as a percentage of all workers	Productivity ratio*
	1913	1938		
Burma	68.6	54.3	69 (1931)	86.3 (1931)
Philippines	38.5	37.7	65 (1939)	58.1 (1939)
Thailand	44.7	44.3	89 (1937)	50.0 (1938)
Indonesia	38.2	34.0	68 (1930)	48.6 (1930)
British Malaya	n/a	n/a	61 (1931)	n/a

* Output per worker in agriculture as a percentage of output per worker in the whole economy.
Sources: Burma: Saito and Lee (1999: 27. 214); Philippines: Hooley (2005: 480-482), labour force data: Commission of the Census (1941: 505-515); Thailand: Ingram (1971: 57), Manurungsan (1989: 251); Indonesia: Van der Eng (2013a), labour force data: Mertens (1978: Appendix Table 1.5); British Malaya: Vlieland (1932: 99-100).

Accommodating Growing Populations in Agriculture

From the latter part of the nineteenth century until 1940, three factors drove agricultural expansion in Southeast Asia. One was the growing population, which, given limited employment opportunities in other parts of the economy, had to be accommodated mainly in the agricultural sector. A second factor was the growth in international demand for many of the tropical agricultural products grown in Southeast Asia, including rice, sugar, tobacco, vegetable oils, tea, coffee, spices, and, after 1900, rubber. This growth was in part due to rising incomes in Europe and the USA; this increased demand for a range of foodstuffs, which had previously been viewed as luxuries by most of the population. But increasingly it was also due to the rise of new industries, such as automobiles and canned foods, which needed tropical products, including tin and rubber, as inputs. A third factor was technological change, which allowed more crops to be grown on existing supplies of land. Probably the best example was the increased use of irrigation, which allowed the double-cropping of rice land. In addition, some progress was made with developing higher-yielding crop varieties; here the most dramatic success was sugar in Java.

In many parts of Southeast Asia, growing populations were accommodated in agriculture simply through extending the land frontier. It is striking that in most parts of Southeast Asia, cultivated area seems to have grown more or less at the same rate as population in the first four decades of the twentieth century. Even in Java, which was already considered densely settled in 1900, harvested area of food crops per capita showed little change between 1915 and 1940 (Tables 2.5 and 2.6). Even if yields of both food and non-food crops did not increase, growing populations could at least maintain output per capita through replicating existing agricultural technologies on more land. The process was analysed by Myint (1958) in terms of 'vent for surplus', a term originally used by Adam Smith. A crucial assumption of this approach was that 'land suitable for the cultivation of food is not a scarce factor' (Findlay and Lundahl 1994: 89). In addition, it was assumed that underutilized labour could easily be drawn out of subsistence food production, or other activities, to meet increased world demand for agricultural exports. These included food crops, such as rice, which had always been cultivated, and exotic tree crops, such as rubber and palm oil, which indigenous cultivators would never have grown had there not been an expanding world market. It was further implied that the land tenure system functioned in such a way that any household willing and able to cultivate larger holdings could easily obtain more land on favourable terms. But how realistic were these assumptions in the context of Southeast Asia by the early twentieth century?

Although Myint developed the vent for surplus concept in the context of colonial Southeast Asia, the evidence on its applicability is in fact mixed. Even if the cultivated land area did grow as fast as the population, was it the case that land was freely available to all those who wished to cultivate it, either to grow more traditional food crops which could also be exported,

Table 2.5: Area of land under food crops per capita (hectares)

	Burma	Philippines	Java
1900	0.42	n/a	n/a
1905	0.45	n/a	n/a
1910	0.45	n/a	n/a
1915	0.46	0.29	0.19
1920	0.46	0.32	0.22
1925	0.47	0.31	0.20
1930	0.46	0.31	0.19
1935	0.45	0.30	0.20
1940	0.42	0.31	0.19

Note; Figures refer to five-year averages centred on the years shown. For 1940 the figures refer to 1940 and 1941 (Burma), 1938 (Philippines), 1938-1940 (Java). For Burma, the figures refer to net sown area; for Philippines, planted area; and for Java, harvested area of indigenous crops. Sources: Burma: Saito and Lee (1999: 37-42); Philippines: Rose (1985: 255-259), population data: Bureau of Census and Statistics (1947: 13); Java: Boomgaard and Van Zanden (1990: Table 4.B1), population data: Central Bureau of Statistics (1947: 5-6).

Table 2.6: Cultivated area of rice land per capita (hectares)

	Thailand	Vietnam/ Cambodia*	British Malaya	Java
1900	0.18	0.21	n/a	n/a
1910	0.21	0.22	n/a	n/a
1911/15	0.23	0.23	n/a	n/a
1916/20	0.24	0.23	n/a	0.10
1921/25	0.26	0.23	0.07	0.09
1926/30	0.25	0.24	0.07	0.09
1931/35	0.24	0.23	0.06	0.09
1936/40	0.23	0.23	0.06	0.09

* Figures for Vietnam and Cambodia refer to calendar years 1900, 1905, 1915, 1920, 1920, 1925, 1930, 1935, 1940.
Sources: Thailand: Manurungsan (1989: Tables 1.1 and 2.7); Vietnam: Giacometti (2000a: 68-80), Banens (2000); Cambodia: Slocomb (2010: Tables 1.2 and 2.8); British Malaya: Barnett (1947: Table 2.6); Java: Boomgaard and Van Zanden (1990: Table 4.B2), population data: Central Bureau of Statistics (1947: 5-6).

such as rice, or to grow exotic export crops, such as rubber? Of particular importance in the Southeast Asian context was the impact of the expansion of estate agriculture. The term 'estate' was not always clearly defined; it was sometimes used to mean any agricultural holding beyond the size which can easily be cultivated by a family, perhaps using some hired labour. But increasingly in Southeast Asia over the twentieth century it came to mean a large-scale agricultural enterprise incorporated as a company and operated along capitalist lines, hiring in labour and selling output to global markets at a profit. Often such companies were owned by shareholders in the metropolitan power or in a third country, although in the Philippines many large estates were owned by local business groups. Ownership was usually separated from management which was carried out by hired managers, who in turn used labour hired on both permanent and temporary contracts. For such companies securing long-term use rights to land was essential. In most parts of Southeast Asia by the early twentieth century, colonial administrations were under considerable pressure from estate companies and their metropolitan owners to formulate land legislation which facilitated the acquisition of large tracts of land to grow export crops.

These pressures reflected the fact that the growth in world demand for export crops was making land in Southeast Asia a valuable asset, even in those regions where it was in relatively abundant supply. It was thus inevitable that, as exports expanded in the last part of the nineteenth century, land markets evolved where none had existed before, and colonial administrations reacted to the increased demand for land by introducing new concepts of land titling, usually imported from other parts of the world and often quite alien to indigenous populations. In Thailand, and in parts of British Malaya and the Philippines, the Torrens system of land titling from South Australia was introduced, although the system required a detailed land cadastre, which was seldom available, even in the more densely settled areas, let alone in the frontier zones. Funds were very limited for both surveying and the drawing up and issuing of title deeds, and many smallholders never received any legal title, thus making them vulnerable to more powerful people seeking to gain control of their land (Pelzer 1945: 109-110; Aquino 1931: 21-27; Feeny 1982: 96-97; Miranda 1991: 58). In the Malay states, the imposition of colonial land legislation 'signified the end of the line for shifting cultivation which was practiced by most Malays in the peninsula outside the long-standing permanent Malay agricultural settlements' (Sundaram 1988: 86).

As large estate companies expanded their operations from the mid-nineteenth century onwards, especially in Indonesia, British Malaya and the Philippines, they used their influence with both colonial administrations and home governments to get access to large blocks of land on long leases or freehold tenure. Many small cultivators across Southeast Asia developed hitherto underutilized land close to their food crop farms so that they could grow more rice, or tree crops such as coffee, pepper and rubber. This was sometimes a reasonably peaceful process, with the smallholders acquiring extra assets, and an extra source of cash income. But often there was the risk of expropriation by powerful land grabbers, both local and foreign, who had the tacit if not open support of ruling elites, both colonial and indigenous. Most vulnerable to predatory behaviour were those who did not cultivate land in their own villages and who had migrated to the so-called 'frontier' regions where they developed homesteads and smallholdings. But even those indigenous cultivators whose families had lived in a particular locality for centuries, farming land under traditional, or communal tenure arrangements, were threatened by new demands for land. Cleary (1992: 180) argued that in North Borneo, a remote region where there had been little European contact, foreign companies in the early twentieth century pushed the local officials to change communal to individual tenures so that a 'proper' land market could develop which would allow them to acquire land with a secure title.

In his discussion of the growth of sugar production in Negros Occidental in the Philippines, Larkin (1993: 60) argued that the peopling and exploitation of the western Negros wilderness had 'much in common with the global frontier phenomenon taking place at this time.' No doubt mindful of its own recent pioneering history, the American administration in the Philippines was, according to Larkin (1993: 68), keen to follow 'America's own ideal of turning the frontier into the realm of the yeoman farmer'. A Congressional Act of 1901, which set out the organization of civil government in the Philippines, stipulated that a maximum of sixteen hectares of public land should be available for each settler family. It seems that fear of land grabbing forced the American Congress to 'appropriate wholesale the public domain of the country' (Aquino 1931: 21). Sixteen hectares was a generous amount for many poor families, and numbers of applications grew steadily over the ensuing years. But a large number of applications for homesteads failed, partly because many potential settlers were often not aware of the legal status of the land they wished to settle. If the land was not considered to be in the 'public domain' the application was refused. In addition, if the homesteader was not able to cultivate at least one-fifth of the land allocated within five years, he lost the claim, which was then given to another applicant (Pelzer 1945: 110-114). In parts of Luzon, some homesteaders found that the land they had cleared and farmed was registered by some of the powerful landlords in the area, and in effect taken from them by a legal titling procedure of which the homesteaders were ignorant (McLennan 1969: 673-674).

Other colonial administrations also stated that their goal was to establish an agrarian system based on small owner-cultivators. Where necessary, the government would facilitate the opening up of 'empty lands' with agricultural

potential on which to settle migrants from the densely settled areas, where
rural poverty was seen as the result of too many people and not enough land.
French policy in Southern Vietnam from the 1860s onwards was 'intended to
settle the majority of the population on the land, and thereby create a secure
social order based on small proprietors' (Brocheux 1995: 30). But often land
under communal tenures were expropriated on the assumption that the
land was not used. Brocheux and Hemery (2009: 156) stated that in the four
decades from 1863 to 1902, 3.7 million hectares were taken over by the state,
at least some of which were under some form of customary tenure. French
policy veered between auctions of the land acquired and free concessions
to indigenous cultivators and to European individuals and companies. By
1942, it was estimated that 2.3 million hectares of land had been sold, of
which 0.9 million hectares was to European companies and individuals.
Native concessionaires, who were mainly Vietnamese, were granted almost
1.4 million hectares (Brocheux and Hemery 2009: 156-157). A high proportion
of the concessions, almost 90 per cent, were in Cochinchina. In Cambodia,
French policy from the 1920s onwards was to grant concessions to both
Cambodians and foreign companies; the latter usually got much larger
amounts of land. Slocomb (2010: 55) argued that only a small fraction of
the land conceded was actually developed; in many cases it appeared that
wealthy Cambodians acquired the land for speculative purposes.

After 1900, the Dutch colonial authorities began an ambitious land settlement programme which involved moving landless families from Java to
Sumatra and Sulawesi (Pelzer 1945: Chapter VII; Hardjono 1977: 16-21). By
1941, it was estimated that almost 174,000 Javanese migrants had settled
in Lampung, the southernmost region in Sumatra, and the closest to Java.
But only 35,000 had actually been moved in the government-sponsored
programmes; the rest had either been born in Lampung or moved without
official assistance. The settlers in Lampung were probably better off than
they had been in Java, as the soil was suitable for rice agriculture and irrigation systems had been built. But the settlers were not given much land and
could not grow cash crops. In addition, the problem of rural indebtedness,
of concern to officials in Java, soon manifested itself in Lampung as well
(Hardjono 1977: 20). Given the small numbers who moved under the official
programme, it was obvious by 1940 that government-sponsored out-migration
was having little impact on the problems of poverty and landlessness in Java.

In the delta regions of central Thailand and southern Burma, large tracts
of agricultural land were opened up for cultivation in the latter part of the
nineteenth and early twentieth centuries (Siamwalla 1972). The impact of
these ambitious schemes differed over time and space, but often they led

to consequences unintended by the governments which had initiated the process of land expansion. These consequences included purchases of land by speculators based in urban areas, and growing tenancy. In Burma, the problem of rural indebtedness became much worse over the 1930s, as more farmers borrowed from Indian moneylenders. When they could not pay back these loans, there was large-scale land alienation and many cultivators became tenants on their own land. It was estimated that only 15 per cent of land in Lower Burma in 1941 was owned by 'genuine agriculturalists and unmortgaged' (Andrus 1948: 81). In the Philippines, in spite of the American policy of supporting the land-owning smallholder, what actually emerged by the 1930s was a pattern of tenure in which around half the holdings were under two hectares in size, while 13 per cent were over five hectares. Over 40 per cent of all cultivated land was in holdings over five hectares (Pelzer 1945: 85). Tenancy was widespread. Only 49.2 per cent of all farmers in 1939 were owners of the land they worked; a further 15.6 per cent owned part of the land and the rest were tenants, mainly sharecroppers. The 1939 population census found that 48 per cent of the male agricultural labour force, of almost three million, were classified as farm labourers, many of them working in rice, corn and coconut farms (Commission of the Census 1941: 505).

Pelzer (1945: 86-89) considered the extent of tenancy in the Philippines 'astonishingly high' and attributed it to Spanish policies which favoured local chiefs (cacique), many of whom acquired substantial holdings and reduced the traditional cultivators to the status of tenant. McLennan (1969: 659-662) stressed the importance of the pacto de retroventa arrangements, whereby moneylenders (often of mixed Chinese-Filipino ancestry) acquired parcels of land when loans secured on the land were in default. American policy, while ostensibly favouring the owner-cultivator, in fact did little to reduce the extent of tenancy, which might have increased in the first four decades of the twentieth century. Owen (1972: 50) argued that the large amounts of land acquired from the church (the friar lands) could have been used to settle landless families, but was in fact sold to wealthy speculators. Larkin (1993: 61) pointed out that in the sugar-growing areas, small landowners were not infrequently dispossessed by 'the new breed of planters' seeking to build up large haciendas, and were forced into a precarious living as agricultural labourers on large plantations, with few alternative sources of income.

Although the high rates of tenancy in the Philippines attracted considerable critical attention from subsequent scholars, the proportion of land under tenancy was in fact lower than Burma by the late 1930s, or indeed in Taiwan (Booth 2007a: Table 3.5). In the central plains of Thailand, Thompson

(1967: 319) found that by the 1930s absentee landlordism was an increasingly serious problem, and more land was being expropriated by moneylenders. The agricultural census of 1937 found that around one-quarter of all land in the central plains was in tenanted holdings; for the country as a whole, the ratio was 15.7 per cent (Ingram 1971: 268). In lower Burma, it was estimated that almost 60 per cent of arable land was operated under tenancy by the late 1930s (Pfanner 1969: 221). The rather low amount of cultivated land per capita in Thailand by the end of the 1930s, together with the high proportion of the labour force employed in agriculture, meant that planted area per agricultural worker was quite low in comparison with Burma, the Philippines or Cochinchina (Booth 2007a: Table 3.1). This, together with the high rates of tenancy, especially in the central plains, would suggest that even in a country which was not a colony, and where foreign-owned estates were almost entirely absent, competition for agricultural land was becoming more intense by the 1930s, and land was not always freely available to all those wishing to cultivate it. The rural survey conducted by Zimmerman in 1930/31 indicated that around 36 per cent of all households in central Thailand owned no land at all (Zimmerman 1999: 25-36). It is probable that most landless households were able to access some land through tenancy arrangements, but in many cases they would have had to supplement income from tenant farming with wage labour and handicraft activities. The consequences of this for living standards are examined further below.

In Java, where data on cultivated area go back further than in most other parts of Southeast Asia, we can trace the growth of both population and cultivated area in the various residencies of the island from 1870 onwards. Those residencies with high rates of population growth also tended to have high rates of growth of cultivated area (Booth 1988: 64-66). Did the causation run from high rates of area growth to high population growth or vice versa? It seems that those regions which were experiencing high growth in cultivated area also experienced high rates of in-migration, and this process continued until the 1930s. The 1930 population census revealed that in some parts of East Java, over 20 per cent of the population was born outside the region, and these people were often found in the regions where growth in rice land was quite rapid. While the Dutch authorities might have had difficulty moving Javanese to other parts of the archipelago, many moved within the island, usually to places where it was possible to open up new land.

But by the early twentieth century it was clear that, in spite of this mobility in Java, the average holding size was falling to below one hectare, and a substantial part of the indigenous population had little or no access to agricultural land, either as owners or tenants. They were largely, if not entirely, reliant on handicrafts, trade and wage labour for their incomes. Boomgaard (1991: Table 1) estimated, on the basis of data collected in 1905, that only 40 per cent of the labour force were agricultural landholders, and 31 per cent landless. Some of the landless got access to land through tenancy arrangements, but on average only 5.3 per cent of all those engaged in agriculture could be classified as tenants, although the percentage was twice as high in parts of West Java and in Yogyakarta (Pelzer 1945: 257). The breakdown of the population of Java given by Meijer Ranneft and Huender in the 1920s indicated that poor farmers comprised 27 per cent of the population and sharecroppers with no land a further 3.4 per cent. Landless labourers were estimated to comprise 32 per cent of the population, roughly the same proportion as in the 1905 survey. Thus over 60 per cent of the population were 'land poor' (Wertheim 1964: 232). Although sharecropping and tenancy appeared to affect only a small proportion of the total rural population, a practice which became increasingly common in the 1920s and 1930s was the leasing of land in return for an advance payment. Usually the landowner continued to work the land, and the lessee received a share of the crop. Such arrangements were informal and seldom registered but surveys indicated they were widespread; in one district of East Java in 1939 it was found that almost three-quarters of landowners had leased part of their land in order to obtain cash (Pelzer 1945: 172).

That access to land, and especially irrigated rice land (*sawah*) was an important determinant of total household income in rural Java by the 1930s can hardly be doubted. Just how important can be estimated from the detailed survey of household incomes carried out in Kutowinangun, in Kebumen in Central Java in 1932 and 1933 (Department of Economic Affairs 1934). While the great majority of the households surveyed, 28 out of 30, did cultivate some *sawah*, most only had access to small parcels. Those who were able to access larger parcels earned higher incomes; around 70 per cent the variation in total household incomes from all sources could be explained by the amount of *sawah* cultivated (Table 2.7). Most households also cultivated the dry land around their houses intensively with fruits and vegetables. On average slightly over 20 per cent of household income came from this source.

In Northern Vietnam (Tonkin), it appears that by the 1930s, cultivated hectares per person were even lower than in Java, and lower than elsewhere in Southeast Asia (Booth 2007a: Table 3.1). As in Java, landholdings were often divided into small parcels, with the great majority of cultivators operating very small, and often fragmented, holdings. Gourou (1945: 278) argued that it was not possible to establish how many households owned no land at all,

Table 2.7: Correlations from the Kutowinangan sample

Land owned per capita and:	
Income from gardens per hectare	-0.458
Percentage of household income from sidelines	-0.397
Household income per capita and:	
Land owned per capita	0.441
Calorie consumption per capita	0.857
Protein consumption per capita	0.875
Percentage from by-employment	-0.393
Total household income and:	
Sawah cultivated	0.839
All land cultivated	0.762

Note: Sample of 30 households.
Source: Ochse and Terra (1934).

although Popkin (1979: 156) claimed that, by 1930, 69 per cent of all families in Tonkin were either landless or cultivated less than 0.36 hectares. As in Java, most cultivators were cultivating small plots with their own labour and there was relatively little land available to be rented or sharecropped out, although it was possible for households to supplement their holding with communal land (Gourou 1945: 283). Much the same was true in Annam, where 94 per cent of all holdings were under 0.5 hectares in 1930, and almost 90 per cent of holdings were cultivated directly by owners (Henry 1932: 211-213).

The situation in Cochinchina, in Southern Vietnam, was very different from the north. Between 1880 and 1910, land under cultivation almost trebled, from 0.52 to 1.52 million hectares. Thereafter, the rate of expansion slowed (Gran 1975: Table 2-2). Although on average, land under rice cultivation kept up with population growth in Vietnam and Cambodia between 1900 and 1940, there were important regional differences, and after 1915 population growth in the north was faster than area growth. In order to bring more land under cultivation in the south, the French invested heavily in land reclamation, dredging and canal building, and to recoup these expenditures, government policy was to sell concessions. Especially after 1913, land was sold 'to the highest bidder' (Brocheux 1995: 30). The result was that the agricultural land was very inequitably distributed; in several provinces between 39 and 66 per cent of all agricultural land was in holdings over 50 hectares (Henry 1932: 189). The process of land surveying and land titling was often farmed out to private companies who 'carried out their duties unsystematically and sluggishly' (Brocheux 1995: 36). Disputes over land rights erupted when squatters were evicted by new owners, who farmed the land out to tenants, often on short leases (Gran 1975: 252ff.). In spite of these problems, the government persisted with the idea that out-migration could solve the problems of Tonkin. In 1932 an office was created to plan migration to supposedly empty lands in the centre and south of the country; it was claimed that 1.2 million hectares could be made available for peasant settlement (Brocheux and Hemery 2009: 276). But experts such as Gourou doubted that this could be anything more than a temporary solution to the problems of Tonkin. There would have to be an improvement in crop output per unit of area, and much greater provision of non-agricultural employment.

It would be wrong to treat the evidence of growing disputes over land in Southeast Asia in the early twentieth century as evidence that the only beneficiaries of the growth in both land area and agricultural exports were powerful corporations or individuals who were closely connected to governing elites, whether domestic or foreign. There is evidence that many millions of small farmers did benefit from growing markets for their output, both domestic and foreign, and were often able to expand that output by opening up new land for cultivation. In those regions where there was potential for expanding the area under cultivation, people did move, even if government-sponsored efforts to encourage migration were not very successful. In addition, local people responded to the opportunities presented by growing world markets, both for traditional staples, and for new crops such as rubber. In Sumatra and parts of Kalimantan, farmers expanded cultivation of smallholder rubber from the 1920s onwards; by 1940, it was estimated that over 700,000 hectares of land were planted to smallholder rubber outside Java, compared to 385,000 hectares planted by large estates (Creutzberg 1975: 94). Most of the smallholder land was under some form of traditional tenure, in which farmers appeared to have confidence.

But in spite of the success stories, very often colonial governments either neglected the welfare of smallholders or actively tried to prevent them from diversifying into different types of agricultural activity. In lower Burma, the government did not prevent the rapid expansion of rice land but neither did it do much to assist the smallholders who had to rely on finance from Indian moneylenders. When rice prices fell over the 1930s and they were forced to default on debt, a substantial proportion of the rice lands passed out of their ownership. In addition, as Adas (1974: 62-65) pointed out, the farmers had little assistance from government officials on cultivation techniques, and simply replicated the primitive rice technologies from the dry zones of Burma in their new surroundings.

A puzzle to some historians is why the British adopted an extreme laissez-faire policy towards land alienation in Burma while taking a much more interventionist approach in Malaya. In 1913, the Malay Reservations Enactment gave the British resident in each of the Federated Malay States (FMS) the power to reserve any land in the state for cultivation by the indigenous population of that state; it could not be sold or leased to any non-Malay party. By the 1920s it was estimated that around 15 per cent of all land in the Federated Malay States was in Malay reservations (Brown 2005: 19). The British policy in Malaya was influenced by the Dutch legislation in Indonesia enacted in the early 1870s, although it was more restrictive in that it prohibited any alienation of land from within the reservations including leasing. Brown argued (2005: 20) that the failure to take any similar action in Burma was mainly due to the fact that Burma was not, until 1937, a colony in its own right but a province of British India, where the authorities were reluctant to impose any legislative restrictions on the freedom of contract in land markets.

Neither the Indonesian nor the British Malayan legislation was intended to stop large estate companies from acquiring land either on long leases or on other forms of tenure. Planted area of estate rubber, which was the most important of the 'new crops' transforming the export economies of both British Malaya and Indonesia after 1900, grew rapidly in both colonies, especially after 1910 (Booth 2007a: Table 3.10). Part of this growth took place in regions where 'empty land' was still available for exploitation by estates but by no means all of it. Estate companies also acquired rights to the use of land in the more densely settled areas of Southeast Asia, where by the early twentieth century land was no longer an abundant factor. Even as late as the 1920s, there was as much land under the control of estate companies in Java as in the rest of Indonesia (Booth 2007a: Table 3.9). Some of this was land rented in from smallholder cultivators, and used for the cultivation of sugar. Planted area of estates in Java in the early 1920s amounted to around 18 per cent of planted area of smallholder food crops and other crops in the early 1920s; this proportion fell over the following two decades but was still over 13 per cent in the late 1930s.

Even in the more land-abundant parts of Southeast Asia, tensions between estates and smallholders over land became more marked after 1920. In British Malaya, the official view of rural Malays was that they were cultivators of rice and other food crops, and should be dissuaded from growing 'speculative' export crops such as rubber, whose prices on world markets were highly unstable (Drabble 1991: 103). These attitudes changed little, in spite of the evidence that growing rubber was considerably more profitable to smallholders than growing rice (Sundaram 1988: 65). Most economic historians of colonial Malaya agree that rubber policies were biased in favour of the estates; this was in part at least because of pressures from the metropolitan government (Drabble 1991: 303-304). That smallholder acreage continued to grow until 1940 testifies to the determination of the Malay farmer to take advantage of the opportunity to earn a cash income, however unstable, from rubber cultivation.

The process of accommodating growing populations in agriculture across Southeast Asia before 1940 varied considerably but some common conclusions can be extracted from the evidence. First, in those areas where population growth was faster than land area growth, especially Tonkin, Annam and parts of Java, it is probable that there was some decline in average holding size over the latter part of the nineteenth and early twentieth centuries. But this was not sufficient to give all households with available labour access to land, and a growing number of agricultural households either became completely landless, or operated only tiny parcels. These households operated whatever land they could access very intensively, but were also forced to seek extra income from other sources. The problem of land scarcity was made worse in at least some areas by the growing concentration of land in fewer households, although evidence on changes in inequality over time is difficult to assemble.

A second conclusion is that, even in regions where arable land grew faster than the rural population, such as in many parts of the Philippines and Cochinchina, tenancy seems to have become more widespread. The reasons for this were complex, but the outcome was that tenants were often in a precarious position, with few rights. At worst their situation was little better than that of landless labourers. But several factors did offset the effects of diminishing holding size, and growing tenancy. One was the growth of double-cropping, which was the result of improved irrigation. Although rice and other food crop yields on average did not increase, double cropping did lead to more land under food crop cultivation. A further development was the growing international demand for export crops. This permitted millions of smallholder producers of crops such as rice, coffee, pepper and, after 1910, rubber to increase production, and their cash incomes. Government policies towards smallholder producers of export crops were seldom supportive and sometimes hostile, especially where the interests of smallholders conflicted with those of the large estates. But governments were unable to prevent the growth of smallholder production for markets, both domestic and global.

A third conclusion relates to the role of large estates, whether controlled by foreign interests or by domestic capitalists. They did provide employment to considerable numbers of workers who depended on wage labour for at least part of their incomes. This was especially the case in Java, and in regions such as North Sumatra and Southern Vietnam where the growth of estates created employment for migrant workers from other parts of Indonesia, and Indochina. In the Philippines, the 1939 census reported that 187,000 workers, over 5 per cent of the agricultural labour force, were employed as labourers on sugar farms, many of them large-scale. In British Malaya and in Burma, where most indigenous households had some access to land, employment in estates and in export-processing industries was considered by many indigenous workers to be both badly paid and demeaning. Most jobs were filled by migrant workers from China and India. But even this was changing by the late 1930s.

A fourth conclusion relates to technological change. By the early twentieth century, yields per hectare of rice were much higher in Japan than in monsoon Asia. The Japanese had learned from German scientists about the key relationships between water control, nitrogen application and higher yields, but these lessons had not spread to other parts of Asia, with the exception of the Japanese colonies of Taiwan and Korea. Agricultural research in the European colonies was mainly limited to estate crops, where there were some impressive achievements, especially in sugar. The new sugar varieties developed in Java led to yields per hectare increasing more than threefold between the 1870s and the 1930s, although much of the economic benefit was lost through falling world prices (Booth 1988: 222-223). In the food crop sector, agronomists working in research stations in India, Java and elsewhere were aware of the difference in rice yields across Asia, but they were unable to bring about any significant improvements. The lack of progress was attributed to low levels of funding for food crop research, the negligible use of fertiliser on food crops, poor water control and a failure to breed higher-yielding varieties which were suited to tropical conditions (Barker and Herdt 1985: 580). Significant breakthroughs had to wait until the 1960s.

The last and most important conclusion is that, in spite of the growth that undeniably occurred in agricultural output in many parts of Southeast Asia, at least until 1930, the goal of an agricultural economy based on land-owning smallholders with secure property rights proved elusive. Increasingly, many millions of households throughout Southeast Asia were cultivating only small parcels of land, or none at all, and were forced to depend on income from non-agricultural activities and wage labour. Even those farmers who had managed to expand their holdings to cultivate export crops usually relied on customary tenure systems to secure their rights to land, including their ability to pass their holdings to heirs. The impact of this on incomes is examined in the next section.

Growth of Non-agricultural Sectors of the Economy

One result of the heavy emphasis on agriculture as the main motor of economic development in colonial Southeast Asia was that rates of urbanization
were low. Indeed, some historians have argued that the proportion of the
population living in towns and cities could well have been lower at the
end of the nineteenth century than during the 'age of commerce' in the
fifteenth and sixteenth centuries (Reid 2001: 59). But between 1891 and 1931,
the populations of what Huff called the seven gateway cities in Southeast
Asia grew to around 2.9 million people (Huff 2012: Table 1). These cities
were all ports, and also provided financial, transport and other services.
By the 1930s, the proportion of the population living in towns over 100,000
was highest in British Malaya, at around 16 per cent. In the least urbanized
parts of Southeast Asia, including Indochina, Burma and Indonesia, this
proportion was under 5 per cent (Booth 2007a: Table 2.3). Chinese and other
migrant groups accounted for a substantial share of the population of the
gateway cities, and dominated the population in Singapore, although in
Jakarta and Surabaya, indigenous people comprised the majority by 1930.
But urban dwellers were in all cases a small minority of the total indigenous
population, and the great majority remained in rural areas where access to
agricultural land remained a key determinant of household income.

But not all rural households could access sufficient land to make even a
basic living. As was argued in the previous section, incomes of rural households were becoming increasingly diversified in most parts of Southeast
Asia by the early decades of the twentieth century. In the more densely
settled regions this was to be expected; given that many households had
only limited, or no, access to agricultural land, they were forced to find other
ways of seeking incomes. The detailed study of farm household incomes
carried out as part of the Kutowinangun (Central Java) study in 1932 and 1933
found that, on average, 'by-employment', which included both wage work
and self-employment, accounted for around 16 per cent of the incomes of
the agricultural households, and a higher proportion of their cash incomes.
For farm households owning less than 0.75 hectares around 30 per cent of
household income came from by-employment. There was a negative correlation between household income per capita, and the percentage of total
income derived from by-employment, suggesting that poorer households
were more dependent on sidelines to supplement their incomes than the
better off (Table 2.7). But by the 1930s, even land-owning households had
become more dependent on wages and other income sources for at least
part of their incomes.

Off-farm employment was also important in more land-abundant parts of Southeast Asia. In Thailand, where average holding size was larger than in most parts of Java, an investigation conducted in 1930/31 found that less than half of the cash incomes earned by rural households came from agricultural activities (crops, animals, fish) in the northern, northeastern and southern parts of the country. Only in the more commercialized parts of central Thailand was the proportion around 41 per cent (Zimmerman 1999: 53-72). In other regions, where access to markets was more limited, it is likely that cash incomes were a smaller proportion of total incomes. But in the north and the south of the country both wage labour and home industry were, by the 1930s, becoming more important to many households as a source of cash. Andrews (1935: 160) probably reflected the official view when he stated that 'Siamese people plainly do not like to perform arduous daily labour on wages, and are very ready to leave this field of occupation to Chinese immigrants'. No doubt it was the perception of the governing elites that Thailand was a land-abundant country, and that the great majority of the population could make a reasonable living in agriculture, without the need to seek wage employment off the farm. But this view was increasingly at odds with developing trends in many parts of the country by the 1930s.

The evidence that cottage industries of various kinds were an important source of income to many households in Southeast Asia in the early decades of the twentieth century is perhaps surprising, given that several scholars have stressed the devastating impact of cheap imports of textile products and other manufactures on native industries in the latter part of the nineteenth century. Legarda (1999: 177-179) discussed the impact of the decline of native textile production in centers such as Ilocos and Iloilo in the Philippines. In Ilocos he argued that the demise of native textile production deprived many households of supplementary income, which could not be replaced by agricultural production. The only solution for many households was out-migration. Furnivall (1957: 161-162) argued that in Burma traditional industries decayed as imports not just from Britain but also from India flooded in. The new industries established during British rule relied on British capital and Indian labour, and did not provide adequate compensation to indigenous Burmans for the loss of their own industries.

While there is little reason to doubt that cheap imports, especially of cotton textiles, did hurt industries in some locations across Southeast Asia, the idea that all cottage and small-scale industry was wiped out, and with it an important source of household income, is simply not correct. Boomgaard (1991: 34) argued that the figures for non-agricultural employment in Java between 1815 and 1905 did not support the deindustrialization case; the percentage of workers employed outside agriculture grew. The advent of cheaper cloth allowed many men and women to take up more profitable tasks, either in agriculture or in a range of non-agricultural employment. By the early twentieth century, household income studies showed that cottage industry was still an important source of cash income; this evidence was supported by employment data collected in censuses carried out during the 1930s. In both Indonesia and Burma, the censuses carried out in 1930 and 1931 found that around 10 per cent of the labour force was employed in industry, including cottage industry. The most important sub-sectors in both colonies were food processing, textiles and clothing, and wood and bamboo crafts (Mertens 1978: Appendix Table 1.6; Saito and Lee 1999: 27). While part of their output was non-tradable, and not directly subject to import competition, it appears that industries such as textiles and garment-making did manage to survive. In some cases these industries were helped by access to imported inputs such as yarn and machinery (Norlund 1991: 87-89). In addition, some handicrafts, such as *batik* in Java, were aimed at niches in the market which imports could not fill.

An important aspect of industrial employment as it developed across the region in the decades after 1850 was that it was often dominated by women workers. In her study of the textile industry in Java in the century up to 1920, Meerkerk (2017) has argued that in spite of increases in imports of cotton goods, indigenous textile production was not destroyed. Workers, especially women, continued to allocate time to hand-weaving and *batik* production, in addition to other household tasks. Van der Eng (2013b: 1038-1040) has argued that the advent of cheap imported plain cotton cloth in Java led to the rapid growth of the *batik* finishing industry, increasingly aimed at a mass market. Both men and women were engaged in turning cotton cloth into a range of inexpensive batik products, often using a stamp to reproduce the designs. In the Philippines, the 1939 census found that manufacturing employed 7.9 per cent of the male labour force but almost 25 per cent of all female workers (Kurihara 1945: 16). Embroidery, dressmaking and native textile manufacture together employed more workers than any other sub-sector of manufacturing, and almost all were women. Women also dominated in hat and mat manufacture. These occupations were often contracted out to homeworkers, and the work could be combined with childcare and other domestic chores. Critics such as Kurihara pointed to the low wages typically received by women workers and the lack of any worker protection. But clearly many thousands of women were prepared to work under what some considered bad conditions in order to supplement household incomes.

As was argued in the previous chapter, the arguments of Williamson about deindustrialization are not supported by the evidence, if the term is defined as a decline in industrial production in absolute terms, or as a proportion of GDP. But another argument can be advanced that colonial governments could have been more active in promoting industrialization as a policy goal. It was often argued by critics of colonial policies in Asia that, even if a range of cottage and small-scale industry did survive in spite of the growth of imports, official policies tried to prevent the emergence of a modern industrial sector, which might compete with imports from the metropolitan economy. While there was some truth in this, at least in the early part of the twentieth century, there is evidence that by the 1930s views were changing. Especially in Indonesia and Indochina, there was growing support for industrialization policies as a means of improving living standards, due in large part to the realization that the growing populations could not continue forever to be accommodated in agriculture. While irrigation and improved crop varieties might allow more output per unit of cultivated land, and out-migration might ease pressures in some densely settled regions, many colonial officials, not to mention indigenous nationalists, realized that these policies would not be enough. The argument became more frequently heard that 'the permanent raising of the standard of living of the backward countries of Southeast Asia can only be obtained by the industrialization of these countries' (Rueff 1945: 14). These were the words of a French businessman with long experience in Indochina, and they found many sympathetic listeners both in the 1930s and after the Japanese defeat in 1945.

In Indonesia, Dutch policy during the 1930s was aimed at restricting the inflow of cheap manufactures from Japan and encouraging the growth of large-scale industry, at least partly by encouraging foreign multinationals to establish plants in the colony (Booth 1998: 41-44). In Indochina, it was argued that abundant reserves of coal and metals, the potential for developing hydro-electricity, and a large and cheap labour force made it highly suitable for the rapid development of manufacturing industry (Shepherd 1941: 13). French policy had in the early part of the century placed more emphasis on extraction of raw materials, but by the 1930s a number of food-processing industries had emerged, including rice mills and alcohol distilleries, as well as a large-scale cement industry and a modern textile industry. Shepherd (1941: 21-22) pointed out that the emergence of textile production was especially surprising, given that French textile producers were very dependent on colonial markets. But the home and colonial industries did not always compete. Part of the Vietnamese industry produced yarn for small-scale weavers, and part produced cheap textiles for poorer Vietnamese who could not afford the more expensive French imports.

Perhaps paradoxically, Thailand, which was not a colony, made little progress with industrialization before 1940. Indeed, until the 1930s, there is little evidence that successive Thai governments attached much importance to industrialization as a policy goal. This view was to change after the 1932 coup, which brought a group of army officers and civilian professionals to power. They embarked on policies designed to 'take the urban economy under state control' by controlling the rice trade, and distribution networks and fostering state enterprises, both in manufacturing and services (Phongpaichit and Baker 1995: 119). But these policies met with only limited success, and the share of non-agricultural activities in total GDP changed little between 1913 and 1938. Thailand also had a much higher proportion of the labour force in agriculture than was the case in the colonial territories (Table 2.4). It was only in the late 1950s that Thai government policies towards private sector involvement in industrial development and towards foreign investment were to undergo a major change of direction.

Summing Up

The last decades of the nineteenth century and the years from 1900 to 1930 saw important changes in economic policies across Southeast Asia, as the colonial governments had to deal with the consequences of growing international demand for tropical agricultural products, and competition for land between indigenous populations and corporations, which needed land to grow crops on a large scale for export markets. At the same time, as a result of both political changes at home, and changing conditions in the colonies themselves, the metropolitan powers were under increasing pressure to spend more at home on welfare policies, while at the same time improving living standards in their colonial possessions. Each colonial power tackled these conflicting demands in different ways, but there were common factors which became more obvious by the early decades of the twentieth century.

Perhaps the most striking concerned access to land. Although all colonial powers claimed that they wanted to build a 'yeoman farmer' class, with secure tenure over enough land to afford their families a reasonable living standard, in practice this proved difficult. In the more densely settled regions, growing populations were leading to smaller holding sizes and, in some areas, many rural families cultivated very small plots, or no land at all. At the same time, business groups were demanding more land to grow commercial crops in regions which were already densely settled such as Java, and in regions which the colonial authorities considered 'empty'. Households in rural areas with little or no land were forced to seek alternative sources of income, from non-agricultural activities or from wage labour. When the global depression hit Southeast Asia in the early 1930s, global markets for tropical products contracted, as did domestic markets for wage labour. The implications of these developments for living standards will be examined further in the next chapter.

3   The Colonial Period: Measures of Welfare and Changing Living Standards

Growth of the Wage Labour Force and Trends in Wage Rates

The growth of both large-scale commercial agriculture and non-agricultural enterprises in mining, manufacturing, construction and services together led to a growth in the wage labour force in most parts of Southeast Asia in the first four decades of the twentieth century. Labour force data collected before 1940 did not usually distinguish between self-employed workers, those working for wages and salaries, and those working as 'family workers' on farms and in other small enterprises, often without direct wage payments. Many workers in the last category were women. It is thus difficult to distinguish between workers who were largely if not entirely dependent on wage employment and those for whom wage employment was only an addition to the family income, the bulk of which was derived from other activities. In the early part of the twentieth century it is probable that most permanent wage employment was provided by large estate companies, and export-processing industries such as sugar refineries, rice mills, saw mills, and mining companies.

But by the end of the 1920s, government employment was becoming more important, especially for indigenous workers. This trend accelerated over the 1930s, as wage employment in parts of the private sector contracted. The special enquiry into industrial (largely wage) labour conducted in Burma in February 1939 found that more than 26 per cent of the industrial labour force was in public employment (Baxter 1941: 64-65). Increasingly over the 1930s, indigenous Burmans rather than Indians and Europeans were taking up government jobs; by 1940 they accounted for around half of all jobs in the government professional services compared with only 22 per cent in 1920 (Saito and Lee 1999: 19). In Indonesia, a report on government reform submitted in 1941 found that by 1938 Indonesians comprised 78 per cent of the civil service; only the more senior ranks were dominated by Europeans (Visman et al. 1941: 55-56). The data compiled by Polak (1943) on wage and salary payments accruing to indigenous Indonesian workers between 1921 and 1939 showed that total payments to government employees, including central and local officials and those in the police and armed forces increased relative to wages and rents paid by estates after 1929, although it lagged behind incomes of foreign Asians and Europeans (Table 3.1).[1]

Table 3.1:   Index of real income accruing to Indonesians, Foreign Asians and Europeans, 1921-1939 (1921-1924 = 100)

Year	Indonesians			Foreign Asians	Europeans
	Government	Trade etc.	Estates		
1921-1924	100	100	100	100	100
1925-1929	103	111	127	148	140
1930-1934	167	116	145	179	146
1935-1939	173	129	124	207	152

Source: Polak (1943: Tables 7.3, 9.1, 10.3, 12.1); deflators: Polak (1943: Table 16.2).

Employment opportunities in large estates and in agricultural processing shrank in the early part of the 1930s in both Indonesia and Malaysia as the impact of the global depression was transmitted through falling demand and declining prices. In the Java sugar industry, which was badly hurt by growing protection in the British Empire, numbers of workers fell from 132,000 in 1929 to only 25,000 in 1935 (Table 3.2). There was also a sharp fall in numbers employed in both rubber estates and tin mining in Malaya, from a peak of 363,000 in 1929 to 167,000 by 1933 (Khor 1983: Table 4.1). There was some recovery after 1934, although the pre-depression level of employment had not been reached again by 1938 in either Java or Malaya. Huff (2001: 302-304) argued that employment fell in Singapore across a range of firms, and this affected real wages. He estimated that real wages for estate rubber workers in Singapore fell by almost half between 1929 and 1932, although there was a recovery in 1933. Choy and Sugimoto (2018: 39), using a different deflator, found the fall was less severe. They also found that wages for skilled construction workers fell less in real terms than those for unskilled workers.

The slump in employment in the Java sugar industry (both field and factory employment) was very severe, and by 1938 numbers of workers were still less than half the 1929 level. Total wage payments (in 1929 prices) also fell after 1929; for the Java sugar estates 1938 wage payments in 1929 prices

---

1   The data given in Visman et al. (1941) used a narrow definition of the civil service; many more Indonesians were employed in the government sector, including local government and village officials, the police, and the army. The 1930 census reported that 492,000 native workers were employed in these categories (7.4 per cent of the non-agricultural labour force).

Table 3.2:   **Trends in total wage bill, numbers of workers and real wages, Java sugar industry, 1921-1940**

Year	Total wage bill (million guilders: 1929 prices)	Total workers (in thousands)	Daily wages (cents: 1929 prices)	
			Male	Female
1921	77	98	41	34
1922	90	101	47	37
1923	90	109	46	36
1924	87	114	43	34
1925	88	115	47	34
1926	86	116	41	32
1927	97	120	45	36
1928	112	129	49	39
1929	102	132	46	37
1930	101	130	48	38
1931	128	119	68	55
1932	109	97	79	62
1933	56	55	84	63
1934	26	29	72	57
1935	17	25	64	52
1936	24	28	60	55
1937	48	54	55	48
1938	54	56	61	52
1939	64	59	64	55
1940	n/a	62	62	53

Sources: Daily wages of factory coolies: Department van Landbouw, Nijverheid en Handel (1922-1930) and Centraal Kantoor voor de Statistiek (1932-1940); Java food price deflator: Central Bureau of Statistics (1947: 125); total wage bill: Polak (1943: 46).

were little more than half those in 1929 (Table 3.2). This sharp fall in real wage payments would obviously have affected demand for a range of goods and services provided by local suppliers. It might have been expected that, given the fall in both employment and the total wage bill in the Java sugar sector, there would have been a sharp decline in real daily wages in the early 1930s. But a marked feature of labour markets, not just in Java but in other parts of Southeast Asia over these years, was considerable degree of rigidity in nominal wages. Although they did fall, the extent of the decline was much less than the decline in prices. Thus real wages actually increased even though wage employment opportunities were declining. By 1934, real wages for unskilled workers in Java, Sumatra, Hanoi, Saigon and Bangkok were all above 1929 levels (Booth 2007a: Table 7.5). The data for workers in the Java sugar industry illustrate the problem very clearly; by 1935 numbers employed as factory and field workers had fallen to less than 20 per cent of the 1929 level, but average daily wages in 1929 prices for both male and female workers were still well above those prevailing in the late 1920s (Table 3.2).

Several explanations have been suggested for these apparently paradoxical trends. First, as often happens in periods of business downturns, it is likely that many employers dismissed the most junior and least experienced workers first. Thus, the average nominal wage might appear to be stable because those receiving the lowest wages had been dismissed, although those more experienced workers remaining in employment could well have been getting a lower nominal wage (Goudal 1938: 145). Second, employers would have been uncertain as to how long the bad conditions were going to last, and thus would have continued to pay their more experienced workers enough to retain their loyalty because they would be needed again when conditions improved. Third, conditions of work probably deteriorated for many workers who remained in employment, even if the nominal wage did not decline; they might have been expected to work longer hours per day, and could have lost some fringe benefits not incorporated in the wage (Ingleson 1988: 309).

Even if nominal daily wages did not fall as fast as prices, for many workers hired on a daily or weekly basis both in Java and elsewhere in Southeast Asia, fewer days or weeks of employment were available, so total earnings per worker on a monthly or annual basis could have dropped sharply. Even if they were lucky enough to keep some wage employment, many millions of workers across the region must have had lower annual incomes, and lower purchasing power, which in turn would have affected many small enterprises in manufacturing, trade, or transport. Thus, the decline in output and the total wage bill in the sugar sector in Java and in the Malayan rubber estates would have had severe repercussions for employment in many other enterprises, which either depended on the sugar and rubber sectors as sub-contractors, or which depended on selling goods and services to their workers.

For all these reasons it would be unwise to interpret apparent increases in real daily wages over the 1930s as indicative of broad-based improvements in living standards. If labour markets were indeed subject to various rigidities, caution should be exercised in using wage data to make any generalization about living standards of the kind that Williamson has made about the Philippines. He argued that living standards in the Philippines doubled under the American occupation because a series on real wages which he compiled showed that real wages more than doubled between 1895-1899 and 1935-1939 (Williamson 2000: Table 1.2). He found that real wages in the Philippines were 80 per cent higher than those in Japan in 1920-1924, and more or less the same as in Japan by 1935-1939, although he cautioned that the deflators he used might not be reliable. After 1910, he argued that real wages in the Philippines were higher than in either Korea or Taiwan, or in Thailand and Indonesia. But other data from the Philippines throw considerable doubt on these assertions.

Certainly it was true that wages for labourers on public works projects in Manila in the late 1930s were high in comparison with most other parts of Asia (Booth 2007a: Table 3.11). But this was a market where minimum wage laws would have been applied, albeit weakly, by the late 1930s. The data from Runes's survey shows that wages for sugar workers in rural areas were much lower than the urban unskilled wage, and indeed lower, in rice terms, than the wage for estate workers in Sumatra. A series on wages for unskilled rural workers in Camarines Sur compiled by Owen (1984: 47-52) showed a very different trend between 1900 and 1939 than the Williamson series. By the 1930s real wages were substantially lower than in 1900-1904 (Booth 2012: Table 8). The surveys conducted by Runes (1939), Lava (1938) and others indicate that many Filipinos in rural areas were living at a very low level in the late 1930s. Their findings, together with other investigations from the Philippines in the 1930s which are examined in the next section, would suggest that living standards were not as high, relative to other parts of the region, as the urban wage data alone might indicate.

A further problem in using wage data to deduce trends in living standards relates to ethnic segmentation in labour markets in several parts of Southeast Asia. Ingram (1964: Table III) produced a long-term series on wages for unskilled coolie labour and rice prices in Bangkok from the late seventeenth century to 1950, and found considerable variation but no rising trend. But for much of the nineteenth and early twentieth centuries, the coolie labour market in Bangkok was dominated by immigrant Chinese, 'recruited from the marginal groups of a Chinese economy in severe crisis' (Phongpaichit and Baker 1995: 177). Thus, trends in real wage rates in Bangkok probably said more about living standards and the availability of wage employment in southern China than in the rest of Thailand. Until the early twentieth century, a system of corvee labour was in place in much of Thailand which restricted the mobility of most Thai men; attempts to reform, or abolish corvee met with considerable opposition (Terwiel 2011: 220). During the 1930s, the government began to encourage more participation by indigenous Thais in the urban labour market, and placed quotas on Chinese employment in rice-milling (Phongpaichit and Baker 1995: 179). This was possibly one reason for the fall in real wages which occurred after 1934.

In many parts of Southeast Asia, it is probable that those who were in full-time wage employment, and kept this employment through the 1930s, were better off than many households who relied on both self-employment and irregular wage employment, which declined as the full force of the world depression was transmitted to Southeast Asia. Given the rigidities which characterized many labour markets, it is unwise to use trends in real wage rates, even for unskilled workers, as an indicator of trends in household incomes. As Huff (2001: 319-320) argued, those Chinese and Indian workers who became unemployed in Singapore had no rural hinterland to fall back on; they had no option but to scrape whatever living they could in self-employment. Even in Java, the workers who lost employment in the sugar industry often came from land-poor households, and would have had few alternative employment opportunities in the rural economy. Their families would have supported them as best they could, but household incomes and expenditures would have suffered.

If wages are an unreliable indicator, and if data on total household incomes from all sources are not available, what other indicators can we use to assess trends in living standards prior to 1940? Are non-monetary indicators such as food availability or mortality rates more satisfactory? The next sections evaluate the evidence on non-monetary indicators, beginning with per capita availability of basic needs such as food and clothing.

Availability of Basic Goods: Food and Clothing

By the early twentieth century, colonial governments in most parts of Southeast Asia collected data on food production and consumption, and for the main food crops, especially rice, it is possible to compare yields per hectare, output growth and per capita availability (Booth 2012: Table 1). Everywhere in Southeast Asia, rice yields were lower than in either Taiwan and Korea. These two Japanese colonies also experienced more rapid growth rates of rice output than anywhere in Southeast Asia. This was in large part due to the successful transfer of Japanese yield-raising rice technologies to its two colonies, which by the 1920s had become important suppliers of rice to the metropolitan Japanese market. But the growth in exports from both Taiwan and Korea meant that less was available for consumption within the colonies, and by the latter part of the 1930s per capita domestic availability in Taiwan was lower than in Indochina and British Malaya. Per capita rice availability in Korea was lower than in any part of Southeast Asia except Java. Many Koreans consumed more millet, and other coarse grains, than rice.

In spite of the greater integration of rice markets within Asia after 1870, there were always fears among colonial officials in regions that depended on imports that exportable surpluses from Thailand, Burma and South Vietnam might diminish, which would inevitably lead to higher prices in local markets. These fears were justified in 1919, when supply from the surplus regions declined and prices in markets in Malaya and Singapore doubled, leading to food riots in several towns. Choy and Sugimoto (2018) estimated that between 1918 and 1921 the real wage of skilled construction workers in Singapore fell, although it recovered rapidly over the rest of the 1920s. In the Philippines, imports fell and prices in urban markets also increased rapidly (Chiba 2010: 534-539). The government distributed rice in Manila at low prices to stave off unrest, and enacted legislation to control stockpiles and speculation and regulate prices. The crisis gradually eased as exports from the three main surplus regions increased again, but in the Philippines the tariff on imports was raised in the hope that domestic production would increase. Domestic production in the Philippines did increase over the 1920s, although imports also accelerated again, suggesting that a broadly based increase in incomes was taking place. In British Malaya, in spite of attempts by the British authorities to increase rice output, around two-thirds of total rice availability was still supplied by imports (Grist 1941: Table 32).

In the years from 1920 to 1940, it was clear that whether a country or region in Southeast Asia was an importer or exporter of rice was not the main determinant of per capita domestic availability. Rather, it was the preferences and purchasing power of the local populations on the one hand, and the price at which rice was available on international markets on the other. In both Java and the Philippines, rice was supplemented by other food staples including corn, vegetables, beans and root crops; this was also true in other parts of Southeast Asia to varying extents. Mears et al. (1974: Appendix 4.1) estimated per capita availability of rice and corn in the Philippines from 1910 to 1940; they found that it reached a maximum in the mid-1920s and fell thereafter. A moving average of both rice and rice plus corn consumption per capita tended to move together, which suggests that corn was not just a substitute for rice. Consumption of both staples were determined by changes in purchasing power, which fell in the Philippines over the 1930s, in spite of declining prices (Booth 2007a: Table 7.3).[2]

---

2   Consumption of rice also fell in Taiwan over the 1930s, although it has been argued that this was in part at least due to substitution of rice for sweet potatoes as rice became more expensive. Booth and Deng (2017: 90-93) examine the evidence on rice consumption in Asian colonies in the interwar years.

In Java, where population densities were higher than in most other parts of Southeast Asia, rice availability per capita fell to around 95 kg per capita in 1928-1932 (Scheltema 1936: Table 2). It was almost certainly low in many regions outside Java as well, with the exception of the less densely settled rice-producing regions such as Aceh, West Sumatra and South Sulawesi. Van der Eng's estimates for Java show a steady decline in calories derived from rice supply between 1880-1885 and 1937-1941, although total calorie supply increased by 26 per cent because of greater consumption of non-rice crops (Van der Eng 2000: Table 1). He estimated that, for Indonesia as a whole, by 1936-1940 food supply in calorie terms had increased to 2,000 per capita, compared to only 1,524 in 1886-1890. By 1936-1940, only around 40 per cent of total calorie consumption came from rice (Van der Eng 2000: Table 6). Given the paucity of data outside Java, these figures must be treated with caution but it is certain that in parts of Java as well as in many regions outside Java, corn, sago, and root crops played an important role in the diets of many people by the early twentieth century. Cassava was eaten in several forms: many poorer families in Java consumed it in dried form (*gaplek*) in the *paceklik*, or months before the main rice harvest. Fresh roots were also consumed, usually with some form of sauce to make the taste more palatable.

Cassava, whether consumed fresh or dried, was a cheaper source of calories than rice and indeed cheaper than corn or sweet potatoes (Van der Eng 1998: Table 7). But in spite of cheap supplements to rice, average calorie consumption per capita in Java by the 1930s was, for most population groups investigated by Dutch officialdom, well below 2000 per day. Polak (1943: 88) estimated that the average per capita daily calorie availability from the seven main food crops was 1,803 in 1921-1925, and fell to 1,658 in 1931-1935. The sample of farmers living near estates investigated in the final report of the Coolie Budget Commission found that average daily calorie consumption was only 1,391, and protein consumption per capita around 35 grams. Plantation factory labourers living off the plantation were consuming about the same, while field labourers were consuming less (Van Niel 1956: 108-111). This report found that calorie consumption rose with increased household incomes, especially among those living off the plantation. This finding appears to hold also for the sample of rural households investigated in the Kutowinangun study in Java in the early 1930s, which found a strong positive correlation between income per capita and calorie and protein consumption (Table 2.7). Nonetheless, the medical experts who participated in the Kutowinangun study found the state of health and nourishment of the entire village to be 'most satisfactory' (De Langen 1934: 405).

One possible explanation for the reasonable state of health in such a densely settled area was that those households who owned little land cultivated their house gardens very intensively. The Kutowinangun study, and other studies carried out in Java in the interwar years, found that as average holding size decreased, the amount of land allocated to house gardens, and the intensity of planting, increased (Ochse and Terra 1934: 355). This is confirmed by the data collected from Kutowinangun, which showed a negative correlation between land owned per capita and household income per hectare from house gardens (Table 2.7). The tendency for those households where land availability per capita was low to exploit their gardens more intensively was to persist into the post-independence era. There was also a significant negative correlation between land owned per capita, and the percentage of household income derived from 'sideline' occupations, which suggests that land-poor households were able to get at least some income from off-farm activities, and this extra income helped them to consume more calories.

Elsewhere in Java, there was evidence of more severe malnutrition in the 1930s, especially in regions where cassava was a staple food, and where opportunities for earning extra cash income were limited. In 1939, the director of public health instructed the National Nutrition Institute (Instituut voor Volksvoeding) to carry out a dietary survey in the Bojonegoro region in northeastern Java, where the food situation was causing grave concern (Penders 1984: 131). In the five villages selected for detailed fieldwork, it was found that most families were consuming well below the stipulated minimum of 1,500 calories per day. Poor diet made the population more prone to malaria, which in turn made hunger oedema more widespread. The governor of the province of East Java, Charles van der Plas, argued that effective programmes to combat hunger oedema across East Java would cost millions of guilders, and the money might be better spent on other policies, including improved irrigation and agricultural extension in poor areas, and better education on subjects such as child nutrition. Other senior officials, such as H.J. van Mook, argued that the situation in Bojonegoro was extreme, although it was widely acknowledged that the growing dependence on cassava as a source of calories was causing dietary problems in other parts of Java, and that, given the expected growth in population, out-migration and the provision of more non-agricultural employment would have to play a greater role in improving living standards on Java (Penders 1984: 142).

It was not just in the densely settled parts of Java that, by the early twentieth century, many households were reliant on non-rice foods for a significant part of their food supply. It has been argued that in many parts

of the Outer Islands of Indonesia, colonial policy encouraged rice cultivation
and consumption in regions where more diversified food consumption
patterns had been the norm. In parts of Sulawesi, root crops were widely
consumed by the common people in the late nineteenth century, and rice
was mainly consumed by elites (Henley 2004: 117-118). In the Philippines,
according to Miller (1920: 78),

> [d]uring the regular annual periods of food scarcity which occur in certain
> backward communities, it is customary to make the chief food go farther
> by adding less appreciated foods. Thus in rice-eating regions, ground
> corn is added to the *morisqueta* [boiled rice], and more root crops are
> consumed. In corn-consuming regions the people resort to cultivated
> roots and even to wild roots and starches from wild palms. In the most
> backward communities the coarsest forms of wild food supplement the
> chief diet. In these localities the period of famine is a time of real want,
> when the hunger belt must be drawn tight.

Miller did not estimate what proportion of the total population was subject
to severe food shortages on an annual basis; he argued that in the most
advanced regions such as Laguna and Pangasinan, where production was
diverse, or in those regions producing export crops such as coconut, where
there were buoyant world markets, annual food shortages were largely
absent, and the effects of periodic droughts less severe. But in those parts of
the country surveyed in the 1930s, there was evidence of persistent shortages.
Lava found that the Ilocano families he investigated were consuming fewer
calories per day than prisoners; indeed, most families of five were consuming
fewer than 6,000 calories (Lava 1938: 24-25). The investigation into living
standards of sugar workers in the Philippines conducted by Runes did not
include estimates of calorie consumption, although Runes suggested that
they might be consuming less than the Ilocano families surveyed by Lava, as
they were often not able to cultivate their own land. His estimates suggested
that sugar workers were spending around 80 per cent of their earnings on
food, much of it inferior in quality (Runes 1939; 22).

In French Indochina, reliance on rice as the staple foodstuff varied
considerably across different regions. Gourou (1945: 322-323) found that,
while rice monoculture often prevailed in Cochinchina, in the centre and
north of Vietnam more diversified cultivation systems were found, and
millet, sweet potatoes, yams, beans and manioc were grown as winter
crops for household consumption. In addition, maize was cultivated
both for local consumption and for export. Given the deficiencies in the

statistics on hectarage and yields, it was not possible to estimate precise production and consumption data even for the Tonkin Delta, let alone the more remote areas. Gourou (1945: 547-553) estimated that the average Tonkinese adult consumed 400 grams of rice per day, and at least 60 grams of root crops. Small amounts of fish were consumed but virtually no meat. These figures suggest a calorie intake of well below 2,000 per day, although other foods were probably consumed as well, especially at feasts and ceremonies. Brocheux and Hemery (2009: 274) quoted the findings of one study in the Red River Delta in Tonkin which found that 80 per cent of the population had only one meal a day for much of the year. Gourou did not think that food availability in Cochinchina would have been much higher than in the north, in spite of the fact that the average household cultivated more land. He argued that living standards in general did not differ greatly between north and south; as in many parts of Java, the population in the densely settled regions of Tonkin cultivated their land more intensively, and derived more income from artisanal pursuits. To some extent this compensated for the very small amounts of land cultivated by most families.

Although Thailand was usually considered a land-abundant country in the pre-1940 era, the available data indicate that planted area per person was lower than in Burma, British Malaya, Cochinchina and the Philippines (Booth 2007a: Table 3.1). Area of rice land per capita was about the same in Thailand as in Vietnam and Cambodia, although higher than Java (Table 2.6). Detailed information on the diets of over 9,000 people in rural Thailand in 1930-1931 was reported by Zimmerman (1999: 273-286). The investigators found very few cases of severe malnutrition, or of diseases such as rickets, scurvy or beriberi. On average, 693 grams of glutinous rice was consumed per adult per day in those areas in the north and northeast of the country where this was the staple, and 553 grams of non-glutinous rice in central and southern regions. Glutinous rice was usually produced by hand pounding, which left more pericarp on the grain, thereby improving the nutritive content. Zimmerman argued that this compensated for the lower amount of fish and meat consumed in the northern part of the country.

If these figures are representative, it would appear that rice availability per capita was considerably higher in Thailand than in most parts of French Indochina, the Philippines or Indonesia. Thus there was less need to gain extra calories from root crops. But Zimmerman pointed to some worrying trends in the diet of many Thais. Hand pounding was in decline, and preferences were shifting towards milled rice, and imported dried fish, rather than fresh, locally produced foods. He argued that 'milled rice without more fish and animal food is probably not a complete diet' (Zimmerman 1999: 276). This study argued that, to the extent that malnutrition existed in Thailand, it was the result of a lack of knowledge and understanding, rather than a lack of food. The problem of the switch from hand-pounded or parboiled rice to polished rice also worried officials in British Malaya, who were worried about the prevalence of beriberi among immigrant Chinese in particular. It was only in the 1920s that scientists understood the association between this disease and vitamin B intakes; beriberi was largely unknown among Malays, who ate hand-pounded rice, and Tamils, who consumed parboiled rice. The possibility that Malays would be tempted into consumption of less nutritious foods was yet another reason why the British wanted to keep them in traditional rural occupations (Manderson 1996: 90-91).

The budget studies which were carried out in various parts of Southeast Asia over the 1930s found that many categories of worker, including small and middle tenants in Cochinchina, small proprietors in Tonkin, farmers in Ilocos, poor coolies in Batavia and field and factory workers on estates in Java were all devoting more than 60 per cent of household expenditures to food (Booth 2012: Table 2). Poorer groups, such as the sugar workers surveyed by Runes, farmers surveyed in Java and landless coolies in Cochinchina, were spending over 70 per cent on food. Other studies did report lower food expenditure ratios; for example, the fifteen farm households surveyed in Kutowinangun in 1932 only devoted about one-third of total expenditures to food, although among the sample studied in the following year the proportion was 59 per cent (Ochse and Terra 1934: Table 9 and Table 22). These high ratios do suggest that many households across Southeast Asia were struggling to provide basic necessities for their families in the 1930s.

Apart from food, the most essential basic need in a tropical climate was cotton cloth. Although domestic production of cotton cloth was growing in several parts of Southeast Asia by the latter part of the 1930s, only in French Indochina did domestic production fill most of the domestic market needs. Elsewhere, with the partial exception of Indonesia, reliance on imports was high (Table 3.3). Imports from Japan amounted to over five yards per capita in Indonesia in the latter part of the 1930s, and almost 31 yards in the Straits Settlements, although many of these imports would have gone to other parts of British Malaya, and to other parts of Southeast Asia, including Thailand and Sumatra. Total imports per capita in dollar terms were much higher in British Malaya than in any other part of colonial Asia, and even allowing for the fact that some of these imports would have ended up elsewhere, it would appear that the inhabitants of British Malaya were spending more on cotton cloth than their neighbours. This, together with the rice consumption data, indicates higher per capita expenditures there than elsewhere. But for a more complete picture of living standards, we need to turn to the demographic and anthropometric evidence.

Table 3.3:   Production and imports of cotton cloth, c. 1939

Colony/ country	Production of cotton cloth (yards per capita, 1939)	Japanese imports (yards per capita, 1937/39)	Total imports ($ per capita 1937/39)
Malaya	n/a	6.85*	4.08
Philippines	1.21	3.31	1.42
Burma	n/a	n/a	1.26
Indonesia	2.01	5.28	0.92
Siam	n/a	n/a	0.79
Indochina	4.08	n/a	0.52
British India	11.79**	1.26	0.20

* Imports are to the Straits Settlements only. It is assumed that they were transported to other parts of British Malaya.
** 1943 figures.
Source: Stewart (1949), Appendix II.

Demographic and Anthropometric Measures

By the early twentieth century, most governments in Southeast Asia were collecting information on demographic indicators, either through improved procedures for registration of births and deaths, or through surveys and censuses. This emphasis on demographic statistics could have been a reaction to a widespread concern about slow population growth, or even population declines in at least some parts of the region in the latter part of the nineteenth century. In Java, there was evidence of population decline in several residencies in the 1880s after the Krakatoa eruption of 1883, which caused substantial loss of life in both West Java and Lampung (Boomgaard and Gooszen 1991: Table 4). In addition, the huge deposits of ash damaged agricultural land across wide areas in western Java and southern Sumatra. Baten, Stegl and Van der Eng (2013: 115-116) argued that the Krakatoa eruption together with a series of droughts, cholera outbreaks and cattle disease all had an adverse impact on food consumption and on population growth in the last decades of the nineteenth century.

In the Philippines, Bassino, Dovis and Komlos (2018) used data on heights of soldiers enlisted by the US military between 1901 and 1913 to argue that

the average height of the cohort born in the mid-1870s was short in comparison with other parts of Asia. Furthermore, the average male height in
the Philippines appeared to be on a downward trend in the last decades of
the nineteenth century, compared with an upward trend in Japan. Their
findings support those of De Bevoise (1995: 12-13), who argued that the
very high mortality rates in 1902 were the result of disease rather than the
military campaigns against the Americans, although the two could have
been connected. Malaria was widespread, as was smallpox and cholera,
as well as deficiency diseases such as beriberi, all of which contributed to
high mortality. Corpuz (1989: II, 521-522) analysed population by province
between the Spanish census of 1887 and the American one of 1902. He found
population declines in 11 out of 30 provinces. There also seem to have been
declines in area under food cultivation.

The demographic information collected after 1900 could in turn be used
for estimating crude birth and death rates, and other demographic indicators
such as infant mortality rates and life expectancies. Most of these estimates
were hedged with caveats about the reliability of both the data and the
estimation techniques. But they do allow some comparisons to be made
of demographic indicators, both across countries, across regions within
countries, between ethnic groups and over time. Infant mortality rates
are perhaps the most important indicator as estimates were quite widely
available by the late 1930s. They show to what extent populations, and
especially nursing women, in a particular country or region had access to
modern healthcare, were eating a good diet and were possessed of sufficient
knowledge to give their babies the right food and protect them from the
main waterborne and insect-borne killers, including diarrhoea, cholera,
and malaria.

By the latter part of the 1930s, the lowest infant mortality rates were
reported in the Philippines, the Federated Malay States, and the Straits
Settlements. Rather higher rates were estimated for the city of Hanoi,
and in Burma and Java (Table 3.4). To place these figures in a broader
international perspective, infant mortality rates in Romania in the late 1930s
were estimated to be 179 per 1,000 live births, 138 in Poland, 65 in France,
54 in England, 50 in the USA and 36 in the Netherlands (Zeldin 1981: 206).
In all the colonial territories, there was a gap between their estimates of
infant mortality rates and those in the metropolitan powers. There was
also by the 1930s a large gap in life expectancies between colonies and
the metropoles; life expectancy in Indonesia was estimated at 34 years
in the 1930s compared with 66 years in the Netherlands (Van Zanden et
al. 2014: 109).

Table 3.4:   Infant mortality rates in Southeast Asia, 1910-1938

	1910	1925	1929	1938
Hanoi	n/a	440	430	190
Philippines	n/a	157	151	139
Straits Settlements	269	194	189	155
Federated Malay States	n/a	n/a	178	147
Burma	233	189	202	186

Note: Figures for Burma refer to 1910, 1925, 1930 and 1935; for the Philippines, 1926-1930, 1931-1935 and 1936-1940; for the Straits Settlements, 1910, 1925, 1929 and 1937.
Sources: Hanoi: Banens (2000: 36); Philippines: Zablan (1978: 105); Straits Settlements: Manderson (1996: 44); Federated Malay States: Evans (1939: 25); Burma: Sundrum (1957: 18).

In all the Southeast Asian colonial territories where data on crude death rates and infant mortality rates are available over a period of years, there seems to have been declines in the first part of the twentieth century. The crude death rates estimated by Vlieland (1932: 109) from the population censuses of 1911, 1921 and 1931 showed quite sharp declines in both crude death rates and infant mortality rates in the Singapore municipality and the Straits Settlements. Gooszen (1999: 205) argued that 'it is likely that the average level of mortality declined in the late nineteenth century in the north coast of Java', most probably because of improvements in the supply of clean drinking water. Vaccination against another killer, smallpox, had in fact begun in Java in the early part of the nineteenth century and by the 1870s smallpox had largely been eradicated, although it was still rife in parts of the Outer Islands (Boomgaard 2003: 610). In spite of increased attention given to public health measures after 1900 in Java, there does not seem to be any evidence of declining mortality rates until the 1920s. Java, like many other parts of Asia, was badly affected by the influenza pandemic which struck at the end of the second decade of the twentieth century, and which caused sharp increases in mortality rates (Brown 1987).

After 1920, infant mortality rates appear to have declined in Hanoi, the Philippines, the Straits Settlements, the Federated Malay States and Burma (Table 3.4). Huff (2001: Table 5) showed that in Singapore death rates and infant mortality actually fell between 1930 and 1933, in spite of the worsening economic conditions. In urban Java, crude death rates fell between 1912 and 1929 in Batavia, Surabaya and Semarang (Boomgaard and Gooszen 1991: 59). In all these cases, colonial authorities would have attributed these declines to increased expenditures on health personnel, and on programmes designed to address specific health problems, especially those of nursing mothers and infants in both urban and rural areas. That such programmes did feature more prominently in colonial government priorities is clear, although the amount devoted to health expenditures in the colonies and in Siam (Thailand) varied considerably, both over time and across countries. The comparative study carried out by Schwulst (1932: 57) showed that in the early 1930s, the Federated Malay States were spending the highest proportion (15 per cent) of the budget on health followed by the Philippines (8 per cent). Other colonies and Siam seem to have given health expenditures a lower priority at that time, compared with public works, and the military.

A further point to emerge from the evidence on infant mortality rates was that there were considerable variations between urban and rural areas, with urban areas often registering much higher rates than rural areas. Perhaps this was not surprising, bearing in mind the evidence from nineteenth-century Europe that urban mortality rates were often very high, to the point where cities only grew because of high rates of in-migration. In British Malaya, the 1931 census data indicated that infant mortality rates were considerably higher in the Singapore municipality than in the more rural Federated Malay States (Vlieland 1932: 110). Higher rates in Singapore than in most of the Malay states persisted into the late 1940s (Smith 1952: 54). In Java, one medical officer found extremely high infant mortality rates, ranging between 400 and 500 per 1,000, in overcrowded kampong areas of Batavia (now Jakarta) in 1917-1919 (Gooszen 1999: 192). Although these rates horrified the Dutch investigators, they were little different from the rates prevailing in Hanoi in the mid-1920s (Banens 2000: 36). Infant and child mortality rates were much lower in the city of Bandung, which was situated in the healthier mountain region of West Java, and in some rural areas, including the regency of Purwokerto in Central Java, where infant deaths per 1,000 lives births in 1935 and 1936 were estimated to be below 100 (Brand 1958: 256-259). Apart from the healthier climate, Brand argued that the higher educational levels of the Sundanese, who were the majority ethnic group in the western areas of Java, made them more receptive to modern medical ideas than the populations of other parts of Java. Outside Java, the evidence assembled by Boomgaard and Gooszen (1991: 63) show that infant mortality rates varied from over 200 per 1,000 in Maluku and the Karo highlands to 170 in Minahasa, although the absence of systematic reporting of deaths in most regions outside Java render the figures unreliable.

Apart from rural-urban differences in mortality in many parts of Southeast Asia, there were also often glaring differences in mortality rates between ethnic groups. The study of infant and child mortality rates in

Batavia (Jakarta) carried out by De Haas in 1935-1937 found that infant mortality rates were around 30 per 100 for native children, 15 per 100 for Chinese and only 5 to 6 per 100 for European infants. Similar interethnic differences prevailed in mortality rates for preschool children (De Haas 1939: 239-240). The rate for Europeans in Batavia was only slightly higher than in the Netherlands in 1929-1932. Although subsequent scholars, including Nitisastro (1970: 113), considered the De Haas estimates of infant mortality to be too high, they did gain considerable currency and were widely cited by other authors (Hull 1995: 5). Other studies, including that carried out by Brand in Bandung, confirmed the large differences between ethnic groups (Table 3.5). Recent scholars have attributed the relatively high mortality rates among the indigenous populations in Java to the slow progress made in the shift from curative to preventive medicine in the interwar years. Certainly the budget cuts in the early 1930s impeded the development of public health programmes aimed at increasing awareness among the indigenous population of modern medical advances (Mesters 1996: 61).

Table 3.5:   Infant mortality rates in Southeast Asia by ethnic group, 1930s

	Indigenous	Chinese	European	Indian
Straits S'ments (1934)	235	154	25	145
Kedah (1928)	112	137	n/a	263
Fed.Malay States (1936)	149	139	n/a	136
Batavia (1935/7)	300	150	50-60	n/a
Bandung (1935/8)	145	111	35	n/a
Saigon (1936)	250	220	n/a	n/a

Note: SS = Straits Settlements; FMS = Federated Malay States.
Sources: Straits Settlements and Kedah: Manderson (1996: 55-56); Federated Malay States: Evans (1939: 25); Batavia: De Haas (1939: 239); Bandung: Brand (1940: 238, 248, 256); Saigon: Statistique Generale de l'Indochine (1937: 832).

There were also very marked differences in infant mortality rates among the various ethnic groups in the Straits Settlements. Manderson quotes official data from 1934 that put the infant mortality rate among the Malay population at 235 per 1,000, compared with 154 in the Chinese population and only 25 per 1,000 in the European population (Table 3.5). In the FMS the gap between Malay and Chinese infant mortality was less marked than in the Straits Settlements, as it was in Saigon. In the northern Malay state of Kedah, infant mortality rates among both Chinese and Indian populations were higher than among the Malays, although this might have been due to under-reporting of deaths among rural Malays. As many of the Chinese and Indians worked as estate labourers, this probably reflected the poor standards of healthcare available on at least some plantations (Manderson 1996: 130-137). Boomgaard and Gooszen (1991: 62) reported higher death rates among Chinese workers than Javanese in Western enterprises in Sumatra's East Coast residency, which might indicate that Chinese workers in both Sumatra and Malaya were more prone to local diseases. By the 1930s, the government of British Malaya had established infant welfare centres in most of the Malay states, as well as in the Straits Settlements, where it was estimated in 1937 that 300,000 mothers and babies had been in contact with clinic staff (Manderson 1996: 216). They received guidance on feeding and on protecting babies and young children against malaria, cholera, respiratory tract infections and other common killers.

Many colonial health officials attributed high infant and child mortality rates to both poor feeding habits and parental ignorance. Doctors deplored the tendency to feed babies with rice as soon as they were weaned, as well as the custom of carrying young children around on the backs of mothers or elder siblings all day. They also pointed out that parents usually ignored minor illnesses, bathed young babies in cold water, and placed them in draughts, which encouraged respiratory diseases (Brand 1958: 265). At the same time, some health officials stressed that, in many parts of Europe until the latter part of the nineteenth century, infant and child mortality rates were as high as those found in many parts of Southeast Asia in the third and fourth decades of the twentieth century. Brand (1958: 256) argued that the mortality situation among the native population of Bandung 'is only a few decades behind the situation in the Netherlands itself'. This optimism was based on an awareness that high infant and child mortality rates were not always the result of economic conditions, but rather of ignorance, which could and should be remedied by better advice and education. But budgetary cuts over the 1930s slowed down the development of more innovative health outreach projects in several colonies.

Further evidence on living standards in Indonesia in the nineteenth and early twentieth century has used evidence on heights of various groups from the 1770s to the twentieth century (Baten, Stegl and Van der Eng 2013). This study found that human stature declined during the mid-nineteenth century, probably as a result of the impact of the cultivation system on food crop consumption. A series of natural disasters, epidemics and cattle plague seem to have led to a further deterioration in stature in the 1870s and 1880s. There was some recovery in the early twentieth century, although the improvement was slow in comparison with other parts of the world. Van Zanden et al. (2014: 127) found that in the 1930s, heights in Indonesia were lower than in Thailand and India, and much lower than in Germany, Britain and the Netherlands. Although the Indonesian evidence refers only to males, and probably suffers from sample selection bias, it would seem to confirm the data on food consumption, which shows a decline in the last part of the nineteenth century and only a slow recovery thereafter.

A large survey of heights and weights of children from birth to 21 years was carried out in the Philippines by Concepcion (1933). She studied data from over 30,000 Filipino children, and compared her findings with studies from China and Japan. While she found some improvement compared with earlier studies carried out by American doctors, she argued that 'compared with Chinese children, the Filipino children compare favourably in weight and stature in certain ages only' (Concepcion 1933: 14). Compared with Japanese children, Filipino girls seemed to be doing less well than boys, which might have reflected a bias towards boys in allocation of food, and expenditure on medical care. Her findings led to the conclusion that 'Filipino children seem to possess all the potentialities found in other races especially during the first two years after birth but somehow they cannot keep up and they are left behind'. She suggested that poor nutrition and the widespread prevalence of intestinal parasites were perhaps the main reasons for this (Concepcion 1933: 15).

Education and Literacy

In the early 1990s, the Human Development Index included both adult literacy rates and mean years of schooling as well as life expectancy and an income variable. In subsequent revisions the literacy variable has been dropped, possibly because of difficulties of definition and estimation across so many countries. In Southeast Asia, questions about literacy were asked in several censuses carried out between 1930 and 1950, although the results have been criticized on the grounds that they often excluded people who were literate in non-European languages and scripts. In both Indonesia and Malaysia, people who had learnt to read Malay-language publications written in the Arabic script were often not considered literate in colonial-era censuses. It is also possible that people who had at least some knowledge of Chinese characters or of Indian scripts such as Tamil were also excluded from census definitions of literacy. This might explain, at least partly, the very high rates of illiteracy found in both Singapore and the Malayan Federation in the 1931 and 1947 censuses (Table 3.6).

Table 3.6:   Percentage of the population illiterate in the Malayan Federation and Singapore, 1931 and 1947

	Male	Female	Total
Malayan Federation:			
1931	59.3	93.3	72.2
1947	43.0	83.5	61.6
Singapore			
1931	53.4	83.6	63.5
1947	35.3	77.5	53.5

Note: Data exclude the aboriginal population.
Source: UNESCO (1957: Table 37).

In Thailand and the Philippines, the censuses held in 1947 and 1948 respectively gave a breakdown of illiteracy by age group. As would be expected the percentage of the population judged to be illiterate rose in the older age groups in both countries (Table 3.7). For males, the proportion illiterate was only 31 per cent in Thailand, and 36 per cent in the Philippines. In Thailand, many boys gained the rudiments of literacy in Thai in the monastic schools, although the curriculum was largely restricted to religious texts. Secular education was slower to develop, although primary education received more government investment after 1932 (Phongpaichit and Baker 1995: 368). In the Philippines, the impact of the expansion of educational facilities in the American period was clear; people born between 1904 and 1928 had lower rates of illiteracy compared with the older age groups. Another striking feature of the Philippine data was the low rates of illiteracy for women compared with both Thailand and British Malaya. This reflects the expanded provision of secular education for both boys and girls in the American era, together with the continued importance of the Catholic church in providing education to both boys and girls.

In Indonesia, no population census was held between 1930 and 1961; the 1961 results showed that around 53 per cent of the population were illiterate, in the sense that they could not read in any script. The percentages were much higher in the older age groups, which confirmed the very limited access to education in the colonial era (Nugroho 1967: 141). The estimate given in the UNESCO study (1957: Table 7) of 80 to 85 per cent of the population illiterate in the early 1950s is probably overstated; other estimates suggest a lower figure, of around 63 per cent in 1947 (Booth 2016: 56). The illiteracy rates for Vietnam and Cambodia given by UNESCO of 80-85 per cent should also be considered rough estimates, given the lack of reliable census data

Table 3.7:   Percentage of the population illiterate in Thailand (1947) and the Philippines (1948)

Age Group	Thailand	Philippines	Thailand	Philippines
	Male	Male	Female	Female
15-19	19.5	24.3	27.3	25.2
20-24	20.4	25.0	44.0	30.9
25-34	26.4	31.5	65.2	38.9
35-44	35.0	36.9	84.0	48.5
45-54	45.0	47.6	91.9	64.6
55-64	52.7	58.8	94.3	76.2
Over 65	59.2	72.0	94.4	83.7
Total	**31.4**	**35.9**	**64.4**	**43.8**

Note: For Thailand the data in the over-55 age groups refer to 55-59 and over 60.
Source: UNESCO (1957: Tables 94 and 109).

in either country. However, it is probable that illiteracy rates were higher in both Indonesia and French Indochina at the end of the 1930s than in other parts of Southeast Asia, given that numbers enrolled in educational institutions as a percentage of the total population were lower than in other colonies, or in Thailand (Table 3.8). By 1940, it was estimated that the average Indonesian had 0.4 years of schooling compared with 6.8 years in the Netherlands (Van Zanden et al. 2014: 96); the gap between French Indochina and metropolitan France was probably just as large.

Even if children in many parts of late colonial Asia were able to enrol for a few years in a primary school, their chances of going on to secondary and post-secondary education were extremely small. Fees were often high relative to average household incomes; in addition, many families could ill afford to lose the labour which a teenager could supply. The Philippines stands out as having the highest total enrolment figures relative to population in colonial Asia, along with Taiwan (Table 3.8). The Philippines was also unusual in having a significant number of students enrolled in secondary and tertiary institutions. The University of the Philippines was founded in 1907 on the model of the state university systems in the USA, and grew rapidly through the American era. By the late 1930s, government and church universities in the Philippines were estimated to be enrolling over 10,000 students, which was far more than in any other colony or in Thailand (Reid 2015: 302-303). When the country was granted self-government in 1935, there was already quite a large educated labour force, including many women, who were able to take over almost all government jobs as well as move into professional,

Table 3.8: Development indicators: East and Southeast Asia, (late 1930s)

Country	Per capita GDP, 1938 (2011 prices)	Infant mortality rates	Crude death rates	Educational enrolments as % of total population*
Singapore	2,296	155	n/a	**(53.5)
Malaya**	2,328	147	21	7.8 (61.6)
Taiwan	2,161	142	21	11.4 (n/a)
Philippines	1,763	139	23	11.5 (40)
Indonesia	1,526	225-250	28	4.0 (80-85)
Korea	1,266	n/a	23	5.8 (60-65)
Burma	1,037	232	30	5.4 (40-45)
Thailand	1,003	n/a	22	10.6 (48)
Vietnam	n/a	190	24	2.5 (80-85)

* Figures in brackets show the percentage of the population over 15 judged to be illiterate in the late 1940s, or early 1950s.
** Crude death rate data refer to Malaysia (British Malaya less Singapore). Infant mortality rates refer to the Federated Malay States only. Educational enrolments refer to British Malaya including Singapore.
Sources: GDP data: Bolt et al. (2018); educational enrolments: Furnivall (1943: 111), with additional data on Korea from Grajdanzev (1944: 264); illiteracy data from UNESCO (1957: Tables 5, 9, 10); data on infant mortality rates and crude death rates for Indonesia: Nitisastro (1970: 113, Table 39) and refer to Java only; Korea: Chang (1966: 268); Philippines: Zablan (1978: 100-105); Taiwan: Barclay (1954: 146, 161); Thailand: Manurungsan (1989: 35); Vietnam: Banens (2000: 36-37), crude death rates refer to Cochinchina, infant mortality rates refer to Hanoi only; Burma: Sundrum (1957: 20, 52); British Malaya: Evans (1939: Table XV), crude death rates: Palmore, Chander and Fernandez (1975: Table 4.1).

administrative and technical employment in the private sector. The situation in Indonesia was much worse; the 1961 census found that only 3 per cent of the population over ten had more than primary education (4.4 per cent for men and 1.9 per cent for women). For those over 25, the percentages were even lower (Nugroho 1967: 143-144).

Gender and Inequality

It was noted in Chapter 1 that the historical evidence suggests that women had a high degree of economic and social autonomy in premodern Southeast Asia, compared with their counterparts in China, India or the Arab world. It has been asserted that they 'monopolized textile and ceramic production, shared agricultural tasks (dominating planting, harvesting and foraging), and most importantly did most of the marketing and business' (Reid 2015: xviii). Some of these tasks were carried out inside the home, but it appears that women also became gainfully employed outside the home, especially in trade. Reid points out that for status reasons men were often reluctant to be involved in managing money or in marketing goods and services. Both European and Chinese visitors to the region in the fifteenth and sixteenth centuries noted the involvement of women not just in the small-scale bazaar economy but also in large-scale trade and transport enterprises, as well as in public entertainment, and even in diplomacy and government. In those regions where Islam gained more adherents, West Asian and North Indian customs such as face veils and *purdah* never really took hold.

In the early nineteenth century, several Europeans with experience in other parts of Asia, including Raffles and Crawfurd, commented on the role of women in employment in various parts of Southeast Asia. Reid (2015: 269) quotes Crawfurd, who found that women in a number of occupations in agriculture and trade in Cochinchina (Southern Vietnam) were as well remunerated as men, which reflected their high skills and intelligence. In Java, Raffles (1978: I, 353) found that, in managing money,

[t]he women are universally considered superior to the men, and from the common labourer to the chief of a province, it is usual for the husband to entrust his pecuniary affairs entirely to his wife. The women alone attend the markets and conduct all the business of buying and selling. It is proverbial to say that the Javan men are fools in money concerns.

What impact did the intrusion of Western colonialism across Southeast Asia, especially in the century up to 1940, have on the economic position of women? There is some evidence that changes did occur over the course of the nineteenth century as new crops were introduced, new farming systems evolved and imports of manufactured goods increased. Where labour demands were imposed on male cultivators, as in the cultivation system (*cultuurstelsel*) in Java, women often had to perform those functions previously carried out by men (Elson 1997: 180). Where households were free to respond to the opportunities offered by the rapid growth of international markets for crops such as rice, sugar, rubber, coffee, pepper and spices, women as well as men became more involved in cultivation and marketing of these crops.

At the same time, there were negative consequences for women's economic opportunities. Boomgaard (1991: 27) argued that over the eighteenth and nineteenth century in Java, large trading houses owned by Dutch and Chinese wrested trade from indigenous Javanese, and women were largely consigned to inter- and intra-village trade. Over the nineteenth century, the importance of spinning and handloom weaving also declined as cheap British and later Dutch textiles poured into Java. This would certainly have had an adverse impact on female employment in those industries but, as was argued above, the decline of certain industries, to the extent that it occurred, did not necessarily force women out of gainful employment. Both male and female workers were able to take up other income-earning opportunities, in agriculture, manufacturing and trade, which often gave higher returns than traditional handicraft industries.

By the early twentieth century, surveys and census data give greater insight into the role of women in the labour force in various parts of Southeast Asia. The labour force data collected for Java in 1905 have been analysed by several scholars, including Fernando (1989) and White (1991). White (1991: Table 1) found that the size of the female labour force was only slightly smaller than the male labour force (6.4 compared with 6.6 million) but almost 60 per cent was in a residual category, not adequately defined. He suggested that most were family workers, rather than those working for wages. The more comprehensive data on the labour force in Indonesia from the 1930 population census found that male workers outnumbered female workers in agriculture, where women were about 25 per cent of all workers. But there were often more women than men employed in non-agricultural occupations. This was especially the case in Java, where women accounted for 54 per cent of the total native non-agricultural labour force (Mertens 1978: 48).[3]

During the 1930s, population censuses were carried out in British Malaya, Burma, Thailand, and the Philippines, as well as in Indonesia. They all collected some labour force data. The 1930 census in Indonesia found that female labour force participation rates were very high in Central Java and Yogyakarta compared to other parts of Java, and most regions outside Java. Almost 60 per cent of adult women were considered to be employed in Yogyakarta and 46 per cent in Central Java. These figures surprised the Dutch enumerators; it is worth noting that in the early part of the twentieth century female labour force participation was very low in the Netherlands, even in comparison with other parts of Europe (De Vries 2008: 212). Whatever the

---

3   Locher-Scholten (2000: 59-63) discusses the evidence on female employment from the 1930 census in detail; her discussion should be read in conjunction with that of Mertens. She argues that the women comprised 44 per cent of the workforce in Java, which is a higher figure than that given by Mertens (1978; Appendix Table 1.3 and 1.5). This disparity might reflect the different figures on female employment in non-agricultural activities given in different tables in the census.

reasons for the emergence of the male breadwinner family in the Netherlands, and in other parts of Western Europe at this time, it did not appear to
have been prevalent in much of Java, or indeed in some parts of Sumatra and
Eastern Indonesia. Around 40 per cent of the female labour force in Java was
employed in non-agricultural occupations, which was a higher proportion
than in the rest of the country, or in any other country in Southeast Asia
except the Philippines (Table 3.9). This reflected the importance of both
manufacturing and trade as sectors which employed women.

At the other extreme, in British Malaya (comprising the Straits Settlements, and the Federated and Unfederated Malay States), only about 23
per cent of women workers were in non-agricultural employment. Women
comprised less than 20 per cent of the total workforce, which was low in
comparison with other parts of the region. In Burma, women were estimated
to comprise around 32 per cent of the total labour force, while in Thailand
and the Philippines, the proportion was almost 50 per cent (Table 3.9). In
Thailand, a very high proportion of both the male and the female labour
force was employed in agriculture. Some of these differences were probably
due to inconsistencies in definitions and enumeration procedures, but
it is arguable that the census data from the 1930s do capture important
differences in female employment patterns across Southeast Asia in the
closing years of the colonial era.

Table 3.9: Percentage breakdown of the labour force, 1930s*

Country	Total (millions)	% Women**	% TIA***	% WIA****
Java	14.7	26.0	64.0	58.9
Outer Islands	6.2	27.5	77.5	74.9
Indonesia	20.9	26.4	68.0	63.8
Burma	6.2	32.0	69.6	72.0
British Malaya	2.0	19.1	60.8	76.9
Thailand	6.8	47.3	88.6	93.4
Philippines	8.5	50.2	40.8	11.2
*****	(5.3)	(20.7)	(65.0)	(43.1)

* Indonesia (1930); Burma and British Malaya (1931); Thailand (1937); Philippines (1939).
** Women as percentage of the total labour force.
*** Percentage of the total labour force in agriculture.
**** Percentage of the female labour force in agriculture.
***** Figures in brackets are estimates excluding those classified as housekeepers and housewives
from the labour force in the Philippines.
Sources: Indonesia: Mertens (1978: Appendix Table 1.5); Burma: Walinsky (1962: 33); British Malaya:
Vlieland (1932: 99); Thailand: Central Service of Statistics (c. 1946: 81-83); Philippines: Common-
wealth of the Philippines (1941: 505-514).

Particularly striking are the figures for the Philippines. The 1939 census figures found that only about 41 per cent of the labour force was employed in agriculture, which was lower than in other parts of Asia. One reason for this was that the census counted both housekeepers and housewives as part of the labour force, which led to high female labour force participation rates and also a high share of the female labour force working outside agriculture. But it appears that many women who gave housekeeping as their primary occupation were also engaged in other tasks, in both agriculture and other sectors. Even when women classified as housewives were excluded from the labour force estimates, only 43 per cent of the female labour force was employed in agriculture, which was lower than elsewhere in the region (Table 3.9). The Philippine census also revealed that, of those employed in agriculture, 48 per cent of all male workers and 86 per cent of female workers were employed not as farmers or farm managers but as agricultural labourers. Many women classified as agricultural labourers were probably working as unpaid family workers.

The Impact of Government on Indigenous Welfare

By the early twentieth century, there were striking differences between Asian colonies in government expenditures and revenues per capita, and in the mix of tax and non-tax revenues (Booth 2007a: Tables 4.1 and 4.3). On the expenditure side, the early years of the twentieth century witnessed a marked change in the role of governments in many parts of the region. Colonial governments across Southeast Asia began to assume responsibility for a much broader range of activities than simply the maintenance of law and order and the collection of revenues. They adopted policies which were intended to enhance the productivity of indigenous workers in agriculture and also equip at least some workers with the skills which would allow them to take on employment outside the rural sector. To a greater or lesser extent, colonial governments in various parts of Asia also began to provide modern healthcare facilities as well as formal schooling. But there were considerable differences across Southeast Asia in the allocation of expenditures. The comparative study produced by Schwulst (1932) found that, in the early 1930s, the Philippines stood out as the colony where a high proportion of budgetary expenditures were devoted to education and healthcare, and very little to defence. This contrasted with both Indonesia and Siam, where defence expenditures accounted for more than 20 per cent of total government outlays (Table 3.10).

Table 3.10:   Percentage breakdown of government expenditures by sector, 1931*

Sector	Philippines	Siam	Indonesia	FMS	French Indochina
Education	28	6	9	5	3
Health	8	2	3	15	1
Public works	8	12	6	20	30
Agriculture	10	3	1	8	6
Administration	31(8)	45(9)	38(6)	34(6)	35(1)
Military	0	22	26	2	13
Public debt	12	9	13	9	4
Other	3	1	4	7	8
Total	100	100	100	100	100

* Percentages in brackets refer to expenditures on law and order. Figures for the Philippines and French Indochina refer to central government expenditures only. All figures are for ordinary budgets only and may understate some capital expenditures.
Source: Schwulst (1932: 57).

On the revenue side, there was by the 1920s considerable variation in revenues relative to population; by 1920 they varied from US$24 per capita in
the Federated Malay States (FMS) to only $3 in Vietnam. Although in the
1930s revenues fell in per capita terms in most Asian colonies as a result of
the global depression, there was still a substantial difference between the
FMS and the Straits Settlements on the one hand and most other colonies
and Thailand (Booth 2007a: Table 4.3). There was also considerable variation in the revenue mix. By the late 1930s, the proportion of total revenues
derived from direct taxes on income and land, and from customs duties
varied from zero in the Straits Settlements to 67 per cent in Burma. There
were several reasons for these variations; in the Straits Settlements and the
FMS, governments relied on excises on tobacco, petroleum products and
alcohol, as well as revenues from the sale of opium. The British authorities
tried to justify this reliance on equity grounds; it was argued that these
revenues fell on the better-off Chinese to a greater extent than the Malays.
In Indonesia, Burma and Vietnam, officials were reluctant to increase taxes
on the indigenous populations for fear of provoking unrest. Government
enquiries into tax burdens in Indonesia in the 1920s found that most of the
indigenous population was being taxed to the limit, and extra revenues
would have to come from taxes on the upper income groups (including
European and Chinese) and on corporate profits.

But in spite of this emphasis on equity, a frequent criticism of colonial
revenue systems in many parts of Asia was that they were regressive in their
impact. Critics pointed to the high reliance on land taxes, excises and export

duties whose incidence fell mainly on the indigenous populations living in rural areas. Income taxes on both corporations and individuals were either not assessed at all, as in British Malaya, or assessed at low rates with many exemptions. The main exceptions were Indonesia and the Philippines, although in the Philippines, the business taxes were often not progressive in their incidence. Excises on petroleum products, tobacco and alcohol, and revenues derived from the sale of opium were thought to fall more heavily on the Chinese, who were on average richer than indigenous populations. But by the 1930s there were worries about their incidence, especially as many poorer labourers, whether Chinese, Indian or indigenous, spent a significant part of their incomes on these products. All colonial governments, as well as Thailand, had to strike a balance between raising more revenues, which could lead to popular unrest and curbing expenditures.

A further aspect of revenue policy in Asia which is often overlooked concerns compulsory labour demands. Pre-colonial governments imposed labour demands on the populations under their control, and slavery and debt bondage were not uncommon.[4] Colonial governments in most parts of Southeast Asia viewed labour shortages as a crucial constraint on the rapid development of both export-oriented agriculture and industries based on the extraction and processing of minerals. But they tackled the problem of labour shortages in different ways. In British Malaya the government decided that indigenous Malays were usually unwilling to work for wages at all, and certainly reluctant to take on arduous regular employment on estates and in mines. Malays were encouraged to stay in their reservations and pursue traditional occupations as farmers and fishermen. Labour was procured cheaply from China and India, and came in large numbers. The 1931 census showed that 1.71 million Chinese lived in the Straits Settlements and the Malay states, and 624,000 Indians. Together these two groups comprised over half the total population of 4.4 million. In Burma, migrants from India also grew rapidly, taking up many of the unskilled jobs in urban areas. In 1931 there were 1.02 million Indians living in Burma, out of a total population of 14.65 million. In both colonies, those migrants who had some knowledge of English, and some entrepreneurial skills moved into non-agricultural jobs as clerks, shopkeepers and traders. A small number moved into the professions. But most were trapped in unskilled jobs, and were prepared to work long hours, which removed any necessity on the part of the British to force indigenous workers into unpaid labour in public works or as plantation workers.

---

4   Lasker (1950) gives a comprehensive historical overview of serfdom, debt bondage, and compulsory public services in Southeast Asia from pre-colonial times to the 1940s.

Other colonies faced different problems. In Indonesia, the 1930 census found that there were 1.23 million Chinese, around 2 per cent of the total population. Some were recent migrants, but many came from families which had already been in the country for several generations. Only a small number of recent migrants took up employment as estate labourers or unskilled workers on public works projects. Many preferred to work in firms owned by more established Chinese migrants. The Dutch authorities encouraged young men from Java to move to the plantation sector in North Sumatra, usually as indentured labourers with penal clauses in their contracts. The harsh treatment of these workers led to campaigns in both Indonesia and the Netherlands to improve their conditions, and a labour inspectorate was established in the early years of the twentieth century.[5] But given the long history of labour coercion through the nineteenth century, both in Java and elsewhere, the Dutch were slow to abolish the various forms of forced labour which had been used by both the colonial government and indigenous rulers. The formal abolition of the cultivation system in Java in the 1870s, and the introduction of more liberal policies which relied on free markets had some impact, and obligations under the *pantjendiensten*, *desadiensten* and *heerendiensten* were reduced or eliminated in most parts of Java by the early twentieth century (Kloosterboer 1960: 42; Lasker 1950: 176-179; Furnivall 1944: 181-187). By the 1920s, they only persisted in the two native states of Yogyakarta and Surakata. But outside Java, *heerendiensten* demands for public works continued until the late 1930s and imposed a considerable burden on the indigenous populations.[6]

In Thailand, a large part of the male population had traditionally been obliged to work for the aristocracy and local patrons, often for several months in the year. This system of corvee labour underwent considerable change over the nineteenth century, as part of wider changes in government revenue policies. There were several reasons for these changes. Migrants from China grew in numbers, and many were willing to work for wages on projects such as canal building. As the rural economy became more monetized, many Thai men began to pay a money tax in lieu of their corvee obligations. These payments were then used to hire Chinese workers, or those Thais who were willing to work for wages (Ingram 1971: 58-59; Baker and Phongpaichit 1995:

---

5   Controversies over the impact of the labour inspectorate and other efforts to improve the conditions of estate labourers in Sumatra continue; see Breman (2002) for one side of the debate.
6   These services were all compulsory and unpaid: *pantjendienstem* services were personal obligations for local rulers, *desadiensten* were for village officials and *heerendiensten* were for supra-village officials.

24-25; Terwiel 2011: 175). By the early twentieth century, most forms of forced labour had been eliminated in central Thailand although they persisted in parts of the north and the south of the country, where laws and regulations passed in Bangkok were implemented more slowly. As late as the 1930s, Andrews (1935: 160) argued that many Thais were still reluctant to work for wages, and a high proportion of non-agricultural wage labour, especially in urban areas, was supplied by Chinese migrants.

In Vietnam, the French authorities introduced regulations which abolished forced labour in Cochinchina in 1898, and in other parts of French Indochina soon after, but implementing these regulations proved difficult (Lasker 1950: 194-195). More regulatory controls on the use of forced labour were issued in subsequent decades, and in December 1936 a law was passed which banned forced labour in Laos and Cambodia, as well as in Vietnam. Thompson (1947: 186) reported that by the late 1930s 'forced labor still existed but only as a vestige and in remote parts of the colony'. The exceptions were obligations to provide labour for public works, although the 1936 law stated that these could be commuted for cash payment in all parts of Vietnam. The length of annual service was reduced to between 16 and 20 days. There were also more controls over the labour contracts used to attract workers from the north into wage employment in the south (Thompson 1947: 204-207). Wages in Saigon were almost twice those in the north in 1931, which should have been a strong incentive for workers to move, and the French government was keen to develop a more unified labour market in Indochina. But employers in Tonkin were worried that large-scale migrations from north to south might deplete their own supplies of cheap labour, and there appears to have been little change in differentials over the 1930s (Giacometti 2000b: 204-205).[7]

Most studies of forced labour in colonial Asia and Africa agree that it should be viewed as a form of taxation, although placing a value on the labour supplied under coercion is not straightforward, given that labour markets in many parts of Asia were undeveloped until well into the twentieth century, and often segmented by region and ethnicity. But where the practice of making money payments to escape corvee duties was widespread, it is possible to value the labour supplied by those who chose to work out their corvee obligations, using the amounts of 'ransom' paid by those who decided to make a cash payment. Estimates for the outer islands of Indonesia (both

7   Giacometti estimated a series for unskilled male workers in Hanoi/Haiphong from 1912 to 1953. He also estimated a series for unskilled male workers for Saigon/Cholon from 1925 onwards. Wages in the south fell behind those in the north after 1945.

the native states and the directly governed territories) in selected years from 1925 to 1937 are given in Table 3.11. In 1930, usually considered the last year before the full impact of the global depression hit the regional economies outside Java, numbers paying the ransom were higher than those contributing labour in the directly governed territories, and the value of labour was thus estimated to be lower than the ransom paid. But by 1934, when the full impact of the global slump was being felt in Indonesia, numbers choosing to pay the ransom fell sharply, while the amount of the ransom increased in the directly governed territories, although it fell in the native states. There was some increase between 1934 and 1937 in the amount of ransom paid, although the total amount of both ransom and work contributed was still less in 1937 than in 1930.

The Dutch authorities claimed that the continued use of corvee labour on public works (*heerendiensten*) outside Java was justified as most regions were not assessed for the land tax. But in 1930, the total amount of the corvee (ransom plus actual labour) was greater in per capita terms than the land tax in those regions where it was assessed. This confirms the argument that the burden of taxation in the regions outside Java in the 1930s was higher than on Java, although it is worth noting that in the native states of Java, and in directly governed Bali and Lombok, cultivators were assessed for the land tax as well as being liable for *heerendiensten* obligations.[8] While the land tax revenues fell sharply over the 1930s, numbers liable for *heerendiensten* fell only slightly in the directly governed territories and actually grew in the native states outside Java, although the value of the ransom per worker paying it did fall after 1930 (Table 3.11).

The continued use of corvee in colonial Indonesia attracted adverse comments internationally, given that other colonial territories in Asia had largely abolished it by the interwar years. A convention of the International Labour Office banning forced labour was ratified in 1930, and became operative in 1932. The Netherlands was a member of the ILO and its conventions applied, at least in principle, to colonies as well as to the metropolitan state. In fact, the value of the *heerendiensten* was by 1930 less than 3 per cent of total government receipts. Why was it not abolished and replaced by paid labour? The most probable answer is that the colonial government was determined to improve infrastructure outside Java, but doubted that sufficient labour would be available at wages which the Dutch authorities

8   Numbers obliged to contribute *heerendiensten* labour in the native states of Java in 1933 amounted to around 362,000 people, or 8.7 per cent of the total population. Most of these (around 275,000 people) were in the native state of Surakarta.

Table 3.11:   **Numbers liable to public works duties (*heerendiensten*), ransoms per worker, total ransoms and value of labour, 1925, 1930, 1934 and 1937**

Sector	Numbers liable (thousands)	Ransom per worker (guilders)*	Total ransom (millions of guilders)	Value of labour	Total (millions of guilders)
1925					
DGOJ**	1,366	6.51 (41)	3.7	5.2	8.9
NSOJ***	1,142	5.87 (24)	1.6	5.1	6.7
1930					
DGOJ	1,469	7.67 (58)	6.5	4.1	10.6
NSOJ	1,306	6.65 (30)	2.6	5.4	8.0
1934					
DGOJ	1,432	5.39 (16)	1.2	5.7	6.9
NSOJ	1,295	4.17 (12)	0.6	4.3	4.9
1937					
DGOJ	1,421	5.47 (23)	1.8	5.1	6.9
NSOJ	1,367	4.10 (22)	1.2	4.1	5.3

* Figures in brackets show the percentage of all those liable who paid the ransom.
** DGOJ refers to directly governed territories outside Java.
*** NSOJ refers to the native states outside Java.
Source: *Indisch Verslag 1938: Part II, Statistical Abstract for the Year 1937,* Tables 405, 427.

deemed reasonable. The only alternative was to maintain the old practices of forced labour, albeit with some restrictions.

To what extent did the emergence of centralized systems of revenues and expenditures across much of colonial Asia in the decades up to 1940 improve the living standards of the indigenous populations? It is true that many governments tried to modify, or in some cases abolish regressive taxes, probably more from a fear of popular unrest than because of any real concern about equity. On the expenditure side, indigenous popula-tions might have benefited from modern infrastructure, including roads, railways and irrigation, and from greater access to educational and health services. But the benefits from these expenditures often accrued to a small part of the population and many were excluded altogether. The perception that colonial fiscal systems benefited particular regions or ethnic groups more than others was exploited by nationalist politicans, keen to use such grievances for their own purposes. After independence, governments throughout Asia had to take these grievances into account in fashioning new revenue policies while at the same time addressing widespread demands for increased government expenditures, both on infrastructure and on health and education.

Winners and Losers in the Colonial Era

A striking feature of Southeast Asian growth in the nineteenth and early twentieth centuries was the fast growth of both population and exports, relative to other parts of Asia, and probably to many other parts of the global periphery. In the century up to 1930, many parts of the region were transformed. Land under various types of agriculture grew rapidly. As far as can be ascertained from the available evidence, cultivated area of food crops more or less kept up with population growth in most parts of Southeast Asia until the 1930s, although this was not the case in some densely settled regions. In addition, millions of hectares were developed for the cultivation of export crops, both by large estates and by smallholders. By 1930, Southeast Asia was no longer an 'empty garden' but an increasingly populated garden buzzing with activity. In parts of Java, and in Northern Vietnam, colonial officials were justifiably worried about population outstripping available supplies of land. Their solution was to try and move people to less densely settled areas, or to non-agricultural employment. Many did move, often without government assistance, either to develop new farms where land was available, or to take up wage employment in estates, mines, offices and factories. In addition, many rural households managed to diversify their income-earning activities away from agriculture, and into manufacturing, trade and other activities. In many regions, women were active in a range of income-earning activities both inside and outside the home.

After 1900, governments across Southeast Asia assumed some responsibility not just for the provision of infrastructure, but also for education and healthcare. The results varied considerably by country and region, but the evidence does suggest that in most colonies there was some fall in crude death rates and infant mortality and an increase in literacy, albeit from very low levels. To the growing numbers of people across the region who had some sympathy with nationalist demands for greater participation by the indigenous majority in government, if not for complete independence, the achievements of the years from 1900 to 1940 seemed a case of 'too little, too late'. But they did lead to more people being able to read and write in both vernacular languages, and the language of the colonial power, even if they were still only a small percentage of the total population. They also led to an expansion of literature and journalism in indigenous languages. For all these reasons, the assessment of Reid (2015: 261) that 'levels of income and welfare rose scarcely at all in most parts of Southeast Asia until the 1970s' seems too pessimistic. Apart from the improvements in health and literacy, millions of small cultivators were able to increase their incomes by cultivating crops for global markets. On the other hand, in all the Southeast Asian colonies, large gaps opened up in life expectancy and literacy between ethnic groups within the various colonies, and with the main metropolitan powers, Britain, France, the Netherlands and the USA.

A further important change in the early decades of the twentieth century concerned employment patterns. By the 1930s, the evidence from censuses and surveys showed that in most parts of the region, the majority of people employed in manufacturing, commerce, trade, government employment and in the professions in most parts of Southeast Asia were indigenous, rather than Europeans or migrant Chinese, Arabs or Indians. The main exceptions were the Straits Settlements and the Federated Malay States, where fewer than 10 per cent of the labour force in manufacturing and commerce were Malays. A larger proportion of the labour force in government and the professions was indigenous but it was still much lower than in other colonies, or in Thailand (Booth 2007a: Table 6.4). It was true that many of the indigenous workers in these occupations were employed in the lower grades and in less responsible positions, but they gained crucial experience which they were able to carry over into the post-1945 era. Another striking feature of labour markets across the region by the 1930s was the high labour force participation rates of women, many of whom were in non-agricultural occupations.

Did Southeast Asia diverge markedly in terms of national income from the metropolitan economies in the nineteenth and early twentieth centuries? In fact, the evidence suggests that there was already a considerable gap in per capita GDP between Southeast Asian colonies and the metropolitan economies in the late nineteenth century, but it does not appear to have widened before 1939 (Table 1.6). But if we compare the performance of these colonies and Thailand with the USA, which had emerged as the leading industrial country by the early twentieth century, a rather different story emerges. In all parts of Southeast Asia for which we have data, GDP per capita grew more slowly than in the USA between 1870 and 1913. This was also the case in Japan (Table 2.1). But between 1913 and 1939, there was some catch-up with the USA in Singapore, Malaysia and the Philippines. Only in Burma and Indonesia was the gap with the USA wider in the late 1930s than in 1913. But everywhere in the region, growth in the 1940s and 1950s was slower than in the USA and by 1960 the disparities in per capita GDP were much wider than they had been before 1939. The reasons for this divergence after 1939 are explored more in the next chapter.

In his study of the global periphery in the decades from 1870 to the 1930s, Williamson (2011) claims that 'the Third World fell behind' although in fact the data on gross domestic output per capita does not really support this argument in Southeast Asia, especially if we compare colonies with the metropoles. He claims that deindustrialization occurred across much of Asia in the era of colonial control, and this led to growing disparities in GDP between the core and the periphery. While it is probable that some indigenous handicraft industries, particularly textiles, contracted as imports from Europe and later from Japan expanded, other industries including those based on agricultural and mineral processing grew. Even in the textile sector, the greatly increased availability of cheap cotton cloth allowed finishing industries to develop. By the 1930s, governments in both Indonesia and Vietnam were adopting policies to foster further industrialization in order to provide more employment for the growing populations. These policies were brought to an abrupt end by the outbreak of World War II, and the subsequent defeat of the colonial powers by Japan. We do not know what the results would have been had the Dutch and the French governments been given longer to pursue these policies but it is wrong to argue that they did not even try.

But in spite of attempts by governments to mitigate the impact of the depression years on indigenous populations, there seems to be little doubt that the years from 1931 to 1936 were ones of hardship for many millions in Southeast Asia. Employment opportunities in the large estate sector contracted in both Indonesia and British Malaya; it is likely that employment opportunities also fell in other parts of the region as well. Falling food prices across the region helped consumers but hurt exporters of rice. Prices of most other export crops also fell, which caused hardship among smallholder exporters of crops such as rubber, coffee, vegetable oils, pepper and spices. Restrictions on exports of most staples made it impossible to increase output and many producers must have experienced falls in money incomes. The sharp fall in the numbers of workers who were able to pay the ransom to escape the *heerendiensten* after 1931 suggests that money became much scarcer in many regions outside Java. Food consumption per capita fell in Java and the Philippines, and possibly in other parts of the region as well.

Authors such as Williamson argued that inequality in income and wealth increased in many parts of Southeast Asia in the century from 1840 to 1940 (Williamson 2015: 35-37). There is certainly support for this hypothesis. Evidence from several parts of Southeast Asia, and from other parts of the periphery, indicates that the wage/rental ratio fell quite rapidly between 1870 and 1913. Williamson (2015: 37) found that in Burma, the ratio fell by 44 per cent from 1890/94 to 1910/14; in Siam it fell by 98 per cent between 1870/74 and 1910/14. The decline for Siam in particular can be contested because of rigidities in the labour market which have already been discussed. But it seems probable that some decline did occur after 1900, especially in the more densely settled parts of Southeast Asia, where extension of the cultivation frontier was becoming more difficult. Figures from Java assembled by Polak (1943: Table 7.3) show that between 1921 and 1939 the ratio of rental payments to wage payments on estates in Java rose continuously from 1921 to 1937, with only a slight decrease in 1938 and 1939. This does indicate that in those parts of the region where arable land was not growing rapidly relative to population, those who could rent out land gained relative to those who relied on wage labour for at least a part of their income.

Williamson (2015: 36) also argued that 'globalization appears to have helped land concentration' in at least some parts of Southeast Asia after 1870. He points to the increase in tenancy in Burma, and in parts of Indochina, and to the increase in land controlled by large estates in the Philippines and Indonesia. By the 1920s, surveys in Java showed that the majority of the rural population were land poor in the sense that they cultivated very small holdings, and had to supplement their incomes from other sources, including wage labour or petty trade. At the same time, an 'official class' of well-paid indigenous workers in government jobs was emerging in several parts of the region. The data put together by Polak (1943) show that while real incomes of most categories of indigenous workers in Indonesia increased between 1921 and 1939, the increase was greatest for those employed in government (Table 3.1). Indeed, their incomes seem to have increased more rapidly than those of Europeans. The argument that inequality grew in Indonesia in the years from 1920 to 1939 receives further confirmation from the estimates of Leigh and Van der Eng (2009: Table 1). They showed that the share of the top 0.5 and 0.1 per cent of the income distribution increased between 1920 and 1934, and fell only slightly until 1939. Their estimates rely heavily on income tax returns over these years.

Williamson (2015: 37-38) also drew attention to the impact of falling terms of trade on agricultural producers across the region from the early years of the twentieth century down to 1940. The net barter terms of trade appears to have deteriorated in most parts of the region, especially after 1913. But the income terms of trade continued to improve, at least until the late 1920s. In the Indonesian context, it appears that the income terms of trade increased steadily from the 1850s right through to the end of the 1920s (Booth 1998: Table 2.1). This reflects the fact that total export earnings continued to grow, in spite of the fall in prices. Many smallholder cultivators across Southeast Asia contributed to the expansion of export production, and they continued to produce and market crops until the international restriction schemes were introduced in the 1930s. In several cases, such as rubber production in Sumatra and Kalimantan, smallholders were challenging the dominance of estate producers well before the end of the colonial era.

By the 1930s, all the evidence points to an increasing stratification of populations throughout Southeast Asia. While Furnivall was correct that part of this stratification was along ethnic lines, it was also increasingly visible within the indigenous majorities which existed everywhere except in British Malaya. Those who controlled reasonable amounts of agricultural land, especially if it was irrigated, were probably able to maintain their real incomes, even if they, and their families, had to seek extra work off the farm. The fortunate few who had access to regular wage employment, either in government or in the private sector, experienced growth in real incomes, even in the depression decade of the 1930s. They also acquired social prestige, and often made advantageous marriages. In some cases, their children were able to access education in schools which taught in the language of the colonial power. They were for the most part men; women were excluded from these jobs because of their low literacy rates, as well as for cultural reasons. Only in the Philippines were female literacy rates catching up with those of men by the end of the 1930s. It was these men who were well positioned to take up senior and more lucrative posts in the post-independence era.

Rankings in the 1930s

Although most colonial governments in Southeast Asia at the end of the 1930s expected to be in control of their various territories for much of the rest of the century, and possibly for longer, in fact matters turned out very differently. The Japanese army inflicted humiliating defeats on the British, the Dutch and the Americans in 1941/42. A pro-Vichy regime in French Indochina remained in place until 1945, but only after many concessions had been made to the Japanese. After 1945, the colonial powers were forced to grant independence, willingly in the case of the Americans in the Philippines, more slowly and often after bitter conflict in the Dutch, French and British colonies. The consequences of the transition to independence for living standards in Southeast Asia will be assessed in more detail in the next chapter. But how should we rank the achievements of the countries in Southeast Asia at the end of the 1930s, in what turned out to be the closing years of colonial control? If we look simply at per capita GDP, it seems clear that Singapore and Malaysia were well ahead of the rest. In 1938, what were to become two independent countries in the 1960s were still part of British Malaya, and per capita GDP in both was above the other colonies in Southeast Asia, and independent Thailand (Table 3.8). They also scored quite well on health indicators. But on educational and literacy indicators they did less well; the percentage of the adult population considered illiterate remained very high until well into the 1950s. British Malaya was also characterized by deep ethnic divisions. By the 1930s, Malays were in a minority. British policy was aimed at keeping them in rural areas as farmers, while Chinese and Indian migrants dominated non-agricultural occupations in urban areas.

Although per capita GDP in the Philippines was lower than in Singapore and Malaysia in the late 1930s, the country was comparable on health indicators, and achieved higher rates of literacy. Indeed, literacy rates, and the proportion of the population in schools were higher in the Philippines than in most other parts of colonial Asia, especially for women. Bennett (1951) ranked 31 countries, including 4 in Southeast Asia, according to nineteen non-monetary indicators in the years from 1934 to 1938. The indicators included calorie intakes, infant mortality rates, physicians per capita, textile consumption, school attendance, pieces of mail handled, vehicles per capita, freight transported by rail, cinema attendance, energy consumption and several other indicators estimated on a per capita basis. On an unweighted average of these indicators, the USA, Canada and Australia were top, followed by several European countries. The Philippines was ranked higher than any other Asian country except Japan. It was also ranked higher than Romania, Turkey and Egypt. Thailand was below these countries, but above India, Korea, Persia and China. French Indochina and the Netherlands Indies were ranked near the bottom; only Nigeria was below them.

Bennett expressed the hope that those countries which were ranked towards the bottom of his table would be able to catch up in the second part of the century, and indeed many countries in Asia and elsewhere have made progress on the indicators which he included. Thailand, Indonesia and Vietnam have moved ahead of the Philippines on the composite HDI index for 2016, although Vietnam was still below the Philippines in terms of per capita GDP (Table 1.1). The reasons for the relatively poor economic performance of the Philippines, in spite of its favourable colonial legacy, have attracted much attention in recent decades, not least from social scientists in the Philippines, and we will examine this literature in greater detail in subsequent chapters.

4   Confronting the Challenges of Independence

The Impact of the Japanese Occupation

The previous chapter examined a number of welfare indicators including availability of basic needs (especially food), demographic indicators (especially mortality rates), anthropometric measures and wage data. The chapter concluded that in spite of the growth in GDP which occurred in most parts of the region between 1900 and 1930, improvements in living standards were modest, and by the late 1930s most colonies still had low educational enrolments and high mortality rates, compared with the metropolitan powers. The Philippines had probably the highest living standards in the region, using educational indicators, mortality rates and per capita GDP estimates. These indicators suggested that living standards in the Philippines were similar to Taiwan and above Korea. But even in the Philippines, rice availability per capita was low and fell over the 1930s. Surveys carried out in the 1930s showed that nutritional levels among some segments of the population were well below acceptable standards. In other parts of Southeast Asia, including independent Thailand, food availability was higher but access to modern healthcare and secular education was very limited.

By the late 1930s, most economies had begun to recover from the ravages of the global depression, and in at least two cases (Indonesia and Vietnam), colonial governments were taking a more activist approach to industrial policy. Per capita GDP increased in many parts of Southeast Asia in the latter part of the 1930s after the decline in the early years of that decade. In the Philippines and Indonesia it was higher in 1940 than in 1929, although in Burma, and in British Malaya excluding Singapore, domestic product per capita in the late 1930s was still lower than in 1929 (Table 2.3). But in spite of the recovery, resentment against the policies of the colonial powers still simmered. In 1941/42, when the Japanese Imperial Army swept across Southeast Asia, inflicting humiliating defeats on the British, Dutch and American armed forces, they were greeted as liberators by many indigenous people. Nationalist leaders who had been imprisoned in remote locations in Indonesia were released although their activities were controlled by the Japanese.

But quite quickly the negative impact of the Japanese occupation on food supplies was felt across much of the region. The Japanese paid little regard to the colonial boundaries in the region, and established governments which suited their strategic purposes. These were chiefly to extract and export the commodities needed for the Japanese military machine, while procuring enough food to feed the Japanese troops across Southeast Asia. Sumatra and peninsular Malaya were governed from Singapore, while the island of Borneo, with its oil fields, was under the control of the navy. Across most of the territories controlled by the Japanese, trade in basic foods was discouraged or forbidden, even within quite limited areas. Rice supplies were commandeered from local populations to feed the armed forces; the local populations survived from what was left, supplemented with whatever non-rice food crops they could grow on the available land.

Those regions, including British Malaya, the Philippines and much of Indonesia, which had depended on rice imports from Burma, Thailand and Vietnam, were severely affected as regional rice trade ceased. For people who had been relatively prosperous before 1942, the occupation was 'life in a time of tapioca' as they supplemented their diet with non-rice foods which they had seldom consumed in peacetime (Bayly and Harper 2004: 327-330). But for others, food scarcity led to famine conditions, especially in 1944-1945. The regions worst affected were those which were already living on borderline subsistence diets in the 1930s, including parts of Java, and Northern and Central Vietnam. Van der Eng (2002: Table 6) estimated that population in Java, which had grown at over 1 per cent per annum through the 1930s, declined between 1943 and 1945. The rate of decline was fastest in Bojonegoro, Pati and Semarang, all residencies where there had been official concerns about food availability in the 1930s. Part of the decline was due to out-migration and part to falling fertility, but the main reason was higher death rates from lack of food, which in turn weakened the resistance of poorer people to common illnesses. Studies have estimated that around 2.4 to 2.5 million premature deaths occurred in Java as a direct result of the occupation (De Jong 2002: 280; Baten, Stegl and Van der Eng 2013: 118).

Famine conditions also prevailed by early 1945 in large parts of Central and Northern Vietnam. Vietnamese nationalists, and several historians, have argued that between one and two million died in Vietnam in 1944/45, although these figures have been disputed (Dung 1995: 575-576). The emergence of famine in Vietnam over this period might seem strange as exports of the rice surplus in the south to other parts of Asia had largely stopped by 1944, leaving more for domestic consumption. Although the rice was badly needed in mainland Japan, and in other regions occupied by the Japanese army, allied bombing had largely brought shipping to a halt by 1944 (Huff 2019). But it seems that transport shortages also prevented the movement of rice from the south to the north, or to Laos (Dung 1995: 614-615; Huff 2019). In addition, abnormally heavy rains led to falls in rice output in both the north and south of the country. Giacometti (2000a: 76) estimated that rice output in Cochinchina was 3.27 million tons in 1943, but had fallen to 2.25 million tons in 1945. Further falls occurred in the years after 1945 in many parts of Vietnam, which suggests that food shortages and high mortality could have persisted after the Japanese were defeated. The full extent of famine mortality remains unclear. The reconstruction of Vietnamese population statistics carried out by Banens (2000: 9) found that 'extra annual deaths' might have numbered between 250,000 and one million in 1944/45, and that total famine-related deaths could have been anywhere between 500,000 and two million. His estimates indicate that the average annual growth of population between 1934 and 1939 was 0.9 per cent per annum. Had this growth rate continued over the 1940s, the population would have been 26.8 million in 1949. In fact, he estimated it to have been 25.9 million, which indicates that the mortality rate over the 1940s must have been much higher than prior to 1940, although it is possible that fertility also fell after 1942.

Another factor which contributed to declining real incomes and increasing hardship for many people across Southeast Asia after 1941 was the high rates of inflation, caused by falling availability of food and other basic needs, and also the large amounts of banknotes issued by the Japanese (Booth 2007a: 154). Price indices showed very rapid growth between 1941 and 1945 in Hanoi, Saigon, Bangkok and Manila. It is unlikely that the incomes of most urban dwellers kept pace with inflation, especially after 1943. High rates of inflation persisted after 1945 in most cities; only in Manila did the price index show some decline, although prices were still much higher in 1953 than in 1941 (Table 4.1). The high inflation in urban centres would have been transmitted to rural areas; farmers with surplus production might have benefited from higher food prices but those depending on food purchases in at least some months of the year would have suffered. Those who depended on wages for at least part of their incomes would also have been hit. In addition to growing inflation, demand for workers in both government and the private sector fell. To the extent that the Japanese conscripted labour for public works projects, workers often received little beyond basic food. Evidence on real wages over the 1940s is limited; in Vietnam, Giacometti (2000b: 192) has argued that there was a continuous decline from 1937 to 1954. It is likely that these trends were also found in other parts of Southeast Asia, at least until the late 1940s.

**Table 4.1:   Index of urban consumer prices in Southeast Asian cities, 1941-1953
(1951 = 100)**

Year	1941	1945	1951	1953
Rangoon	29	n/a	100	92
Bangkok	10	66	100	n/a
Singapore	24*	n/a	100	102
Jakarta	6*	n/a	100	111
Manila	28	196	100	90
Hanoi	2	24	100	149
Saigon	3	10	100	156

* 1938.
Sources: Rangoon: Central Statistical and Economics Department (1963: 257); Bangkok: Ingram
(1971: 164); Singapore: Sugimoto (2011: 181); Jakarta: Central Bureau of Statistics (1959: 229); Manila:
Journal of Philippine Statistics, Vol 13 (10/12), p. 229; Hanoi and Saigon: Giacometti (2000b: 211-212).

The Japanese occupation, together with the post-1945 attempts to reimpose colonial control in Indonesia and French Indochina, led to a sharp decline in real GDP in most parts of Southeast Asia. Only Thailand, Malaysia and Singapore had regained pre-war levels of per capita GDP by 1950 (Table 4.2). In Burma where the British had granted full independence in early 1948, per capita GDP was little more than half the pre-war level, and was still below the 1938/39 levels in 1960.[1] Recovery was also slow in Indonesia. The Dutch were determined to regain control of their most important colony after the Japanese surrender, and ignored the declaration of independence issued by Sukarno and Hatta on 17 August 1945. The struggle between the Dutch and the Indonesian nationalists lasted for over four years, and the economic consequences were severe. When the Dutch finally conceded independence in late 1949, it was on terms which were far from favourable to the new republic (Booth 2016: 36-39). In 1950, per capita GDP was estimated to be only about 72 per cent of the 1940 level.

In the Philippines, per capita GDP in 1950 was also around 70 per cent what it had been in 1940; it had only just caught up in 1960 (Table 4.2) The American re-conquest of the Philippines, led by General McArthur, caused substantial loss of life and destruction of infrastructure. There was bitter fighting in the capital, Manila, large parts of which were almost completely destroyed. Nevertheless, it was decided to honour previous promises and

---

1   Estimates published by the Ministry of National Planning (1960: 16) showed that total
GDP in Burma only returned to the 1938/39 figure in 1957/58, by which time population was
considerably higher.

Table 4.2:   Index of per capita GDP in pre-war peak, 1950, 1960 and 1975 (pre-war = 100)

Country	c. 1940	1950	1960	1975
Singapore (1939)	100 (2,671)	100	89	245 (6,556)
Malaysia (1940)	100 (2,186)	122	113	229 (5,014)
Philippines (1940)	100 (1,845)	71	96	145 (2,033)
Indonesia (1940)	100 (1,627)	72	91	122 (1,977)
Burma (1938)	100 (1,037)	54	76	83 (863)
Thailand (1938)	100 (1,003)	99	136	256 (2,569)
Taiwan (1940)	100 (1,880)	74	113	336 (6,320)
South Korea (1940)	100 (1,238)	91	120	416 (5,146)

Note: Figures in brackets show per capita GDP in 2011 dollars.
Source: Bolt et al. (2018).

grant full independence in 1946. The transfer of power was largely peaceful, and American economic support continued for some years. The favourable educational legacy left by the Americans meant that there was a relatively large educated class to fill jobs in the civil service, as well as in private business and the professions. But in the Philippines, as well as in Indonesia and Burma, independence brought about a massive rise in expectations on the part of populations who felt they had been deprived of economic opportunities in the colonial era. Meeting these expectations proved difficult in all three countries, whatever the political orientation of the governments which assumed control in the immediate post-independence years.

The four protectorates and one colony which comprised French Indochina had a different experience, both during the Japanese occupation and after the Japanese defeat. In 1941-1942, the Japanese cooperated with the pro-Vichy government, which in turn was instructed to give the Japanese military the support it demanded. But as famine conditions took hold in the north, the Japanese finally ousted the French in March 1945 and tried to set up a local government structure which had been installed in Burma in 1943 (Bayly and Harper 2007: 143-144). The Japanese initiatives were welcomed by some Vietnamese, but little was achieved before the Japanese surrender and the arrival of a British force of Indian troops commanded by General Gracey. Gracey displayed little knowledge of, or sympathy for Asian nationalism; his mission as he saw it was to pacify Indochina and hand the country back to France. Although the British commander who was dispatched to Java took a more sympathetic approach to the Indonesian nationalists, neither he nor his superiors could control the returning Dutch, who viewed the nationalist leaders as Japanese collaborators with no following among the Indonesian masses.

The Netherlands in 1945 had a devastated economy, with limited capacity to fight a prolonged colonial war on the other side of the world. As the USA became more convinced that the Indonesian nationalists were not pro-communist, they were not prepared to help the Dutch reassert control. France was in a rather different position regarding French Indochina. Although the colony did not have the same economic significance to France as Indonesia had to the Netherlands, there was an awareness in France that surrender in Indochina could lead to the dissolution of the French Empire in Africa. This was unacceptable to large parts of French public opinion in 1945, not least because of the influence of the large settler community in Algeria. The French fought on in Indochina, with some American help, until their defeat at Dien Bien Phu in 1954. There followed a conference in Geneva, when a decision was taken to divide Vietnam into two parts, and grant independence to four new nations. Far from solving the problems of Indochina, the partition ushered in two more decades of conflict, which ended with the reunification of Vietnam in 1975. Communist governments took control in Vietnam, Laos and Cambodia. As will be seen in subsequent chapters, the consequences for the living standards of the people of Indochina were very serious.

Responding to the Challenges of Independence

In the immediate aftermath of independence, most governments in Asia were concerned with accelerating economic growth and diversifying their economies away from what was perceived as the colonial pattern of production. The expectation was that faster economic growth would lead over time to a broad-based improvement in living standards. The governments which had assumed power across the region in the decade after 1946 differed in their political views, but all shared a common reaction against what they saw as the colonial economic pattern. Almost without exception, it was argued that, while export growth might have been rapid in the colonial era, the benefits to indigenous populations were often meager. Even moderate nationalists thought that colonial economic policies were aimed at extracting profits from the exploitation of agricultural and mineral resources in the colonies, and that most of these profits had been remitted abroad. Although the colonial governments might have built infrastructure, including roads, railways and irrigation systems, it was widely believed that the benefits of infrastructure development accrued mainly to foreign estates and mining companies.

There was also considerable bitterness that most colonial governments had paid so little attention to improving the skills of the indigenous populations. In Malaysia there was added resentment that the British had done little to educate Malays, compared with the Chinese. This resentment was also felt in Indonesia. Although the Chinese were a much smaller percentage of the population than in British Malaya, only around 2 per cent, they had managed to get better access to Dutch-language education through the network of government schools for the Chinese resident in Indonesia (Govaars 2005). These produced graduates with a command of Dutch, who often moved into clerical and administrative jobs in the private sector. More wealthy Chinese families sometimes sent their children abroad for post-secondary education. Almost everywhere it was argued that more overt government interventions in the economy were needed, which would repair the deficiencies of the colonial period. Most politicians and senior officials across Asia in the 1950s and 1960s would have agreed with the assertion of Singapore's deputy prime minister that the policies of the colonial era had led to 'little economic growth, massive unemployment, wretched housing and inadequate education. We had to try a more activist and interventionist approach' (Goh 1976: 84).

But did this mean turning away from involvement with the international economy? Singapore had experienced negative economic growth in per capita terms through the 1950s, as had Malaysia (Table 4.2). Rapid population growth in Singapore after 1945 had aggravated the problems of overcrowding and inadequate housing which were already obvious in the 1930s. The government felt that its future lay with the Malayan Federation, and in 1963, Singapore had joined with the Federation, and the British territories of Sarawak and North Borneo on the island of Borneo to form the new federal state of Malaysia. But the Singapore leadership, ruling over an island with a Chinese majority, found it impossible to cooperate with the Malay-dominated government in Kuala Lumpur, and broke away to become an independent state in 1965. This presented difficult problems. Could Singapore become a viable economy on its own, having abruptly severed links with the hinterland of which it had been part for over a century of colonial rule?

The Singapore government sought advice from several foreign experts; one of the most influential was a Dutch economist who had been involved in framing the policies which led to the recovery of the Dutch economy after 1945. Dr Winsemius encouraged the government to develop the port as a container hub, as Rotterdam was doing in Europe, and recommended several industrial sectors where the government should attract foreign investment (Peebles and Wilson 2002: 35). The domestic Singapore market was small, and it was recognized that those industries which located in Singapore should aim to produce for export. The Economic Development Board had in fact been established in 1961; after independence it became the lead agency for attracting foreign investment into the Singapore economy.

The Malaysian government also realized that it would need to continue to produce for the international economy, although after 1957 economic planners gave higher priority to import-substituting industrialization than had been the case in the colonial era. Foreign investors were encouraged to locate in Malaysia, but it was expected that they would produce largely for the domestic market, with tariff protection. This strategy was also adopted in Thailand and the Philippines, albeit with some restrictions. But Burma and Indonesia seemed to have had serious doubts about the benefits of links to the international economy from the early 1950s onwards. Although in the immediate aftermath of independence, some ministers recognized the importance of foreign investment in Indonesia, by the late 1950s the forces of economic nationalism had gained the upper hand. Dutch enterprises were nationalized without compensation, which gave Indonesia a bad reputation in international investment circles (Lindblad 2008: 177-208).

Burma also adopted an increasingly hostile approach to foreign investment after 1960. Myint (1971) termed these two economies 'inward-looking', and contrasted their policies with the more 'outward-looking' policies adopted in Singapore, Malaysia, the Philippines and Thailand. According to Myint (1971), while these four countries also reacted against what they saw as the colonial economic pattern, they realized that it would be easier and quicker to change the pattern of distribution if the economy was growing than if it was stagnating. Myint argued that Burma and Indonesia were still 'obsessed by the fear that once the foreign enterprises were allowed to re-establish themselves in the export industries, they would regain their old stranglehold on the economy'. Post-independence governments must prevent foreign enterprises from reasserting their control, even if there was a cost in terms of economic growth.

In the case of Burma, Brown (2013: 205) argued that the extremely strong character of Burmese nationalism, including its 'ferocious rejection of the colonial economic structure' was the result of the Indian domination of the colony, as much as of British policies. It can be questioned whether the rejection of the colonial economic structure in Burma was stronger than in North Vietnam, where the Viet Minh had taken control after the 1954 Geneva Accords, or indeed in Indonesia after 1957. But there can be little doubt that many in government in both Burma and Indonesia, together with large swathes of public opinion, were doubtful about the benefits of continual links with the global economy, and especially with the Western economic powers. In the Indonesian case, the moderate pragmatists who supported at least some role for foreign investors in the national economy after 1949 became increasingly marginalized over the 1950s, while those advocating more extreme measures gained more popular support (Booth 2016: 40-46).

But whatever their doubts about continued links with the global economy after 1950, most Asian governments felt that a more activist and interventionist approach on the part of government was needed, and that this would involve medium-term economic planning. Such plans would set targets across a range of economic sectors, and then government agencies would implement policies designed to achieve these targets. New government planning agencies were established in most former colonies and in Thailand. But it soon became clear that, while establishing plan targets was relatively easy, implementation was far more difficult. Planning agencies often faced difficulties in getting cooperation from the government departments which were responsible for plan execution in sectors such as transport, irrigation, agricultural extension, education and health. Sometimes the sectoral agencies had different ideas about projects to be prioritized, but even where they agreed with the plan targets, they faced severe shortages of skilled people and, crucially, of financial resources.

The problem of mobilizing resources for the implementation of development projects, whether in infrastructure or in social sectors, including education and public health, proved to be difficult in most of the newly independent countries of Asia. The International Bank for Reconstruction and Development (IBRD, later the World Bank) began to give loans for infrastructure projects but the amounts were usually small. By the early 1960s Indonesia had severed links with both the International Monetary Fund and the IBRD, as well as with the United Nations agencies. In spite of much rhetoric about socialism, especially in the Guided Democracy years, Indonesia struggled to maintain real per capita government revenues and expenditures at the level they had reached at the end of the 1930s. By 1958, real per capita expenditures were lower than in 1938; in the Philippines they were no higher (Table 4.3). They were higher in Burma, but as Brown (2013: 122-124) pointed out, the increased expenditure was devoted to achieving the three key goals of post-independence policy: nationalization, Burmanization and industrialization, mainly through the creation of state enterprises. These goals were criticized by the American advisers who worked in Burma in the 1950s. But most Burmese, even the more critical ones, argued that given the complex political and economic difficulties which the country faced, there was no alternative.

Table 4.3:   Index of real per capita government expenditures in local currencies
(1953 = 100)

	1938	1953	1958
Indonesia	130	100	117
Philippines	129	100	130
Burma	58	100	104
Thailand	52	100	89

Note: Price indexes for Burma: GDP deflator from Ministry of National Planning (1960); for Indonesia, 1938-1953: Average retail prices in Jakarta of 30 home-produced and imported products, 1953-1958: ECAFE (1964: 240); for Thailand: cost of Living index in Bangkok and after 1951 GDP deflator; for the Philippines: cost of Living of lower income groups in Manila.
Sources: Indonesia: Creutzberg (1976: Table 4), Central Bureau of Statistics (1971: 317), population data from Van der Eng (2002); Burma: Ministry of National Planning (1960); Philippines: Commonwealth of the Philippines (1941: 164) and Central Bank of the Philippines (1956, 1960); Thailand: Ingram (1971: 329-330).

A further problem which affected development planning in many parts of Southeast Asia in the 1950s was a shortage of reliable statistics (Chander 1980: 88-89). While most planning agencies were primarily concerned with increasing economic growth, they were also under considerable political pressure to demonstrate that growth was leading to improved incomes and living standards for the indigenous populations. But how were they to do this, when they often had only unreliable estimates for even basic indicators such as population? In most Southeast Asian colonies, population censuses had been conducted in the 1930s, although in some areas the census information was incomplete. Statistics were also collected on production, foreign trade and prices, which have been used by subsequent scholars to assemble GDP series. But the decades from 1940 to 1960 were often not conducive to the orderly collection of data. Statistical agencies were reconstituted after independence, but they often suffered from lack of both funds and qualified personnel. After 1945, the Philippines led the way with household surveys and population censuses. These were also conducted in other parts of Southeast Asia in the late 1950s and early 1960s, although the coverage was often incomplete. Agricultural and industrial censuses and labour force surveys were also initiated. By the early 1970s, the availability of data had improved in most parts of the region, although there were still problems of quality. In the next chapter, the statistical evidence used for monitoring living standards will be examined for six countries: Philippines, Malaysia, Singapore, Thailand, Indonesia, and Burma, with particular emphasis on the use of household survey data for the estimation of poverty and income distribution.

The International Debate on Growth, Poverty and Distribution

After 1945, new international agencies were established which were mandated to promote development planning and assistance. Former colonial powers, which had never provided development aid to their colonies before they were granted independence, established aid agencies, which often concentrated their assistance on the countries which had been their colonial possessions. The international agencies were usually not permitted to become involved in the internal political processes of the countries they were operating in. This was true of the IBRD, and also of the United Nations agencies, which were also constrained by a lack of funds, and in some cases by internal arguments over what their role should be. The articles of agreement of the IBRD expressly prohibited the organization from engaging in political activity. Its lending was almost entirely directed to infrastructure projects aimed at improving productivity in agriculture and industry (Konkel 2014: 281). Although many countries in Latin America, Asia and Africa did experience some growth through the 1950s, by the 1960s, doubts began to be expressed about the extent to which the benefits of economic growth were benefiting the poorest sections of society. The United Nations decided to term the 1970s a 'development decade' in order to focus global attention on the problems of these countries, and their specialist agencies were encouraged to promote research on issues relating to the distributive consequences of economic growth.

One agency which responded to this challenge was the International Labour Organization (ILO), which had been established in 1919 to encourage tripartite cooperation between governments, employers and trade unions, so that working conditions and terms of employment could be improved in various parts of the world. After 1945, the ILO became an agency of the United Nations, and in 1969 it established the World Employment Program (WEP), with the ambitious goal of encouraging research on poverty eradication, employment promotion and economic growth (Ghai 1999). Several important studies were carried out in Southeast Asia under the auspices of the WEP, including a report on the Philippines, written by a team led by Professor G. Ranis of Yale University. Research carried out by the WEP tried to answer a number of key questions on the links between poverty, income distribution and employment. Were poor people usually unemployed, conventionally defined as those without employment but actively seeking work? Or were they working long hours, but trapped in low-productivity work, in sectors such as agriculture and small-scale manufacturing and trade, with no opportunity to move to more productive employment either

as wage workers or as self-employed workers? If the poor were mainly in
the latter category, what policies should governments adopt to encourage
the generation of more productive employment opportunities across the
economy in agriculture, industry and services?

The WEP research, while of considerable value to the scholarly community with an interest in development issues, inevitably had only a limited
impact on the policies of national governments, either in Southeast Asia or
elsewhere. The ILO report on the Philippines received considerable publicity
but the Marcos government displayed little appetite for the kind of policy
reform that the report advocated. A World Bank country economic report
on the Philippines published in 1976, which contained extensive analysis
of agricultural and industrial growth, as well as demographic and labour
force trends, also had little discernable impact on policy. The problem of
limited policy impact also affected other research carried out over the
1970s, including the influential series of studies on trade and development
carried out by the OECD. These studies stressed the costs of high rates of
protection in countries such as India, Pakistan and the Philippines. While
many academics involved in development research became convinced that
the problem of mass poverty in much of Asia, Africa and Latin America
could only be tackled through comprehensive reform of fiscal, monetary,
and trade policies, it was often difficult, if not impossible, to persuade
governments that such reform was needed. The IBRD was reluctant to
attach overt conditions to its lending and anyway it was still a small player;
one estimate claimed that its total lending financed less than 1 per cent of
all development spending in poor and middle-income countries (Konkel
2014: 283).

The World Bank stance on poverty-related issues changed over the 1970s,
after Robert McNamara became president. The watershed is often seen to
be the speech McNamara gave to the Board of Governors of the World Bank
(IBRD) in Nairobi in 1973, where he argued that reducing absolute poverty
should become an important, if not the main, goal of development policy.
He defined absolute poverty as a condition of life 'so limited as to prevent
realization of the potential of the genes with which one is born; a condition
of life so degrading as to insult human dignity' (Konkel 2014: 289). The
World Bank commissioned a study jointly with the Institute of Development Studies at the University of Sussex in 1974. Its title, *Redistribution with
Growth*, implied that growth alone would not necessarily bring about an
improvement in the incomes of the bottom two quintiles of the population
(Chenery et al. 1974). The report argued that greater attention must be paid
to the problems of employment, poverty and income distribution. Inevitably,

this emphasis raised a number of issues relating to the measurement of both poverty and income distribution, which influenced subsequent research in Southeast Asia as in other parts of the world.

The *Redistribution with Growth* (RWG) study suggested two approaches to the measurement of poverty. The first was to use household survey data to measure the percentage of the population below poverty lines of $50 per capita and $75 per capita per year. The second was to define the poor as the bottom 40 per cent of the income distribution (Ahluwalia 1974: 10-21). Although it was not made clear, the poverty lines expressed in terms of dollars were converted into the currencies of the countries in the study using market exchange rates. The results for the headcount measures of poverty in 1969 showed that the problem was worse in Asia than in either Latin America or Africa (Table 4.4). But the Asian data were heavily influenced by India and then undivided Pakistan. No estimates for China were available and only four Southeast Asian countries were included (Burma, Thailand, Philippines and Malaysia). The estimates showed over half the population of Burma was below the $50-a-year line, although the estimates were apparently made using only the survey carried out in Rangoon in 1958. The estimates also showed that the percentage of the population below the $50 line was almost 27 per cent in Thailand, more than twice as high as in the Philippines or Malaysia.

Table 4.4: Estimates of the population below two poverty lines, 1969

Region/Country	% below poverty line		Numbers (millions)	
	(1)	(2)	(1)	(2)
Latin America	10.8	17.4	26.6	42.5
Africa	30.9	48.2	370.4	578.2
Asia	36.7	57.2	320.0	499.1
Burma	53.6	71.0	14.5	19.2
Thailand	26.8	44.3	9.3	15.4
Philippines	13.0	30.0	4.8	11.2
Malaysia	11.0	15.5	1.2	1.6

Note: (1): poverty line of US$50 per year. (2): poverty line of US$75 per year.
Source: Chenery et al. (1974: Table 1.2).

Critics of the new emphasis on poverty and distributional issues pointed to the difficulty of generalization across a large number of countries in Asia, Africa and Latin America. As Little (1976: 105) argued, 'it is very difficult to write with great cogency and relevance about the forces which affect the lot of the poor in so many, and such different countries, and especially so when there are so few solid figures and so little research has been done'. In addition to the problems of data, there were disagreements about how the poor should be defined. Ahluwalia (1974: 18-19) argued that the poor could be defined as the lowest 40 per cent of the population, distributed by income, and this approach was used by several World Bank studies in Indonesia. But this method of measuring poverty contrasted with that advocated in India, where debates about poverty measurement had begun soon after independence. In the early 1960s, a study group established by the government recommended a minimum national consumption level of 20 rupees per capita per month (1960-1961 prices). Indian economists pointed out that that the basis for calculating this figure was never clarified (Dandekar and Rath 1971: 8; Rudra 1974: 36). Dandekar and Rath (1971: 9) argued that a more satisfactory poverty line should be based on calorie consumption of 2,250 per capita per day. A poverty line set in terms of calories could incorporate differences across regions in prices of basic foods. It could also be adjusted upwards to include the cost of non-food needs, including clothing and shelter.

The concept of a poverty line set in terms of calories in fact became widely used, both in Asia and elsewhere. But that concept in itself was ambiguous. The monetary value of a poverty line sufficient to purchase 2,250 calories could vary depending on what foods were selected and what adjustments were made to allow for non-food expenditures. Some analysts used linear programming techniques to determine 'least-cost' diets, but these often did not reflect consumer preferences.[2] While a national poverty line could be set in terms of averages for the whole country, most governments in Asia realized that regional variations in both prices and consumption patterns meant that different poverty lines would have to be set for different regions. It was also assumed the cost of living was higher in urban than in rural areas, and urban poverty lines should reflect this. But how much higher should urban poverty lines be? What allowance should be made for higher housing and transport costs in urban areas? Or for the fact that many people bought prepared food from market stalls, whereas in rural areas they were able to obtain food from their own holdings, even if these holdings were small house gardens?

2   A linear programming exercise carried out in Indonesia using the 1969/70 Household Expenditure Survey data (Susenas) found that a least-cost diet, providing adequate calories, protein, iron and vitamins, comprised four staples: cassava, fish, buffalo meat and spinach (Beenstock 1980: Table 5.3). But this diet ignored the strong preference for rice among most Indonesians.

Although the RWG report had considerable influence on development debates over the 1970s, the idea of a common poverty line, which could be used to measure poverty across countries and indeed continents, did not immediately catch on. The *World Development Report*, published in 1980, which included a section on poverty and human development, emphasized the difficulties inherent in measuring poverty. This report argued that 'absolute poverty means more than low income'. Malnutrition, poor health and lack of education were all factors which both caused poverty and made it difficult for people to overcome it. This report also pointed out that there was often 'disagreement about where to draw the line between the poor and the rest, and about the correct way to calculate and compare incomes and living standards at different times and in different places' (World Bank 1980b: 33).

It was these problems, together with changes in personnel after McNamara left office, that led to changes in World Bank thinking on development issues, and a change of focus in the 1980s. Both the World Bank and important bilateral donors turned away from the concerns expressed in the RWG volume, and concentrated more on macroeconomic reform and also reform of trade and investment policies. 'Structural adjustment' policies became the order of the day, and most of these paid only cursory attention to the impact of these policies on the poorer groups. It was only after agencies such as UNICEF began to point out that the impact of structural adjustment on the least prosperous groups was often adverse that the global development debate changed direction again, and economists once more began to address issues relating to poverty. The consequences of this for the countries in Southeast Asia will be examined in Chapter 5.

To produce headcount or other measures of poverty, statisticians had long realized the need to adjust the poverty lines set in dollars to allow for differences in living costs between countries, which are often not fully captured in exchange rates. In his pioneering study of national income in the years from 1920 to 1939 in Indonesia, Polak (1943: 90-94) had stressed that the difference between per capita GDP in Indonesia and the USA narrowed once differences in prices were allowed for. But a thoroughgoing attempt to estimate the extent of these price differences, and to assess their implications for estimates of global GDP, only began in the 1960s, with the establishment of the United Nations International Comparison Project (ICP), based at the University of Pennsylvania and led by Professor Irving Kravis. This project published several reports in the 1970s, which examined price and output data for a limited number of countries. The range was increased in subsequent studies.

The early work of the ICP included estimates of gross domestic product (GDP) converted using market exchange rates, and 'international dollars', which were dollars which purported to have the same overall purchasing power in the particular country as the American dollar had in the USA. Fifteen countries were included in the 1978 report, including two from Southeast Asia (Philippines and Malaysia). The results for both countries, together with the Republic of Korea, are given in Table 4.5. In all three countries the difference between per capita GDP converted using the market exchange rate, and per capita GDP in international dollars is considerable. The exchange rate deviation index was around three in the Philippines, although it was lower in both Malaysia and Korea. The main reason for the disparities was the lower prices of non-traded goods and services in Asian countries compared with the USA and Europe, which reflected lower wages rates.

Table 4.5:   Estimates of GDP in US$: exchange rate and PPP conversions, 1970 and 1973

	Philippines	Republic of Korea	Malaysia
1970			
Per capita GDP (exchange rate)	185	258	388
Per capita GDP (PPP $)	576	580	915
Deviation index	3.11	2.25	2.36
1973			
Per capita GDP (X Rate)	259	366	633
Per capita GDP (PPP $)	755	904	1,180
Deviation index	2.91	2.47	1.86
Percentage breakdown of GDP: 1973 (Int $)			
Consumption	75	68	62
Investment	15	20	26
Government	10	11	11
Total	**100**	**100**	**100**

Source: Kravis, Heston and Summers (1978: Tables 1.2, 1.6).

Southeast Asia: An International Perspective in the 1950s and 1960s

The poverty estimates given in Table 4.4 indicate that, in spite of their best intentions, the governments in Asia which became independent in the two decades after 1946 struggled to deliver the improvements in income and living standards which their populations had been promised. Although there was some growth in per capita GDP in all countries in the years from 1950 to 1965, only in Singapore, Malaysia and the Philippines were estimates high by Asian and African standards in 1965 (Table 4.6). Thailand had experienced some growth, from a low base in 1950, but by 1965 per capita GDP was still lower than in several North and West African states (Algeria, Ivory Coast, Senegal and Ghana). Indonesia had about the same per capita GDP as Nigeria, while Vietnam, then divided, was only slightly higher than India. Cambodia, Laos and Burma were all lower than India. The estimates of poverty prepared by World Bank economists showed that the headcount measure of poverty in Thailand was only slightly lower than the African average (Table 4.4). With rapidly growing populations, all the countries in Southeast Asia struggled to provide the improved education, healthcare and housing that their populations had expected as a result of independence.

Table 4.6: **Per capita GDP: Southeast Asia and international comparisons, 1950 1965, 1980 and 1996 (1990 international GK$)**

Southeast Asia	1950	1965	1980	1996
Singapore	2,219	2,667	9,058	19,160
Malaysia	1,559	1,804	3,657	7,608
Thailand	817	1,308	2,554	6,820
Indonesia	817	990	1,898	3,576
Philippines	1,070	1,633	2,376	2,267
Vietnam	658	877	757	1,490
Laos	613	712	876	1,077
Cambodia	482	687	828	1,056
Burma	396	617	828	1,005
Other Asia				
Taiwan	916	1,810	5,260	14,050
South Korea	854	1,436	4,114	12,860
China	448	702	1,061	2,892
India	619	771	938	1,635
Africa				
Algeria	1,365	1,870	3,152	2,702
Ivory Coast	1,041	1,581	2,041	1,378
Nigeria	753	944	1,305	1,028
Senegal	1,259	1,511	1,268	1,212
Ghana	1,122	1,393	1,157	1,207

Source: Maddison Project Database, 2013; for more details on estimation, see Bolt and Van Zanden (2014).

In the latter part of the 1960s, Southeast Asia had become an arena of great power conflict; some saw the war in Vietnam as a proxy war between the USA and the USSR. Not only was the war causing serious problems for a divided Vietnam but it was threatening to spill over into neighbouring countries, including Laos, Cambodia and Thailand. It was far from clear that the political systems in these countries could deal with external threats while at the same time delivering higher living standards to their own populations. Even in those countries with relatively high GDP and less immediate threat from the war in Vietnam (Singapore, Malaysia and the Philippines), and where poverty was lower than the Asian average, there were doubts about the ability of governments to deliver sustained economic growth, and improved living standards for their populations.

But these doubts did at least mean that the non-Communist governments across the region were encouraged to take the measurement of poverty and inequality more seriously, both by international agencies and also by various pressure groups in their own countries. They had to demonstrate that the economic growth to which they were committed as a policy goal would lead to improved living conditions for all their people, in both urban and rural areas. The next chapter reviews the measurement initiatives which were adopted in six countries. With its favourable legacy from the colonial era, the Philippines was the leader, followed by Malaysia, Singapore, Thailand, Indonesia and Myanmar (Burma).

5 Estimating Poverty and Inequality: Country Estimates from the 1950s to the 1970s

Estimates from the Philippines, 1965 to 1975

In the 1950s the Philippines, with its relatively favourable legacy from the American period, was widely considered to have the best economic prospects of any country in Asia. Self-government had been granted in 1935, after which Filipinos occupied almost all the key posts in the civil service, and were prominent in business and the professions as well. In spite of the devastation of the war, the American government honoured promises to confer full independence in 1946. Together with the British territories which became the Federation of Malaysia in 1963, the Philippines was considered to have the best capacity for implementing and analysing household surveys (Chander 1980: 90). In the decades from the 1950s to the 1970s, the Philippines led the way in the analysis of poverty and income distribution in Southeast Asia, mainly because of its more abundant statistical data, together with a well-staffed research system. A number of studies were carried out, some by government statisticians, and some by university-based researchers, especially faculty members of the University of the Philippines School of Economics. A survey of research on the distribution of income and wealth in the Philippines compiled in the late 1970s ran to almost 140 pages (Mangahas and Barros 1979).[1]

The main statistical source was the Family Income and Expenditure Surveys (FIES) carried out by the Bureau of the Census and Statistics from the mid-1950s onwards.[2] The results of these surveys were analysed by government statisticians and articles were published in the *Journal of Philippine Statistics*[3] The analysis revealed some growth in average real household incomes in the years from 1957 to 1965, but also a very skewed

1   Another survey of the literature on the Philippines is given in Alburo and Roberto (1980).
2   Chander (1980) gives details on the history and design of these surveys, including the sampling frame used.
3   The Journal of Philippine Statistics commenced publication around 1950, and was published by the Bureau of the Census and Statistics, now the Philippine Statistics Authority (PSA). In recent years it has been published quarterly. It contains statistical series and special articles written by employees of the government statistical agency, which are not signed.

distribution of household income. The ratio of the income share of the top 10 per cent to the poorest 40 per cent of the distribution was over three in 1956/57 and increased over the next decade (Table 5.1). The FIES data were also used in several academic studies including Abrera (1976), Berry (1978), Tan and Holazo (1979), Mangahas (1979, 1982), and Boyce (1993). They were also used in a book-length study on social indicators in the Philippines (Mangahas 1976). In addition, the National Economic and Development Authority published a series of studies on national income accounts and food balance sheets, as well a series on demographic data.[4] Several scholars also computed real wage series.

Table 5.1:   **Share of total family income received by quintile groups, and top 10 and 5 Per Cent: Philippines, 1956/57, 1961 and 1965**

	1956/57	1961	1965
Quintile Groups:			
Lowest 20%	4.5	4.2	3.5
Second 20%	8.1	7.9	8.0
Third 20%	12.4	12.1	12.8
Fourth 20%	19.8	19.3	20.2
Top 20%	55.1	56.4	55.4
Top 10%	39.4	41.0	40.0
Top 5%	27.7	29.0	28.7
Palma ratio*	3.1	3.4	3.5

* Top 10 per cent as a ratio of the bottom 40 per cent.
Source: *Journal of Philippine Statistics*, Vol 19 (2), 1968, Table 4.

These studies produced conflicting evidence, and led to a debate on the impact which the growth in per capita GDP between 1950 and 1975 had had on the lower income groups. Between 1950 and 1975, real per capita GNP in the Philippines doubled (NEDA 1978: 10). What was the impact on living standards of different groups in both urban and rural areas? The paper by Tan and Holazo (1979) was a pioneering attempt to tackle this question. These authors identified a basket of basic needs which met what they considered to be a minimum subsistence standard, including nutritional standards, shelter, health and educational requirements (Tan and Holazo 1979: 467-468). The poverty line was estimated for a household of six (mother, father and four children), using price data for ten regions of the country. A

4   A series on national income from 1946 to 1975 were published in NEDA (1978). Food balance sheets were published in NEDA (1975).

linear programming model was then used to find the least-cost basket of food that met the nutritional needs recommended by an official committee. Two poverty lines were estimated, one based on food requirements and the other including not just food, but also shelter, fuel, clothing, medical care and education. These poverty lines were then applied to the FIES data for 1965, 1971 and 1975 to give estimates of the percentage of the population below the poverty line. The results showed considerable variation across regions and some increase in the headcount measure of poverty, especially between 1971 and 1975. Using the full poverty line, they found that the percentage of families below the poverty line increased from 41 per cent in 1965 to 44 per cent in 1971 and 51.5 per cent in 1975 (Tan and Holazo 1979: 473-474).

Tan and Holazo qualified their findings in several respects. They pointed out that ideally the estimates should be prepared for urban and rural areas separately. Prices for food were usually lower in rural areas while prices for non-food items might be higher. But in the absence of rural price data they could not prepare separate estimates. They also tried to adjust their estimates for family size, making reasonable but arbitrary assumptions about marginal increments in consumption as family size increases. These adjustments led to some fall in the poverty incidence estimates for 1965 and 1971. They also argued that, given the strong tendency for households in the lower income deciles to dis-save, poverty incidence might better be estimated from the expenditure data rather than the income data.[5] Poverty incidence based on household expenditures was found to be much lower than that estimated from the income data in both 1965 and 1971 in all regions and for the country as a whole. But they stressed that all their estimates showed an upward trend in poverty incidence between 1965 and 1975, a decade in which per capita GNP increased by thirty per cent. They did not present any detailed explanation for this, but pointed out that both fiscal and monetary policies might have been regressive over this period.[6]

Other studies including that by Abrera (1976: 245) found that there was an increase in the proportion of the population below a stipulated poverty threshold between 1961 and 1971, with a sharp increase between 1965 and 1971. These findings were supported by the drop in the share of the lowest 20 per cent of households in total incomes between 1961 and 1971 (Berry 1978:

5   An earlier study by Abrera (1976: 228) also argued that poverty estimates based on expenditure data would be more satisfactory but pointed out that income data were more readily available.
6   Tan (1975) carried out a study of the incidence of taxes and expenditure in the Philippines in the early 1970s. She found that the regressive impact of the tax system was just offset by the slight progressive impact of government expenditures.

316). Berry also drew attention to the evidence of declining agricultural wages between the late 1950s and the early 1970s, a decline which was confirmed by Boyce (1993: Table 2.7). This decline might seem surprising given that agricultural output was increasing, in part as a result of increased yields for rice and corn. The government did increase the legislated wage rates for non-plantation workers in agriculture between 1974 and 1980, but it was widely believed that compliance with this legislation was low (Bautista 1994: 100).

Bautista (1994: 99-100) argued that by 1965 around 20 per cent of all rural households in the Philippines were landless, in the sense that their incomes were derived mainly from wage labour in agriculture. By 1975, the labour force survey of that year showed that around 15 per cent of male agricultural workers were classed as employees, and a further 19 per cent as family workers (Table 5.2). Bautista suggested that they probably did not benefit much from the accelerated growth in agricultural output, especially as it was accompanied by increased use of labour-displacing machinery on larger farms. He also pointed out that the distribution of income gains from agricultural growth was influenced by the distribution of landholdings, which in the 1970s was very different from that in Taiwan (Booth 2002b: Table 2). Around one-third of all land was in holdings over ten hectares in 1971; much of this land was rented out in small holdings to farmers who owned little or no land. It was argued that many tenants had to pay over half of their output to the landowner and were frequently forced into debt (Berreman 1956: 27).

The studies of Tan and Holazo and others using the FIES data were not without their critics. While concurring that poverty in the Philippines probably did worsen through the 1960s, and remained high in 1975, Mangahas (1979) raised several problems. He pointed out that the linear programming approach used by Tan and Holazo resulted in a consumption basket that contained no rice, and was weighted towards other foods which, while affording the basic number of calories, might not reflect the known preferences of most consumers. In another paper he raised the problem of the divergence between the FIES data on household consumption and those from the national accounts. In the surveys carried out in 1961, 1965 and 1971 the FIES income coverage amounted to between 60 and 67 per cent of the national accounts data (Estudillo 1997: Table 2) but in 1975 it fell to about half (Mangahas 1982: 133-134). Mangahas argued that the undercoverage revealed in the 1975 survey meant that the data should not be used to estimate inequality indicators, including decile shares and the Gini coefficient.

Setting aside the problems with the 1975 FIES, the poverty estimates for the Philippines over the 1960s do present puzzles. This was a decade

Table 5.2:   Labour force indicators in Thailand (1971), the Philippines (1975) and
             Indonesia (1980)

	ALF/ TLF	Wage/ ALF	Family/ ALF	Wage/ TLF
Thailand 1971				
Male	75.5	4.8	42.0	20.1
Female	83.5	3.4	91.9	10.5
Total	79.3	4.1	64.4	15.6
Philippines 1975				
Male	63.3	14.8	18.8	37.3
Female	34.4	15.0	30.2	45.9
Total	53.5	14.8	22.7	40.2
Indonesia 1980				
Male	57.0	15.9	18.2	30.6
Female	53.8	17.2	41.5	23.3
Total	55.9	16.4	25.5	28.2

Note: ALF = agricultural labour force; TLF = total labour force; Wage/ALF = percentage of the ALF
working as wage labourers; Family/ALF = percentage of the ALF from within the family.
Sources: Thailand: National Statistical Office (1976: 79-80); Philippines: National Census and Statistical Office (1976: Tables 1 and 17); Indonesia: Central Bureau of Statistics (1983: 175-177, 247-249).

when per capita GDP in the Philippines grew by around 25 per cent, and
there were also improvements in per capita calorie and protein consumption, and in infant mortality rates (Table 5.3). There appeared to have
been little change in total inequality between 1956 and 1971, at least as
measured by the Gini coefficient, although the ratio of income received
by the top quintile to the bottom quintile did increase between 1961 and
1971. The poverty estimates presented by Abrera showed a marked increase,
especially from 1965 to 1971. Those presented by Tan and Holazo, using
expenditure data from the FIES, also show some increase between 1965
and 1971, although not as large as the Abrera estimates. The evidence of
declining real wages in the agricultural sector supported the argument
that poverty increased, but the wage data were not easy to reconcile with
improved calorie and protein intake. The ILO report, published in 1974,
which drew on the work of many of the researchers cited above, did find
evidence of increasing inequality in rural areas, as shown in an increase
between 1956 and 1971 in both the index of quintile inequality and the
Gini coefficient.[7]

7   Boyce (1993: Table 2.12) estimated the ratios of the top 10 per cent of the real income distribution to the bottom 30 per cent for 1961 and 1971, using three different approaches. He found that
that in each of the three approaches, the ratio in rural areas increased between 1961 and 1971.

Table 5.3:   Per capita GDP, infant mortality rates, food availability and poverty estimates: Philippines, 1961-1971

	1961	1965	1971
Per capita GDP (1990 Int GK$)	1,512	1,633	1,808
Infant mortality rates	73.0	65.5	63.7
Daily food intake per capita:			
Calories	1,846	2,047	2,092
Protein	44.9	50.1	54.0
Gini Coefficient	0.50	0.51	0.49
Top 20%/Bottom 20%	11.6	13.7	13.5
Poverty (Headcount: 1)	51.2	48.3	56.9
Poverty (Headcount: 2)	n/a	25.0	25.9
Wages (1965 pesos)	3.49	2.93	2.25

Sources: Per capita GDP (1990 International GK$): Bolt and Van Zanden (2014); infant mortality rates: Zablan (1978: 105), data refer to averages for 1958-1962, 1963-1967, and 1968-1972; daily food take: NEDA (1975), Gini and quintile shares: Estudillo (1997: Table 1); poverty headcount (1): Abrera (1976: 245); poverty headcount (2): Tan and Holazo (1979: Table 18), using expenditure data; wages: Berry (1978: 325); figures refer to a series compiled by the ILO, using data from the Bureau of Agricultural Economics.

Some researchers claimed that output growth, and especially growth in the agricultural sector, did not lead to poverty decline in the 1960s and 1970s because most of the income gains in the rural sector accrued to the already better off part of the rural population (Bautista 1990: 63; Bautista 1994: 99-107). Bautista argued that the larger farmers operating ten hectares or more benefited from the improvement in the agricultural terms of trade, and that the 'effect on the structure and growth of rural consumption demand was to favour capital-intensive products and imported goods rather than labour-intensive, locally produced goods' (Bautista 1990: 63). This pattern of demand reinforced the anti-employment bias of import-substituting industrial development which favoured large firms concentrated in the Metro Manila region. There was agreement among many researchers that the problems in rural areas in many parts of the Philippines were made worse by the high degree of protection afforded the manufacturing sector from the 1950s onwards, which had resulted in slow growth of both output and employment opportunities, and a failure to take advantage of the opportunities of growing world demand for labour-intensive manufactures. It was clear that the Philippines was not following the Taiwan model of a successful land reform followed by policies which encouraged the growth of small- and medium-scale industry producing for both local and international markets.

An International Labour Organization (ILO) report concurred with this analysis. It argued that 'the particular growth path chosen in the past has tended to be adverse to the interests of the average worker, and still more so to that of the below-average worker' (ILO 1974: 13). The report recommended that a two-pronged strategy be adopted in the Philippines, which would involve agrarian reform on the one hand, and a labour-intensive industrial export drive on the other. The Marcos administration did implement a land reform programme in the 1970s; its impact will be examined in greater detail in Chapter 8. The main focus was on tenancy reform, which did enable rice and corn farmers in some parts of the country to purchase the land they were cultivating, but large farms cultivating other crops were for the most part untouched. Little was done to promote the development of labour-intensive industries. In addition, population growth remained high in the Philippines in comparison with Taiwan and Southeast Asian neighbours, including Singapore, Thailand and Indonesia, which had begun to sponsor family planning programmes in the 1960s and 1970s.

The relative abundance of data on income and expenditure distribution for the Philippines meant that the country was included in several cross-country comparisons of income distribution. A study prepared under the auspices of the World Employment Programme included the Philippines with a number of countries from Europe, Asia, Africa and Latin America for which comparable estimates of income per household could be generated for years ranging from 1967/68 to 1979 (Van Ginneken and Park 1984). The results indicated that the Philippines had a rather skewed distribution of income, although the Gini coefficients and Palma ratios were not as high as for Mexico, Iran, Panama, which had higher per capita GDP than the Philippines, or for Zambia and Kenya, which had lower per capita GDP (Table 5.4). These results throw some doubt on the widely held view that the distribution of income in the Philippines was by the 1970s similar to that found in parts of Latin America.

Estimates from Malaysia, 1957 to 1980

Along with the Philippines, Malaysia was considered by the 1970s to have reasonably good household survey data. It was the only Southeast Asian country selected by Visaria (1980) for detailed examination in his comparative study of poverty and living standards in Asia.[8] But in the

---

8   The other countries were India, Nepal, Sri Lanka and Taiwan. The Philippines, Singapore and Thailand were initially selected but their surveys were not analysed in depth.

Table 5.4:   **Per capita GDP, Palma ratio and Gini coefficient: Philippines and selected countries, c. 1970**

	Per capita GDP (1970)	Palma ratio	Gini coefficient
Mexico	6,214	5.1	0.56
Iran	6,173	3.7	0.52
Panama	4,504	6.1	0.57
Philippines	2,196	2.8	0.46
Egypt	2,137	2.0	0.40
Sierra Leone	2,154	2.5	0.44
Zambia	2,031	4.3	0.56
Kenya	1,701	5.1	0.59

Sources: GDP data: Bolt et al. (2018), 2011 prices; decile shares and Gini coefficient: Van Ginneken and Park (1984: Table 1).

Philippines most of the work on income distribution and poverty was done by university-based academics and published either in academic journals or in publications sponsored by international organizations. In Malaysia, early estimates were made by both Malaysian and foreign scholars, but after 1970 the government also began to publish 'official' estimates of poverty in planning documents. In one of the early analyses of the five surveys carried out between 1957/58 and 1970, Snodgrass (1975b: 254) argued that none could be accepted as wholly accurate. He used three of them to estimate trends in poverty and distribution between 1957/58 (when the first household budget survey was carried out) and 1970 (when a post-enumeration survey was attached to the population census of that year).

In spite of the problematic data base, Snodgrass argued that the trend was towards increasing inequality in the distribution of personal income, both within ethnic groups and for the population as a whole. In 1970, the median income for ethnic Malays was well below that for the Indian and Chinese populations, but the Gini coefficient for the three groups was broadly similar. The lower average income meant that the proportion of Malay households with incomes of less than RM120 per month was much higher than for Indian or Chinese households (49 per cent in 1970 for Malay households, 20 per cent for Indian households and 14 per cent for Chinese households). These proportions had not changed much between 1957/58 and 1970, but as the population was growing quite rapidly, the absolute numbers below this line had increased (Snodgrass 1975b: 261-264).

As in the Philippines, increasing absolute numbers of households below the poverty line in Malaysia had occurred in spite of growing per capita GDP. Between 1960 and 1975, GDP growth was faster in Malaysia than in the Philippines. But the growth did not appear to have reduced the incidence of poverty. Snodgrass argued that the distributive pattern was somewhat improved by fiscal policy (taxes and expenditures). Anand (1983: 273) in his analysis of the 1970 post-enumeration survey cast doubt on the comparability of this survey with earlier surveys, and disputed the claim that inequality had worsened between 1957 and 1970. He found that in 1970 the Gini coefficient for all racial groups was 0.51; the Gini estimates for each ethnic group separately were slightly lower but still in the region of 0.47 to 0.49 (Anand 1983: Table 6-5). Using a poverty line of 25 Malaysian ringgit per capita per month, he found that 40 per cent of the total population of Peninsular Malaysia was under this line. The difference in poverty between ethnic groups was large; 56.2 per cent for Malays, 33.4 per cent for Indians and 18.3 per cent for Chinese (Anand 1983: Table 4-2).

These figures confirmed the widespread perception, especially among Malays, that they were not benefiting from the economic growth which had occurred since the granting of self-government in 1957. They suggested that rural Malays were falling behind urban dwellers, the majority of whom were not Malay. The Malays were behind not just in terms of income but also education, which was the passport to white collar occupations in both the public and private sectors. Violent race riots, which erupted after disputed election results in 1969, led to the adoption of the New Economic Policy in 1970. This was an ambitious affirmative action policy, designed to increase Malay incomes and assets relative to those of other ethnic groups, and bring more Malays into non-agricultural employment. The NEP led to the publication of detailed estimates of poverty and distribution in official documents. Estimates published in the Fourth Malaysia Plan claimed that in 1970, 49.3 per cent of the total population was below the poverty line. In the agricultural sector, which was dominated by Malays, the figure was 68 per cent (Jomo 1990: Table 7.1). These proportions fell only slightly between 1970 and 1975, and the numbers of poor increased.

The data published in the plan documents attracted criticism from independent scholars who pointed out that the surveys on which the estimates were based were only available to government analysts. There was no way that outsiders could verify the figures. Shari (1979: 421) claimed that the official data did not even specify the poverty line used, although independent researchers deduced that it was RM33 per household member per month which was a higher figure than that used by Snodgrass or Anand.[9] The

9   It appears that the poverty lines were only made public in the mid-term review of the Fifth Malaysia Plan. See Government of Malaysia (1989: 45).

Economic Planning Unit, attached to the Office of the Prime Minister, did finally disclose the methodology for estimating the poverty line; it was based on a minimum cost food basket plus expenditures deemed to be sufficient for other essential non-food items. Shari's own estimate of the poverty line, applied to 1973 data, gave a poverty estimate of 49.7 per cent, almost the same as the official estimate given for 1970. Broken down by ethnicity, the percentage of the population below this poverty line was 68.5 per cent for Malays, 29.7 per cent for Chinese and almost 40 per cent for Indians. Shari's estimate of the incidence of poverty among households earning most of their income from agriculture was 67.5 per cent, which was little different from the figure given in the official publications (Shari 1979: 428).

Estimates published in the Fourth Malaysia Plan document showed that the proportion of the population below the poverty line fell sharply between 1975 and 1980, from 43.9 per cent to 29.2 per cent of the population. In spite of population growth, a fall of this magnitude was sufficient to reduce the absolute numbers below the poverty line from 835,000 to 666,100 (Jomo 1990: Table 7.1). Almost 80 per cent of the fall in numbers below the poverty line took place in the agricultural sector. While this was at least partly due to government rural development policies, including an ambitious land settlement programme aimed mainly at rural Malays with little land, and to increasing output per hectare on rice and rubber farms, higher prices for export crops such as rubber also helped. Rubber prices more than doubled over the 1970s which probably explained much of the fall in poverty among rubber cultivators between 1970 and 1980 (Shari and Ragayah 1990: 121).

It seemed clear that the fall in poverty over the 1970s was not the result of declining inequality in the distribution of income. Lim (1975: 184) estimated that the Gini coefficient of household income had increased from 0.42 to 0.5 between 1957/58 and 1970. Shari and Ragayah (1990: Table 1) gave estimates of the Gini of household income for 1970, 1976 and 1979. There was some increase between 1970 and 1976, especially in rural areas, and only a slight fall between 1976 and 1978. In 1979 they estimated the Gini to be 0.49, compared with 0.5 in 1970. The share of income accruing to the top 20 per cent of households did fall between 1976 and 1979 (from 58 to 54 per cent) but the share accruing to the poorest 20 per cent also contracted slightly. Only in the 1980s did the share of the bottom 20 per cent show some increase. This was true for the Malay population as well as the total population.

Since 1970, it has been difficult for independent scholars, whether based in Malaysia or abroad, to access the household survey data on which the estimates of poverty and distribution published in the official plan documents are based. It is therefore difficult to assess the reliability of the survey results. Visaria (1980: 17) found that per capita expenditure, as reported in the household expenditure survey of 1973 was only about 15 per cent smaller than the component in the national accounts. This might suggest that the surveys at that time were quite accurate. In subsequent chapters, more recent evidence on, and criticisms of, the Malaysian figures will be evaluated.

Estimates from Singapore, 1953/54 to 1997/98

From the 1950s onwards, Singapore was a very different economy from most other parts of Southeast Asia. Until 1942, it was the dominant part of the British colony known as the Straits Settlements, along with Melaka and Penang. After the end of the Pacific War it became a separate colonial territory. Compared to other parts of Southeast Asia it was highly urbanized with only a small agricultural sector. It had by far the largest port in the region, and its entrepôt function embraced not just the other parts of British Malaya but also Sumatra and the Indonesian territories on the huge island of Borneo, which historically had looked to Singapore as the main market for their commodities, especially rubber. In addition, Singapore was an important banking centre and a naval base. In the 1950s, the population was growing rapidly as a result of both in-migration and high rates of natural increase. Housing had already been a serious problem before 1942, and the problem became worse after 1945, with increases in population leading to massive overcrowding in some parts of the city.

The report on the Social Survey of Singapore carried out in 1953/54 found that 20 per cent of households were living in acutely overcrowded conditions compared with 21 per cent in 1947. Acutely overcrowded was defined as two adults and four children, at least one over ten years, living in one room (Goh 1956: 73). A further 28 per cent lived under conditions of overcrowding, and only 15 per cent were deemed to be living in spacious conditions. Official documents also admitted that a large part of the population, not just the poorest, lived in very crowded conditions (Colonial Office 1955: 47). Using a poverty line which included the costs of food, clothing and housing but not education, 21 per cent of all households were estimated to be poor, and 29 per cent of households consisting of a man, wife and children (Goh 1956: 141). About a quarter of all people in the households surveyed were considered poor. It was hardly surprising that, when the author of the 1953/54 report became deputy prime minister of the independent Republic of Singapore, a national family planning programme was launched, together with an ambitious public housing project.

In 1966, after Singapore had become an independent state, the Ministry of National Development together with the Economic Research Centre at the University of Singapore carried out a further sample survey of households (Rao and Ramakrishnan 1976: 97). Analysis of the results produced a Gini coefficient of around 0.5.[10] Further surveys were carried out in 1972, 1973, 1974 and 1975, although these were not primarily household income surveys, and there were issues of data comparability. Rao and Ramakrishnan thought that the 1966 and 1975 data could be compared; between these years the Gini dropped slightly. They argued that the decline was mainly the result of the decline in rates of unemployment together with an increase in female labour force participation rates. They also pointed out that the decline in real income inequality was higher when post-tax real income distributions were adjusted for the imputed benefits from public housing (Rao and Ramakrishnan 1976: 121).

In a subsequent paper, Rao (1990: 147) found a slight decline in the Gini coeffcient between 1972/73 and 1977/78, and an increase in the share of the bottom four deciles in total income (from 15.8 to 17.7 per cent). But Rao stressed the problem of undercoverage in the income data he used, relative to the national income figures on private consumption expenditures. A rather different approach to the estimation of income disparities in Singapore was that taken by Atkinson (2010). Using income tax data, he calculated the share of the top 1 per cent in the distribution from 1947 through to 2005, and the share of the top 5 and 10 per cent from 1969 onwards. His results showed that in 1947, the share of the top 1 per cent was almost 11 per cent, and increased to 14.8 per cent in 1951, but by 1960 had fallen back to where it had been in 1947. From then on, the share of the top 1 per cent was quite stable until the Asian crisis of 1998. Following Rao (1990: 155-156), Atkinson suggested that the extreme openness of the Singapore economy together with the proactive wage policy followed by government led to a fairly stable distribution of income over three decades when per capita GDP was growing fast.

Estimates from Thailand, 1962/63 to 1981

The first household survey of Thailand was held in 1962/63 and a further one in 1968/69. As in the Philippines, the analysis of these surveys, and

10   Rao and Ramakrishnan (1976: 121) estimated a higher Gini (0.527) using a generalized Pareto model.

subsequent ones, was carried out by academics, often with support from the International Labour Organization and the World Bank. The 1968/69 survey confirmed the widespread belief that regional variations in household incomes per capita were large; average household per capita incomes in Bangkok were well over three times those in the northeast which was the poorest part of the country. In order to estimate poverty, Meesook (1975: 349-353) used a cut-off of 1,000 baht ($50 at the prevailing exchange rate) as an annual poverty line and found that, in 1968/69, 24 per cent of all households had incomes below this threshold. Almost 53 per cent of all poor households were in the northeast and a further 30 per cent in the north. Meesook also found that the incidence of poverty increased directly with household size, and with numbers of children under fifteen. Poverty was much lower in households where the head had at least some secondary education (Meesook 1975: 354).

Meesook stressed the importance of including income in kind in estimates of poverty. Income in kind was a much higher proportion of total income in the lowest income groups, especially in rural areas. On average it accounted for 22 per cent of total income in rural areas and 4 per cent in towns. Excluding income in kind led to a substantial increase in the incidence of poverty (41 per cent compared with 24 per cent). But it did not make much difference to the extreme concentration of poor households in the north and northeast of the country. The 1962/63 household survey did not collect data on income in kind, which limited the extent to which comparisons could be made with the 1968/69 survey.[11] Based on money incomes alone, the incidence of poverty did decline between the two surveys from 61 per cent of all households to 41 per cent. Meesook (1975: 371) also found that average money incomes had grown rapidly in the north and northeast of the country between the two surveys, but much of the growth occurred in households which were already above the poverty threshold in 1962/63. In spite of slower income growth in the south of the country, the incidence of poverty fell rather more there than in the northern regions.

A further analysis of the 1968/69 data was carried out by Krongkaew (1979) using a rather different poverty line from Meesook. He introduced the concept of the poverty band, based on upper and lower limits of the poverty threshold, which were estimated using consumer expenditure patterns. Using the lower limit income threshold, he found that 52 per cent of rural families and 11.2 per cent of urban families could be categorized as poor in

11   For these and other reasons Visaria (1980: 153) excluded the Thai data from his detailed examination of poverty and living standards in Asia.

1968/69. In total, 46.8 per cent of all households fell below the threshold. He also found that there were considerable regional differences; 75 per cent of rural households in the northeast fell below the threshold compared with only 7.3 per cent of the population in urban Bangkok. Another household survey was carried out in 1975/76; an analysis by Meesook (1979: 52-55) found that between 1968/69 and 1975/76 the headcount measure fell from 39 to 31 per cent. The fall was especially pronounced in the northeast (from 65 per cent to 44 per cent). But in spite of this decline, 50 per cent of the poor population was still located in the northeast in 1975/76, and a further 23 per cent in the north of the country.

Various other estimates of the headcount measure over the 1970s are available from other sources. Warr (2009: Table 9) showed a steep decline from 1962 to 1975, but his estimate in 1962 of 88.3 per cent of the total population below the poverty line (96.4 per cent in rural areas) was much higher than that estimated by Meesook. One has to assume that a different poverty line was used. It also appears that income in kind was excluded from Warr's poverty estimates for the 1960s, which probably overstated these estimates in relation to the later estimates. Another series on the headcount measure of poverty for the years from 1962/63 to 1981 was given in Krongkaew and Kakwani (2003: 742-744). They also found a consistent decline, from 57 per cent in 1962/63 to 31.3 per cent in 1981. They acknowledged that the estimates might not be strictly comparable, but claimed that the decline was not in doubt. Krongkaew and Kakwani also gave estimates of the Gini coefficient from 1962/63 to 1975/76; they found an increase from 0.56 to 0.605. They also found a further increase in the Gini coefficient between 1975/76 and 1981. As in Malaysia, it appears that the decline in poverty over the two decades from the early 1960s to the early 1980s took place in spite of an increase in inequality.

A comparative study of income distribution across countries in Africa, Asia and Latin America using data from the 1970s found that the Gini coefficients in Malaysia, the Philippines and Thailand were roughly similar (Lecaillon et al. 1984: Table 6). Using data on household income, the study reported estimates of 0.52 for Malaysia, 0.49 for the Philippines and 0.50 for Thailand. These estimates were lower than for most, although not all, of the Latin American and African countries in the study, although among the Asian countries they were on the high side. Hong Kong, India, Sri Lanka and the Republic of Korea all had lower estimates. The study supported the view that these three Southeast Asian countries were not especially egalitarian around 1970, although the distribution of income was less skewed than in some African countries (Zambia, Zimbabwe, South Africa and Kenya). It was also less skewed than in Brazil, Mexico, Honduras and Peru. This study also cast doubt on the assertion that income distribution in the Philippines was more unequal than in other parts of Southeast Asia, and similar to countries in Latin America such as Brazil and Mexico.

Estimates from Indonesia, 1963/64 to 1980

Apart from a small number of village-level studies, few studies were carried out on poverty in Indonesia until the 1970s, although many observers suspected that, given Indonesia's low per capita GDP, the problem must be worse there than in the Philippines, Thailand or Malaysia.[12] Compared with these three countries, the Indonesian Central Bureau of Statistics was slower to implement nation-wide household income and expenditure surveys. The National Socio-economic Survey, usually known by its Indonesian acronym Susenas, was first carried out in 1963/64 but only in Java. A further survey in 1964/65 covered most, but not all provinces outside Java, while the one carried out in 1967 again only covered Java. The Susenas surveys carried out in 1969/79, 1976, 1978 and 1980 covered most of the country although Maluku and Irian Jaya were excluded in 1969/70 and Irian Jaya in 1976. In subsequent surveys, rural areas of both Irian Jaya and East Timor were excluded; indeed, the first truly national Susenas was not carried out until 1987. The samples were not large enough to permit a breakdown by province until the early 1990s; until then data were only published for Java and the rest of the country.

An early analysis of the Susenas data for Java between 1963/64 and 1969/70 was carried out by King and Weldon (1977). They found little change in expenditure distribution over these years in rural Java, but evidence of growing disparities in urban areas, and especially in Jakarta. They did not attempt to estimate the changing percentage of the population below a stipulated poverty line, although they noted the estimates made by Sajogyo for 1969/70, which are discussed below. Their estimates of weekly rice consumption by quintile group in both rural and urban areas showed a considerable increase in rural areas, especially between 1964/65 and 1967 for the poorest 20 per cent. There was little change for the bottom quintile in urban areas. Real per capita food expenditures increased for the top 80 per cent in both urban and rural areas between 1967 and 1969/70 but fell

12   A brief summary of work carried out in the early 1970s is given in King and Weldon (1977: 699).

for the bottom 20 per cent (King and Weldon 1977: Table 6). The authors concluded that the evidence suggested some decline in the real standard of living for the poorer groups and growing disparities between rich and poor in urban areas.

Indonesia could be used as a case study of the impact of rapid inflation, culminating in hyperinflation, on the distribution of income and expenditure but data for the years from the late 1950s to the late 1960s for the entire country are very difficult to assemble. It seems probable that most urban households suffered real declines in income in the early and mid-1960s as prices for food and other basic needs increased. Government employees and some private sector workers received part of their salary in rice and thus were partially protected from price rises, but most other urban workers, who were usually poorer than government workers, had little protection. In rural areas, the landless and near landless who depended on food purchases for at least part of their income would also have suffered. Only those farmers with a marketed surplus would have benefited from rising prices. Timmer (2015: 102-103) found that in 1963/64 there were sharp differences in rice consumption per capita by expenditure quintile in both urban and rural areas in Java. In rural areas the top quintile consumed more than three times the amount of the poorest quintile. Timmer found convergence in rice consumption by quintile group only after 1976.

The finding of Van Leeuwen and Foldvari (2016: Table 4) that employees in agriculture and farmers operating less than 0.5 hectares increased their share of total consumption expenditure between 1960 and 1975, while those operating over one hectare saw a decline in their consumption share seems implausible, even if employees and small farmers did experience an improvement in real consumption after prices stabilized in the late 1960s. The finding of these authors that the Gini coefficient declined from 0.55 in 1953 to 0.51 in 1959, and 0.28 in 1975 also seems dubious. There is little evidence that any country has experienced such a massive decline in inequality over less than two decades. It seems doubtful that such a decline occurred in Indonesia after 1959. It is likely that the departure of Dutch and other foreign nationals after 1945 would have had some equalizing impact on incomes, as these people were highly paid compared to most indigenous Indonesians. But this cannot explain the large drop in the Gini coefficient between 1959 and 1975, as almost all foreigners had left by the late 1950s. Given the differential impact of inflation by income class over the 1960s, it is probable that inequality in real expenditures would have increased, rather than declined, over that decade.

The first attempt to propose a poverty line for Indonesia and measure the proportion of the population below the line was made by Sajogyo (1975). He set the poverty line in terms of rice: 240 kg per year for rural areas and 360 kg for urban areas.[13] The use of milled rice equivalent as a 'basic needs standard' has a long history in Java in particular, where it extends back to the rural welfare surveys carried out by the Dutch in the early decades of the twentieth century. A number of investigations of rural poverty in Java adopted the concept in one form or another. Penny and Singarimbun (1973) in their study of Sriharjo in Yogyakarta claimed that villagers had a concept of 'sufficiency' (*cukupan*) which they expressed in terms of rice, and many studies have used rice prices to deflate rural wage data.[14] In fact, if it is accepted that rice is the most 'basic' of basic needs in Indonesia, its use in determining a poverty line would seem to be close what Lipton (1983: 6) had in mind in suggesting that poverty be defined in terms of the fulfilment of one 'key' need.

When the rice-based poverty lines were converted into rupiah and applied to the National Socio-economic Survey (Susenas) data for the years from 1963/64 onwards, there was an increase in the proportion of the population considered poor in Java until 1967, from 61 per cent to over 67 per cent. Then there was a steady decline until 1980, when only 32 per cent were below the Sajogyo poverty line. Outside Java, the proportion fell from 52 per cent in 1964/65 to 14.5 per cent in 1980 (Booth 1988: 193). But in spite of these declines, several studies suggested that nutritional standards in Indonesia were far from satisfactory in the late 1960s and early 1970s. An analysis of the 1969/70 Susenas data by Van Ginneken (1976: 32-33) showed that average per capita intake of both calories and protein was low in comparison with recommended standards, and lower than in Pakistan, Mexico, Tanzania and Tunisia. While it is possible that food consumption was understated in the Susenas, especially in urban areas, the evidence suggested that in both urban and rural areas there was still a wide disparity in calorie and protein intake by expenditure group in the late 1960s. In rural areas the bottom 10 per cent of the population were consuming only 1,117 calories per day, compared with an average intake of 1,885 calories per day. Protein intake was only 29 grams per day, compared with the average of 44 grams. These

13   There was a history of using rice as a standard in determining poverty lines and minimum wages, not just in Indonesia but also in other parts of Southeast Asia; for a discussion of the rice-wage formula in the Philippines, see Abrera (1976: 232-233).

14   This is particularly true of the numerous village studies carried out by the Agroeconomic Survey. See Collier et al. (1982) for a survey of this literature.

disparities by expenditure class were larger than in Pakistan. The 1969/70 data confirmed that the very marked differences in food consumption by expenditure class, found in the Kutowinangun study in the 1930s, were still evident 30 years later.

Sundrum and Booth (1980: 463) extended the Sajogyo analysis to 1976, breaking down the poverty data into urban and rural areas. They found that the percentage of the population below the 240 kg poverty line in rural areas of both Java and the Outer Islands fell, although in Java the fall was not very rapid (from 39.5 per cent to 33.7 per cent). In urban areas, both in Java and elsewhere, the fall was greater. Other estimates, including some put forward by the World Bank, showed a greater decline in the headcount measure of poverty between 1970 and 1976, especially in rural Java.[15] But several analysts pointed out that using rice, or a price index heavily weighted towards rice, probably underestimated the impact of the inflation over these years on the poor. It was argued that the consumption basket of the poor, especially in rural Java, contained more non-rice staples, especially corn and cassava, whose prices had risen faster than rice. Thus the rate of inflation for the bottom 40 per cent in rural areas was higher than for upper income groups (Dapice 1980: 71; Asra 1989a: 107). Asra (1989a: 104-105) also argued that the Gini coefficient for household expenditures increased slightly over these six years, once corrections had been made for the differential impact of inflation on different expenditure groups.

Whatever the statistics showed, there can be no doubt that many people concerned with poverty issues in Indonesia, and especially in Java, over the decade from the mid-1960s to the mid-1970s felt disappointed that the real per capita GDP growth in Indonesia which had occurred (67 per cent over the decade from 1966 to 1976) was not having a more dramatic impact on the incomes of the poorer sections of the population, whether in Java or elsewhere. Some analysts put the blame on the impact of the oil boom, which had led to a sharp increase in revenues accruing to the central government budget. This in turn led to increased expenditures on salaries for government employees, who were mainly based in urban areas and had a higher propensity to consume on luxury and semi-luxury goods and services. An analysis of the cost of living surveys carried out in urban areas in 1968/69 showed that families where the household head was in government service were already earning well above the average for all

---

15   Asra (1989b: Table 1) presented estimates which showed quite a rapid decline in the headcount measure of poverty between 1970 and 1976 in both urban and rural areas, but the measures were presented for Indonesia as a whole.

urban households (Booth and Sundrum 1981: 198). The disparity probably grew over the 1970s. The evidence from the Susenas surveys for 1970 and 1976 showed that urban-rural disparities in per capita household expenditures had widened, although they were not as high as in Malaysia or Thailand (Sundrum and Booth 1980: 459-460).

The latter part of the 1970s saw a moderation in the rate of inflation in Indonesia, and also considerable growth in agricultural production, especially rice. Numbers falling below the rice-based poverty line fell steeply between 1976 and 1981. But by the early 1980s, it was argued that the changes in consumption opportunities which had occurred in Indonesia since 1965 made the Sajogyo poverty line an anachronism. This was partly because many Indonesians, especially in Java, were living in urban and peri-urban areas where the Sajogyo poverty concept was never very satisfactory anyway.[16] But also a diminishing number of Indonesians anywhere in the country by 1980 embraced the concept of *cukupan*, expressed exclusively in terms of rice. The proportion of total consumption expenditures devoted to purchase of cereals had fallen steadily everywhere in Indonesia since 1970, and other expenditures, including housing and education, assumed a much greater role in both actual consumer budgets and in concepts of basic needs.

The series on poverty published by the Central Bureau of Statistics (CBS) in the 1980s used a broader poverty line although one which became increasingly controversial in the last part of the Suharto era.[17] Between 1976 and 1980, the CBS series showed the percentage of the population in poverty to have fallen from 40.1 per cent to 28.6 per cent, and the absolute numbers of poor to have fallen from 54 million to 42 million (Central Bureau of Statistics 1997: 570). Other Indonesian economists queried the use of a rice-based poverty line. Esmara put forward a poverty line concept in terms of average per capita expenditure on a package of basic needs (Esmara 1986: 286-349). Using the household expenditure data from successive rounds of the Susenas for 1970, 1976, 1978 and 1980, Esmara estimated average expenditures on this basic needs package, which included cereals and tubers, nuts, fish, meat, vegetables, fruit, clothing, housing, education and health. The package for urban and rural areas was broadly similar although a few extra food items were added for rural areas. The Esmara approach was a novel one in that

16   The Sajogyo poverty line in urban areas was simply the rural poverty line increased by 50 per cent, although no justification was given for such an arbitrary markup. In Eastern Indonesia, where rice was often not the staple food, and was a relatively expensive source of calories, the use of a rice-based poverty line led to overestimates in the headcount measure of poverty.
17   The CBS began to publish data on poverty in 1984; the series, published in the annual statistical yearbooks, was taken back to 1976.

it explicitly allows for the concept of 'basic needs' to change over time by using average per capita expenditure on the basic commodities rather than expenditures on a fixed basket of needs (however defined).

Much of the change in per capita expenditures on the basic needs package over the 1970s reflected changes in prices. But a part also reflected a decision on the part of households to consume more food, clothing, housing, education etc. According to the Esmara approach, this revealed a change in social attitudes to, and perceptions of, what comprises basic needs which should be incorporated in the poverty line concept. The Esmara poverty line, like that of Sajogyo and the CBS, was higher in urban areas than in rural, and the gap widened over the decade of the 1970s. But in spite of this, he found that the percentage of the population below the poverty line in rural Indonesia had consistently been higher than in urban areas.

Esmara acknowledged that his concept of a 'dynamic poverty line', which altered not just with changing prices but also with changing real consumption patterns, was open to objections. He also proposed a more orthodox alternative, which derived a poverty line for the years 1976-1980 from the 1970 data simply by adjusting for changes in the Jakarta Cost of Living Index. This alternative poverty line in rural areas was not very different from the 'dynamic' poverty line except for 1980. But in urban areas it was much lower (Esmara 1986: 329). Thus the estimate of the percentage in poverty is also lower using this measure. But there were obvious problems with this approach as well. Why should the Jakarta index be used to adjust an all-Indonesia poverty line for inflation? To the extent that the rate of inflation had not been the same in urban and rural areas, or in different regions of the country, the use of the Jakarta index to adjust the poverty line for changes in prices could have under- or overstated changes in poverty.

Beginning in the 1970s, the World Bank also paid considerable attention to issues of poverty and income distribution in Indonesia and published a number of estimates of the proportions of the population in poverty and its changes over time. Most of these estimates were made in internal documents, but publicly available estimates were given in a country study published in 1980 (World Bank 1980a). In addition, two staff working papers by Chernichovsky and Meesook (1984a and 1984b) used the 1978 Susenas. The 1980 World Bank study used a poverty line of Rp 3,000 per month everywhere in the country although to correct for regional differences in price levels, rupiah consumption expenditures were adjusted to Jakarta prices (World Bank 1980a: 84). The most striking aspect of these estimates was the very marked difference in poverty incidence in urban and rural areas; the disparity was much greater than that shown by either of Esmara's estimates. Whereas according to Esmara, 16.3 per cent of the poor were located in urban areas in 1976, the World Bank found only 8 per cent.

Chernichovsky and Meesook (1984b: 2) tried to avoid the problem of choosing a poverty line altogether by simply defining the 'poor' as the bottom two deciles of the population ranked by household per capita consumption expenditure. Using this approach they found a large disparity between urban and rural poverty incidence in 1978 (14.1 per cent of urban households were considered poor compared with 41.7 per cent of rural households). By contrast, the CBS estimates for the same year found that 30.8 per cent of urban households were below the poverty line compared with 33.4 per cent of rural households. Chernichovsky and Meesook criticized absolute poverty lines as 'incorporating many arbitrary assumptions' but their method appeared just as arbitrary.

The bewildering diversity of estimates of the incidence of poverty, numbers in poverty, and the location of the poor, together with evidence that, as in the Philippines, the Susenas surveys seemed to be underestimating total household expenditures, encouraged other analysts to adopt different approaches to the measurement of poverty in Indonesia. Papanek (1980) compiled several series on real wages; the longest was for real wages for both temporary and permanent plantation workers in Java and Sumatra from 1951 to 1978. He found that real wages fell fairly consistently from 1953 to 1968, although the fall was steeper in Java; by 1968 wages in Java were well under half those in Sumatra. Part of the fall between the 1950s and 1963 might have been the result of increased employment; total numbers of workers increased in all plantations except coffee (Papanek 1980: 86). Employers could have been reacting to the economic difficulties of the late 1950s and early 1960s, as well as to increasing opposition by trade unions to laying off workers, by keeping workers on, but reducing their remuneration. From 1968 to 1972, real wages increased sharply although numbers employed fell. But after 1972, the various wage series he examined did not show much sign of real increases. Papanek (1980: 102) attributed the improvement in real wages between 1967 and 1972 to the rebuilding of a shattered economy. But given that total plantation sector employment fell after 1967, it is probable that the reduction in trade union power made it easier for the estates to get rid of older, less productive workers, which must have impacted adversely on their living standards.

Living standards were almost certainly lower in Indonesia than in the other four ASEAN countries in the mid-1960s, and poverty incidence higher, but were they still lower in 1980, after more than a decade of rapid growth of GDP? Comparisons of the national headcount measures of poverty are not really feasible, given that the poverty lines in Indonesia were lower in dollar terms than in Malaysia, Thailand or the Philippines (Booth 1993: Table 11).[18] Even allowing for differences in the purchasing power of the rupiah compared with the other Southeast Asian currencies which might not have been fully incorporated in the exchange rate, it is probable that the poverty line in Indonesia allowed for a lower basket of goods and services than in Malaysia, Thailand and the Philippines.[19] In 1972, the consumption of cereals in Java was well below that in the Philippines; in spite of higher consumption of roots and tubers, the total intake of calories was lower, although it was higher outside Java (Table 5.5). Protein intake was much lower in both Java and the Outer Islands than in the Philippines. By 1981, the percentage of the Indonesian population below the Malaysian poverty line was more than five times that in Malaysia, and over twice that in Thailand (Table 5.6). Even those resource-rich provinces which had a much higher per capita GDP compared with the national average also had a higher headcount measures of poverty than in Malaysia.

Table 5.5:   Estimated food availability in the Philippines and Indonesia, 1972
                   (grams per day)

Food Type	Philippines	Java	Outer Islands	Indonesia
Cereals	363	297	347	325
Roots/Tubers	66	216	202	211
Sugar	51	27	45	34
Pulses/Nuts	15	33	10	24
Vegetables	77	36	19	30
Fruits	99	90	100	94
Meat	43	8	10	9
Eggs	9	1	3	2
Fish	107	3	18	8
Fats/Oils	10	7	16	11
Calories Per Day	2,047	1,850	2,208	2020
Protein Per Day (grams)	53	36	42	39

Sources: Philippines: NEDA (1975); Indonesia: Nicol (1974: Tables 1-4).

18   Mangahas (1983) compared the various poverty lines used in Southeast Asian studies in the late 1970s and early 1980s. He came to the conclusion that, once adjustments had been made for differences in purchasing power, there was not a great difference between them, although the Malaysian poverty line was higher than most of the others.
19   It is worth noting that the effect of the rice premium and other export taxes in Thailand was to lower the domestic price of rice in Thailand in dollar terms, compared with other countries in Southeast Asia.

Table 5.6: Percentage of the population below a 'Malaysian' poverty line, 1980-1981

	Percentage of the population below the poverty line	Average monthly per capita consumption expenditures in US$ (Kravis $ in brackets)
Indonesia (1981)	76.1	17.29 (37.24)
Aceh	67.5	20.53 (44.22)
North Sumatra	73.2	18.49 (39.82)
West Sumatra	68.0	20.32 (43.77)
Riau	60.3	22.14 (47.69)
East Kalimantan	49.6	25.17 (54.21)
Peninsular Malaysia (1980)	14.7	61.27 (110.77)
Thailand (1981)	30.9	34.36 (82.30)
Bangkok	4.8	62.60 (149.94)
North	34.6	31.10 (74.48)
Northeast	49.1	22.96 (54.99)
Central	17.3	40.45 (96.88)
South	36.9	34.82 (83.40)

Note: The poverty line estimated by the Economic Planning Unit for 1977 (as reported in Shari [1979]) was adjusted upwards to 1980 and 1981 prices using the Peninsular Malaysia CPI. This was converted into rupiah and baht at the prevailing exchange rate and adjusted to allow for differences in purchasing power using the 1980 index for consumption expenditures supplied in Summers and Heston (1991). Indonesian and Malaysian data refer to the percentage of the population; Thai data refer to the percentage of households whose per capita consumption expenditures fall below the poverty line. Average per capita consumption expenditures for Malaysia in 1980 were adjusted to 1981 data using the Peninsular Malaysia CPI. Per capita consumption expenditures were converted into 1981 dollars at the prevailing exchange rates and to Kravis dollars using the indices for 1980 reported in Summers and Heston (1991).
Source: Booth (1997a Table 3.12).

Estimates from Burma in the 1950s

The government of Burma conducted a household survey in Rangoon in 1958, and in four rural areas in 1960-1963. Samples were small; in Rangoon 500 households were surveyed, with incomes of not more than 400 kyats per month. The four rural areas surveyed were the Irrawaddy Delta, Central Burma, Arakan and Tenasserin; 6,000 households were surveyed. The statistical yearbooks, published in the 1960s, included tables which compared the food consumption data collected in 1958 with those collected in a 1927 enquiry into the standard of living of the working classes in Rangoon. The proportion of household budgets spent on food had increased from 53 per cent to 66 per cent. This increase could have indicated a decline in living standards although it might also have been the result of lower housing costs in the post-independence years. Per capita consumption of rice, pulses, vegetable oils and sugar had increased, although consumption of meat and fish had declined (Table 5.7). Perhaps a better indicator of improvement in living standards is the improvement in infant mortality rates which took place over the 1950s. In 1930, Sundrum (1957: 18) estimated that the infant mortality rate in Burma was around 200 per 1,000 live births, although this could have been an underestimate as some infant deaths were probably not reported. The figure was little different in 1954, but dropped after that to 130 in 1961 (Central Statistical and Economics Department 1963: 42).

Table 5.7:   Household consumption in Rangoon, 1927 and 1958

	1927	1958
Food as percentage of total expenditures	52.8*	66.1

Food consumption (per capita per month)		
Rice (Kg)	12.4	13.2
Pulses (Kg)	0.1	0.4
Meat (Kg)	1.2	0.75
Eggs (Unit)	0.3	2.6
Fish (Kg)	2.2	1.2
Oils/Fats	0.6	0.9
Sugar	0.1	0.2

* Burmese households only.
Sources: Bennison (1928: 97); Central Statistical and Economics Department (1963: 313-314).

During the 1960s and 1970s, real per capita consumption expenditures did increase, although the data did not separate out government and private expenditures, and much of the growth was probably due to the government (Booth 1997a: Table 3.1). On the other hand, per capita rice availability increased steadily from the 1950s to the early 1970s (Booth 2003: Table 12). This improvement could have been partly due to an increase in real per capita expenditures, but was also the result of the government policy of diverting the exportable surplus to the domestic market at prices well below the world market price. While the government probably wanted to devote more resources to sectors such as health and education, it was constrained by falling tax revenues relative to GDP. By the mid-1970s, government revenues were only 12 per cent of GDP, which was much lower than in the late 1950s (Booth 2003: 146). Defence expenditures continued to have top priority in the allocation of government expenditures.

Lessons from the Country Studies

The considerable body of research on inequality, poverty and living standards in Southeast Asia from the 1950s to around 1980 highlighted a number of issues which were to recur in more recent research. Measurement problems were of concern to most of the studies cited here. How should be poverty line be set? How should it be adjusted for differences in prices between regions, and for changes in prices over time? How should the urban poverty line be set relative to the rural one? Several studies emphasized the differential impact of inflation on different expenditure groups. This was likely to be important in those economies experiencing high rates of inflation. Governments often tried to control prices of some basic staples such as rice, but not of corn and cassava, which in some regions were more important in the consumption baskets of the poor.

Another problem which emerged was whether the headcount and other measures of poverty should be estimated using household income or expenditure data. The Malaysian figures used income data, as did most estimates from the Philippines and Thailand. But in Indonesia, the Central Bureau of Statistics only published expenditure data. Opinions varied as to whether income or expenditure figures were likely to be more accurately reported in the household surveys. Visaria (1980: 29) suggested that 'it would be advisable to emphasize the data on expenditure over those on income and to collect them for relatively short reference periods to reduce the problems of recall lapse'. Others argued that income data collected over a longer period would be less prone to temporary fluctuations. The broader issue of the accuracy of the survey data was of concern to most analysts in the 1970s. Chander (1980: 88-98) concluded his analysis of the household survey results for Malaysia and the Philippines by drawing attention to four key lessons; these related to the sampling frame, the questionnaire design, the implementation of field operations and the problems of data processing and publication of the final results. He stressed the importance of keeping the sampling frame up to date, of keeping questionnaires short to avoid respondent fatigue, of proper supervision of field staff, and of recruiting trained staff to carry out data processing. These points might seem obvious, but as will be seen in subsequent chapters, they are as relevant today as when they were written almost four decades ago.

Van Ginneken (1976: 61) argued that 'the reliability of the findings of a sample survey of households varies with the size of the sample'. He followed other statisticians in suggesting that one way of checking the reliability of the sample survey data was to blow up the expenditure data using population figures and then compare the survey estimates of household expenditure with those of private final consumption expenditure in the national accounts. Household survey data were likely to be lower, because consumption of non-household institutions was excluded. But if the disparity was greater than 30 per cent, it was probable that the survey data were underestimating total expenditure (Van Ginneken and Park 1984: 4). It was noted in the discussion of the FIES surveys in the Philippines that some analysts argued that when the ratio of FIES expenditures to those in the national accounts fell much below 70 per cent, the resulting measures of inequality were unlikely to be accurate, especially if the disparities were the result of under-reporting in richer households. But could the results still be used to measure poverty? The problem of disparities between survey and national accounts data, far from being resolved, continues to be debated down to the present.

Most of the studies cited in this chapter found that the headcount measure of poverty was high in the 1960s and declined only slowly through to the mid-1970s or early 1980s, even in those economies where per capita GDP growth was quite rapid. Where there were rapid declines, as in the Indonesian case using a rice-based poverty line, critics argued that the poverty line was no longer suitable by the end of the 1970s. The poverty line introduced by the Central Bureau of Statistics (CBS) in Indonesia in 1976 was based on a broader basket of goods and services. The headcount estimates of poverty based on the CBS poverty line also showed a significant decline between 1976 and 1981, which was to continue down to 1996 (Central Bureau of Statistics 1997: 570). But the methodology used to construct the CBS poverty line was not transparent; this was also true of the estimates published by the Malaysian government in official documents. Some researchers argued that, given the problems with both the household survey data and the poverty line estimates, headcount measures of poverty should be abandoned. Other estimates of living standards should be computed using demographic data, wage data or food consumption figures from food balance sheets.

The problems can be illustrated in the case of the Philippines. Not only did per capita GDP grow over the 1960s, but average calorie and protein consumption increased and infant mortality rates dropped (Table 5.3). Educational enrolments and literacy also increased from the already high figures recorded in the late 1930s. But at least according to some estimates, the headcount measure of poverty also increased. Certainly there was little evidence that it had declined. How could these apparently contradictory trends be reconciled? Was it the case that average improvements in non-monetary indicators such as literacy and mortality rates masked large, and growing disparities by income class, regions or ethnic groups? This question also arose in the other countries which achieved improvements in educational and health indicators from the 1950s onwards. To what extent did improved performance go along with growing inequalities in access to both healthcare and education? If inequalities were increasing, then some young people on entering the labour market were far better prepared than others to seize the opportunities which came with faster economic growth.

In both Indonesia and the Philippines, some researchers argued that the benefits of accelerated growth after 1966 in the agricultural sector accrued mainly to those who owned agricultural land, or were able to access land on reasonably favourable terms. The problem of landlessness received some scholarly attention, although as Boyce (1993: 132) pointed out in the context of the Philippines, the definition of landlessness proved 'slippery'. After 1950, population censuses and labour force surveys in many parts of Asia made a distinction between family and hired labour, but in practice in many rural settings the boundary between the two was often unclear. In addition, not all people classified as wage workers were landless; village surveys found that some of those who worked for wages also hired in labour to cultivate their own land. Many rural households were found to be employed in more than one sector. Earnings from agriculture, whether from cultivating a small holding or from wage labour in agriculture, were often supplemented with earnings from other sectors, including trading, transport, construction and manufacturing.

In spite of all these difficulties, Boyce did find some support for the oft-repeated argument that 'a distinct class of landless wage labourers' had emerged in the Philippines by the 1960s. He argued that longitudinal studies in parts of Luzon had found that the number of households headed by landless labourers was increasing over time. In 1975, the labour force survey attached to the National Sample Survey found that the proportion of the male agricultural labour force working as employees was around 15 per cent; it was slightly higher in Indonesia in 1980 (Table 5.2). Other estimates of landlessness in Indonesia produced different results, although it was clear that the problem was worse in Java than in the other islands (Booth and Sundrum 1981: 189). A detailed breakdown of rural households by landownership in the district of Klaten, in Central Java, found that almost 30 per cent were landless in the sense that they did not own any land at all, and a further 37 per cent owned only house gardens (Booth 1974: 136). The

1971 census found that this district had a low percentage of the economically active rural population working in agriculture compared with rural Java as a whole. How many were forced to seek non-agricultural employment through lack of access to agricultural land was not clear. But by the 1980s, many agricultural households in Java were supplementing their incomes from agriculture with off-farm jobs; the evidence for this will be reviewed in more detail in subsequent chapters.

A further set of issues concerned trends in inequality. In those economies where there was some economic growth, and the headcount measure of poverty did decline over the 1960s and 1970s, such as Malaysia, Indonesia and Thailand, the fall did not appear to have been due to a dramatic reduction in income inequality. In most parts of Southeast Asia, there was not much evidence of redistribution with growth in the decades up to 1980. Rather, the distribution of household incomes or expenditures, as shown by the Gini coefficient or the shares of the top to bottom deciles of the distribution, remained stable, so the decline in poverty, where it occurred, was the result of an increase in average incomes. This appears to have been the case in the Philippines and Thailand over the 1960s, and in Indonesia and Thailand over the 1970s.[20]

For much of the period under review, almost all the research on poverty and distribution was carried out by the International Labour Organization and the World Bank, or by independent scholars, sometimes with assistance from bilateral and international donors. Most government statistical agencies did not begin to publish figures on poverty or income distribution until the 1980s or later. In the Philippines, the FIES results were not published between 1975 and 1985, and the Marcos government in its final years did not encourage debate about trends in poverty. Malaysia was the only country to publish official estimates of poverty, and these were often criticized for their lack of clarity. The Malaysian government was reluctant to publish the results of household income surveys, which made it difficult for academic researchers to check the government claims about trends in poverty and income distribution. Estimates of the headcount measure of poverty made by academics or international organizations in Southeast Asia often produced very different results, because different methods for estimating poverty lines

---

20   The estimates of the Gini coefficients in Indonesia for 1964 and 1970 given in Van Leeuwen and Foldvari (2016: Table 5) show a decline from 0.39 to 0.35. The two figures may not be comparable because of differences in survey coverage, although it is possible that the dramatic drop in inflation at the end of the 1960s did bring about some improvement in real incomes for the poorer groups relative to others.

were used as well as different approaches to adjusting poverty lines over time. This understandably caused confusion and some degree of cynicism. Some political activists thought that the whole approach to poverty measurement in Southeast Asia was motivated mainly by a concern on the part of national governments and international agencies to demonstrate that accelerated economic growth was helping the poor, regardless of whether that was true or not. These doubts persisted in subsequent decades.

Rankings in 1980

By 1980, Singapore, Brunei and Malaysia were well above other countries in Southeast Asia in terms of per capita GDP, and were also making progress on health and educational indicators. Thailand's per capita GDP was above that of the Philippines, although the country was still well behind on educational indicators. The Philippines was still above Indonesia in terms of both per capita GDP and health and educational indicators, in spite of the gains which Indonesia had made over the 1970s. Vietnam, Laos and Cambodia were well behind in terms of per capita GDP, and were struggling with the legacies of more than three decades of conflict. Myanmar had achieved some growth in per capita GDP since the 1950s, but was still behind the peak achieved in the early 1930s. A ranking of 48 of the world's poorest countries compiled by Dasgupta (1993: Table 5.2) included three Southeast Asian countries, Indonesia, Thailand and the Philippines. Singapore, Brunei and Malaysia were presumably excluded because they were not considered poor, while Vietnam, Laos, Cambodia and Burma were excluded through lack of data. Six indicators were used including per capita GDP, life expectancy and infant mortality, adult literacy and two indexes of political and civil rights. Thailand and the Philippines were ranked sixth and eighth from the top, with Indonesia further back at seventeenth. Indonesia was below both China and India. It fell behind China on GDP and demographic indicators, and behind India on political and civil rights.

The Human Development Index was not published until the 1990s, but the twentieth anniversary edition did publish estimates for some countries from 1980 to 2010 (UNDP 2010: 148-151). Estimates for 1980 were only available for Malaysia, Thailand, the Philippines and Indonesia. In 1980, the Philippines had a composite score below that of Malaysia, but above Thailand and Indonesia. Thailand in 1980 had very low mean years of schooling, only 3.5 years for adults over 25, compared with 6.6 years in the Philippines (UNDP 1991: 128). In that year, the Philippines was still above several countries which had by 2010 moved into the high human development category, including Algeria, Turkey, Jordan and Tunisia. Indonesia was still well behind a number of other countries in the medium human development group, which it would overtake in the next three decades, including Syria, Nicaragua, Guatemala and the Congo (Brazzaville). In subsequent chapters the reasons for the relative success of Indonesia and the weaker performance of the Philippines are further investigated.

6   The 1980s and the 1990s: The Fast and the Slow in Southeast Asia

Rapid Growth in the ASEAN Four in the 1980s

Within Southeast Asia, the policy reforms which were discussed in Chapter 4 began to have an impact on economic growth in the years from 1965 to 1980. Singapore, which was troubled by a range of political, economic and social problems in the aftermath of the Japanese occupation, had experienced very little economic growth in per capita terms until 1965, but between 1965 and 1980 per capita GDP more than trebled. The development strategy implemented after Singapore's break from Malaysia was far more successful than most observers had predicted in 1965 and by the latter part of the 1970s was influencing policy in neighbouring countries. Rapid growth was sustained until 1996, when real per capita GDP was almost nine times the 1950 level (Table 4.6).

Accelerated growth in both Thailand and Malaysia in the 1960s and 1970s was in part the result of growth in the traditional export sectors (agriculture and mining), but both countries began to attract foreign investment into manufacturing industries oriented not just to local markets but also to export markets. The Philippine economy also achieved some success in diversifying its export base, although growth was slower between 1965 and 1980 than in Malaysia and Thailand, and by 1980 per capita GDP had fallen behind that of Thailand and was little more than half that of the Republic of Korea (Table 4.6). Over the 1980s, both Thailand and Malaysia forged ahead while the Philippines fell behind. In 1996, per capita GDP in the Philippines was slightly below the 1980 figure. Indonesia which had achieved rapid growth over the 1970s as a result of improvement in the terms of trade, managed to sustain growth from 1980 to 1996 by a successful policy of export diversification. After two devaluations in 1983 and 1986, and the introduction of a duty drawback scheme, non-oil exports grew rapidly in the decade up to 1996 (Hill 1996: 161-164).

The perceived success of these economies in achieving rapid growth began to influence thinking over the 1980s in the leading development agencies. It was pointed out in Chapter 4 that in the 1980s both the World Bank and important bilateral donors turned away from many of the concerns expressed in the 1970s about poverty and distribution and concentrated more on macroeconomic reform and also reform of trade and investment policies. 'Structural adjustment' policies were implemented in a number of countries, but they appeared to have been most successful in Malaysia, Thailand and Indonesia which by the early 1990s were considered success stories along with the four tigers (Singapore, Hong Kong, Taiwan and the Republic of Korea). These seven countries, together with Japan were the focus of the 'East Asian Miracle' report, published by the World Bank in 1993.

The message was that the 'fast-growing four' in Southeast Asia had managed to achieve growth if not with equity at least with a substantial decline in absolute poverty, through open-type trade and investment policies which other countries, both in Asia and elsewhere, should learn from and emulate. These countries had encouraged foreign investment in export-oriented manufacturing and, particularly in the case of Malaysia, had reduced the role of government in the economy through privatization of state enterprises. But some reviews of the 'Asian Miracle' report pointed out that the evidence that the four Southeast Asian countries included in the report had got their policies right, and were following in the footsteps of Japan, Taiwan and Korea, was open to question. The vulnerabilities in the financial sectors of Thailand, Malaysia and Indonesia which were a causal factor in the crisis of 1997/98 were largely ignored in both World Bank and other evaluations until 1997. The claims made about educational attainment were also misleading. Although the report claimed that the eight countries were all characterized by 'higher initial levels and growth rates of human capital', in fact it was clear by the 1980s that several Southeast Asian countries, especially Thailand, had neglected education, at least beyond the primary level. In 1992, when per capita GDP in Thailand was about the same as in South Korea in 1984, the secondary enrolment rate was only 37 per cent, compared with 91 per cent in South Korea (Booth 2001b: Table 2.3). Indonesia, Malaysia and Thailand had more favourable resource bases than the northeast Asian economies and had developed as exporters of agricultural products and minerals. The ready availability of rents from the exploitation of natural resources meant that the nature and purpose of government intervention in countries such as Indonesia and Malaysia differed from Taiwan and South Korea (Gomez and Jomo 1997: 177-181).

In the 1980s, some doubts were raised about the sustainability of the Southeast Asian model. One economist went so far as to call capitalism in Southeast Asia 'ersatz' or fake, and by implication unsustainable (Yoshihara 1988). Yoshihara stressed the high dependence on foreign capital and technology, the dominant role of entrepreneurs of Chinese descent, and the tendency of many business groups to focus on rent-seeking activities. The large conglomerates which emerged in Indonesia and Malaysia from the 1970s onwards were often controlled by people with close links to powerful politicians. 'Crony capitalism', which had flourished in the Philippines under Marcos, spread to other parts of the region. But according to the World Bank and many other economists in the region and elsewhere, these problems were belied by the growth figures. By the 1990s, Thailand had outperformed not just the Philippines but also most of the African countries which had had similar levels of per capita GDP in 1965. Indonesia's successful policies of post-oil boom restructuring could be contrasted with other petroleum economies such as Nigeria. Indonesia's per capita GDP almost doubled between 1980 and 1996, whereas in Nigeria, it had decreased over these years by over 20 per cent (Table 4.6).

Estimating the Changes in Poverty and Living Standards in Southeast Asia: The Achievements of the 'Miracle Economies'

An important part of the World Bank message in the early 1990s was that the fast-growing economies in East Asia had also experienced rapid declines in poverty. The 1990 *World Development Report* put forward a new international poverty line, this time set at between $275 and $370 per capita per year, converted not using market exchange rates but the 1985 exchange rates derived from the International Comparisons Project. It was argued that this range 'was chosen to span the poverty lines estimated in recent studies for a number of countries with low average incomes – Bangladesh, the Arab Republic of Egypt, India, Indonesia, Kenya, Morocco, and Tanzania' (World Bank 1990: 27). The lower limit coincided with the poverty line commonly used for India. Because the upper limit of the poverty lines suggested in this report corresponded to roughly a dollar day, this was the poverty line which became the standard one used by the World Bank for much of its comparative work on poverty for the next two decades. With some adjustments, it remains in use. For some observers, especially those who welcomed the renewed emphasis on problems of global poverty, the choice of a global poverty line 'was a sensible yardstick for the Bank to adopt in order to focus its work and to measure progress' (Konkel 2014: 298). The use of an income-based measure was defended on the grounds that non-monetary measures were usually highly correlated with monetary measures. In addition, it permitted a relatively straightforward way of measuring the relationship between economic growth, measured in terms of GDP, and poverty alleviation. The old debate about whether, and to what extent, growth helped the poor could be settled more easily if changes in poverty could be measured using a money metric.

A further reason for the introduction of a global poverty line was implied in several World Bank publications, as well as those put out by other agencies, although often not addressed directly. This related to the greater availability of statistics. By the 1980s, the work of the International Comparison Project had been extended to a much greater number of countries than were covered in the reports discussed in Chapter 4. The World Bank eventually took over responsibility for producing these estimates. Another crucial requirement for the estimation of global poverty estimates were household surveys; they were needed for every country included in the global estimates. Some countries, where violent conflict over a long period prevented the implementation of household-level surveys or even population censuses, were excluded from the early World Bank estimates. But for many countries with a history of conflict, including several in Southeast Asia, survey data did become available through the 1990s, although the coverage and accuracy of these surveys remained a matter of dispute.

The 1990 *World Development Report* used the global poverty lines of $275 and $370 per capita per year, in 1985 PPP dollars, to estimate the headcount and poverty gap measures for all developing countries, and for broad geographic regions (World Bank 1990: Table 2.1). But when the report discussed changes in poverty indicators in a group of sixteen countries in Asia and Latin America, it used the national poverty lines in these countries. The report noted that several countries in Asia had experienced rapid declines in poverty in the 1970s and 1980s. Indonesia was singled out as an especially strong performer, cutting its headcount measure of poverty by 41 percentage points in just seventeen years. This led to a very sharp decline in the numbers of poor, in spite of the fact that population growth had been quite rapid over these years (Table 6.1). The estimates in this table were also used in the Asian Miracle report (World Bank 1993: 4-5). It was claimed that not only had the headcount and other measures of poverty declined rapidly, but other economic, social and demographic indicators had improved, and income distribution had either improved or stayed constant.

There was little attempt in these reports to analyse the poverty data produced by national governments in detail, although the figures shown in Table 6.1 did raise some perplexing questions. Why, for example, was the headcount measure of poverty in Indonesia in 1987 lower than in Thailand, and only slightly higher than in Malaysia, in spite of the fact that per capita GDP, and other indicators such as life expectancy, were higher in both Malaysia and Thailand than in Indonesia? In fact, the answer to this question should have been quite obvious: both the Malaysian and Thai estimates

Table 6.1:   Estimates of the headcount measure of poverty and the population below national poverty lines (World Bank estimates)

Region/Country	Percentage below the poverty line		Numbers (millions)		GDP Per Capita (1987)*
	(First Year)	(Final Year)	(First Year)	(Final Year)	
Indonesia (1970, 1987)	58	17	68	30	2,138
Thailand (1962, 1986)	59	26	17	14	3,421
Malaysia (1973, 1987)	37	15	4	2	4,218
Singapore (1972, 1982)	31	10	0.7	0.2	11,743
Philippines (1971, 1988)	52	44	19	26	2,019

*Per capita GDP in 1990 international GK$.
Sources: World Bank (1990: 41); Philippines: Balisacan (1994: Table 2.4). GDP data from Bolt and Van Zanden (2014).

used poverty lines which were considerably higher than the Indonesian one. The World Bank in several publications issued in the early 1990s claimed that the poverty lines used in comparing headcount and other measures of poverty were broadly comparable in that they permitted similar calorie intakes. But in fact they were not comparable; in Thailand the basket of foodgrains contained higher quality and more expensive foods than in Indonesia. In addition, the mark-up for non-food expenditures was higher (Booth 1997b; Asra 2000). When in the latter part of the 1990s, the World Bank began to publish estimates of poverty using the $1 a day poverty line, it became clear that the headcount measure was much lower in Thailand than in Indonesia (World Bank 2001: 280-281).

Comparisons were also made in the measurement of poverty between Indonesia and the Philippines. It was argued that, when comparable estimates of poverty incidence (the percentage of the population below the poverty line) in the 1980s were estimated, the difference was in fact quite small, and certainly far lower than shown in Table 6.1. This was because the national poverty lines were estimated according to different methodologies. Using the national poverty lines, the headcount measure of poverty in Indonesia was only 17 per cent in 1987, compared with 44 per cent in the Philippines. But the adjusted estimates showed that the difference was much less; 47.3 per cent of the population were below the poverty line in Indonesia in 1987, compared with 55 per cent in the Philippines in 1988 (Asra, David and Virola 1997: 271).[1]

1   The Indonesian figures, relative to those from the Philippines were also queried by Balisacan (1997: 2).

But the different poverty lines used by national statistical agencies, and by academic researchers, were not the only reason for the rather questionable results shown in Table 6.1, and in some other World Bank publications issued in the 1990s. In addition, there were queries about the survey data used to estimate the headcount measure. Several commentators pointed to the disparity between the household income and expenditure estimates shown in the survey data and those derived from national accounts data. In the Philippines, the survey data on household expenditures were estimated to be around 80 per cent of the national accounts data in 1971, falling to 69 per cent in 1991 (Balisacan 1994: Table 2.3). In Indonesia the ratios fell from 71 per cent in 1970 to 61 per cent in 1990 (Booth 2016: 177). The reasons for these disparities are complex, and may reflect problems with the national accounts data as well as the household survey data. But they do suggest that caution is needed in comparing poverty estimates from household survey data both over time in one country, and between countries.

Even allowing for the problems with both poverty lines and household survey data, there were good reasons for arguing that living standards did improve in Malaysia, Thailand and Indonesia in the three decades from 1965 to 1995, compared to other parts of Asia, and other parts of the developing world. Already by 1980, these three countries had an HDI which was above the 'medium human development' average, and in all cases it increased through to 1995 (Table 6.2). By that year, the HDI in these three countries was above Vietnam, Laos and Cambodia. Most observers expected that the improvement would continue into the new century. What they did not anticipate was the serious growth collapses which occurred in 1998. The implications of this for living standards are examined below.

Table 6.2: Human Development Index, 1980 to 2010

Year	1980	1995	2000	2010
Malaysia	0.541	0.659	0.691	0.744
Thailand	0.483	0.581	0.600	0.654
Philippines	0.523	0.569	0.597	0.638
Indonesia	0.390	0.508	0.500	0.600
Vietnam	n/a	0.457	0.505	0.572
Lao PDR	n/a	0.388	0.425	0.497
Cambodia	n/a	0.385	0.412	0.494
Myanmar	n/a	n/a	n/a	0.451
Medium Human Development (Average)	0.361	0.480	0.510	0.586

Source: UNDP (2010: 150-151).

Trends in Inequalities in Thailand, Indonesia, Malaysia and Singapore

As the international debate on poverty gathered pace through the 1990s, attention was also given to inequality issues. For any given rate of growth, the impact on poverty would obviously be greater if incomes of the poorer groups were growing at the same or a faster rate than the better off groups. But to the extent that the better off were benefiting from growth to a greater extent than the poorer groups, growth would be less 'pro-poor'. Definitions of pro-poor growth have in fact varied in the literature. Some studies assume that if growth is accompanied by a decline in the headcount measure of poverty or a decline in numbers of poor people, then it can be termed 'pro-poor'. Timmer (2004: 184-185) argued that growth in Indonesia, and several other Asian countries was pro-poor in the decades from the 1960s to the 1990s in the sense that the incomes or expenditures of the bottom quintile of the income distribution grew at roughly the same rate as average incomes. According to Timmer's analysis, growth was pro-poor in Indonesia the sense that incomes of the bottom quintile grew faster than the average in some years between 1967 and 2002 but not in others. Other studies have argued that pro-poor growth should imply that the poor benefit from growth to a greater extent than the non-poor (Kakwani and Pernia 2000).

Over the 1980s, the Thai case received considerable attention. Some economists argued that the rapid GDP growth over that decade was having little impact on the poor, especially in rural areas. Real per capita GDP increased by 75 per cent between 1981 and 1990, but the numbers below the poverty line, as estimated by Warr (2009: 67), dropped by only about 1.6 million, or 9.4 per cent over these years (Table 6.3). The household survey data also showed that the rapid growth in incomes until 1992 was accompanied by an increase in inequality. Between 1981 and 1992, the share of the top 10 per cent as a ratio of the bottom 40 per cent increased from 2.3 to almost 3.9 (Phongpaichit and Baker 2016: 10). Tinakorn (1995: 224-225) found that most of the poor in the latter part of the 1980s were in rural areas and were mainly farmers and farm labourers. The headcount measure of poverty was especially high in the northeast, where many households still lacked basic amenities such as piped water, toilets and electricity. She questioned whether the 'trickle down' mechanism had in fact worked well in Thailand, at least over the 1980s.

But it did appear to be working more strongly over the early part of the 1990s. Both the headcount measure of poverty and numbers below the poverty line fell sharply between 1990 and 1996, and there was some fall in inequality from the high level reached in 1992 (Table 6.3). Over the decade from 1986 to 1996, per capita GDP more than doubled, and numbers in poverty fell by more than half. Kakwani and Krongkaew (2000: 152-153) disaggregated the data by region, and showed that the decline in the head-count measure of poverty was particularly rapid in the northeast region. In 1988, 48.4 per cent of the population were below the poverty line. By 1996 that had fallen to 19.4 per cent. For all rural areas, the headcount measure of poverty over these years fell from 40.3 per cent to 14.9 per cent. At the national level, the headcount measure of poverty fell from 32.6 per cent to 11.4 per cent. But Kakwani and Krongkaew argued that, even given these impressive rates of decline, significant numbers of Thais in 1996 remained poor, especially among the elderly and children.

Table 6:3:   Headcount measure of poverty, poor population and Palma ratio:
             Thailand, 1975 to 1996

	Headcount (% below poverty line)	Poor population (millions)	Palma ratio
1975	48.6	20.6	n/a
1981	35.5	17.0	2.3
1986	44.9	23.8	2.7
1990	27.2	15.4	3.4
1992	23.2	13.4	3.9
1996	11.4	6.9	3.4

Sources: Warr (2009: Table 9); Palma ratio: Phongpaichit and Baker (2016: 10).

An important reason for the fall in poverty in rural Thailand between 1988 and 1996 was the improvement in the performance of the agricultural sector. In response to the weak growth of the agricultural sector in the mid-1980s, the government implemented several reforms including removing most export taxes, especially on rice. These policies helped to boost farm gate prices. In addition, the booming economy in the Greater Bangkok region created employment opportunities for many migrants from the poorer regions in other parts of the country, and their remittances boosted incomes in their home regions. But as Warr (2009: 75) argued, low standards of education in rural areas placed many rural migrants at a disadvantage in urban labour markets, where they could not compete with better educated graduates from urban schools and tertiary institutions for the well-paid jobs. The government used minimum wage legislation to improve incomes of unskilled workers. But this policy had negative effects as well. By the early 1990s higher wages, especially in the Greater Bangkok region were forcing many labour-intensive industries to relocate to other parts of Asia, including China and Vietnam, where wage rates were less than half of those in the Greater Bangkok region.

The Indonesian estimates of the Gini coefficient of household expenditures using the Susenas data were quite stable between 1976 and 1990. Between 1990 and 1996 there was some increase (Asra 2014: 34). Even allowing for problems with the survey data in Indonesia, which will be discussed in more detail in the next chapter, it is probable that there was some increase in income and expenditure inequalities in the decade up to 1996. The estimates of relative poverty (the percentage of the population below half the average per capita consumption expenditure) also showed some increase between 1984 and 1996. The increase occurred entirely in urban areas, especially in Jakarta (Booth 2016: 171). This indicator has been criticized for conflating poverty estimates with inequality, but it can be argued that by the 1980s many Indonesians were comparing their living standards not with some abstract poverty threshold set by government officials, but with those of their neighbours and others with whom they came into contact on a regular basis. To the extent that some people felt left behind in a comparative sense, they probably experienced a sense of grievance, even if their absolute living standards were improving.

In Malaysia, most studies of poverty and inequality from 1970 to 1997, and beyond, have relied on the figures published in official documents. They showed a very rapid decline in the headcount measure of poverty between 1970 and 1997, from 49.3 per cent to 6.1 per cent. The decline took place across all ethnic groups; by 1997 the headcount measure for the Malay population was only slightly above the national average (7.7 per cent). Over these years there was also some decline in the Gini coefficient of household income from 0.53 to 0.47 (Ragayah 2012: Tables 11.3 and 11.5). Milanovic (2006) analysed changes in the distribution of earnings between 1984 and 1997. He found that both the Gini coefficient and the Theil index of real earnings fell. Together with the official data, his findings supported the view that Malaysia did experience some redistribution with growth, although the redistribution was modest. Much of the poverty decline was the result of sustained growth of income over the decades from the 1970s to the late 1990s.

An analysis of the distribution of earnings in Singapore also found little change in the Gini coefficient between 1984 and 1997, and some decline in the Theil index (Mukhopadhaya 2014: 65). Over these years, the composition of the labour force began to change in Singapore, with more migrant workers being employed in both skilled and unskilled occupations. Malaysia also began to use more foreign workers, especially in agriculture and construction. Shari (2000: 121) argued that growing numbers of unskilled workers imported from Indonesia and Bangladesh depressed wages for local workers. But this trend did not appear to have had much impact on earnings inequality in either Singapore or Malaysia, at least until 1997. In 1997, the Gini coefficient of earnings in both countries was around 0.47. Comparable data on earnings were not available for other Southeast Asian countries in the 1990s, but the Gini coefficient for earnings in Taiwan was much lower than in either Singapore or Malaysia, even allowing for the inclusion of property incomes in the Taiwanese data. Mukhopadhaya (2014: 76) pointed out that if property income had been included in the estimates for Singapore, the Gini would have been higher.

An important aspect of the debate on growth, poverty and inequality in Southeast Asia, beginning in the 1970s, was the regional dimension. In Thailand, the much higher headcount measure of poverty in the north and northeast of the country, compared with other regions, was already obvious in the 1960s. This was the result of lower per capita GDP in what were predominantly agricultural regions. But as more figures on regional GDP became available in Indonesia and Malaysia, as well as poverty data broken down by region or province, it became clear that there were a number of states in Malaysia and provinces in Indonesia where per capita GDP was close to or above the national average, but where poverty was above the national figure. In Malaysia in 1987, the national headcount measure of poverty was reported to be 17.3 per cent, but state-level estimates ranged from 36.1 per cent in Terengganu to 5.2 per cent in the Federal Territory of Kuala Lumpur. Some of the states where poverty was higher than the national average, such as Kedah and Kelantan, had lower per capita GDP than the national average, but others including Terengganu, Sabah and Sarawak had per capita GDP that was as high or higher than the national average (Government of Malaysia 1989: 45-51). In Indonesia, when headcount measures of poverty by province began to be published in the 1990s, it was clear that in several resource-rich provinces where per capita GDP was higher than the national average, the headcount measure of poverty was also close to, or even higher than the national average.

The extreme outlier was the province then known as Irian Jaya, now divided into the two provinces of Papua and Papua Barat. Poverty was estimated to be almost twice the national average in 1993 and 1996, but regional GDP was 60 per cent above the national average.[2] The reason

---

2   Estimates of the provincial headcount measures of poverty in Indonesia reported in Asra and Santos-Francisco (2003: Appendix 1) use a different approach to the estimation of regional poverty lines from that used by the Central Bureau of Statistics (CBS). They showed that the proportion of the population below the provincial poverty line in Irian Jaya in 1993 was not as

for this was that much of the GDP produced in the province did not stay there; revenues from mining and other resource-based industries were either remitted abroad, or accrued to the central government. Thus, per capita consumption expenditures were only a small fraction of regional output. Even in those resource rich provinces where poverty was below the national average, such as East Kalimantan, poverty was much higher than in the neighbouring Malaysian state of Sabah, although per capita GDP was higher in East Kalimantan in 1993 (Table 6.4). Drains from the resource-rich provinces to the centre remained high in Indonesia until the reforms in regional finance implemented after Suharto's departure in 1998; in East Kalimantan they persisted into the 2000s (Booth 2015: Table 2.4)

Table 6.4:   Headcount measures of poverty: Indonesia and Malaysia, 1993

	National poverty line (% below)	Malaysian poverty line (% below)	GDP per capita (Rupiah '000) ***
Sabah	33.2	33.2	4750
Sarawak	19.1	19.1	6517
Peninsular Malaysia	10.5	10.5	7136
East Kalimantan *	13.8	79.4	7630
Riau **	11.2	80.6	4779
Aceh **	13.5	86.7	3019
Irian Jaya **	24.2	81.5	2641

* Using the Sabah poverty line.
** Using the Peninsular Malaysia poverty line.
*** Exchange rate: Rp 811 = Malaysian ringgit.
Sources: Department of Statistics: Malaysia (1997), Department of Statistics: Sabah (1996), Department of Statistics: Sarawak (1998), Central Bureau of Statistics (1997).

Estimating Changes in Poverty and Living Standards in the Non-miracles in the 1980s and 1990s: The Philippines, Vietnam, Cambodia, Laos and Myanmar

Although the Philippine economy grew quite rapidly from the 1950s to the 1970s, the growth was increasingly viewed as debt-driven and much of the

high relative to the national average as the CBS figures. In that year Irian Jaya was ranked 25th in terms of the headcount measure out of 27 provinces using the CBS poverty line; using the alternative estimates it was ranked 11th. The difference resulted in part from the higher weight given to rice, and the lower weight given to root crops in the food basket in the CBS poverty line.

foreign borrowing was used for prestige projects which often did not yield reasonable economic returns. The report of a World Bank mission published in 1976 argued that the economy could grow at around 4 per cent per annum in per capita terms if appropriate economic reforms were adopted in both the public and the private sector (Cheetham and Hawkins 1976: 38-41). But in the latter part of the 1970s and the early 1980s, growth slowed as the country found it more difficult to borrow abroad. After 1983, both the economic and the political situation deteriorated further until President Marcos was forced to resign after popular protests in 1986. Balisacan (1994: Table 2.4) estimated that the headcount measure of poverty increased from 52.2 per cent in 1971 to 53.9 per cent in 1985. This might not appear to be a large increase, given the economic problems the country endured in the latter part of the 1970s and the early 1980s. But population growth was rapid by Asian standards, and numbers in poverty increased substantially from 19.5 million in 1971 to 29.15 million in 1985. Boyce (1993: Table 2.13) presented estimates of the headcount measure of poverty which showed a greater increase, from 43.8 per cent in 1971 to 58.9 per cent in 1985, although he emphasized the problems of data comparability.

There were high hopes that the economic situation would improve after 1986, but in fact the economic recovery was patchy. Reforms were implemented by President Cory Aquino, who was elected in 1986, but a combination of political instability and natural disasters meant that business confidence was slow to recover, and per capita GDP only returned to the 1982 level in 1988. During the Ramos presidency, there was some acceleration in growth, and the economy was not as badly affected by the Asian crisis as Thailand, Malaysia and Indonesia (Balisacan and Hill 2003: 5). Given the slow pace of the economic recovery after 1986, it might have been expected that there would have been an adverse impact on poverty, and on non-monetary indicators of development in the Philippines. But in fact the evidence does not support this pessimistic view. The poverty indicators presented by Balisacan (2003: Table 10.1) showed that both the headcount measure and the poverty depth measure fell between 1985 and 1997. The fall in poverty between 1985 and 1988 was due to the economic recovery which occurred over these three years from the trough in 1985.[3]

---

3   It should be noted that the estimates prepared by Balisacan used the expenditure data from the FIES, whereas estimates prepared by the government statistical agency (the official estimates) used the household income figures, which gave higher estimates of poverty. Balisacan (1997) gives more detail on the differences between his methodology and that used in the official estimates.

It seems probable that a considerable number of people had fallen slightly below the poverty line by 1985, so even the modest economic recovery was enough to push their expenditures back above the line. A further fall between 1994 and 1997 was due to the increase in real per capita expenditures of 21 per cent over these three years (Balisacan 2003: 319). In spite of population growth, which was still rapid by Asian standards, numbers below the poverty line also fell by almost four million from 1985 to 1997 (Table 6.5). As the Gini coefficient increased slightly, these falls could not be attributed to an improvement in income or expenditure distribution; changes in real per capita expenditures were the crucial factor. In an earlier paper, Balisacan (1999: 39) argued that the agricultural sector led the way in poverty allevia-tion, at least until 1994. This was in contrast to the experience in the 1960s, where it had been argued that growth in the agricultural sector had not led to rapid poverty decline (Bautista 1994).

Table 6.5:   **Poverty incidence and depth, numbers in poverty and Gini coefficient, Philippines, 1985-2000**

Year	Poverty estimates		Numbers of poor (millions)	Gini coefficient	GDP per capita*
	Incidence	Depth			
1985	40.9	13.2	22.2	0.41	1967
1988	34.4	10.1	20.2	0.40	2105
1991	34.3	10.6	21.8	0.43	2136
1994	32.1	8.7	21.9	0.40	2144
1997	25.0	6.4	18.3	0.43	2331
2000	27.5	7.2	21.4	0.45	2336

* 1990 international GK$.
Sources: Balisacan (2003: Table 10.1); GDP: Maddison Project Database, 2013.

The estimates of household income inequality for the Philippines compiled by Estudillo (1997) showed a decline in the Gini coefficient between 1965 and 1985 (Table 6.6). It is not clear what caused this decline, although it is possible that the growth slowdown over the years from 1970 to 1985 had a more serious impact on higher income households than on those on lower incomes. Estudillo's estimates confirm those of Balisacan that there was an increase in inequality between 1985 and 1991, although her estimates refer to household income, not expenditure. Her estimates also suggest that by the 1980s, household income distribution in the Philippines was not much higher than in Malaysia, Indonesia and Thailand. The estimates in Table 6.6 are all derived from household income, rather than expenditure, but

still might not be fully comparable, as definitions of income could well
have varied, both across countries and over time. But they do not support
the view that household income distribution in the Philippines was more
unequal than in other parts of Southeast Asia in the years from 1965 to 1990.[4]

Table 6.6:   **Gini coefficient of household income distribution, 1965-1982:**
               Philippines, Malaysia, Thailand and Indonesia

Year	Philippines	Malaysia	Thailand	Indonesia
1965	0.50			
1969			0.43	
1970		0.51		
1971	0.49			
1975			0.43	
1976		0.53		0.49
1978				0.50
1981			0.43	
1982				0.45
1985	0.45			
1986			0.48	
1990		0.45	0.52	
1991	0.48			

Note: Estimates for Indonesia, the Philippines and Malaysia 1970 refer to household income.
Estimates for Thailand refer to household per capita income.
Sources: Indonesia: Asra (2000: Table 6); Philippines: Estudillo (1997 Table 1); Thailand: Warr (2009:
67). Malaysia: Ragayah (2012: Table 11.5).

In contrast to the Philippines, where there was some optimism about growth
prospects, at least until the mid-1970s, the three countries which emerged
from the French possession of Indochina had a far more difficult post-
independence experience. In Vietnam, the struggle against the French ended
in 1954, but the subsequent division of the country was not accepted by many
who had participated in the battle against the French. The prolonged and
destructive war in Vietnam, which spread to both Cambodia and Laos, was
finally brought to an end with the reunification of Vietnam in 1975 under the
Vietnamese Communist Party, and the emergence of communist regimes in
both Laos and Cambodia. In Cambodia, the Pol Pot government embarked
on a brutal policy of 'de-urbanization' which destroyed the educated middle

---

4   The estimates of the Gini coefficient based on household expenditures given by Asra (2000:
Table 4) for Indonesia and Balisacan (2000: Table 2) for the Philippines show that inequalities
were higher in the Philippines in the years from 1985 to 1994.

class; most of those who were not killed fled the country. Even after Pol Pot was deposed in 1978, the Cambodian economy was slow to improve. Per capita GDP in 1990 was little different from a decade earlier.

For more than a decade after 1975, Vietnam, Laos and Cambodia had few diplomatic or commercial ties with other countries in Southeast Asia. Vietnam relied heavily for rehabilitation of its war-shattered economy on aid from the former Soviet Union and from Eastern European countries and Sweden. Economic growth, and growth in per capita consumption expenditures, were positive but slow in real terms, at least until the mid-1980s.[5] In the latter part of the 1980s, influenced in part by the Deng reforms in China, the government embarked on a process of structural reform, aimed at reducing inflation and opening up the economy to trade and investment from other parts of Asia and Europe. These reforms had some success, although in the early 1990s, Vietnam was still considered a low-income economy whose per capita GDP was well below the six member states of ASEAN. The collapse of the Soviet Union deprived the country of its major source of foreign assistance, and many Vietnamese who had worked in Eastern Europe were repatriated, depriving the country of an important source of foreign exchange. The birth rate had surged after reunification, and more young people were entering the labour force by the early 1990s. This, combined with the return of migrant workers and the reduction in the military, created serious problems of unemployment.

A report published by the World Bank in 1995 stated that there was 'little systematic knowledge about the prevalence and distribution of poverty on a national scale'. Using a calorie-based poverty line, and data from the living standards survey conducted in 1992/93, the report estimated that 51 per cent of the population was below the poverty line. There was considerable regional variation, with the highest incidence of poverty in the north-central region, and the lowest in the southeast (World Bank 1995: 10-11). Subsequent revisions produced a somewhat higher estimate of poverty incidence in 1993, of 58 per cent. Almost 25 per cent of the population was estimated to be below the extreme poverty line which meant they were not able to afford sufficient food. Almost 64 per cent were below the World Bank's international poverty line of $1.25, in 2005 PPP prices (Demombynes and Vu 2015: Table 2). A further survey carried out in 1997/98 found a sharp fall in the headcount measure, from 58.1 per cent of the population to 37.4 per

5   Dollar (2004: 33) quotes World Bank estimates of growth over the 1970s and 1980s. In per capita terms, growth accelerated from 3 per cent per annum in the 1970s to 3.5 per cent per annum over the 1980s.

cent.[6] In spite of quite high population growth over this period, numbers below the poverty line fell from 40.46 million in 1993 to 28.22 million in 1998.

The HDI in 1995 showed that Vietnam remained well behind other parts of ASEAN, including the Philippines (Table 6.2). This reflected not just lower per capita GDP in Vietnam compared with the Philippines, Indonesia, Thailand and Malaysia but also problems in the delivery of both health and education. Haughton and Haughton (1997: 542), using the 1992/93 Living Standards Survey, found that 22 per cent of children under 13 were severely stunted, which was similar to the results of a survey in the Philippines in 1978. Prescott (1997: 2-5) argued that school enrolments actually fell after 1987, especially at the secondary and post-secondary levels. He attributed this fall to the rising costs of education, in terms of both fees and other costs, including uniforms and books, and also to the rising opportunity costs to the family of keeping a young person in school beyond the primary level. With accelerated growth, and a return to household responsibility, came greater opportunities for households to develop businesses in both agriculture and other activities, and this encouraged many parents to withdraw children from school after the completion of the primary cycle. But this trend seems to have been reversed by the early 1990s. Glewwe (2004a: 269) found that net enrolment rates at the secondary level had returned to the 1985 levels by 1993/94, and grew after that.

Improving secondary enrolments after the early 1990s reflected a growing awareness among parents in Vietnam that education was the key to obtaining well-remunerated jobs, especially in urban areas. Glewwe, Gragnolati and Zaman (2002: 790) found that Vietnam's gains in terms of poverty reduction between 1992/93 and 1997/98 were striking, in spite of a small increase in inequality. But the gains were not evenly shared among all regions and classes. The growth in export-oriented activities benefited those who were best able to take advantage of the new employment opportunities. They were usually the better educated living in urban areas, although improvements in agricultural productivity helped to boost incomes in rural areas. Poverty among ethnic minorities remained very high. These problems were to persist into the new century.

Social surveys were also carried out in both Cambodia and Laos in the early 1990s. The first Socio-economic Survey of Cambodia (SESC)

6   Dollar (2004: 39-40) claims that the rate of poverty reduction in Vietnam between 1992 and 1998 was higher than in India but lower than in China. Haughton and Khandker (2009: 13) claimed that the 1997/98 survey oversampled the sparsely populated central highlands and undersampled the dense and populous Red River delta. They do not speculate on what impact this had on poverty estimates.

was implemented in 1993/94. An analysis by Prescott and Pradhan (1997) found that 39 per cent of the population were below a poverty line set in terms of food and non-food expenditures.[7] The regional disparities were quite marked; the headcount measure was only 11 per cent in Phnom Penh, compared with 43 per cent in rural areas. These authors argued that 'reliable comparisons between Cambodia and other countries cannot be made at the national level because a large part of the country was excluded from the SESC sample frame' (Prescott and Pradhan 1997: xi). They did however suggest that the results were broadly in line with those from Vietnam and Laos. Another examination of the Cambodian data from the 1990s argued that 'no robust poverty trends for the 1990s can be calculated from these irreconcilable data' (Gibson 2005: 137). A further study of the surveys carried out in 1997 and 1999 found little evidence of any improvement in the poverty measures, although the authors pointed out that there were very wide differences in the results between the two rounds in the 1999 survey, which cast doubt on the accuracy of the data (Beresford et al. 2004: Table 1.1).

Beresford et al. (2004) also drew attention to Cambodia's low HDI compared with other countries in Southeast Asia (Table 6.2). They argued that there had been some improvement in infant and child mortality rates after 1978, when the Pol Pot regime was driven out of most parts of the country, but little change in more recent years. Laos also began to implement living standards surveys in the 1990s. An analysis prepared for the Swedish International Development Agency found some decline in the headcount measure of poverty between 1992/93 and 1997/98, from 46 per cent to 39 per cent, although doubts were raised about sample coverage (Andersson, Engvall and Kokko 2006: Table 2). By 1997/98 a gap had opened up between the capital, Vientiane, where the headcount measure was only 13.5 per cent, and most other regions of the country. In spite of some progress in health and education, the HDI was almost as low as in Cambodia in 1995, and considerably lower than in other parts of Southeast Asia (Table 6.2).

Little can be said about trends in living standards in Burma, or Myanmar as it was called, over the 1970s and 1980s. By the 1990s, many observers considered the country to be a development disaster, whose economic performance had little in common with most other parts of Southeast Asia. In the previous chapter, it was argued that some indicators pointed to rising living standards in the two decades after independence in 1948.

7   A report published by the Asian Development Bank in 2012 found that 47 per cent of the population in 1994 was below the poverty line, which was presumably higher than the one used by Prescott and Pradhan. See Asian Development Bank (2012: 4).

But for most of the time Ne Win was in power there was little enthusiasm for comprehensive economic reform, and trade and investment policies did not encourage greater links with the regional or the global economy. Over the 1980s, growth in real GDP was erratic, and growth in per capita consumption expenditures was negative (Booth 1997a: Table 3.1). There were hopes that economic policies would change after the coup which ousted Ne Win in 1988 and which led to the establishment of a new military regime apparently more committed to economic reform. Real per capita GDP did increase over the 1990s, but there was little evidence that this led to a marked improvement in living standards. A report prepared by the UNDP argued that four factors constrained human development in the country: low revenue mobilization, high defence expenditures, weak public administration and an uncertain policy environment (UNDP 1998: 32). The report pointed out that budgetary expenditures on defence were almost twice as high as those on health and education; the latter comprised less than 2 per cent of GDP, which was lower than in most other Asian countries.

In 1997, a household income and expenditure survey was carried out which claimed to be comprehensive. An analysis of the survey by the World Bank was contained in a report that was never made public, although it received some circulation in non-government circles. The report estimated that 23 per cent of the population fell below a poverty line set in terms of a packet of basic needs. There was wide variation by region; as would be expected, poverty was higher in rural areas than in urban areas. A headcount ratio of 23 per cent might appear quite low, at least compared with figures from Laos, Cambodia and Vietnam, and even the Philippines from the latter part of the 1990s. But the poverty line was probably not comparable with those used in other parts of Asia, and it is likely that some more remote regions in Myanmar were excluded altogether. On the other hand, the policy of keeping rice prices low did reduce the costs of calories in Myanmar compared with neighbouring countries (Booth 2003: 164).

An Emerging Consensus in the Mid-1990s?

By the mid-1990s, it seemed that a consensus was emerging in Southeast Asia that rapid economic growth was leading to a broad-based improvement in living standards and a fall in poverty. This was the message which the World Bank (1993) put forward; even allowing for the problems with their poverty estimates, it was widely accepted that poverty had fallen in Malaysia, Thailand and Indonesia in the decades from 1965 to 1996.

Balisacan (2000: 137-138) argued that the Philippine evidence from 1985 to 1994 confirmed the 'usual story about growth and poverty reduction in East Asia. [...] [T]he main reason for the relatively high poverty in the Philippines is primarily the short duration of growth and the slowness of this growth.' These views influenced the international debate at the time, but even before the tumultuous events of 1997/98 it was clear that there was some dispute about the policy mix which had produced the poverty decline. The experience of several countries in Southeast Asia in the 1980s and 1990s revealed anomalies which did not always fit with the received wisdom. In particular, it was clear that there were important differences between Taiwan and the Republic of Korea on the one hand and the Southeast Asian countries on the other (Booth 1999). While there were some similarities between the 'northeast Asian' model and the high-growth Southeast Asian economies, including the high levels of investment, and government policies which encouraged export growth, there were also a number of differences. Partly because of their natural resource wealth, governments in Southeast Asia were less inclined to invest in post-primary education, with the result that most countries in the region had fallen well behind Taiwan and South Korea in terms of educational enrolments by the 1980s. The lack of educated workers with the skills needed in rapidly growing economies, combined with restrictions on recruitment from abroad, meant that skilled workers often earned large salaries. This contributed to the greater disparity in incomes of the top decile compared to the bottom two deciles in Thailand, Malaysia, Singapore and the Philippines compared with Taiwan in the 1970s (Booth 1999: Table 8).

It was clear by the early 1990s, that the problems of poverty and skewed distribution of income in the fast-growing four were rather more serious than both the World Bank and some academic observers appeared to think, especially in Indonesia. When comparable poverty lines were used, the Indonesian headcount measure was well above that in Thailand, and not much below the Philippines in the 1980s. Estimates of inequality using household income showed that there was little difference between Indonesia and the Philippines over the 1980s (Table 6.6). A further problem was the regional disparities; in Indonesia the relatively rich provinces in Sumatra and Kalimantan where per capita GDP was closer to the Malaysian level had much higher levels of poverty than in Malaysia. By the 1990s, many Indonesians were crossing to Malaysia to work in sectors such as agriculture and construction, attracted by the higher wages. Inevitably they began to question why regions with broadly similar resource endowments differed so much in the living standards of their populations.

In Chapter 5 it was noted that, in the Philippines, a number of studies emphasized the problem of landlessness in rural areas. It was argued that, by the 1960s, many rural households had little or no access to land, and were forced to rely on wage labour for most of their income. This was also the case in parts of Indonesia. Ranis and Stewart (1993) in their comparison of employment growth in Taiwan and the Philippines pointed out that after the comprehensive land reform implemented in Taiwan in the early 1950s, growth of rural incomes appears to have been both rapid and remarkably egalitarian. They argued that the difference between Taiwan and the Philippines did not lie in the growth of agricultural incomes which were quite similar in the two countries in the 1960s and 1970s. Rather, it lay in the very different growth rates of rural non-farm income (RNFI). In the Philippines between 1965 and 1985 RNFI grew slightly less rapidly than farm incomes while in Taiwan between 1962 and 1980, it grew more than three times as fast (Ranis and Stewart 1993: Table 14). They found that an important reason for the rapid growth of RNFI in Taiwan was the fast growth of exports of processed non-traditional crops; part of this production took place in rural areas.

Many of the reasons for the rapid growth of Taiwan's non-traditional exports lay with reforms in trade and exchange rate policy which have been extensively discussed in the literature. Vested interests made such changes much more difficult to implement in the Philippines. In addition, the more skewed distribution of land in the Philippines meant that in 1971 much more land was in larger holdings compared with Taiwan, where there was greater use of labour-displacing machinery (Ranis and Stewart 1993: Table 10). In 1980, more labour per hectare was employed in rice agriculture in Taiwan than in the Philippines, while at the same time rural workers in Taiwan had greater access to off-farm employment. The result was much faster growth of rural incomes in Taiwan which led to rapidly expanding demand for a range of goods and services produced in both urban and rural areas.

To what extent did the Ranis and Stewart arguments hold in other parts of Southeast Asia? In Indonesia, the agricultural census of 1983 found that a higher proportion of land was in holdings under one hectare than in the Philippines, and a smaller proportion was in holdings over ten hectares (Booth 2002b: Table 2). By 1993, the proportion of land in holdings under one hectare had risen further, although it was still lower than in Taiwan in 1975 (Table 6.7). The linkage ratio between growth in farm and off-farm incomes between 1984 and 1993 was higher than in the Philippines especially in Java and Bali, but still lower than the high ratios achieved in Taiwan (Booth 2002b: Table 4). In Thailand, the proportion of agricultural land in holdings under five hectares was lower than in Indonesia in 1993, and much lower than in Taiwan in 1975 (Table 6.7). The linkage ratio in Thailand over the 1970s was lower than in Taiwan in the previous decade, although slightly higher than in Indonesia over the 1980s. Although they performed rather better than the Philippines, neither Indonesia nor Thailand was as successful as Taiwan in generating rapid growth of rural non-farm incomes in the years from the 1970s to the 1990s.

Table 6.7:   Distribution of land by holding size in hectares: Taiwan (1975), Indonesia (1993), Thailand (1993) and the Philippines (1980)

Holding Size (ha)	Taiwan 1975	Indonesia 1993	Thailand 1993	Philippines 1980
Under 1.0	39.0	26.4	3.0	3.8
1-3	48.0	38.7	22.8	25.9
3-5	9.2	13.1	17.9	21.2
5-10*	3.8	7.5	32.0	23.1
Over 10	n/a	14.3	24.2	26.0
Total	100	100.0	100.0	100.0

* Data for Taiwan include land in all holdings over five hectares.
Sources: Booth (2002: Table 2), with additional data for Indonesia from Central Bureau of Statistics (1995: 43-44).

But even if the faster-growing economies of Southeast Asia were not following the Taiwan model of egalitarian development, many observers of Asian development in the 1990s argued that poverty decline had been substantial in Thailand, Malaysia and Indonesia. Even if fast economic growth had produced greater inequalities, the reduction in poverty was still significant. Part of the poverty decline was the result of progress within the agricultural sector, but part was also due to the relocation of labour from agricultural to non-agricultural occupations. It was expected that export-oriented growth would continue in the countries which had already achieved sustained growth in the decades from the 1970s to the 1990s, and this model would spread to Vietnam, Laos, Cambodia and Myanmar, if the governments in these countries were willing and able to implement the necessary policy reforms. What many observers, both in Southeast Asia and abroad, did not fully appreciate was that growth had been achieved in spite of serious shortcomings in economic institutions. The growth collapses which occurred in 1997/98 were not just the result of vulnerabilities in the financial sectors of several economies in the region, but also of deficiencies in governance.

Growth Collapses in 1997/98

To many people, both in Asia and elsewhere, the crisis which struck in mid-1997 appeared like a bolt from the blue, a meteor crashing from outer space into what many development experts had considered to be the most dynamic and successful part of the world economy. As the crisis deepened, it became clear that its economic and political consequences would be serious, especially for the three worst affected economies in Southeast Asia, Thailand, Indonesia and Malaysia. Not only were their currencies depreciating rapidly but real GDP was also contracting. Other countries in Southeast Asia experienced some collateral damage; the Philippine peso experienced a substantial fall, but there was only a slight fall in real GDP. In Vietnam, the official figures showed that real GDP continued to grow, and by 2000 was 40 per cent higher than in 1995 (Table 6.8).

Table 6.8:   Index of GDP growth, 1995-2005

	Malaysia	Indonesia	Thailand	Philippines	Vietnam
1995	100.0	100.0	100.0	100.0	100.0
1996	110.0	107.8	105.9	105.8	109.3
1997	118.1	112.9	104.4	111.3	118.3
1998	109.4	98.1	93.5	110.7	125.1
1999	116.1	98.9	97.6	114.5	131.0
2000	125.8	103.7	102.3	119.0	139.9
2001	126.8	107.3	104.5	123.0	149.6
2002	132.3	112.0	110.0	129.8	160.2
2003	139.5	117.3	117.9	136.3	171.9
2004	149.6	123.2	125.3	143.0	185.1
2005	157.3	130.2	130.9	149.9	200.9

Sources: International Monetary Fund, *International Financial Statistics*, various issues, with extra data from Bank Negara Malaysia (2006) and Bank of Thailand website (www.bot.or.th) accessed 20 December 2010).

In Thailand, real GDP had already fallen in 1997, and the further decline in 1998 meant that real GDP in that year was around 12 per cent less than in 1996. In 1996, GDP growth, although positive, was slower than in the decade from 1985 to 1995, prompting some comments in the international media that the era of high growth in Thailand was probably over. It was argued that, although the growth of export-oriented manufacturing had been impressive, the government had made a serious error in the early 1990s in removing most controls on capital inflows, while at the same time maintaining the peg against the dollar. The resulting inflow of capital led to a real estate boom, faster inflation than Thailand's trading partners, and a real appreciation of the baht.[8] Wage rates, although low in comparison to the OECD economies, were higher than in China and Vietnam, and, in the absence of any compensating fall in the value of the currency, export industries were moving off-shore to take advantage of lower production costs. Export growth slowed to almost zero in 1996.

But in spite of the problems in Thailand, and the accelerating capital outflow which in early July 1997 finally forced the Bank of Thailand to float the baht, many observers both in the Asian region and elsewhere thought that it was unlikely that there would be serious contagion to other countries, where economic fundamentals were considered to be sound. There is now a considerable literature on why the contagion spread from Thailand to other parts of Southeast Asia, with commentators blaming the decline in the influence of technocrats in economic decision-making, as well as premature financial liberalization in the context of weak regulation of the financial sector. Other, mainly foreign, commentators argued that fundamentals in these economies were indeed sound and that the real problem lay with foreign speculation and the response of the International Monetary Fund. Still others blamed the growth in cronyism and corruption, which affected public confidence in the ability of governments across the region to deal with the crisis once it had erupted (Booth 2001a). These debates have continued down to the present, and may never be fully resolved. But it was clear by 1999 that, in two economies in particular, output appeared to have been very seriously affected by the crisis. They were Indonesia and Thailand, where GDP in 2000 was still below 1996 levels. In Indonesia, per capita GDP only returned to pre-crisis levels in 2004. In Malaysia, GDP fell by over 7 per cent in 1998, but had recovered by 2000. Elsewhere the impact of the crisis on output growth appeared to have been less serious (Table 6.8).

The Impact of the Crisis on Poverty: Thailand, Indonesia and Malaysia

Given the magnitude of the GDP decline, especially in Thailand and Indonesia, coming after decades of solid growth, it was hardly surprising

8   Although commentators in Europe and North America were openly discussing the weaknesses in the Thai economy at least a year before July 1997, the Thai government appeared to be in denial, and discouraged any open debate about the economic situation.

that there was widespread concern about the impact on poverty. Many observers, both inside and outside the region, predicted an increase in the headcount measure of poverty. Such an increase did indeed happen. In Thailand, Krongkaew and Kakwani (2003: Table 5) estimated that the headcount measure of poverty rose from 11.4 per cent in 1996 to 16.2 per cent in 2000. Sarntisart (2005: Table 4.4), using a lower poverty line, found that the headcount measure increased from 6.35 per cent to 8.45 per cent between 1996 and 2000. His estimates were valuable in that they broke down the headcount measures by region, and by farm and non-farm employment He found little change in the headcount measure in Bangkok (which was already very low by 1996), but a sharp increase in the northeast region, which historically had always been the poorest part of the country, although there had been a decline in the headcount measure of poverty between 1986 and 1996. Breaking down the headcount measure by farm and non-farm employment, he found that the largest increase was among farmers not owning land. For the country as a whole, numbers in poverty increased from 3.8 million in 1996 to 5.3 million in 2000 (Table 6.9).

Table 6.9:   Headcount measures of poverty in Thailand, 1990, 1996 and 2000

Region	1990	1996	2000
Bangkok	2.0	0.1	0.1
Bangkok Vicinity	2.7	1.0	0.5
Central Thailand	13.9	3.1	2.7
North Thailand	17.8	5.8	8.4
Northeast Thailand	30.9	10.4	15.1
South Thailand	20.0	6.9	7.7
Thailand*	20.1 (11.4)	6.4 (3.8)	8.5 (5.3)
Non-farm	9.9	2.8	3.6
Owners	29.3	12.1	16.0
Non-owners	33.1	13.6	20.2

* Figures in brackets show population in millions.
Source: Sarntisart (2005: Tables 4.4 and 4.8).

The series given by Warr (2009: Table 9), which was based on estimates from the National Economic and Social Development Board, found that there was an increase in the headcount measure from 11.4 per cent in 1996 to almost 16 per cent in 1999, although the headcount measure fell after 1999 and by 2002 it was lower than in 1996. The estimates of Sarntisart showed that the impact of the crisis on poverty was more severe in rural than urban areas and was most severe in the northeast and among farmers not owning land.

This contradicted the view of some commentators that the crisis was largely urban, and that the brunt of the income decline was borne by the urban middle classes. Boonyamanond and Punpuing (2012: 351) argued that an important reason for the more severe impact on rural areas was the return of migrant workers from the cities whom the rural sector had to absorb. The households to which the migrant workers returned had extra mouths to feed, while at the same time they were deprived of their remittances. Bresciani et al. (2002: 12) found that farm households which depended most on off-farm income experienced the biggest decline in income, because much of the off-farm work was tied to those sectors most affected by the crisis, especially construction.

In Indonesia, given the extent of the GDP decline in 1998, a lively and at times acrimonious debate emerged about the consequences for poverty. A full round of the National Socio-economic Survey was carried out in 1996 and another was planned for 1999. In the absence of solid statistical evidence on the impact of the crisis, several different estimates were circulated in the latter part of 1998 (Booth 2003: 122-123). The World Bank took the view that the decline in GDP of around 12 per cent (in fact it was slightly higher than this) could push the headcount measure of poverty up to around 14 per cent compared with an estimated 10.1 per cent in 1997. Their argument was that the decline in GDP affected investment expenditures more than household consumption expenditures, although it was acknowledged that the *El Niño* drought would also have a serious impact on rural incomes in some parts of Eastern Indonesia. A much more pessimistic set of estimates was prepared by the Central Bureau of Statistics (CBS) and published in the appendix to the state speech of President Habibie in August 1998. These estimates showed that by mid-1998 the headcount measure of poverty had increased to almost 40 per cent compared with 11.3 per cent in 1996. Numbers below the poverty line increased from 22.5 million to 79.4 million (Department of Information 1998: Table IV-1).

These estimates, and some even more alarming ones contained in an ILO/UNDP report, received wide circulation, but were not subject to much critical scrutiny at the time. They were based on an assumption that poorer groups in both urban and rural areas would experience a sharper decline in incomes and expenditures than the fall in real GDP. Certainly it was true that inflation was high through 1998 and into early 1999, and real wages declined sharply. But at the same time it was also argued that many of those who had lost their jobs in sectors such as construction had returned to their homes and managed to get some employment in the agricultural sector, or elsewhere. As a result, open unemployment figures increased only slightly

between 1997 and 2000. But on the other hand, further analysis of the 1999
Susenas, when the results became available, showed a substantial increase
in the headcount measure of poverty. The figures published by the CBS
showed an increase in the headcount measure between 1996 and 1999 from
17.5 per cent to 23.4 per cent. An alternative set of estimates prepared by the
Social Monitoring and Economic Response Unit (SMERU) using the same
data found an even greater increase in the headcount measure, from 15.7
per cent to 27.1 per cent (Table 6.10). The methodology adopted by the CBS
used a higher poverty line in urban areas relative to rural areas than did the
SMERU estimates, so that their results found that around 44 per cent of the
increase in numbers in poverty occurred in urban areas, compared with 32
per cent in the SMERU estimates. These differences in the measurement of
urban and rural poverty persisted after 2000.

Table 6.10:   **Headcount measures of poverty and numbers below the poverty line
in Indonesia: Central Board of Statistics and SMERU estimates, 1996
and 1999**

	1996		1999	
	CBS	**SMERU**	**CBS**	**SMERU**
Percentage below the Poverty Line				
Urban	13.4	7.2	19.4	16.3
Rural	19.8	20.5	26.0	34.1
Total	17.5	15.7	23.4	27.1
Numbers in Poverty (Millions)				
Urban	9.4	5.1	15.6	13.2
Rural	24.6	25.3	32.7	42.4
Total	34.0	30.5	48.0	55.6

Sources: Central Board of Statistics (2009: 181), Pradhan et al. (2000: Tables 2 and 4).

A further set of estimates were prepared by Ravallion and Lokshin (2007:
37). They used a price index based on consumption patterns of those at the
poverty line to adjust the poverty line from 1996 onwards. This index gave
greater weight to food prices which had increased more rapidly than the
general price index. According to their estimates, the headcount measure
of poverty almost trebled between 1996 and 1998, from 12.1 per cent to 36.5
per cent which was only slightly lower than the figure in the appendix to
the president's speech. But they also found that the headcount measure
fell sharply after 1998, and by 2001 was lower than in 1996, whereas the
CBS estimates found a slower decline. Ravallion and Lokshin (2007: 53-54)

concluded that the diverse impact of the crisis across the country was partly explained by initial conditions; poorer and more remote regions were less affected than those which were well integrated into the national economy. The integrated regions were richer in the pre-crisis years, but more vulnerable to the fall in national output. Bresciani et al. (2002) found that urban-rural linkages were weaker in Indonesia than in Thailand, and the impact of the contraction in the rural economy less severe. Farmers growing export crops benefited from the rapid depreciation of the rupiah.

Malaysia was the third country to experience a significant drop in income in 1998, but the fall in real GDP was less marked, and the impact on poverty was less dramatic than in Thailand and Indonesia, at least according to the estimates given by Ragayah, which were based on official data (2012: Table 11.1). The headcount measure of poverty rose from 6.1 per cent to 7.5 per cent between 1997 and 1999; numbers in poverty increased from 274,200 to 360,100. Around 57 per cent of the increase in the poor occurred in rural areas, and 43 per cent in urban areas.[9] Ragayah (2012: 237) claimed that poverty remained stable in rural areas, and increased in urban areas, but this claim did not appear to be supported by her figures. Poverty increased in both Penang and the Federal Territory of Kuala Lumpur, albeit from very low levels in 1997, but there were also increases in states such as Kedah, Perak and Sabah, which were more rural. While it might have been true that government policies protected the rural population in some states, this was not the case everywhere in the country.

The Impact of the Crisis on Poverty: The Philippines, Vietnam, Laos and Cambodia

Other countries in Southeast Asia did not experience declines in gross domestic product between 1996 and 1998 of the same magnitude as Thailand, Indonesia and Malaysia. In the Philippines, there was a slight decline in GDP in 1998, but a recovery in the following year. Between 1995 and 2000, total GDP increased by 19 per cent (Table 6.8), although in per capita terms there was little change. But according to the estimates compiled by Balisacan, the headcount measure of poverty increased between 1997 and 2000. Numbers in poverty, which fell between 1994 and 1997, rose again between 1997 and

---

9   The estimates given by Ragayah (2012) in Tables 11.1 and 11.2 show that the headcount measure of poverty was 7.5 per cent in 1999; in Tables 11.3 and 11.4 a figure of 8.5 per cent is given. No explanation is offered for the disparity.

2000 (Table 6.5). The increase was partly due to the impact of the severe *El Niño* weather effect in 1998. In addition, after a jump between 1994 and 1996, employment fell between 1996 and 1998 (Herrin and Pernia 2003: Figure 9.6). For many people who were just above the poverty line in 1997, even a small fall in income was enough to push them back into poverty.

Vietnam, Laos and Cambodia all began to carry out household surveys in the 1990s; it was pointed out above that problems were raised about the coverage of the surveys, especially in Cambodia. Given that all three countries were not severely affected by the 1997/98 crisis, there was little reason to expect that poverty levels would increase. In fact, the available data show that headcount measures fell steadily in the decade from the early 1990s to the early 2000s. In Vietnam, which achieved a faster growth of GDP in the decade from 1995 to 2005 than any other country in the region, the headcount measure fell between 1993 and 2002 according to various measures (Table 6.11). The series compiled by the General Statistics Office and the World Bank showed a fall in the headcount measure of poverty from 58 per cent in 1993 to 29 per cent over these nine years. Such a rapid decline was probably due to the fact that many were close to the poverty line in the early 1990s, so the increases in household income which occurred after 1993 were sufficient to push many millions of Vietnamese above it. But it should be noted that the fall in numbers under the $2-a-day poverty line was much less spectacular.

Table 6.11:   Headcount measures of poverty in Vietnam: Results from different poverty lines

Year	Molisa	GSO/WB	$1.25	$2.00
1993	26.0	58.1	63.8	85.7
1998	16.0	37.4	49.4	78.1
2002	11.4	28.9	40.1	68.7
2004	6.8	19.5	31.4	60.4
2008	12.1	14.5	16.8	43.3
2010	14.2	20.7	3.9	16.8
2012	9.6	17.2	2.4	12.5

Note: The Molisa poverty line was revised in 2001, 2005 and 2010, so the headcount estimates are not comparable over these years. In 2010 there were several survey and methodology revisions so the GSO data are not comparable with previous years.
Source: Demombynes and Vu (2015: Table 2).

The estimates of poverty given in Tables 6.9 and 6.10 are derived from the household income and expenditure surveys which had been carried out in Thailand and Indonesia since the 1960s. The figures in Table 6.5 use data from the Philippine surveys which began in the 1950s. Most analysts using these surveys, including those in the World Bank and the Asian Development Bank, appear to have accepted the results without too much scrutiny of their reliability. The data for Vietnam, Cambodia and Laos were derived from surveys initiated in the 1990s, which followed the World Bank Living Standards Measurement Survey (LSMS) template, which was introduced in the 1980s. Pyatt (2003: 345) argued that the primary concern of the LSMS 'was to provide information on who was benefiting from development and by how much. This put a premium on the consistency of survey results, and, therefore, on the consistency of survey design over time.' But in spite of these goals, doubts were raised about the accuracy of the LSMS. The problem of survey reliability will be addressed in greater detail in Chapter 7.

The Impact of the Crisis on Inequality

In the immediate aftermath of the 1997/98 crisis, some analysts argued that income inequality might be reduced, as the fall in incomes was more severe among relatively highly paid urban workers in sectors such as construction, banking, finance and other modern services. Incomes of rural workers were less affected, and some rural producers might have benefited from the increase in prices of export commodities such as rice, rubber, vegetable oils and spices. The evidence from household income and expenditure surveys across Southeast Asia from 1996 to 1999 offered some support for this argument. Gini coefficients were either stable or fell between 1996 and 1999 (Table 6.12). Only in the Philippines did expenditure inequalities show a slight rise.

But these estimates are derived from nominal data and ignore the possibility that real incomes of the poor in both urban and rural areas fell sharply as a result of the rapid rise in prices of basic needs, especially food. This argument was most relevant to the Indonesian case, where inflation accelerated rapidly as the crisis worsened, and the rise in the cost of basic needs led to falling real incomes for wage earners. In their analysis of a rural survey conducted in 100 villages in Indonesia in 1998, Skoufias, Suryahadi and Sumarto (2000) found that, once adjustments had been made for price increases, inequality did increase after the crisis erupted. Similar studies are not available for Thailand or Malaysia, although inflation was lower in these economies than in Indonesia in 1997 and 1998.

Table 6.12:   Gini coefficients in Southeast Asia, 1996, 1999, 2004 and 2011

Country	1996	1999	2004	2011
Singapore	0.47	0.48	0.49	0.53
Malaysia	0.47	0.44	0.46	0.44
Thailand (1)	0.52	0.52	0.53	0.48
Thailand (2)	0.43	0.43	0.43	0.37
Indonesia	0.35	0.31	0.32	0.41
Philippines	0.43	0.46	0.44	0.43
Vietnam	0.37	0.35	0.37	0.36
Laos	n/a	0.35	0.33	0.37

Note: Estimates for Malaysia refer to 1997, 1999, 2004 and 2009; for the Philippines 1997, 2000, 2003 and 2012; for Vietnam, 1996, 1998, 2004 and 2012; for Laos, 1997/98, 2002/3 and 2012/13. Countries are ranked according to estimates of expenditures per capita using 2011 PPP data, from World Bank (2014a: Table 6.2). Estimates are based on household expenditures, except for Singapore (earnings), Malaysia (income), Thailand (1) (income)
Sources: Singapore: Mukhopadhaya (2014: Table 3.1); Malaysia: Ragayah (2012: 240); Thailand (1), Warr (2009: Table 9); Indonesia: Asra (2014: 34); Laos: Warr, Rasphone and Menon (2015: Table 7). Other estimates from UNU-WIDER (2018).

What happened to the share of the highest income groups in total income after the crisis? There is some evidence from Indonesia that the income share of the top decile dropped slightly between 1996 and 1998, which is consistent with the argument that these households were more adversely affected by the crisis than other income groups. But the very rich households (the top 1 per cent of the distribution) appear to have increased their share of total income in the years after 1996. Leigh and Van der Eng (2009: Table 1) estimated that in 1996, the top 1 per cent received slightly less than 10 per cent of total income; that share increased steadily after the crisis and peaked at 15.5 per cent in 2001. If these estimates are correct, it appears that the incomes of the very rich were largely protected from the immediate impact of the decline in GDP in 1998, even if their net wealth might have declined.

7   Growth, Poverty and Distribution in the Early Twenty-first Century

The Impact of Accelerated Growth after 2004: The Evidence from National Poverty Lines

From the early 2000s onwards, the Southeast Asian countries put the events of the late 1990s behind them, and growth rates of GDP recovered, although there was some variation across countries. In the decade from 2005 to 2015 most experienced fairly robust growth in GDP, ranging from 3.3 per cent in Thailand to almost 7 per cent in Cambodia, and 7.8 per cent in Laos, although in this case the figures may well be overstated (Table 7.1). The global financial crisis (GFC) which erupted in the USA and Britain in the latter part of 2007 did affect growth in Southeast Asia, but the impact was not nearly as severe as the Asian crisis of a decade earlier. The impact was transmitted to Southeast Asia mainly through a fall in demand for manufactured exports in the developed world, and a decline in numbers of tourists. Malaysia and Thailand experienced a slight contraction in GDP in 2009, while there was almost zero growth in Cambodia. But in all three countries growth rebounded the following year, although Thailand experienced a further fall in output in 2011, mainly as a result of catastrophic floods. In most other countries in the region, including Indonesia, the Philippines, Vietnam, Laos and Myanmar, GDP continued to expand in 2009, although at a lower rate. Demand for commodities continued to be buoyant, especially from China.

Some commentators predicted that the GFC would affect poverty across Asia, but in fact the statistical evidence showed that the impact was small. Most countries in Southeast Asia were by the early 2000s publishing estimates of the headcount measure of poverty using 'official' poverty lines. There was a general tendency for the improved growth performance to lead to a decline in the headcount measure of poverty, although there were some critical voices. The Eleventh Malaysia Plan, scheduled to run from 2016 to 2020, claimed that poverty had declined from 3.8 per cent of the population in 2009 to only 0.6 per cent of the population by 2014. But no details were given about the poverty line used, and Malaysian officials were still reluctant to publish the household survey data on which the estimates were based. To some informed observers, the discussion of poverty was both perfunctory and non-transparent (Chander and Welsh 2015: 7). They pointed out that the problems of East Malaysia received very little

Table 7.1:   Growth in GDP, 2005-2015, and Gini coefficients

Country	Average annual GDP growth (%) 2005-2015	Gini coefficients*	
		c. 2005	c.2015
Singapore	5.7	0.42	0.39
Malaysia	4.9	0.46	0.40
Thailand	3.3	0.43	0.36
Indonesia	5.7	0.33	0.41
Philippines	5.4	0.43	0.40
Vietnam	6.1	0.35	0.34
Lao PDR	7.8	0.33	0.37
Cambodia	6.9	0.35	0.31

* Singapore: 2006 and 2014; Malaysia and Vietnam: 2004 and 2014; Thailand: 2004 and 2015; Indonesia: 2005 and 2015; Philippines: 2006 and 2015; Laos: 2002-2003 and 2012-2013; Cambodia: 2004 and 2012. The Ginis are comparable for each country over time, but not comparable across countries, as some are estimated from income data and some from expenditure data.
Note: GDP data refer to constant prices in local currencies from the websites of national statistical agencies.
Sources: Indonesia: Asra (2014: 34) and Central Board of Statistics (2015a: 27); Laos: Warr, Rasphone and Menon (2015: Table 7); Vietnam: Benjamin, Brandt and McCaig (2016: Table 1); Singapore: Department of Statistics (2015: Tables 4.6 and 4.7). Other countries: UNU-WIDER (2018).

discussion; indeed, the plan documents had very little to say about poverty alleviation strategies in either urban or rural areas. It remains to be seen whether the new coalition government which was elected in 2018 will address issues relating to poverty and inequality in more depth. In Indonesia, the headcount measure of poverty as measured by the Central Board of Statistics (CBS) had been trending downwards since 1999, but it increased from 16 per cent of the population in 2005 to 17.8 per cent in 2006. Numbers below the poverty line jumped from 35.1 million to 39.3 million. This increase preceded the global crisis, and was attributed in large part to the increase in domestic rice prices, which resulted from increased protection against foreign imports. Both the headcount measure of poverty and the numbers in poverty fell after 2006. By 2010 the headcount measure was 10.7 per cent and numbers in poverty 31 million, which was lower than the numbers of poor in 1996, in spite of the population growth which had occurred (Central Board of Statistics 2015b: 175).

In the Philippines, as in Indonesia, the global recession also hit at a time when the country was still affected by the increase in rice prices in 2007/8 (Balisacan et al. 2010: 8). But the impact on poverty was modest. Estimates prepared by the Philippine Statistics Authority showed that the headcount measure of poverty was almost constant between 2006 and 2009, although numbers below the poverty line increased because of population growth (Table 7.2). Using a different poverty line, Balisacan et al. (2010: Table 4) estimated that there was a continual decline in the headcount measure from 33 per cent in 2006 to 29.7 per cent in 2009. They also found a small decline in numbers of poor. They also gave a counter-factual estimate of what poverty might have been, had there not been a slowdown in growth of GDP in 2008/9. These authors claimed that numbers of poor people could have declined to 25.6 million in 2009. In other words the global crisis meant that over four million people in the Philippines stayed poor who might otherwise have moved above the poverty line.

Table 7.2: **Headcount measure of poverty and numbers below the poverty line: Philippines, 2006, 2009, 2012 and 2015**

Year	Percentage below poverty line	Numbers below poverty line (millions)
2006	26.6	23.1
2009	26.3	23.9
2012	25.2	24.0
2015	21.6	21.6

Sources: Philippine Statistics Authority (2016); population data from *Philippine Statistical Yearbook* (Manila: National Statistical Coordination Board and Philippine Statistics Authority), various issues.

In Thailand, where GDP did decline in 2009, and the dollar value of merchandise exports fell by 19 per cent, the net impact on real spending was small. Haughton and Khandker (2014: 90) concluded that the only demographic group to be affected were young adults, especially those residing in the Bangkok region. They were hurt by the decline in jobs in export-oriented manufacturing, and in tourism. In Vietnam, the headcount measure of poverty did increase between 2008 and 2010, but this was the result of changes in the way the poverty line was estimated. Even before the impact of the global crisis, a surge in inflation had led to a reduction in real wages. A World Bank report argued that, as GDP growth slowed in Vietnam in 2009, there was a negative impact on living standards but only of short duration. The group most affected were migrant workers; to the extent that their remittances to rural areas were reduced, there was also an adverse impact on those rural households which relied on remittances (Kozel 2014: 37).

In Cambodia, both government and World Bank estimates showed that there was a decline in the headcount measure of poverty between 2004 and 2011, with much of the decline taking place before 2009. The Cambodian government introduced a new poverty line in 2013 and revised the headcount measures from 2004 to 2012. Much of the fall at the national level took place between 2007 and 2009 (48 per cent to 23 per cent). In 2012 the national headcount measure had fallen further to 19 per cent, although there was an increase in the headcount measure in Phnom Penh between 2011 and 2012, which could have been a delayed reaction from the impact of the global crisis on exports (Asian Development Bank 2014b: 3-5). In Laos, Estudillo, Phimmavong and Quimba (2017: Table 4) estimated that the headcount measure of poverty fell from 35.5 per cent in 2002 to 14 per cent in 2012; again most of the fall took place in the years from 2002 to 2007. In the southern region of Laos, there was actually an increase in the headcount measure of poverty between 2007 and 2012. Estudillo, Phimmavong and Quimba (2017: 42) found that poverty was lowest in urban areas, especially the capital (Vientiane) and in those rural areas which had access to roads and electricity.

In the previous chapter, the problem of comparability of national poverty lines in the 1980s and 1990s was noted. It was clear from the 2011 estimates that the problem had not gone away in the early twenty-first century (Table 7.3). Although most countries claimed to be using the 'cost of basic needs' approach to setting both national and regional poverty lines, by the early twenty-first century it appeared that the different approaches used by different statistical agencies across Southeast Asia were producing poverty lines which varied considerably. There was a tendency for the countries with higher per capita GDP to have a higher poverty line, but this was not always the case. In 2011, Indonesia stood out as having a low poverty line in comparison with the Philippines and Cambodia, in spite of the fact that Indonesia's per capita GDP was higher.[1] National poverty lines also varied as a proportion of household consumption expenditures, although the variation was greater using the national accounts data than those from household surveys (Table 7.4). The reasons for this will be discussed further below.

Over the years, the national poverty lines estimated by statistical agencies in Southeast Asia have attracted criticism from various quarters, including academics and NGO activists. In Indonesia there were criticisms in the early 1990s that the poverty line estimated by the Central Bureau of Statistics (CBS) was not only low, and falling relative to per capita consumption expenditures,

---

1   Bhalla (2010: 137) regressed national poverty lines on per capita consumption from the national accounts data for a cross section of countries; there was a clear trend for countries with higher per capita consumption to have higher poverty lines. But several large countries in Asia, including China, India and Indonesia, were below the trend line; their national poverty lines were lower than would have been expected given their per capita consumption expenditures.

Table 7.3:   National poverty lines, 2011 (per person per month)

Country	$ (exchange rate)	$ (PPP)
Thailand	79	188
Indonesia*	27	57
Philippines	37	84
Vietnam**	25	68
Cambodia (2009)***	29	77

* The poverty line is the population-weighted average of the urban and rural poverty lines given in Central Board of Statistics (2012). The poverty line for the March quarter is used.
** The poverty line is the population-weighted average of the urban and rural poverty lines given in General Statistics Office (2013).
*** The poverty line of 3,871 riels per day is used, as reported in Asian Development Bank (2014b: 5).
Sources: Thailand: National Statistical Office (2015); Indonesia: Central Board of Statistics (2012): Philippines: Philippine Statistics Authority (2014); Vietnam: General Statistics Office (2013); Cambodia: Asian Development Bank (2014b). Exchange rate and PPP data from World Bank (2014a, 47).

Table 7.4:   National poverty lines as a percentage of household consumption expenditures from surveys and national accounts estimates

Country	Household surveys	National accounts
Cambodia (2009)*	45.7	61.2
Vietnam (2010)**	57.4	47.4
Vietnam (2010)**	37.8	31.3
Vietnam (2012)**	38.0	29.1
Philippines (2009)	47.4	25.6
Philippines (2012)	43.6	22.9
Indonesia (2010)	43.0	16.6
Thailand (2009)	45.1	32.2
Thailand (2011)	44.6	29.7

* Estimate made using the poverty line of 3,871 riels per person per day, as reported in Asian Development Bank (2014b: 5).
** Estimate made using revised poverty line of 653,000 dong per person per month for 2010, given in Kozel (2014: 5). The other estimate for 2010 and that for 2012 uses the lower poverty lines given in General Statistics Office (2013).
Sources: Thailand: National Statistical Office (2015); Cambodia: National Institute of Statistics (2014); Philippine Statistics Authority (2014); Vietnam: General Statistics Office (2013); Indonesia: Central Board of Statistics (2012).

especially in urban areas (Booth 2016: 177). In 1996 the CBS came up with a new set of poverty lines for both urban and rural areas. The justification for the increase was that, as per capita GDP increased, Indonesians were consuming a broader range of goods and services, including more education and healthcare. The new poverty lines for 1996 were 10 per cent higher than the old ones in urban areas and 14.4 per cent higher in rural areas (Central Board of Statistics 2009: 181). In Vietnam, the poverty lines used by both the Ministry of Labour, Invalids and Social Affairs (MOLISA) and the General Statistics Office were revised upwards in 2010 reflecting the decision to use a more comprehensive consumption welfare aggregate.[2] The new poverty lines were almost twice as high as the old ones in urban areas and exactly twice as high in rural areas (Demombynes and Vu 2015: 16). These changes meant that in both Indonesia and Vietnam it is not possible to compare the headcount measures of poverty over the long term: in Indonesia the break came in 1996 and in Vietnam in 2010.

In the Philippines, a debate emerged in the 1990s when academic economists at the University of the Philippines criticized the approach to poverty measurement used by the National Statistical Coordination Board (NSCB). One issue concerned the use of income rather than expenditure data from the Family Income and Expenditure Surveys. Professor A. Balisacan from the University of the Philippines argued that expenditure data should be used because it is a household's spending rather than its income which determines its welfare. In this he was following the recommendation of a number of international experts, in the World Bank and elsewhere.[3] Following their reasoning, he argued that it was likely that households would give more accurate information on expenditure rather than income (Balisacan 1997: 4-5). But statisticians from the NSCB argued that, faced with a lengthy and complicated questionnaire which took several hours to complete, many respondents were likely to have better recall about their income over a period of months than about their expenditures. They conceded that the diary approach might avoid at least some of the recall problems, but experience in the Philippines had shown that it had not worked well in 1979 (Virola, Ganac and Bacani 2000: 4). These problems with household survey data are examined further below.

If expenditure data are used to measure the proportion of the population below a given poverty line, the results will usually be lower than if income data are used, especially when households can draw down savings in hard times or when they receive assistance, in cash or kind, from outside the household. Balisacan (2003: Table 10.1) calculated that 32.1 per cent of the population were below his poverty line estimate in 1994 using the

2   See Kozel (2014: 68-74) for a discussion of the changes which were made in the estimation of the poverty line.
3   See Haughton and Khandker (2009: 183-184) and World Bank (2017: 38-44) for further discussion of the income versus expenditure debate.

expenditure data from the FIES. This was lower than the estimates using the official poverty line and household income data from the FIES. Other statistical agencies in Asia also use the income data from household surveys to measure both poverty and inequality. In Thailand and Malaysia, income data are used for the official estimates, although in the case of Thailand estimates of poverty using the household expenditure data collected in the household surveys have been published by UNU-WIDER (2018). This of course means that the headcount and other estimates of poverty in these two countries published in official documents are not directly comparable with those from Indonesia (where the estimates of the Central Board of Statistics use expenditure data from the household surveys).

By the 1990s, Myanmar was considered a development disaster by many in international development circles. Some estimates of poverty were contained in a World Bank report which had limited circulation in the late 1990s, but the survey data on which they were based were not publicly available. In the early years of the twenty-first century, the government of Myanmar published estimates of GDP growth which were considered very high, but verification of the figures was difficult, given the fact that Myanmar was subject to strict international sanctions, and was cut off from contact with most development agencies. After political liberalization and elections, most sanctions were removed and a process of economic reform began. But it was only in 2017 that the Ministry of Planning and Finance, together with the World Bank published an analysis of poverty in Myanmar based on household surveys carried out in 2004/5, 2009/10 and 2015. These surveys found a substantial decline in both the headcount measure of poverty and numbers below the poverty line, especially between 2009/10 and 2015 (Table 7.5).

Table 7.5: Headcount measures of poverty in Myanmar and numbers in poverty, 2004/5, 2009/10 and 2015

Year	Headcount measure of poverty			Numbers (millions)
	national*	urban	rural	
2004/5	48.2 (44.5)	32.2	53.9	23.3
2009/10	42.2 (37.5)	24.8	48.5	22.2
2015	32.1 (26.1)	14.5	38.8	16.8

* Estimates refer to the headcount measure using 2015 living conditions poverty line. Figures in brackets refer to the headcount measure of poverty, using the 2009/10 living conditions poverty line.

Source: Ministry of Planning and Finance and World Bank Group (2017: Part 01, p. 19; Part 02, p. 25).

Creating Internationally Comparable Poverty Estimates

Because national poverty lines often reflect not just the economic, but also the social and political concerns of national governments and are not comparable across countries, or even over time in the same country, efforts have been made in recent decades by international agencies to establish 'international poverty lines'. These are supposedly more comparable across national boundaries, and can also be used to monitor poverty trends at the regional and global level over time. The World Bank used the 'dollar a day' measure until the early years of the twenty-first century, when $1.25 and $2 lines were introduced.[4] These poverty lines were converted into national currencies using data on the purchasing power of the national currency, relative to the American dollar (PPP adjustments). In Chapter 4, the original work on the development of purchasing power adjusted GDP figures by economists at the University of Pennsylvania was discussed. The early work included data for only two Southeast Asian countries, the Philippines and Malaysia (Table 4.5). In both cases the estimate of per capita GDP after the PPP adjustments was considerably higher than using the official exchange rate. Over time the country coverage was greatly expanded, and the estimates were published by the Penn World Tables (PWT) project.

It has been argued that the PPP-corrected estimates published by the PWT had been developed as a means of comparing national accounts figures, and were not well suited to poverty comparions (Aten and Heston 2010: 155-156). In many countries, the price data were mainly collected in urban areas; it was often considered too expensive, and sometimes too dangerous, to collect information from remote rural locations (Ravallion 2015: 15-16). The World Bank began to generate its own PPP data in 1993; new estimates were published in 2005 and 2011. In 2005 the country coverage was expanded, and China was added for the first time, although the data for China were confined to eleven large cities and could not claim to be nationally representative. In 2011, further changes were made to the methodology which led to significant changes in the estimation of poverty in Asia and elsewhere; these changes will be discussed below.

The Asian Development Bank also became involved in the measurement of poverty in developing member countries, and took an approach which differed from that of the World Bank. An important study which endeavoured to estimate poverty using PPP data incorporating prices paid by the poor

---

4   A detailed discussion of the changes in the World Bank methodology up to 2005 is given by Ravallion, Chen and Sangraula (2009).

was published by the Asian Development Bank (ADB) in 2008 in its *Key Indicators for Asia and the Pacific*. Together with the national statistical agencies in sixteen developing member countries (China was not included), the ADB carried out a series of poverty surveys which estimated prices paid by the poor for 2005. For several countries in South and Southeast Asia, the headcount measures of poverty measured using the PPPs derived from the poverty surveys were lower than those derived from the unadjusted PPP data. This was true for India, Pakistan and Sri Lanka, as well as for Indonesia and Vietnam (Table 7.6). These findings were greeted with some surprise, as it was often assumed in the literature, based mainly on evidence from rich countries, that the poor pay more for basic needs that the better-off, who buy in bulk from large stores (World Bank 2017: 75-78).[5]

Table 7.6:   Headcount estimates of poverty, 2005 ($1.35 Per Person Per Day)

Country	Headcount Index		
	Consumption PPP	Poverty PPPs	
		ICP	PS
Thailand	0.1	0	0
Vietnam	25.6	24.2	16.0
Philippines	27.0	24.1	29.5
Indonesia	39.2	38.7	24.1
Cambodia	35.4	36.2	36.9
Lao PDR	48.8	52.5	53.6

Note: Poverty PPPs are estimated using the data on the consumption basket of the poor; poverty survey PPSs are estimated using prices paid by the poor, derived from the poverty survey.
Source: Asian Development Bank (2008: 32).

It is possible that the results for South Asia were influenced by the fact that many of the poor purchase basic staples in government 'fair price' stores. In Indonesia the post-1998 policy of supplying rice at subsidized prices was also likely to have helped the poor, although critics argued that the targeting was weak. Most analysts have acknowledged that this is a topic which needs more research, both in Asia and elsewhere, although there has been some

5   For a more detailed discussion of the importance of using prices paid by the poor, see Aten and Heston (2010: 158-160). They cite evidence that in India the poor tend to buy smaller quantities of food and other goods and often pay a higher price per kilo compared with those who buy in larger quantities. This point has often been made in the Southeast Asian context as well.

criticism of the ADB approach. Deaton and Dupriez (2011: 161) pointed out that it is difficult to control for quality differences; poor people tend to buy lower-quality rice and other foodgrains, which may not be reflected in the PPP data. It is also important to look at the prices the poor pay for services such as healthcare and education, as the cost of these services is now included in most official poverty lines. A study in Thailand found that the poorest quintile of the population in the urban area studied (a town in the centre of the country) were paying a much higher proportion of their income on health services than the richest quintiles. The authors argued that the generous health benefits enjoyed by civil servants explained this result (Pannarunothai and Mills 1997). It is likely that these findings also apply to other middle-income countries in Asia.

In 2014, the Asian Development Bank (ADB) suggested a poverty line of $1.51, again converted into local currencies using exchange rates adjusted for differences in the purchasing power of currencies. The higher poverty line compared with the World Bank one of $1.25 was justified on the grounds that developing member countries in Asia are on average rather better off than those in Africa, whose lower national poverty lines influence the World Bank line. The estimates of the headcount measure of poverty in 2010 were given in Table 1.2. As was noted in Chapter 1, these estimates raised a number of questions. Why, for example, was the headcount estimate for Indonesia higher than for Vietnam and Cambodia, in spite of the fact that per capita GDP in these two countries was much lower? Did these disparities reflect problems in the household survey data? I return to this question below, but first it is important to examine the most recent World Bank poverty estimates for Asia, based on the 2011 PPP data.

The new estimates of GDP and household expenditures based on the 2011 PPP estimates were published by the World Bank in 2014, and were greeted with some surprise, and a degree of skepticism. The data showed that there was a large increase in PPP-adjusted GDP figures for the non-OECD countries relative to the USA. China's total GDP was thus close to that of the USA, while India's GDP was larger than Japan. The ten ASEAN countries had a combined GDP which was around 38 per cent of that in China, and about the same as the combined GDP of Germany, the Netherlands, Switzerland, Norway and Sweden. Researchers were not slow to spell out the implications of these new estimates for world poverty. Dykstra, Kenny and Sandefur (2014) argued that, as a result of the new PPP data, the proportion of the population in the developing world below the poverty line of $1.25 fell from 19.7 per cent to 8.9 per cent, with a particularly large drop in South Asia, whose share of the global poor population dropped from 49 per cent

Table 7.7: **Headcount measures of poverty in Southeast Asia using World Bank and national poverty lines**

Country	$2.00*	$1.90**	$3.10**	national
Malaysia (2009)	2.3	0.3	2.7	3.8
Thailand (2012)	3.5	0.1	1.2	12.6
Indonesia (2013)	43.3	9.8	39.4	11.4
Philippines (2012)	41.7	13.1	37.6	25.2
China (2012)	18.6	6.5	19.1	n/a
India (2011)	59.2	21.2	58.0	n/a
Vietnam (2012)	12.5	3.2	13.9	17.2
Laos (2012)	62.0	16.7	46.9	23.2
Cambodia (2012)	41.3	2.2	21.6	20.5 (2011)

* Estimates using the $2 poverty line converted into local currencies using the 2005 PPP data. Estimates refer to 2009 for Malaysia, 2010 for Thailand, 2011 for Cambodia, Indonesia, India and China and 2012 for Laos and Vietnam.
** Estimates using the $1.90 and $3.10 poverty lines converted into local currencies using the 2011 PPP data.
Sources: $2 poverty line estimates from Asian Development Bank (2015: Table 1.9); estimates using $1.90 and $3.10 poverty lines from wdi.worldbank.org/table/1.2,(accessed 20/3/2016):
Malaysia: Ragayah (2012: Table 11.2); Thailand: National Statistical Office (2015: Table 8.12); Indonesia: Central Board of Statistics (2015b: Table 4.6.1); Philippines: Philippine Statistics Authority (2016); Cambodia: World Bank (2014b: Table 1); Laos: Warr, Rasphone and Menon (2015: Table 10); Vietnam: Demombynes and Vu (2015: Table 2).

to 29 per cent. The explanations for these results were complex; to some extent they were due to overestimation of poverty, especially in Asia, in 2005.[6] The literature on the implications of the new PPP estimates has grown rapidly, and will no doubt continue to grow when further PPP data become available.

The World Bank used the new PPP data to produce new estimates of both GDP and consumption per capita in PPP dollars (World Bank 2014a: Tables 6.1 and 6.2). New poverty lines were adopted of $1.90 and $3.10, adjusted for the new PPP data. The headcount measures of poverty for seven Southeast Asian countries, together with India and China, using the new PPP data are given in Table 7.7. The most striking difference with the earlier data using the $2-a-day line is that the new headcount measures were much lower. For example, using the $2-a-day measure, it was reported that around 42 per cent of the population in the Philippines was below the $2 line in 2012 (Table 7.7). Two years later, using the new $1.90 line and new PPP data, the percentage drops to 13.1 per cent. In Indonesia there was a drop from 43 per

6   A useful overview of the reasons for the changes can be found in Deaton and Aten (2017).

Table 7.8:   Actual individual consumption expenditures per capita: Southeast Asian Countries, China and India, 2011

Country	Expenditures per capita PPP $	Expenditures per capita Exchange rate $	Price level Index (World =100)
Singapore	24,725	21,960	110.7
Brunei	15,683	10,124	80.5
Malaysia	11,082	5,354	60.2
Thailand	8,477	3,343	49.2
Indonesia	4,805	2,044	53.0
Philippines	4,490	1,831	50.8
Vietnam	2,991	978	40.8
Laos	2,341	740	39.4
Cambodia	2,277	760	41.6
Myanmar	2,273	638	35.0
China	4,331	2,341	67.4
India	3,023	907	37.4

Note: Actual individual consumption includes all household consumption expenditures, as well as general government and NPISH (non-profit institutions serving households) expenditures on goods and services, such as health and education.
Source: World Bank (2014a: Table 6.2).

cent in 2011 to just under 10 per cent in 2013. Using national poverty lines, the Philippine Statistics Authority showed a far more modest decline in the headcount measure from 25.2 per cent in 2012 to 21.6 per cent in 2015 (Table 7.2). In Indonesia, the CBS headcount measure showed a decline from 12 per cent in 2012 to 11.2 per cent in 2015. Perhaps unsurprisingly, many statisticians and economists in Southeast Asia, confronted with the very large revisions in the World Bank figures, argued that the poverty estimates based on national poverty lines gave a more reliable guide to policy.

The new estimates based on the $1.90 poverty line and the 2011 PPP data gave headcount measures of poverty for several countries in Southeast Asia which were closer to the headcount measures derived from the national poverty lines than were the older estimates. But there were still quite large disparities in the Philippines, Vietnam and Thailand. There were also differences between the ranking of countries according to the per capita estimates of actual individual consumption expenditures using the 2011 PPP data (AICE), and the headcount measure of poverty using the $1.90 poverty line (Tables 7.7 and 7.8). Vietnam's estimates of per capita AICE was less than $3,000 in 2011, which was considerably lower than either the Philippines or Indonesia. But the headcount measure of poverty was lower in Vietnam. Did this reflect greater equality in expenditure distribution in Vietnam? Or does it suggest that the 2011 PPP figures have not captured important differences in the price of basic goods such as rice in Vietnam compared with Indonesia and the Philippines? In principle, differences in the price of basic needs such as rice and housing should be reflected in the PPP data but in practice this might not be the case. In addition, there may be problems in the sample coverage of the household surveys which lead to the exclusion of poorer households. These questions are addressed further in the next two sections.

Trends in Inequality, 2005 to 2015

The decade from 2005 to 2015 was one where most countries in Southeast Asia experienced growth in GDP of between 5 and 7 per cent per annum (Table 7.1). In most cases, this growth was accompanied by either a fall in income/expenditure inequality, as shown in the Gini coefficients, or only a slight increase. The important exception to this trend appears to have been Indonesia. But there are a number of caveats which must be attached to the estimates of the Gini coefficients given in Table 7.1. First, although in most cases they relate to inequalities in household expenditure per capita, as reported in household surveys, this is not the case for Singapore and Malaysia. In Singapore the estimate is derived from household income from employment, and is adjusted for the impact of taxes and transfer payments. In Malaysia, the data refer to household income, and is not fully comparable with the estimates from expenditure data. Second, even for those countries where the Gini is derived from household expenditure per capita, they may not be comparable because of different approaches to measuring expenditure in household surveys. Third, the survey data themselves may be flawed because certain groups of households are undercounted, or omitted altogether.

Even where inequality estimates are comparable both across countries and over time, they are often not accepted as useful indicators of changes in the distribution of income and wealth. While conceding that the household survey figures on income and expenditure in Thailand did show some fall in inequality between 1992 and 2013 (the Palma ratio fell from almost four to under three), Phongpaichit and Baker (2016: 12-13) identified three problems which had emerged since 2000. First, there appeared to be a '1 per cent' problem in Thailand in that the richest households had over time increased their share of both income and wealth by amassing not just financial assets but also property. Second, the least advantaged 5 per cent of the population, who were mainly rural and uneducated, were not able to increase either their physical assets or their human capital. Third, while spatial inequalities may have been reduced over time, disparities in education and skills increased. Phongpaichit and Baker quoted studies which showed that while the quantity of education has increased sharply in Thailand since the 1990s, there were still sharp differences in quality. PISA tests showed that students at the best schools in Bangkok performed as well as, or better than, those in most OECD countries. But those in rural areas, especially in the northeast, performed even worse than in parts of Africa.

Among the countries for which data are available, the largest increase in inequality in the decade from 2005 to 2015 was found in Indonesia. It is now widely believed, both in Indonesia and in international circles, that in spite of, or perhaps because of, the progress towards greater democracy since the fall of Suharto, inequalities in income and wealth have increased. It has not infrequently been claimed that Indonesia has become a very unequal society, both in comparison with the Suharto era, and with other parts of Asia. But there are several problems with this argument. The Indonesian Statistics Agency (CBS) has in recent years changed both the way the Gini coefficient has been calculated, and the sample frame for the household surveys (Susenas). Both these changes have consequences for the increases shown in Table 7.1. Asra (2014: 34-35) has shown that the CBS moved from using grouped data to individual household data, and this led to an increase in the Gini from 0.33 to 0.36 between 2006 and 2007.[7] Between 2010 and 2011 there was a further increase in the Gini, from 0.38 to 0.41, which was at least partly due to a change in sampling methodology (World Bank and Australian Aid 2016: 41). Given these problems, and also other problems with the Susenas surveys which will be discussed in the next section, the conclusion given in a report published in 2016 by the World Bank and Australian Aid that the Gini coefficient increased 'from 30 points in 2000 to 41 points in 2014' must be treated with considerable caution (World Bank and Australian Aid 2016: 7). Using the year 2000 as the base year is also misleading insofar as there had been a very sharp decline in GDP in 1998, and no recovery in 1999, which was accompanied by a fall in the Gini. A better comparison would be between 1996 and 2006; according to Asra (2014: 34), the Gini did fall over this decade but only from 0.35 to 0.33. There has probably been

7   Van Ginneken and Park (1984: 13-16) discussed the bias which the use of grouped data can introduce.

some increase in inequality in the decade from 2005 to 2015, but bearing in mind the changes in the estimation methodology, it is far from clear how large this increase was.[8]

In Myanmar, figures from the 2015 household survey were used to estimate several measures of inequality. The Gini coefficient of household expenditure was estimated at 0.32, which was lower than most other Asian countries. The proportion of total expenditure made by the top decile of the expenditure distribution was also quite low at 26 per cent, although the report noted that households in the top decile had seen a faster growth in their expenditures between 2009/10 and 2015 than other households (Ministry of Planning and Finance and World Bank Group 2017: 25). The share of expenditures made by the bottom 40 per cent of the expenditure distribution fell over this period. Inequality in expenditures in urban areas were considerably higher than in rural areas. Given that urbanization rates are still low in Myanmar compared with most other Asian countries, at only 30 per cent, and given that they are likely to increase rapidly in coming decades, it is probable that inequalities will also increase.

Recently some attention has been given to the estimates of the distribution of wealth in parts of Southeast Asia. Laovakul (2016: 37) estimated the Gini coefficient of asset distribution in Thailand, based on the data collected in the Socio-Economic Household Surveys of 2006, 2007 and 2008. For all assets he found that the Gini coefficient was 0.68 in 2006, falling to 0.66 in 2009. The Gini was higher for financial assets and for land and buildings used for business and agricultural purposes. Both Thailand and Indonesia were also ranked among the countries with highly skewed wealth holdings, as reported in the Credit Suisse *Global Wealth Databook* for 2017 (Table 7.9). In Thailand it was estimated that 56 per cent of the total wealth of the economy was owned by the richest 1 per cent of the population, which was about the same as Russia, and higher than China or India.[9] In Indonesia, the richest 1 per cent owned around 45 per cent of total wealth. The only other Southeast Asian country to be investigated was Singapore, where the top 1 per cent owned 34 per cent of the wealth, a higher proportion than in South Korea or Japan.

8   Yusuf and Warr (2018: 136) claimed that the post-crisis rise in measured inequality in Indonesia was one of the largest increases found in any country in recent times, second only to that in Russia following the collapse of the Soviet Union. That might be true if 2015 is compared with 2000, but not if 2015 is compared with 1996.

9   Credit Suisse (2018) estimated the Gini coefficient of the wealth distribution in Thailand to be 90.1, which was the highest for all the countries investigated.

Table 7.9:   Share of total wealth: Ten countries

Country	Share of total wealth		
	Richest 1 per cent (%)	Richest 10 per cent (%)	Poorest 10 per cent (%)
Thailand	56.2	78.7	0.1
Russia	56.0	77.4	0.2
China	47.0	71.9	0.2
Indonesia	45.4	74.8	-0.1
India	45.1	73.1	-0.9
Brazil	43.5	72.3	-0.7
South Africa	41.2	75.0	-1.1
Singapore	34.0	63.1	0
Taiwan	29.6	57.9	0.4
Japan	14.6	45.2	0.3

Source: Credit Suisse (2017: Table 6.5).

Flaws in the Household Survey Data

Previous chapters have discussed the results of the household income and expenditure surveys which have been carried out in the Philippines, Indonesia, Thailand and Malaysia since the 1960s. These surveys, and similar surveys from other parts of the world, have come under criticism for several reasons. The most frequent allegation is that they underestimate the incomes and expenditures of both the upper and the lower income groups (Milanovic 2016: 15-16). It is often claimed that homeless, internally displaced and migrant populations are not included in the sample if they lack a fixed abode, and these groups are likely to be poorer than average. In addition, workers living in accommodation provided by employers are often not included. Whether all these people are really poor can be debated; construction and factory workers living on-site in urban areas may in fact be quite well-paid and they or their family may own a home in another part of the country. Even those migrants who lack a fixed abode in the town or city to which they move may own property in their place of origin. At the other end of the scale, the very affluent people living in gated housing complexes are often hard to approach, and if they are included, they may under-report their income and expenditure, probably through fear of tax demands. A study carried out in eighteen Latin America countries found not just that high earners do tend to under-report their incomes, but also that there was a general tendency to under-report earnings from self-employment (Pyatt 2003: 343). This is probably true in many parts of Asia as well.

The exclusion of high earners, or their tendency to under-report income and expenditure is almost certainly one reason for the gap between the estimates of household income and expenditure in household surveys, and that given in the national accounts in Indonesia and the Philippines in recent years.[10] Under-reporting of income by the richest households is likely to produce lower measures of inequality, and to the extent that such households refuse to participate at all, the headcount and other measures of poverty could be overstated (World Bank 2017: 31). On the other hand, the exclusion of other groups of the population such as migrant workers, or those in camps for internally displaced people could lead to underestimates of poverty, if indeed these groups are poorer than those households which are captured in the surveys. Even if they are not poor, their exclusion could help to explain the gap between the survey and the national accounts data, which has widened in several countries in Southeast Asia in recent years (Table 7.10). In Indonesia, the gap seems to have been widening since the 1980s, and by the early 2000s the survey data was well under 50 per cent of that in the national accounts (Booth 2016: 177). The reasons for the decline do not seem to have attracted much scholarly attention, at least compared with India where the problem of the disparity between the National Sample Survey (NSS) data on household consumption and the national accounts has been widely discussed since the 1970s.[11] While there are valid reasons for disparity between the two data sets, there appears to be some consensus that when the survey data fall below 50 per cent of the national accounts figures, there is likely to be a problem with the coverage of the household surveys.

Deaton (2010: 194) pointed out that in the OECD countries, where the quality of both household survey and national accounts figures is assumed to be higher than in the rest of the world, surveys tend to pick up around three-quarters of the estimated consumption expenditure in the national accounts. The difference is due to items such as imputed value of owner-occupied housing, which is usually excluded from surveys, and expenditures by non-profit institutions serving households (NPISH). While expenditures by various non-governmental organizations, including religious charities, have

---

10   In the Philippines, it has also been argued that the FIES has been increasingly underestimating the flow of remittances, especially among high-income groups (Ducanes 2010). But Ducanes also argued that understatement of remittances is unlikely to explain the large difference between the national accounts data and the FIES.

11   See, in particular, Deaton and Kozel (2005), Chapters 4 to 8.

Table 7.10:   Household survey consumption data as a percentage of national accounts consumption expenditures, 2000-2013

	Thailand	Cambodia	Philippines*	Indonesia	Vietnam**
2000	74	n/a	70	42***	74
2004	74	251	60	42	76
2007	67	n/a	55	38	75
2009	72	132	54	37	n/a
2011	67	n/a	53	45****	83
2013	66	126	n/a	44****	77

* Data refer to 2000, 2003, 2006, 2009 and 2012.
** Data refer to 2000, 2002, 2006, 2010 and 2012.
*** 1999 data.
**** March quarter data.
Sources: Thailand: *Statistical Yearbook of Thailand* (Bangkok: National Statistical Office), various issues. Cambodia: *Statistical Yearbook of Cambodia* (Phnom Penh: National Institute of Statistics), various issues. Philippines: *Philippine Statistical Yearbook* (Manila: National Statistical Coordination Board and Philippine Statistics Authority), various issues. Indonesia: Booth (2016: Table 8.5). Vietnam: *Statistical Yearbook of Vietnam* (Hanoi: Statistical Publishing House), various issues.

certainly been growing in many parts of Southeast Asia, and are now given in the national accounts data for both Thailand and Indonesia, it appears that they are very small relative to household consumption expenditures (less than 2 per cent in Indonesia). A more important reason for the disparities in the Philippines and Indonesia could be that the household expenditure component of the national accounts is estimated as a residual. Total gross domestic product is estimated from the production side, and estimates of government consumption expenditures, investment expenditures and exports less imports are subtracted from total GDP. The residual thus incorporates the errors in the other components of expenditure, which may be underestimated, thus inflating the estimate of household consumption expenditures. But even allowing for these problems, the survey figures on household income and expenditure are probably underestimated, although the extent of the under-reporting is very difficult to assess. It might not be confined to the richest decile of the distribution, but could well affect the returns of many households further down the distribution.

The evidence from both Cambodia and Vietnam raises different problems. In Cambodia, the survey data have been higher than the national accounts since 2004, although the disparity has been narrowing (Table 7.10). Ratios greater than unity have been found in some African countries where they have been attributed, in part at least, to underestimation in the national accounts (Deaton 2010: 194). Pyatt (2003: Table 4) compared national accounts data with those on household consumption expenditure from the Living Standards Measurement Surveys (LSMS), and found that the LSMS figures exceeded those from the national accounts not just for Tanzania, Ghana, Cote d'Ivoire and Morocco but also for Russia, Kyrgyzstan and Pakistan.[12] It is possible that understatement in the national accounts explains the Cambodian result, although it is likely that the problems with the household survey coverage in Cambodia which were discussed in the previous chapter have persisted after 2000. The World Bank claimed that in 2004 a more standardized methodology was introduced in implementing the household surveys, with assistance from the Swedish International Development Cooperation Agency (SIDA). This was intended to promote best practice and to limit comparability problems over time (World Bank 2014b: 6). This report did not directly address the disparity between the national accounts figure and the survey data. More recently, the World Bank's poverty estimates for Cambodia, based on the 2011 PPP data, show that the country had a lower headcount measure than Indonesia, the Philippines and Vietnam, in spite of the very low estimate of expenditure per capita compared with these other countries (Tables 7.7 and 7.8). Are these figures plausible? It seems probable that the measurement problems in Cambodia have not been fully resolved.[13]

In Vietnam, the household survey data have also fallen short of the national accounts figures: the ratio has fluctuated between 74 and 83 per cent between 2000 and 2013 (Table 7.10). This might suggest that the household surveys in Vietnam are of high quality, although some critics have suggested that this is not in fact the case. Pincus and Sender (2008) argued that many poor migrants to urban areas are excluded from the sample which only includes registered households, and this leads to understatement of numbers under the poverty line. Poorer households in remote rural regions are also likely to be undercounted, or missed out completely in the surveys.[14] Undercounting of the poor in Vietnam might explain the apparently paradoxical results that the proportion of the population in Vietnam below the $1.90-a-day poverty line was lower in 2012 than in Indonesia or the Philippines, in spite of the fact that average consumption expenditures

12   Haughton and Khandker (2009: 192) argue that there is a universal tendency for average national accounts data to be higher than the figure obtained by grossing up data from household surveys. But the evidence from several parts of the world refutes this argument.

13   The World Bank stopped publishing poverty estimates for Cambodia in the World Development Indicators in 2018. No estimate for Cambodia was included in Asian Development Bank (2018).

14   A report by the World Bank acknowledged that some unregistered short-term migrants were probably vulnerable to short-term shocks such as the 2009 growth slowdown (Kozel 2014: 60).

per capita, in PPP terms, were considerably lower in Vietnam (Tables 7.7 and 7.8). But it is also likely that poor migrant households are excluded in Indonesia and the Philippines as well.

Part of the puzzle could be explained by the fact that economic growth in Vietnam has been more egalitarian, and more consistent since the early 1990s. Vietnam introduced comprehensive land reform policies after reunification and, at least until the early 1990s, private enterprise was strictly controlled, public sector salaries were low, and there were very few 'rich' people. Thus the accelerated growth in the 1990s until recently might have begun from an unusually egalitarian base.[15] But in 2005 and 2010, it appears that the Gini coefficient for household per capita expenditures in Vietnam was about the same as in Indonesia, although lower than in the Philippines (Table 7.11). Only in 2012 and 2014 was the Gini in Indonesia higher. So the argument that the higher headcount measure for Indonesia was the result of higher inequalities does not seem plausible, at least until after 2010. Perhaps a more important factor in explaining the low poverty headcount measures for both Vietnam and Cambodia in recent years is the lower prices of basic needs, including food, housing, education and medical care. In principle this should be captured in the PPP figures, and it is true that in 2011 the general price level was lower in Vietnam and Cambodia than in Indonesia and the Philippines (Table 7.8). But it is possible that the PPP data derived from the 2011 exercise do not capture fully the difference in the cost of living of households at or near the poverty threshold in these countries.

Table 7.11:   Gini coefficient of household consumption expenditures

	Vietnam	Indonesia	Philippines*	Thailand
2002	0.34	0.32	0.41	0.42
2004	0.35	0.32	n/a	0.43
2006	0.34	0.33	0.43	0.42
2008	0.33	0.35	0.42	0.40
2010	0.38	0.38	n/a	0.39
2012	0.35	0.41	0.42	0.39
2014	0.34	0.41	n/a	0.37

* Estimates for the Philippines refer to 2003, 2006, 2009 and 2012.
Source: Vietnam: Benjamin, Brandt and McCaig (2016: Table 1); Indonesia: Asra (2014: Table 6.1);
Thailand and the Philippines: UNU-WIDER (2018).

15   The estimates of the Gini coefficient for 1993 given in Glewwe (2004b: Table 1.4) indicate that the Gini coefficient of household income was 0.33 in 1993 and rose to 0.35 in 1998.

To sum up, it seems probable that flaws in the household surveys themselves, together with problems in the PPP estimates, explain at least
some of the differences between countries in the poverty estimates of
the Asian Development Bank for 2010 given in Table 1.2, and in the more
recent estimates of the World Bank, given in Table 7.7. Problems in the
household surveys can result from non-compliance, or under-reporting,
which might affect not just the richest households but those households
whose incomes and expenditures are closer to, or even below the poverty
threshold. It is also likely that non-compliance may result from a reluctance
on the part of householders to devote many hours to keeping a diary, or to
responding to a long questionnaire. In the Philippines, the Family Income
and Expenditure Survey (FIES) takes place every three years, and involves
a lengthy questionnaire of 78 pages, with 24 questions on income and 47
on expenditures. It takes five hours to administer (Albert, Dumagan and
Martinez 2015: 4). In Indonesia, the full Susenas survey as administered in
the 1990s included 320 questions (Pradhan 2009: 391). In Vietnam the Living
Standards Measurement Survey has also been criticized for its length (Kozel
2014: 60). Unsurprisingly, it seems that many households simply refuse to
participate if they have other demands on their time. Enumerators will try
to find other, more cooperative, households to fill their quota. These may
well be households which are easier to access, and also smaller, given that
obtaining data from large households takes more time. To the extent that
richer households value their time more highly, they may be more likely to
refuse to cooperate than poorer ones.

Given how crucial household survey data are to the estimation of both
poverty and distributional indicators, it is surprising how little research
has been carried out on 'best practice' ways of designing and adminis-
tering such surveys in middle- and low-income countries. In the 1970s
experienced statisticians were pointing out that long questionnaires risked
respondent fatigue and possible non-compliance. But it appears that the
World Bank did not always heed this advice in compiling the global poverty
estimates. In the early 2000s, they financed an experiment in Tanzania
which administered eight different types of survey to 4,000 households.
It was found that the surveys based on recall were much less expensive to
administer than those based on diaries, especially when diary-keeping was
combined with frequent visits from enumerators. But they were sometimes
less accurate. Attempts to cut costs by reducing the number of questions
led to a substantial loss in accuracy. This study concluded that a long-list
recall module with a reference period of one to two weeks might produce
the best results, given cost constraints (Beegle et al. 2012: 17). But it was

clear from their results that there was a trade-off between the time taken
to administer a survey and accuracy. The World Bank report on monitoring
global poverty recommended that there should be an investigation into
the extent to which people are missing from household surveys, and the
extent of under-representation and non-coverage of surveys (World Bank
2017: 33). But such an investigation would be expensive, and would require
the cooperation of national statistical agencies. It is far from clear that such
cooperation would be forthcoming, either in Southeast Asia or elsewhere.

Should Monetary Estimates Be Abandoned?

The various estimates using internationally comparable poverty lines published by the World Bank since the 1990s were no doubt done in good faith.
But it is difficult to avoid the conclusion that the World Bank has consistently
underestimated the difficulties not just in designing and implementing
household surveys across the developing world, but also in estimating
purchasing power parities (PPP). As a result of the changes in the PPP data,
in both 2005 and 2011, major changes had to be made in their estimates of
global poverty. This in turn has led to a loss of credibility regarding their
estimates. Statisticians in countries such as the Philippines and Indonesia
can reasonably point out that, if they want to monitor poverty trends over a
period of years, it is preferable to use their own poverty lines, which generate
data that are more useful to domestic policymakers.

It is now widely acknowledged that the data requirements for comparable
estimates of poverty across countries are formidable. The authors of the report
on the 2011 PPP revisions set out these requirements with admirable clarity:

> Global poverty numbers require a large and varied set of data collected
> from different places, time periods, and sources. Five unique data sources
> are required for the World Bank's calculation of global poverty numbers
> and global poverty lines: household surveys, population censuses, national
> accounts, consumer price indexes, and PPPs from the ICP. Each new round
> of the ICPs brings revisions of the PPPs, and these revisions, like revisions
> of the other data sources, can have large effects on global, regional and
> national poverty counts. The global poverty line itself is calculated as an
> average of the PPP equivalents of the poverty lines of the world's poorest
> economies. In general, therefore, the global line will also change with the
> new PPPs, even if the underlying national poverty lines remain unchanged.
> (World Bank 2014a: 24)

These data requirements would tax the capacity of even the most advanced, and well-funded, statistical offices. It is hardly surprising that in many parts of the developing world, poverty estimates using 'internationally comparable' poverty lines have produced results which have conflicted with estimates using national poverty lines, which themselves may have serious flaws, and with evidence from national accounts. The ranking of countries in Southeast Asia according to per capita consumption expenditures published by the World Bank might appear broadly plausible, given what we know from the national accounts across the region. Singapore and Brunei have the highest per capita consumption expenditures, and Laos, Cambodia and Myanmar the lowest. Perhaps surprisingly, both Thailand and Indonesia had higher per capita consumption expenditures in PPP-adjusted dollars in 2011 than China (Table 7.8). This could reflect the higher level of prices in China, and also the higher proportion of GDP devoted to investment expenditures in China. As would be expected, the price level relative to the world average is highest in Singapore and Brunei, and lowest in Vietnam, Laos, Cambodia and Myanmar.

It might therefore be expected that the headcount measure of poverty would broadly follow this ranking as well, unless income or expenditure inequalities were much higher in some countries compared with others. But it seems that there are some anomalies, especially in the case of Vietnam and Cambodia. In the case of Cambodia, it appears that successive surveys have under-represented poorer, more remote, parts of the country. This might also be the case in Vietnam. In both Indonesia and the Philippines, it appears that in recent years, the survey data have underestimated the incomes and expenditures of the upper income groups, or perhaps excluded them altogether. If the sample is biased towards poorer households, it is likely that the poverty estimates are too high.

Does this mean that attempts to rank countries according to monetary estimates of poverty and inequality should be abandoned? Should more reliance be placed on non-monetary estimates of welfare? The Human Development Index was devised by the United Nations as a tool for ranking countries according to GDP and several non-monetary indicators relating to life expectancy and education. As was pointed out in Chapter 1, the HDI has attracted criticism over the years from several quarters, not least because, like other composite indicators including both monetary and non-monetary components, arbitrary assumptions have to be made about weights attached to each component. These assumptions often change over time. For example, Ravallion (2016: 284–289), who has been very critical of what he terms 'mash-up indicators' pointed out that changes to the HDI made in 2010 greatly reduced the implicit weight on longevity in poorer countries.

Another 'mash-up' indicator which has attracted considerable attention in recent years is the Multidimensional Poverty Index (MPI) developed by a group working at Oxford University. This index incorporates ten non-monetary indicators grouped into three dimensions: education, health and living standards. It is an attempt to measure poverty using what its designers term the direct method, which 'shows whether people satisfy a set of specified basic needs, rights, or – in line with Sen's capability approach – *functionings*' (Alkire and Santos 2014: 251). The MPI has been used to rank low- and middle-income countries according to a composite index derived from the ten non-monetary indicators. The rankings for seven Southeast Asian countries together with China and India were given in Table 1.8. The rankings differ in several respects from those derived from the headcount measures of poverty given in Tables 7.6 and 7.7. Cambodia, which had a very low headcount measure of poverty, ranks below all the other countries in the table except Laos and India according to the MPI index. The Philippines ranks above Indonesia according to the MPI index, although its headcount measure of poverty was above Indonesia's. Vietnam is below China in the MPI rankings, although its headcount measure of poverty was lower than China.

There are good reasons why the MPI rankings might differ from the ranking according to the headcount measure of poverty. They are exclusively non-monetary, whereas the headcount measures of poverty derive from household survey data on income or expenditure, and PPP-adjusted poverty lines. The problems associated with both household surveys and PPP data have already been discussed, but how reliable are the data used to compile the ten indicators used in the MPI? In most cases they are derived from the Demographic and Health Surveys which have been conducted in most countries in Southeast Asia for several decades. It has been suggested that these surveys may be biased towards poorer households. On the other hand, the results of the MPI estimates in Southeast Asia do confirm that some countries have achieved more in health, education, sanitation, electrification and housing than others, at similar or even higher levels of per capita GDP. Vietnam stands out as a relatively poor country which seems to have done especially well, in comparison with richer countries such as the Philippines and Indonesia.

Vietnam also appears to have achieved good results in child health indicators (prevalence of wasting and stunting) compared with both Indonesia and the Philippines (Table 7.12). This is in spite of the fact that FAO estimates show that the percentage of the total population which is undernourished in Vietnam was in fact slightly higher than the average for Southeast Asia, although lower than in the Philippines. In 2014/16, the percentage of the population considered undernourished was highest in Cambodia, Laos and Myanmar, although these countries have all experienced some reduction since 2004/6. The evidence assembled by the FAO indicate that most countries in Southeast Asia still face problems with both child and adult nutrition, which policymakers will need to address.

Table 7.12:   **Percentage of the population undernourished and stunting and wasting in children**

Country	Percentage undernourished (total population)		Stunting in children		Wasting in children
	2004/6	**2014/16**	**2005**	**2016**	**2016**
Malaysia	3.9	under 2.5	17.2	17.7	8.0
Thailand	12.3	9.5	15.7	16.3	6.7
Indonesia	18.6	7.9	n/a	36.4	13.5
Vietnam	18.2	10.7	33.3	24.6	6.4
Philippines	16.3	13.8	33.8	30.3	7.9
Laos	26.8	17.1	47.6	43.8	6.4
Cambodia	20.0	15.3	43.7	32.4	9.6
Myanmar	32.1	16.9	40.6	29.2	6.4
Southeast Asia	18.1	10.2	34.1	25.8	8.9

Note: Countries ranked according to their HDI position in 2015. Stunting in children refers to the percentage of children too short for their age. Wasting in children refers to the percentage of children too thin for their height.
Source: FAO et al. (2017: Table A1.1).

Human Development Rankings

The second decade of the twenty-first century has seen the publication of several studies which rank countries according to composite indicators of human capital. The most ambitious in terms of country coverage was a measure of expected human capital defined for each birth cohort as the expected years lived from ages 20 to 64, and adjusted for educational attainment, learning or educational quality, and functional health status (Lim et al. 2019). The results, for 195 countries, were published for 2016 and also for 1990. In 2018 the World Bank published its Human Capital Index, which ranked 157 countries according to a number of educational and health indicators (probability of survival to age five, adult survival rates, under-five stunting rates, expected years of schooling, harmonized test scores, and learning-adjusted years of schooling). In 2017 the World Economic Forum published its Global Human Capital Index which was another composite index comprising indicators of capacity (the existing stock of education), deployment (skill accumulation through work experience and adult education), development (current efforts to educate coming generations) and 'know-how' (the breadth and depth of specialized skills used in the economy).

Country rankings for the ten countries of Southeast Asia, plus the Republic of Korea, China and India, are given in Table 7.13. Broadly the rankings follow per capita GDP, but there are outliers. Vietnam has a higher place than its per capita GDP alone would indicate; this was especially the case in the World Bank index, where it was ranked higher than any other Southeast Asian country except Singapore. Indonesia was ranked lower than Vietnam according to both the World Bank index and that compiled by Lim et al. (2018). It did rather better on the World Economic Forum index, probably because that index did not include any health indicators, where Indonesia does rather badly in comparison with other countries in Southeast Asia. The indexes compiled by Lim et al. (2018) for 1990 and 2016 show that neither Indonesia not the Philippines improved their rankings over these 26 years; the Philippines slipped back six places.

Table 7.13: Human Development Indexes: Rankings

Country	World Bank 2017	Lim et al. 2016 (1990)	World Economic Forum 2017
Southeast Asia			
Singapore	1	13 (43)	11
Brunei	n/a	29 (35)	58
Malaysia	55	79 (106)	33
Thailand	65	72 (103)	40
Indonesia	87	131 (130)	65
Philippines	84	130 (124)	50
Lao PDR	111	149 (157)	84
Vietnam	48	85 (116)	64
Myanmar	117	140 (152)	89
Cambodia	100	153 (158)	92
Other Asia			
Republic of Korea	2	6 (18)	27
China	46	44 (69)	34
India	115	158 (162)	103

Note: Countries ranked according to 2017 per capita GDP. The World Bank ranked 157 countries, Lim et al. (2018) ranked 195 and World Economic Forum ranked 130.
Sources: World Bank (2018), Lim et al. (2018), World Economic Forum (2017b).

The composite indicators shown in Table 7.13 are only as good as the data on which they rely. Doubts have been expressed about the reliability of the educational indicators, especially those relating to educational quality. To the extent that many countries do not include schools in more remote rural areas in the international tests, the results are probably overstated. The same arguments apply to the figures on childhood wasting and stunting. On the other hand, it does seem that several countries in Southeast Asia are not performing as well on several of these indicators as their per capita GDP alone would predict. When the scores of 157 countries in the World Bank sample were plotted against per capita GDP, Malaysia, Indonesia, Laos and Myanmar were all found to be below the regression line. To the extent that GDP is a reasonable indicator of national economic capacity, these countries should have been achieving rather more in terms of health and education outcomes than is currently the case.

Inequality in Non-monetary Indicators

Therborn (2013: 48-54) has argued that three types of inequality should be of interest to social scientists in all parts of the world. The first is what he terms resource inequality, which usually emphasizes inequalities in income and wealth. This is the type of inequality which has attracted most attention from social scientists, both in rich countries, and in the developing world. A second type of inequality, which has generated a considerable body of research in the rich countries, concerns what Therborn (2013: 49) terms vital inequality, or 'socially constructed unequal life-chances'. Typically the study of this type of inequality involves differences in life expectances and mortality rates, across regions and social classes, as well as evidence from surveys of hunger and malnutrition. It can also include inequality in access to education, although this might more properly be placed under resource inequality, given the tight link which exists between education and earnings in most societies. The third type is existential inequality which is inequality based on attributes which people are born with, such as gender, race and social status.

Research on vital inequality in many low- and middle-income countries has been hampered by inadequate, or non-existent, systems of vital registration. Births and deaths in poor households, with poorly educated parents are often the least likely to be officially registered. The main change in recent decades has been the growth in comprehensive population censuses and surveys, although these often do not ask questions about household income and wealth. The Demographic and Health Surveys do attempt to estimate household assets. Since the 1980s these surveys have been monitoring population, health and nutrition developments in over 70 countries, mainly in Asia and Africa. These surveys have been used to estimate the MPI (Table 1.8), and have also been used by researchers investigating socio-economic inequalities in infant and child mortality in a number of low- and middle-income countries.

A survey of this research came up with several important findings (Houweling and Kunst 2010). The first was that the poorer and less educated groups exhibited considerably higher childhood mortality rates than better-off ones. In almost all of the 55 countries investigated by these authors, child mortality among the poorest households (based on ownership of household assets) exceeded that of the richest group, often by a large margin. The authors argue that huge population health gains could be made if these inequalities were directly addressed by policymakers. A second point made by Houweling and Kunst (2010: Figure 2) was that inequalities in under-five mortality did not always exhibit a linear gradient; especially in sub-Saharan Africa, the most obvious gap was between the top one or two deciles and the rest. There were also striking differences in under-five mortality between Asian countries at broadly similar levels of per capita GDP; Vietnam, for example, had lower levels of child mortality in each quintile group than India.

Houweling and Kunst argued that these differences between countries in childhood mortality, as well as improvements in the same country over time, showed that the problem was amenable to policy intervention. They cited earlier work by Houweling et al. (2006) which found that socio-economic inequalities in childhood mortality declined in Indonesia between 1982 and 1997, a period of rapid economic growth. Over these years there were equally strong declines in under-five mortality among households with poorly educated mothers as in households with well-educated mothers, although the paper also drew attention to the gap between the more remote parts of the country and Java-Bali. Research by Hodge et al. (2014), also using the Demographic and Health Surveys but extending the period to 2010, found that absolute inequalities in under-five mortality across wealth and education in Indonesia showed a decreasing (and statistically significant) trend over three decades.[16] But there did appear to be an increase in inequalities

16   Lieberman, Capuno and Minh (2004) found that there were still high disparities in infant and child health mortality by wealth categories in Indonesia in the late 1990s compared with other countries in South and Southeast Asia.

by wealth and education, both for under-five and for neo-natal mortalities after the 1990s. The absolute disparities across island divisions remained and showed some signs of increasing. These authors suggested that the decentralization reforms, which began in 2001, might have contributed to a slowdown in mortality rate reduction, and also to the widening gap between Java-Bali and the rest.

A comparative analysis of the consequences of decentralization reforms for health policies in the Philippines, Vietnam and Indonesia made the important point that the implementation of decentralization, especially in Indonesia, but also in the Philippines and Vietnam, took place at a time of considerable macroeconomic instability associated with the Asian crisis and its aftermath (Lieberman, Capuno and Minh 2004). In all three countries, government budgets came under pressure. The high cost of bank restructuring after 1998 in Indonesia meant that budget resources for health, education and infrastructure policies were very limited (Booth 2016: 101-102). In addition, the central governments were reluctant to give more taxing powers to regional and local governments, which meant that they continued to depend on grants from the centre to fund health, education and other services. There were also problems of poor targeting, although given the dearth of information on who and where the poor were, governments at the sub-national level could hardly be blamed for an inability to concentrate resources on localities where they were badly needed.

The Philippines has had the longest experience with decentralization reforms, which began in the early 1990s. By the mid-1990s, gaps across regions in infant and child mortality rates were closing, although they widened again after 1998. Local governments were spending a significant proportion of their budgets on health; on average the ratio had increased to almost 21 per cent by the early 2000s (Lieberman, Capuno and Minh 2004). But after 2000, in spite of accelerated rates of GDP growth, the evidence pointed to a slowdown in rates of decline of both infant and under-five mortality rates while neo-natal mortality rates remained high (Kraft et al. 2013). This study found that important within-country inequalities in child health persisted in the Philippines. Child mortality rates varied substantially across several dimensions, including rural/urban locations, provinces and wealth status. The study also identified a lack of health professionals in some regions, together with geographic inaccessibility of facilities, as causes of high infant and child mortality. These problems appear to have persisted in spite of decentralized funding.

Several comparative studies have suggested that, by the early twenty-first century, Vietnam had achieved very high rankings in infant and child mortality, as well as in life expectancies, compared with other Asian countries with similar or higher per capita GDP (Table 1.1). But an analysis of data on Vietnam over the 1990s found that the fall in under-five mortality which occurred was not spread evenly across the whole population (Wagstaff and Nguyen 2004: 320-323). The top two quintiles in the wealth distribution had a rapid fall, while the bottom quintile saw little improvement. Lieberman, Capuno and Minh (2004) found that inequalities in infant and child mortality in Vietnam were about the same as the Philippines in the late 1990s, but after that, Vietnam experienced faster declines in child mortality than the Philippines. Houweling and Kunst (2010: Figure 2) in their comparative survey found that the differences in under-five mortality by wealth quintile in Vietnam were much lower than in India or Brazil. The Vietnamese experience confirms the argument of Houweling and Kunst that government policies do make a difference, given that outcomes can vary so much in countries at similar levels of per capita GDP.

In most countries in Southeast Asia, governments have been trying for decades to increase school attendance. Most claim to have come close to achieving universal primary enrolments (UPE), and have plans for a compulsory nine-year cycle. But even at the primary level, many children drop out before completing the full cycle. At the secondary level progress in reaching universal enrolments has been much slower; even at the lower secondary level, not all children complete the cycle in many parts of Southeast Asia. In 2010, there were striking differences in the percentage of the population over 25 with at least secondary education. In Singapore almost 65 per cent of men had secondary education and 57 per cent of women (Table 7.14). As would be expected the poorer countries in terms of per capita GDP had lower percentages, and in the case of Laos and Cambodia wider gaps between men and women. Adult literacy was over 90 per cent in all countries except Laos and Cambodia.

Several points emerge from the figures on secondary education. The Philippines, which had the most favourable legacy from the colonial era, still had high rates of secondary attendance among the adult population in 2010 compared with Thailand and Indonesia, in spite of lower per capita GDP. The Philippines also continues to have high tertiary enrolment rates in comparison with most other parts of Southeast Asia. Singapore and Malaysia have both invested heavily in education since gaining independence, and by 2010 had achieved high rates of secondary and tertiary enrolments, while Indonesia in 2010 still had less than 30 per cent of the adult population with secondary schooling. In Thailand which only began to expand post-primary

Table 7.14:   Educational indicators and gender inequality index

Country*	Population with at Least Secondary Education (Female, Male)**	Adult Literacy 2005-8	Tertiary Enrollment 2001-9	Gender Inequality Index Ranking***
Singapore (27)	57.3, 64.8	95	n/a	10
Brunei (37)	66.6, 23.5	95	16	n/a
Malaysia (57)	66.0, 72.8	92	30	50
Thailand (92)	25.6, 33.7	94	n/a	69
Philippines (97)	65.9, 63.7	94	28	78
Indonesia (108)	24.2, 31.1	92	18	100
Vietnam (113)	24.7, 28.0	93	10	58
Lao PDR (122)	22.9, 36.8	73	13	88
Cambodia (124)	11.6, 20.6	77	7	95
Myanmar (132)	18.0, 17.6	92	11	n/a

* Figure in brackets show rankings according to the Human Development Index for 2010 in which 169 countries were ranked.
** Figures refer to the percentage of the population over 25 with secondary education, 2010
*** Gender Inequality Index rankings for 2008 in which 137 countries were ranked.
Sources UNDP (2010: 144-159).

enrolments in the 1990s, the proportion of the adult population with secondary qualifications was only slightly higher than in Indonesia.

Thailand has seen a dramatic expansion in upper secondary enrolments since the 1990s, in spite of the fact that education is only compulsory to the lower secondary level. Furthermore, the expansion has been most rapid for the poorer income groups, with the result that the very large gap in enrolments between income groups which existed in the 1980s has narrowed considerably (Lathapipat 2016: 44). This outcome is the result of expanded facilities on the one hand, and growing parental awareness of the importance of education for a child's earning capacity on the other, especially after the post-1997 growth slowdown. But at the tertiary level there appears to have been an increase in enrolment inequality between income groups, although for most income groups enrolment growth slowed after 2000. Lathapipat suggests that the implementation of fees, and the introduction of the Education Loan Fund, may have had a deterrent effect, especially on potential students from poorer households.

The available evidence from Indonesia and the Philippines, as well as Thailand, suggests that access to education at the tertiary level is still to a considerable extent determined by household income, and that people with tertiary qualifications earn more, and are less likely to be poor. In Indonesia, successive rounds of the Susenas have showed quite marked differences in educational participation rates by expenditure groups, especially in the over-sixteen age groups. In 2012, around one-third of people in the 19-to-24 age groups in the top 20 per cent of the expenditure distribution in urban areas were enrolled in educational institutions (Booth 2016: 186). But in the bottom 40 per cent of the expenditure distribution in rural areas, less than 5 per cent of those in the 19-to-24 age group were still in education. In the Philippines, Ducanes and Tan (2014: Table 4) have shown that poverty incidence falls steeply when the most educated household member has graduated from high school or college. Using the 2009 FIES data, they estimated that at the national level, poverty incidence was 41 per cent for households where the most educated member had only primary education, falling to 2.4 per cent when the most educated member was a college graduate. Households with at least one college graduate earned more than other households from all income sources, including remittances.

Ducanes and Tan (2014) did find that there was some improvement in educational attainment among the younger age cohorts in poor households, although the improvement was slow. Poor households where at least one younger member managed to reach college were more likely to move out of poverty, especially if that member completes college. But the gap in college graduates between poor and non-poor households remained very large. Among the adult population aged 25 to 40 in poor households, only 1.6 per cent were college graduates, compared with 23.2 per cent in non-poor households. Narrowing the educational gap between poor and non-poor households remains a crucial challenge for educational policy not just in the Philippines but elsewhere in Southeast Asia as well. As long as most young people from poor households fail to at least graduate from high school they are likely to face a lifetime of low and unstable earnings.

The third aspect of inequality to which Therborn drew attention was what he termed existential inequality, which refers to inequality based on attributes which people are born with, such as race or gender. In recent years there have been several attempts to rank countries according to gender inequality and gender gaps. The Gender Inequality Index, published in the *Human Development Reports*, showed that in 2010 Singapore achieved the highest ranking among the Southeast Asian countries, at tenth out of 138 countries, followed by Malaysia and Vietnam (Table 7.13). The Global Gender Gap Index (GGGI) has been published since 2006 by the World Economic Forum. Its focus is on measuring gaps rather than levels, and examines gender disparities in four broad categories. These were economic participation and opportunity, educational attainment, health and survival, and political empowerment. The 2017 ranking places the Philippines in the tenth spot, out of 144 countries (World Economic Forum 2017a: Table 3). It was ranked above France, the United Kingdom, Germany, Canada, and Australia. The other nine ASEAN countries were ranked much lower, from 64 (Laos) and 65 (Singapore) to 104 (Malaysia). Another ranking, which used OECD data to compile a Social Institutions and Gender Index, ranked 101 countries according to a range of criteria. The Philippines was ranked seventh and Thailand sixteenth, although the Philippines slipped eighteen places when an abortion rights indicator was added (Branisa et al. 2014).

The high ranking achieved by the Philippines, especially in the GGGI, reflects the fact that gender disparities were quite low by global standards, even if absolute levels achieved in areas such as economic participation, education and health were not especially high. Critics point out that the GGGI does not take into account inequalities in economic opportunity, or in access to education and health facilities, or in political empowerment, across regions and social classes. Given that these disparities remain considerable, and may be getting worse, the high ranking of the Philippines in the GGGI may not fully reflect the reality of gender relations, where many girls from low-income families struggle to get education beyond the primary level, and where the women who have achieved high political office have often come from elite families. But the fact that no other country in Southeast Asia is in the top 60 countries in the GGGI, and only two are in the top 60 countries in the UNDP index, should be a cause for concern among policymakers.

8 Government Policy Interventions

Introduction

Since the 1950s, most governments in Southeast Asia have implemented policies which are intended to increase incomes and improve living standards
for their populations. Because in the 1950s and 1960s, the great majority
of the populations across the region derived most of their income from
agricultural activities, the agricultural sector was often given priority in
development plans. In some countries, especially those which had inherited
a skewed pattern of land distribution from the colonial era, it was argued
that land reform should be a crucial component of agricultural policy.
Where rural population densities were already high, and extending the
cultivation frontier was no longer possible, settling surplus rural populations
in less densely settled areas also became a focus of government policy. In
addition, the importance of providing rural non-farm employment (RNFE)
was recognized. This could be done by government through employment
on labour-intensive public works projects; following models developed in
South Asia, a number of programmes were initiated in various parts of
Southeast Asia.

Family planning programmes were also initiated in several countries, in
the expectation that slowing population growth would make it easier for
governments to improve child health and educational attainment, which in
turn would allow young people to move to more productive employment.
More recently, following the model developed in parts of Latin America,
some countries are implementing cash transfers which are conditional on
children attending school and receiving healthcare. In the expectation
that regional and local governments often have a better idea of what sorts
of policies might be most effective in their areas, several countries have
implemented decentralization and community empowerment policies.
They have also intervened in markets for basic commodities, especially food.

Given that most countries in Southeast Asia have tried to implement
at least some of these policies over the last five decades, and several have
experimented with most of them, is there strong evidence that at least
some of them have produced positive results in terms of improving the
incomes of the poorest people? Have some policies, such as labour-intensive
public works, land reform, land settlement or community empowerment
programmes, been more successful in alleviating poverty in some countries
than others, and if so why? Is it, for example, possible to identify those

who have been left behind, even in the fast-growing economies, and offer them assistance through cash transfers? The rest of this chapter attempts to answer some of these questions by examining the experience of various countries in the region since the 1950s.

In assessing the impact of these policies, two points need to be emphasized. The first is that most governments have had multiple objectives in implementing them, of which poverty alleviation was often not the most important. Rural public works projects, for example, were intended to rehabilitate and improve infrastructure; the benefits from these improvements often accrued, at least in the short run, to segments of the population which were not poor. The second point is that government budgets in many Southeast Asian countries have been, and are still, small relative to populations. Thus the amount of money in per capita terms available to spend on anti-poverty programmes has often been very small. To the critics, this means that many of these programmes are unlikely to have much impact, and are often implemented for political reasons, to appease particular interest groups. These points are important, and will be taken up again in the concluding section.

The Challenge of Land Reform

All the countries of Southeast Asia, with the exceptions of Singapore and Brunei, emerged into independence with a large fraction of their populations dependent on agriculture for at least part of their income. Across the region, access to agricultural land and problems of land tenure were of paramount importance to many of the nationalists who had come to power after 1945. In several countries, including Indonesia (especially Java and Sumatra), Malaysia, the Philippines and Southern Vietnam, the available land was divided between smallholders and large estates, the latter often owned by foreign interests.[1] Even among smallholdings, the distribution of land was skewed and many rural households operated only small parcels from which it was difficult to earn incomes above the poverty threshold. In several

---

1   The definition of an estate has varied between countries and over time in Southeast Asia. Often it has referred to any holding above the size which can be cultivated by a family, using some hired labour, although there are differences between countries, and even within countries over time, on how large that holding is. But in some countries a legal definition has been used; an estate is an enterprise incorporated as a business under the relevant legislation. This definition probably excluded some holdings which might have been considered estates under the former definition.

countries, a considerable part of the land controlled by smallholders in the latter part of the colonial period was tenanted.

In Burma it was estimated that almost 60 per cent of land was under some form of tenancy arrangement (Pfanner 1969: Table 15). In the Philippines, the 1939 census found that 30.7 per cent of cultivated land was tenanted, and 49 per cent was in wholly owned holdings. The remainder was mainly in part-owned holdings. Only in one province (Negros Occidental) was a significant proportion of cultivated land in holdings run by managers (Spencer 1952: Table 8). Spencer (1952: 120-121) reflected a widespread view among both Filipino and American observers that the land tenure system had created widespread discontent, especially in those parts of Luzon where more than half of the cultivated land was under tenancy. Spencer argued that there were wide variations in the extent of tenancy which could not be explained just by population pressure alone. Some regions, especially in northern Luzon, had low rates of tenancy in spite of high population pressures.

Given these problems, land reform was a major concern of successive governments, both during the American and Commonwealth periods, and after the transfer of power in 1946. The reform agenda consisted of the regulation of landownership in less densely populated provinces, and the appropriation and redistribution of land above a stipulated threshold. But progress was often slow, and opposition from landed interests in the congress was considerable, although in the face of considerable pressure from radical groups the Congress did pass the Code of Agrarian Reform in 1971 (Fuwa 2000: 3). After Marcos declared martial law in 1972, one of his first presidential decrees was PD 27, which set up Operation Land Transfer (OLT). The main purpose of OLT was to convert tenant farmers in rice and corn areas to landowners by allowing them to purchase the land they were cultivating. Landowners were permitted to retain up to seven hectares of their land, which could continue to be leased out. Above that limit, land had to be transferred to the tillers. It was estimated that around 400,000 tenant farmers out of a total of between 900,000 and one million were in a position to benefit, each operating 1.8 hectares (Mangahas 1985: 221). By 1981, it was claimed that almost 90 per cent of potential farmer-beneficiaries had been identified, and 80 per cent had been issued certificates of land transfer. But a much smaller fraction had actually benefited in the sense that they were either full owners or amortizing owners of their land. Fuwa (2000: Table 2.5) argued that only about 15,000 hectares of land had actually been transferred, which was less than 3 per cent of the total.

Critics of OLT pointed out that the Marcos programme was riddled with loopholes; for example, farmers could avoid land transfer if they planted crops other than rice or corn. The decree also adversely affected landless labourers, who were a large segment of the rural poor. They had gained nothing directly from OLT, but their access through tenancy contracts was often prevented because landowners were worried that renting out land would lead to confiscation (Balisacan, Fuwa and Debuque 2004: 249). Their exclusion, together with the exclusion of many tenant farmers cultivating land below the owner's retention limit, or cultivating land growing crops other than rice and corn, meant that the impact of OLT on rural poverty was limited. Mangahas (1987a: 150) argued, 'OLT has not come close to such sweeping reforms as were implemented in Taiwan or in South Korea but can be rated as a moderate, somewhat long-drawn-out beginning at land reform.' Other evaluations were more critical. Putzel (1992: 154) claimed that Marcos depended on both the landed oligarchy and the military to maintain martial law, and neither supported comprehensive agrarian reform. A more complete programme would clearly have to include all land irrespective of tenure status or crop grown, and potential beneficiaries would have to include landless workers as well as tenant farmers.

Such a programme was in fact embodied in the Comprehensive Agrarian Reform Law (CARL) passed by the Aquino administration in 1988. The first phase of this reform covered rice and corn land as well as idle, foreclosed and abandoned land and private land voluntarily offered by owners. The second phase included all public land which could be alienated and private land in excess of 50 hectares. The third phase covered all other private land above the retention limit of five hectares. Thus CARL covered an estimated 9.77 million hectares or about 50 per cent of all productive forest and cultivated land in the country (Balisacan 1990: 94). Of this, two-thirds was public alienable and disposable land. Much of this was not vacant but cultivated by an estimated 15 million 'squatters' who required security of tenure. Beneficiaries of land reform in the public sector would not receive permanent title but 25-year non-transferable stewardship titles, which could not be used as loan collateral.

Such an ambitious programme of land reform, embracing so much land and so many potential beneficiaries, was bound to run into implementation difficulties. Putzel (1992: 212-213) argued that the first Aquino cabinet was dominated by conservative reformers, with at best lukewarm support for CARL. Even the more radical ministers were urban-based and lacked a deep knowledge of rural problems. But Fuwa's estimates indicate that during the Aquino presidency, much more was achieved than under the OLT programme during the Marcos era, although some parts of the CARL legislation ran into problems. One issue which received much publicity involved the provision that corporations owning agricultural land could transfer stock to potential beneficiaries rather than land. Many corporations were thought to have undervalued their stock for the purposes of transfer. Financing the programme also became a major problem, especially in the light of the very substantial pressures being put on the Philippines by international agencies to cut the budget deficit and control bank lending. There were endless controversies about the retention limits, exemptions, land valuations, grace periods and definitions. The Department of Agrarian Reform, essentially a bureaucracy left over from the Marcos regime, proved ill-equipped to meet the challenge of a new and greatly expanded agrarian reform programme. Even where officials were sincerely committed to implementation of the land reform programme, they ran into opposition from powerful vested interests in the legislature and in local governments who had little desire to see the power of the landowning class reduced.

Some analysts pointed out that successful implementation of comprehensive agrarian reform in the Philippines would not be possible until there was a radical shift in the political balance of power in favour of tenants and landless workers. The 'EDSA Revolution' which deposed Marcos and installed Cory Aquino did not produce such as shift, and thus it was hardly surprising that implementation of CARL was so slow (Balisacan 1990: 103; Putzel 1992: 193-216). Some argued that a less ambitious programme targeted more specifically towards landless agricultural labourers and marginal farmers in the poorest parts of the country would have been easier to implement, and might have incurred less fierce political opposition than the comprehensive strategy enacted by the Aquino administration. It was also suggested that more indirect methods of inducing large landowners to divest themselves of at least part of their land, such as progressive land taxes, might be more effective than mandatory land ceilings. The ILO report on the Philippines published in 1974 recommended a progressive tax on presumptive income from agricultural land as a means of encouraging greater utilization of agricultural land (ILO 1974: 264-265). Hayami, Quisumbing and Adriano (1990: 163) also argued in favour of a progressive land tax coupled with a progressive land rent on public lands so that the large corporations currently renting these lands could be induced to use more small contract farmers. Unfortunately it proved difficult to implement progressive land taxes for the same reasons as it was difficult to implement programmes involving land redistribution.

The Ramos administration which succeeded that of Cory Aquino pushed ahead with the various parts of the CARL programme. Ramos appointed a new head of the Department of Agrarian Reform (DAR), who came from the

NGO sector. Under his leadership the OLT programme was largely completed. Around 584,000 hectares were redistributed under the voluntary offer of sale and voluntary land transfer sections of CARL. Another important development was the acceleration of land settlement policies, which had begun during the Marcos presidency, and were expanded under CARL. It was estimated that 193,000 hectares were resettled during the Aquino presidency and a further 352,000 hectares under Ramos (Fuwa 2000: Table 2.5). Much of this resettlement took place in Mindanao; its consequences will be examined in more detail in the next section.

Implementation of the CARL legislation continued under the presidents who succeeded Ramos, although in the opinion of some commentators the political commitment declined, especially in the second Aquino administration (2010-2016), where it was argued that redistribution proceeded at a snail's pace (Tadem 2015: 3). In June 2014, there was supposed to be at least one million hectares of land still remaining to be redistributed, although some analysts contested this. Ballesteros (2019) pointed out that the budget for land acquisition and distribution declined from 0.44 per cent of GDP in 1988-1991 to only 0.15 per cent in 2010-2016, and that the Department of Agrarian Reform was forced to redirect its priority from land acquisition to the provision of support services for the 2.8 million beneficiaries of land reform. But even given the declining political support for land reform Ballesteros argued that a major achievement of the land reform programme has been to abolish the hacienda estate system in most parts of the country, with the exception of the sugar estates in Negros Occidental. After 40 years of land reform initiatives, the average holding size in the country had fallen to 1.29 hectares, and only 0.03 per cent of farms exceed 50 hectares.

But the abolition of large estates, and the consequent reduction in farm size does not appear to have led to a more dynamic and competitive agricultural sector in the Philippines. In 2010-2016, the sector only managed to grow at 1.7 per cent per annum, and contributed only a small part of the total growth in GDP of over 6 per cent per annum (Batalla 2016: 173). Can this poor performance be attributed to land redistribution, or are there other explanations? Balisacan and Fuwa (2004: 1902) analysed the processes of growth and poverty reduction in the Philippines and found that greater implementation of CARL provisions was positively related to provincial growth, although other factors were also significant. But Fabella (2014: 13) claimed that the land reform legislation 'effectively chased away private capital from agriculture with the five-hectare ownership limit'. He argued that the constraints placed on the selling or renting of land by beneficiaries had forced the land market to go underground, and created a new class of landed poor in rural areas. These criticisms were not shared by all researchers, although Ballesteros, Ancheta and Ramos (2017: 39) in their evaluation argued that 'land reform as a policy lever to address inequalities and poverty in the agricultural sector has become obsolete'. They advocated policies to improve productivity on small holdings, and suggested that government support for land consolidation and contract farming may be necessary to boost productivity on smaller farms.

Debates over the effect of land reform on rural poverty in the Philippines are likely to continue for some time. But the Philippines is not the only country in Southeast Asia which has pursued land reform policies since independence. It has frequently been argued in the literature that land reform in the Philippines has had so much policy attention because the country has a much more skewed distribution of land than other parts of Southeast Asia, and the problems of tenancy and landlessness are much worse (Balisacan, Fuwa and Debuque 2004: 234). But the empirical evidence to support these assertions is not very strong. If we examine the data on the distribution of holdings by size in Thailand, Indonesia and the Philippines for the 1980s and 1990s, we find that in 1980, well before CARL was initiated, around 51 per cent of agricultural land in the Philippines was in holdings under five hectares. This was lower than in Indonesia, but higher than in Thailand. The proportion of land in holdings over ten hectares was much higher in the Philippines than in post-reform Taiwan, but this was also true in both Indonesia and Thailand (Booth 2002b: Table 2; see also Table 6.7).

In Burma, immediately after independence, the government adopted a radical solution to problems of land tenure by nationalizing all land, and in the latter part of the 1950s the government enacted further land reform legislation. But the impact on the country's agrarian structure, and especially on the growing numbers of agricultural labourers was small. The reforms covered only 17 per cent of the targeted area, and 6 per cent of the total area (Fujita 2009: 247). The government gave priority to tenant farmers, but Steinberg (1981: 126) argued that in effect tenants just experienced a change of landlord from the private sector to the government. This did not always eliminate insecurity of tenure. By banning mortgages and tenancy, the government made it almost impossible for landless rural households to get access to land, and their numbers grew in subsequent decades. Than and Nishizawa (1990: 91) argued that the main result of government agrarian policy from 1948 to the 1980s was to replace the old landowner-tenant relationship with a new relationship between the government and owner-cultivators which strengthened government control over the agricultural sector, while not conferring any obvious benefits on land-poor farmers.

In Thailand, the government in the 1950s and 1960s also faced a series of problems in the agricultural sector. Population growth was rapid and job creation outside agriculture was limited, so much of the growing population had to be accommodated in the agricultural sector. But increasing population pressure was creating serious land shortages, especially in the central part of the country. Radical land policies such as nationalization had been advocated by Pridi Phanomyong in the 1930s but rejected by the government of the time. In 1954 a land reform act was passed, but the limit was high (eight hectares) and applied only to individuals, so families could easily get around the limit by distributing land among relations. After the student protests in Bangkok in 1973, a more reformist government took office and in 1975 a further land reform act was passed (Suehiro 1981: 318). The act tried to deal with the high levels of tenancy (41 per cent of all farm households were classified as tenant household in the central region in the mid-1970s, and 27 per cent in the northern provinces), and also with the growing problem of illegal squatting on land, which was nominally under the control of the government. Squatters in theory at least could be evicted at any time, even if they had cultivated the land for years, which was a deterrent to investment in improving land productivity. A further problem which worried the government was growing agricultural debt, which often led to loss of land.

Suehiro (1981: 341-343) in his evaluation of the 1975 legislation argued that political changes had an important impact on implementation. The Khukrit government was not as committed to land reform as was its predecessor, and it gave greater priority to the *tambon* public works programme. After the military coup of October 1976, government commitment declined even further. The more moderate Kriangsak government, which took office in 1978, was supportive of assistance to the agricultural sector, but favoured debt relief rather than land redistribution. As a result, the distribution of land in Thailand by holding size changed very little between 1978 and 1993 (Booth 2002b; Table 2). The major achievement over the 1980s and 1990s was in giving legal titles to cultivators who previously had none. The Thai government with support from the World Bank and the Australian government implemented what has been viewed as a successful policy of land titling, aimed at the northern and northeastern provinces. As much of the land to which titles were granted was controlled by the government rather than private owners, this policy ran into fewer problems than policies which involved compulsory redistribution from private owners.

In Indonesia, the Dutch colonial government had begun to worry about the problem of 'overpopulation' in Java in 1900, when the population of the island was around 30 million. They offered several solutions, including agricultural settlement outside Java, a policy which continued after independence, and will be discussed in the next section. Land redistribution in Java and other densely settled islands such as Bali and Lombok was not part of the Dutch policy agenda. But after independence, and especially during the Guided Democracy era, land reform became an important part of Sukarno's emphasis on Indonesian socialism. The Agrarian Law of 1960 was one of the few pieces of socialist legislation which was enacted in the years between 1958 and 1967. The aim was to prohibit ownership of land above stipulated maximum amounts, and absentee ownership, and to take surplus land for redistribution. The maximum amount of irrigated land which a household might own varied from five hectares in densely populated regions to 15 hectares in regions of low population density; slightly higher maximum amounts applied to non-irrigated land. The government stated that every nuclear household should have a holding of at least two hectares (Mortimer 1974: 286).

It was obvious to any informed observer that these maximum and minimum amounts were quite unrealistic, given the amount of arable land available, and the numbers in rural areas available to cultivate land, especially in the densely settled parts of the country. The minister for agriculture, who drew up the law, was reported as stating that 60 per cent of all cultivators were landless, although no definition of what this really meant was given. Senior officials appeared to assume that redistribution of land from 'large farmers' could make a significant difference (Utrecht 1969: 78). The results of the 1963 agricultural census showed that the real problem in Java, Bali, and several other provinces in Sumatra and Eastern Indonesia was that the average size of holdings was low (under one hectare) and that many rural households across the country were cultivating holdings which could not, given the prevailing yields of both food and non-food crops, give them a basic income.[2] How many households were landless in the sense that they operated no land at all was open to dispute, but what was clear was

2   The 1963 agricultural census was the first such census to be carried out in Indonesia, and it was implemented at a time of considerable tensions in rural areas in many parts of the country. There seems to be little doubt that the total amount of land under cultivation in various parts of the country was under-reported. In Java, the agricultural census found that 5.64 million hectares were under cultivation, compared with 8.42 million hectares reported by the Central Bureau of Statistics (Nugroho 1967: 235-237). The 1963 census excluded land in holdings under 0.1 hectares, but this is unlikely to explain the difference. On the other hand, the land area reported by the CBS was based on pre-1942 data, which might not have been accurate in the post-independence period.

that many millions of farm households controlled less than two hectares, and there simply was not enough land above the maximum limits stated in the law to give every household the minimum amount. Some government ministers suggested that the problem could be solved by moving people from Java to less densely settled provinces, but in the two decades after 1950 the numbers moved were small, and it seemed clear that migration could not solve the basic problem of too many people and not enough land, not just in Java but in other parts of the country as well.

There were other problems, including protecting the rights of squatters on land controlled by large estates, which the 1960 legislation did not really address. Figures from the 1963 estates census showed that large estates controlled 1.59 million hectares in 1962, of which almost 237,000 hectares was 'not in their possession', which implied that it was controlled by squatters (Nugroho 1967: 262). The Indonesian Communist Party pressed the government to grant these people secure title. It also advocated lower maximum ceilings, the nationalization of those foreign estates which had not already been converted to state enterprises in the late 1950s and the abolition of grants of land to village officials in lieu of salary (Mortimer 1974: 287-288). It used these demands to gain popular support, especially in Java, but it did not have enough votes in parliament to make radical changes to the legislation. Mortimer argued that in the years from 1961 to 1965, the party was playing consensus politics, demonstrating its moderation and loyalty to President Sukarno. It did not want to further rock what was already a very unstable boat.

After the failed coup of 30 September 1965, the army and Muslim youth groups set out to destroy the Communist Party and their supporters through killings and imprisonment. This slowed down the redistribution of land, and some land which had already been redistributed appears to have been taken back by the previous owners or passed to third parties. But the redistribution programme did continue through 1968; by the end of that year Utrecht (1969: 87) estimated that around one million hectares had been reallocated to one million households. Some of this land was probably former estate land, and also land which had been owned by people killed in 1965/66. Exactly who the beneficiaries were has never been clarified but to the extent that they were households farming very small holdings, they would have received some boost to their income from the extra land even if it was of poor quality. But the government of President Suharto showed little enthusiasm for continuing land redistribution. Instead, it was much more interested in a massive increase in government-sponsored migration from Java and Bali to other parts of the country. The results of this policy are examined in the next section.

The history of land reform in Vietnam is very different from other parts of Southeast Asia, partly because of the colonial legacy, and partly because of the course of Vietnamese history after 1945. Data on landownership and land tenure were considered sparse and unreliable until the 1930s, when a detailed report on landownership was published by the colonial Agricultural Department under the direction of Yves Henry. The economic geographer Pierre Gourou also undertook major surveys in various parts of the country (Murray 1980: 396-397). Their work has been used by most subsequent scholars. In Tonkin, the data collected by Henry showed that the great majority of rural households (over 90 per cent) possessed less than five mau (1.8 hectares), and over 60 per cent were farming less than one mau (0.36 hectares). On the other hand, a very small group of large landowners (less than 0.1 per cent of the total) owned about 17 per cent of the total land in Tonkin. A further set of data from 1941 found that 66 per cent of cultivators were farming holdings under 0.36 hectares, while 0.9 per cent controlled holdings over five hectares. López Jerez (2014: 129-135) argued that those landowners controlling more than five hectares probably rented out the land in smaller parcels. The government of Tonkin found that there were 17.7 million parcels of land in 1941, so on average a cultivator could be cultivating up to ten parcels.

In Cochinchina, where the amount of cultivated land had been expanding rapidly since the nineteenth century, it was estimated that around one-quarter of all landowners owned between 5 and 50 hectares, and 2.5 per cent owned in excess of 50 hectares. This small group owned around 45 per cent of all the land in Cochinchina. Many were absentee landlords who rented out the land and lived in urban areas (Wiegersma 1988: 77). In some parts of the Mekong Delta around 45 per cent of the land area was in holdings over 50 hectares, according to the figures compiled by Henry, and cited in López Jerez (2014: Table 4.3). López Jerez also found evidence that between 1930 and 1936, the middle class of landowners in Cochinchina lost land to the larger landowners controlling over 50 hectares.

After 1945, as the Viet Minh gained greater political control over much of the country, agricultural development was given high priority, but land redistribution was not at first accorded much attention. But by 1949, the Viet Minh realized that the skewed landownership was a matter of great concern to many Vietnamese, including those who were fighting against the French. In 1953, the Land to the Tiller (LTT) policy was adopted. Wiegersma (1988: 110) argued that this policy was designed to show the soldiers fighting the French that they could expect grants of land when the French were finally driven from the country. But after the French were defeated, the Geneva

Accords partitioned the country and only the northern part was controlled by the Workers' Party. After the fifth plenum in March 1955, the decision was made to accelerate land reform by destroying the landlord class. As Chinese influence became more pronounced, radical cadres pressed for the establishment of collective agriculture, but the Maoist model was never fully implemented, and the peasant family economy continued in many, if not all rural areas. In the decade from 1955 to 1965, this model was successful in raising production of food staples, mainly through the construction of small-scale water control projects (Wiegersma 1988: 149-151).

In the south, the Diem government was not supportive of land redistribution policies, and even more moderate LTT programmes were opposed. Although the government of France handed over 230,000 hectares of land formerly owned by French citizens to the Diem regime, most remained under the control of local officials who profited from the rental incomes. Putzel (1992: 100) claimed that the American advisers who wanted the Diem government to pursue a Taiwan-style reform policy became very disillusioned. Diem was killed in 1963, but little progress was made with land reform in the south until President Thieu signed a LTT law in 1970. The law was the result of American pressure, and was modelled on Taiwan and Korean experience, but by the time it was passed large parts of the south were effectively controlled by the National Liberation Front. Even in areas nominally under the control of the Saigon government the LTT programme was seen as favouring better-off farmers and offering few benefits to smaller cultivators, let alone landless labourers.

After reunification in 1975, the victorious Communist government quickly realized that it would be difficult to impose the northern system (semi-collectivization) on the south. They encouraged cooperatives but by the early 1980s the country faced severe food shortages. Prices of staples were controlled, but black markets emerged, and popular unrest mounted with what was seen as the inefficiencies of the socialist system. As liberal reformers gained more power in the planning system and in the party itself, the scene was set for the major reforms of the Doi Moi era. In 1988 a new land law was passed which granted individual long-term use rights over land to cultivators who had formerly been members of cooperatives or collectives. This law did not permit voluntary re-contracting of cultivation rights and land sales were still banned. Debates raged about whether Vietnam should move towards a free market in land-use rights, or whether the system of controls should continue, including the periodic reallocation of land by the cooperative or the collective. By 1993 the debate was resolved in favour of those who advocated the market model. The Land Law of that year went some way towards establishing free markets in land use across the country (Ravallion and Van de Walle 2008: 25-26).

There has been considerable controversy over the impact of these reforms which went further than the Chinese reforms in freeing up land markets. On the plus side, many rural households appear to have used the money they have gained from selling or leasing the land they were allocated before 1988 to diversify into non-agricultural activities, such as trade and transport. Some have tried their luck in urban areas, seeking wage employment in the manufacturing sector. Inevitably there have been some whose diversification strategies failed, and they have found themselves without the assets necessary to obtain the credit which could help them find other sources of income. Ravallion and Van de Walle (2008: 172) argued that 'the landless poor are not being well served by the market and non-market institutions that have emerged in Vietnam's agrarian transition'. This neglect was a problem on both efficiency and equity grounds. Given the evidence of growing inequalities in household incomes, at least until 2010, it could be argued that Vietnam still faced a need for targeted programmes which addressed the particular needs of those who found themselves without assets in the brave new world of market capitalism.

Land Settlement Policies

Land settlement programmes have figured prominently in the poverty alleviation strategies of several Southeast Asian governments since the colonial era, and have sometimes been viewed as an alternative to land reform. In Indonesia, the policy of moving people from overcrowded to underpopulated islands was initiated in the colonial era. After independence, the policy was revived, and was used by the Sukarno government to justify pro-natalist policies. It was argued that if there really was a problem of overpopulation in Java, Bali, and some islands to the east, then it could easily be dealt with by moving people to the supposedly empty lands outside the densely settled core of the country. In fact, it appears that between 1950 and 1968, around 416,000 people were moved, the great majority to Sumatra (Suratman and Guinness 1977: 83). While this was more than the numbers moved in the colonial era, it was insufficient to make much impact on population growth in Java, bearing in mind that there was also considerable in-migration to Java in the early post-independence years. The 1961 population census showed that the proportion of the total population in Java had changed little since 1930.

The New Order government of President Suharto, once it had abandoned the land reform policies of the early 1960s, embarked on an expanded programme of subsidized migration from Java and Bali to other parts of the archipelago. The motives of the government were mixed; on the one hand, some economic planners did genuinely believe that migration from Java would ease the pressure on resources in that island and also help to develop the areas to which they were sent. On the other hand, there were those, especially in the military, who thought that the movement of Javanese to other parts of the archipelago would mitigate the separatist tendencies which had emerged in the decade from 1955 to 1965, and create a national identity which supported Javanese hegemony.

During the first five-year plan of the New Order (1969-1974), the total number of families moved amounted to around 40,000, a modest figure when set against the increase in the population of Java over these years. In addition, there was rapid growth in the population of the islands outside Java, which was leading to greater pressure on land in Sumatra, Kalimantan and Sulawesi, the three islands which were expected to receive most migrants. The second five-year plan (1974-1979) proposed a target of 250,000 families, although government figures indicated that only about 20 per cent of the target was achieved (Table 8.1). There were several reasons for this result. First, accelerated growth in Java as revenues from the oil boom fed into the domestic economy created new employment opportunities even for those with few skills. In addition, the cities in Java continued to be a magnet for young people looking for advanced education and professional, technical and managerial jobs. But even allowing for the tug of Java, net out-migration did increase over the 1970s: in 1971, the census of that year showed that net outward migration was almost one million, while in 1980 it had increased to 2.35 million (Hugo et al. 1987: 178).

Table 8.1:   **Transmigration in Indonesia: targets and actual movement (numbers of persons)**

Years	Target	Moved with assistance	Moved without assistance
1969/74	38,141	39,436	n/a
1974/79	250,000	55,083	7,281
1979/84	500,000	365,977	169,497
1984/89	750,000	228,422	521,728
1989/94	550,000	94,864	152,136
1994/98	n/a	122,316	193,579

Sources: Department of Information (1993: Table XII-16), Department of Information (1994: Table XII-16), Department of Information (1998: Table IX-35).

In spite of the relatively poor performance of the transmigration programme in meeting plan targets in the decade from 1969 to 1979, many influential policymakers in the government continued to support subsidized movement of people from Java to other islands in the archipelago. The third development plan of the Suharto era (1979-1984) doubled the target of families to be moved from 250,000 to 500,000. An important reason for setting this increased target was that the World Bank had committed substantial funding to the programme; between 1976 and 1985, loans to transmigration projects totalled almost $600 million. An estimated 163,550 hectares of land was cleared (Fearnside 1997: Table 2). Official figures show that almost 366,000 family heads did move under the official programme. In addition, almost 170,000 moved as voluntary migrants (Table 8.1). It is probable that many of these voluntary migrants were friends or family of those who moved officially.

The fourth five-year plan (1984-1989) contained an even more ambitious target of 750,000 families although in the event the government only managed to move 228,422 families through the official programme. The target was 'achieved' through the somewhat dubious procedure of counting in almost 520,000 unofficial migrants who had, according to the government, moved of their own accord. One reason for the fall in families moved under the official programme after 1984 was the contraction in the government development budget, necessitated by the oil price fall and the sharp increase in government debt-service obligations. But the transmigration programme suffered a much larger cut than most other sectors in the development budget over the fourth plan (Asher and Booth 1992: 60). This reflected growing disenchantment with the whole policy in many parts of the Indonesian bureaucracy, as well as in the international development community.

The reasons for this disenchantment were several. First, it was becoming increasingly obvious that there were not abundant supplies of 'empty' land suitable for agriculture in Sumatra, Kalimantan and Sulawesi. Much of the land onto which settlers were moved was of poor quality and food crop yields were low and erratic. The World Bank acknowledged that in many sites food crop production was inadequate to meet even subsistence needs and advocated increased emphasis on tree crops to support viable farm enterprises (World Bank 1988: 128). In fact, it appeared that many migrants were earning a considerable part of their income from wage employment. To the extent that this wage employment was dependent on short-term site development, what would happen when this was terminated? A second problem concerned the environmental impact of large-scale clearing of forest and swamp land for agricultural settlement. Little consideration was paid to the environmental consequences of the programme until a vociferous international campaign was launched, which forced the Indonesian government to give the problem greater attention. A third problem concerned the relationship between the mainly Javanese migrants and the indigenous inhabitants. This was especially sensitive in Irian Jaya where the transmigration programme exacerbated existing conflict between indigenous separatist movements and the central government. But tensions were also growing between migrants and the local population in parts of Kalimantan and Sulawesi as well, and these erupted into violent conflict over the 1990s.

Behind all these problems was the increasing awareness that the alleged 'overpopulation' of rural Java which had given rise to the whole preoccupation with moving people away from Java, both in colonial times and since independence, was no longer such a pressing concern. Although population densities in Java and Bali continued to be much higher than in other parts of the country, by the early 1990s many rural people were obtaining an increasing proportion of their incomes from off-farm activities. The 1993 agricultural census showed that in that year almost half of total farm household incomes were derived from off-holding sources (Booth 2002a: Table 3). The rapid growth in food crop production in Java combined with the growth in the manufacturing, construction, transport and trade sectors led to increased employment opportunities for both men and women in a range of activities. Some rural people relocated to urban areas to take advantage of new employment opportunities while others commuted on a daily, weekly or monthly basis. Still others found that their rural homes were fast becoming part of spreading urban areas, which offered new employment opportunities to people without having to move. The increased migration combined with urban growth and falling fertility in Java and Bali had led to a marked slowdown in rural population growth; indeed, the results of the 1990 population census indicated that the rural population in many parts of Central and East Java and Bali was scarcely growing at all. Some argued that the slowing population growth combined with rising incomes indicated that over time a smaller proportion of the rural poor would be located in Java and a rising proportion in other parts of the country, especially in Eastern Indonesia.

Given such developments, it was increasingly argued that, even before the crisis of 1997/98, moving people from Java and Bali to other parts of the archipelago was no longer a sensible poverty alleviation strategy for the sending regions, and could lead to serious problems in the receiving areas. While it was probably true that the movement of substantial numbers of poor people from Central Java and parts of East Java to the Outer Islands in the early 1980s did contribute to a fall in poverty in the sending regions, it was less clear what impact the migrants were having on the economies of the receiving provinces. On the basis of surveys carried out in the early and mid-1980s, the World Bank argued that most migrants improved their incomes and living standards as a result of their move (World Bank 1988: 18ff.). But at the same time these surveys also showed that transmigrant households were crucially dependent on off-farm earnings for much of their income. If their farms could be made viable, or if off-farm employment could be found in the local area, they would stay where they were, but otherwise it was argued that many would return to Java, move on to other parts of the country, or go abroad. As a result of doubts about the economic viability of many of the projects, and in the face of mounting criticism from environmental groups, the World Bank withdrew from funding new projects. Around $220 million was disbursed over the 1990s in the 'second stage' transmigration programme which, as critics pointed out, mainly comprised attempts to remedy problems in the design and implementation of earlier projects (Adhiati and Bobsien 2001).

The transmigration programme was always viewed as integral to the Suharto vision of Indonesia's economic and political development, and when he resigned in May 1998, it rapidly became clear that focus of the government policy would shift away from government-financed land settlement projects. The fiscal constraints imposed after the 1997/98 crisis meant that financing for development projects through the budget was very limited. In addition, the decentralization reforms introduced by President Habibie empowered the district governments in the receiving regions, and made them less willing to cooperate with projects 'dropped' from the centre, which they did not view as being in their interests. The unrest in several provinces outside Java in the latter part of the 1990s led to large numbers of internally displaced people. As the government struggled to cope with the refugee problem, there was a tendency both within the government and in the NGO community to blame population movement for many of the economic and social problems in parts of Kalimantan, Sulawesi, Maluku and Papua. Stopping government-sponsored land settlement would not prevent movement of people around Indonesia in search of better economic opportunities, but those who moved would not be the responsibility of the central government.

As fiscal constraints were gradually eased, and as government concern about food imports grew during the Yudhoyono presidency, it seemed that the central government might once again finance land development projects outside Java. But there were continuing controversies about what projects were likely to be viable. There were increasing worries about the development of peatlands in Sumatra and Kalimantan for both palm oil and other crops; these worries appeared to be justified when serious fires erupted in the dry season in 2015. That there is still land of agricultural potential outside Java seems clear; the debate is over what crops are likely to be most profitable for farmers, and least damaging to regional ecologies, which in many parts of Indonesia are still poorly understood. Some have argued that the appropriate strategy would be to focus on tree crops, and to rely more on imports of staple foods. Others queried the role of large estates, especially in the palm oil sector. Many were controlled by companies outside Indonesia.

Inevitably because of its size, and the controversies which it has aroused, the Indonesian transmigration programme has dominated the literature on land settlement in Southeast Asia. But other governments have also implemented similar programmes. After the introduction of the New Economic Policy (NEP) in 1970, the Malaysian government invested heavily in land development as a means of rural poverty alleviation. The main vehicle was the Federal Land Development Authority (FELDA), which had in fact been established in 1956, and was intended to assist those rural Malays who were poor because they did not have enough land through resettlement on new land. The FELDA schemes were mainly confined to peninsular Malaysia, but there were also a number of other land development schemes at both state and federal level. Between 1971 and 1980 FELDA succeeded in opening up some 373,705 hectares, and settling some 42,000 families, while other federal and state programmes brought the total to 866,000 hectares (Osman-Rani 1987: 284). Although the pace of land development slowed somewhat in the 1980s, FELDA was still targeted to develop some 175,000 hectares between 1986 and 1990; total resettlement schemes, including state and joint-venture projects were targeted to cover 287,000 hectares (Government of Malaysia 1989: 141).

But as in Indonesia, the impact of both FELDA and other land settlement schemes on rural poverty alleviation was controversial. There was little doubt that the great majority of the settlers chosen were poor, unskilled rural Malays with no access to land of their own, and that their incomes increased as a result of participation in the FELDA scheme. MacAndrews (1977: 196) quoted several studies which concluded that the scheme benefited between 15 and 20 per cent of the country's poor – which seemed a reasonable achievement. However, many of the schemes were expensive to develop and critics argued that greater numbers of the rural poor would have benefited from alternative uses of the funds. In addition, as Jomo (1990: 100) argued, much of the land development was carried out by large contractors, often close to the ruling party, who made substantial profits. The policy of concentrating on only two crops, rubber and palm oil, was also criticized, as this made the incomes of settlers very vulnerable to fluctuations in their prices. In addition, observers pointed to the possibly adverse demographic impact of the FELDA and other schemes on both the sending and the receiving areas. The sending areas lost many of their most productive workers, while the newly settled areas had large numbers of households, both indigenous and migrant, at the same stage in their life cycles. They would eventually face a problem of aging populations and young people in their turn leaving the FELDA sites for urban areas or other resettlement sites (Osman-Rani 1987: 288-289). If the younger generation stayed, the original holdings might have to be sub-divided into uneconomic units.

By the 1990s, it was considered that the programme of land settlement had largely achieved its purpose, and no new land was allocated. FELDA itself diversified into a range of businesses. FELDA Global Ventures Holdings was established as a private venture, and has become one of the largest plantation operators in the world. Less is known about the other land development projects in Malaysia, although King (1986) examined various schemes in Sarawak. He concluded that 'given the financial resources, time, energy and personnel devoted to these schemes, the yield has not been very great'. He argued that the schemes had been very expensive relative to the numbers of settlers involved, and failed to provide a solution to the long-term poverty problems in Sarawak, which were due to poor soils, primitive technologies, inappropriate cropping practices and poor infrastructure rather than landlessness as such. He concluded that, especially in the interior of the state, the goal of poverty reduction would be better achieved by spending the available funds on improving existing farming practices, rather than embarking on ambitious land development programmes which the state government did not have the capacity to implement. This argument was also relevant to the problems of Indonesia's Outer Islands, especially those provinces where poverty incidence has in recent years been as high or even higher than in parts of Java. Rather than developing new land in marginal areas, the need was, and continues to be, to improve agricultural technologies and infrastructure in existing settlements and thus increase incomes and improve the living standards of both indigenous populations and those migrants who are already in place.

In Vietnam, land settlement policies were also pursued with considerable vigour in the years after reunification. There appeared to be at least four objectives behind Vietnamese population redistribution policies adopted at that time (Desbarats 1987). One was the need to boost food production and provide employment. A second was the perception, which had persisted since the colonial era, that population must be moved away from the densely populated Red River Delta region in the north. A third was the desire to move people out of the cities in the south, into which many thousands of rural people had fled during the war. After reunification, urban employment opportunities were limited, and there was official fear that urban unemployment would lead to political unrest. A fourth objective was the strategic one of populating the border regions close to Cambodia, Laos and China. These objectives were translated into a set of targets for population movement in the second and third plans of five million people.

As was the case in both Indonesia and Malaysia, the Vietnamese government had considerable difficulty in achieving these targets. Desbarats (1987: 61) quoted official statements to the effect that 2.4 million were resettled between 1975 and 1984, although there was considerable return migration, especially from the New Economic Zones. Many of these were prepared in haste and turned out to be quite unsuited to intensive food crop agriculture. The combination of return migration from the New Economic Zones and accelerated migration to towns and cities in the north in the 1980s frustrated official targets for reducing urban populations. The 1989 population census indicated that the urban population was growing at around 3 per cent per annum, compared with 2.3 per cent for the population as a whole. As in other parts of Asia, the Vietnamese authorities were by the mid-1980s forced to concede that the goal of accelerated agricultural production could be better achieved by improving agricultural technologies and cultivation practices on existing farms, rather than through ambitious and costly land settlement schemes, whose results were often disappointing. This change of thought ushered in the market reforms of the late 1980s and early 1990s.

In the Philippines, the data assembled by Fuwa (2000: Table 2.5) indicated that over the Aquino and Marcos presidencies, around 546,000 hectares of land was devoted to 'resettlement projects'. In fact, resettlement projects have a long history going back to the American era; even before the presidency of Quezon in the latter part of the 1930s, land settlement in Mindanao had been seen as a solution to the problem of landlessness in Luzon and Cebu (Spencer 1952: 142-149; Paderanga 1987: 10-12; Fuwa 2000: 4). The thinking of the American, Commonwealth and post-1946 governments in the Philippines was not dissimilar to that in both Indonesia and Malaysia. Given that population densities varied considerably in different parts of the country, and that land tenure disputes were becoming more violent in the densely settled regions, surely the obvious solution was to move people to those parts of the country where land of arable potential was still available?

Paderanga (1987: Table 6) estimated that 52,728 households were moved under the auspices of the land settlement projects administered by the Ministry of Agrarian Reform between 1950 and 1976; they were allocated a total of 737,000 hectares. This was a lower total than the 127,000 families who were moved in Indonesia between 1950 and 1974, although the Indonesian families were given, on average, less land.

The official figure cited by Paderanga refers only to those who moved with assistance, although (as in Indonesia), it appears that many people moved on a voluntary basis, often following family and friends. Where did these families move to? Increasingly, the destination was the island of Mindanao. By the 1970s, there was growing evidence that land settlement by mainly Christian people from other parts of the country was causing tensions with the local Muslim population in Mindanao (Abaya-Ulindang 2015). The region of Mindanao-Sulu experienced faster population growth than the country as a whole over the twentieth century; total population was around one million in 1918, increasing to 14.1 million in 1990 (Costello 1992: Table 3.1). This rapid growth had inevitable environmental consequences, including the destruction of much of the upland forest. Repeated attempts by successive administrations from Marcos to the present have failed to solve the religious and demographic problems and violence remains a fact of life for much of the population.

Employment Creation through Labour-Intensive Public Works

Labour-intensive public works programmes began to be implemented in several countries in both South and Southeast Asia in the 1960s. Their fundamental rationale was that the demand for labour in many parts of rural Asia was very seasonal, and that for some months of each year, there were considerable numbers in rural areas who were able and willing to work, but could not find employment within a reasonable distance of their home. Some were able to migrate to where work was available, usually in larger towns and cities, but many could not move because of family responsibilities or other constraints. The purpose of rural public works programmes was to provide work for such people in the agricultural slack season, with a focus on constructing or repairing infrastructure such as irrigation works, roads, bridges, grain silos etc. To the greatest extent possible, it was argued that the planning and implementation of such projects should be decentralized, so that regional and local governments who supposedly understood the needs of a particular region, could decide what sorts of projects should be constructed.

In Indonesia, a rural public works programme was initiated in 1970, as one of the initiatives adopted by the Suharto government to address what was then seen as a serious problem of rural underemployment. Although the funds were disbursed from the central government budget, the responsibility for selecting and implementing projects was delegated to the district (*kabupaten* and *kota*) governments. This was the level of government immediately below the province, and in Java the average population approached one million in 1971. Although this level of government had its own technical and administrative staff, operated its own budget and had some autonomous sources of finance, its capacity to implement projects in the field of infrastructure rehabilitation and extension was severely constrained by lack of funds. The programme of government grants to districts (which became known as the Inpres programme) was designed to alleviate this financial constraint. The subsidy was disbursed on a per capita basis, and its use was limited to infrastructure projects which were to be implemented using labour-intensive techniques. The programme achieved considerable initial success, and at the beginning of the second plan of the Suharto era (1974-1979) Inpres grants were also given to the provincial governments although the disbursement criteria were somewhat different (Van Leeuwen 1975). A further innovation was to allocate regional development subsidies for specific purposes, such as the construction of primary schools, rural health clinics and village markets as well as reafforestation.

The various Inpres allocations allowed regional governments (provinces, *kabupaten* and villages) throughout the archipelago to rehabilitate and extend physical infrastructure, and build primary schools and health clinics in areas where none had existed before. Improved infrastructure in turn meant better access to markets and allowed previously isolated rural populations to link up with the growing national economy. The Inpres grants were thus one element in the government's success in reducing rural poverty in the years from 1976 onwards. By 1981 the various regional grants accounted for 16 per cent of development expenditures and 2 per cent of GDP (Asher and Booth 1992: 68). But their importance diminished through the 1980s relative to total government expenditures and relative to GDP. This was mainly because most government development expenditures were squeezed during the decade, as oil revenues contracted, and the rupiah value of government debt service obligations grew. Some observers argued that the reduction in Inpres expenditures would have a more direct and severe impact on rural welfare, because they were targeted to rural areas and to labour-intensive projects.

In practice, it was difficult to assess the full impact of Inpres expenditures on the alleviation of rural poverty in Indonesia. Evidence on their direct employment generation effects were only available for the Inpres grants to the *kapupaten* and *kota*. The number of 'jobs' of 100 days each grew from around 200,000 in 1970/71 to over one million in 1975/76 (Asher and Booth 1992: 69). It was estimated in the early years that wage payments comprised 60 per cent of total programme expenses (Patten, Dapice and Falcon 1980: 169). Employment generation reached its peak in 1975/76, and declined thereafter, so that by the latter part of the 1980s only about 500,000 to 600,000 jobs were available, even though in real terms expenditures continued to increase until the early 1980s. After the mid-1970s there was a switch in the type of project selected away from irrigation works and towards roads and bridges, which utilized less labour per rupiah of expenditure. Of course, the indirect impact of building roads and bridges on rural incomes and employment may have been considerable, but such indirect effects were more difficult to assess. What was clear from an examination of Inpres allocations by province was that there was a tendency from the 1980s onwards for the smaller, less densely settled provinces to receive higher Inpres grants, both in per capita terms and relative to provincial GDP. By the early 1990s, many of the grants were skewed to regions outside Java; certainly there was no 'Java bias' in their allocation (Booth 2014a: 37).

Other labour-intensive public works implemented in the 1970s included the Padat Karya programme, which was revived in 1997, as one of the social safety net programmes implemented in the wake of the 1997/98 crisis. An evaluation of these labour-intensive public works programmes claimed that they were 'hastily developed by sectoral or line ministries to absorb recently retrenched workers, especially in rural areas' (Perdana and Maxwell 2005: 101). Some observers thought that the main reason for these programmes was that the relevant ministries wanted to capture a share of the budget allocations for emergency relief projects. Many of the projects were criticized for poor results; while the aim of the projects may have been to provide some employment for those desperate for some work and income, in practice the rules were often flouted and the supervision lax. Targeting was weak. One study found that 70 per cent of those who participated in the Padat Karya activities were from non-poor households. Most were young men, as the work was physically quite demanding. Older men and women could not participate.

With the introduction of the sweeping decentralization reforms implemented after Suharto left office, the Inpres grants were abolished, and instead districts received several new grants from the centre, and were given more discretion about how to use these grants. Critics of the labour-intensive works programmes pointed out that, by 2001, the unemployed, and especially young people seeking work for the first time, did not see their future as unskilled workers, sitting by the side of the road breaking up stones, or doing other forms of manual labour. They wanted work which would lead to permanent jobs, with secure career prospects. The challenge for governments at all levels was to implement policies which would expand employment opportunities, especially for young, first-time job seekers graduating from the school and college system.

Another country in Southeast Asia which devoted considerable budgetary resources to rural employment generation schemes was Thailand. In the 1960s, the Thai Ministry of the Interior began to rationalize local government and improve the calibre of the personnel. By the mid-1970s, after a more democratic government came to power, it was decided that a sub-provincial level of government (*tambon*) had the capacity to implement labour-intensive public works. In 1974/75 the Tambon Development Programme was initiated with funding of 2.5 billion baht (about 0.8 per cent of 1975 GDP).[3] This money was spread among 5,027 rural *tambons*. In 1975/76 funding was increased to 3.5 billion baht (Poot 1979: 16-19). These funds came from the central government budget, and were to be used for labour-intensive infrastructure projects, especially irrigation works, roads and bridges, in the agricultural slack season. It was estimated that between 45 and 50 per cent of total disbursements were spent on wage payments, and some 56 million person-days of employment were created. The average wage paid was quite high in comparison to that paid in alternative jobs, and there was little difficulty in procuring labour (Poot 1979: 58). Most of the projects were either roads or irrigation works, and although simple construction techniques were used there were problems of quality control, so that roads constructed in one dry season were in need of repair again by the next year.

The Tambon Development Programme was suspended after the military coup in 1976, although in 1978 a programme of public works was initiated as a drought relief measure. In 1980, the Rural Job Creation Programme (RJCP) was implemented along the same lines as the Tambon Development Programme (Krongkaew 1987: 238-239). In 1980, 3.5 billion baht was allocated to the RJCP, about the same amount in nominal terms as was allocated to the Tambon Development Programme five years earlier, although in real terms and as a proportion of GDP the allocation was lower. Throughout

3   The *tambon* is a unit of local government below the province.

the 1980s the budgetary allocation fell in nominal terms and relative to GDP so that by 1989 the total allocation was 2.35 billion baht or only 0.1 per cent of GDP. There was also a sustained drop in the number of projects implemented, and in the number of workers employed. Whereas in 1980 an estimated 3.75 million workers were given employment, by 1989 only 415,450 were employed (Krongkaew 1990: Table 6). Some argued that this decline was caused by declining demand for off-season employment in rural areas as a result of increased migration to urban areas, and especially to Bangkok. While it was true that employment opportunities in Bangkok and surrounding areas had expanded rapidly over the 1980s, the evidence from the labour force surveys indicated that there were still significant numbers of men and women in rural areas who reported themselves as 'unemployed and available for work' in the late 1980s. In 1988 over 1.2 million were enumerated in this category in the slack season.

Several commentators pointed to the apparent mismatch between allocations of RJCP funds and levels of income and poverty by region. In his evaluation of the original *tambon* programmes, Poot (1979: 19) showed that the northeast, the poorest region in the country, received the least funds in per capita terms, while the central region, the richest after metropolitan Bangkok, received the most. Jitsuchon (1990: 54) found that this disparity continued with the RJCP programme after 1980, and in 1985 the average additional income per head received as a result of the RJCP was over 2,000 baht in the central region, where poverty incidence was least, and only 870 baht in the northeast where the majority of the rural poor were concentrated. This indicated a failure to target funds to the regions where the incidence of poverty was most severe. Furthermore, Krongkaew (1987: Table 3) showed that the ratio of wage to non-wage expenditures in all parts of the country fell sharply after 1980, and by 1984 wage payments accounted for only 32 per cent of total expenditures. This change in the focus of the programme from labour-intensive public works to more capital-intensive infrastructure projects was a response to public criticism about the poor quality of the infrastructure built by labour-intensive means. Inevitably, as less labour was hired, and contractors looked for skilled rather than unskilled labour, the impact of the RJCP on rural poverty was reduced (Krongkaew 1987: 250-257).

Under the Marcos regime, the Philippines did not place much emphasis on mobilizing underutilized rural labour for labour-intensive public works. With the advent of the Aquino administration in 1986, the Community Employment and Development Program (CEDP) was initiated. The CEDP was part of the government's 'short-term development strategy of stimulating recovery by inducing demand through increased incomes', especially in rural areas (Mangahas 1987b: 170). As such, the programme was expected to be discontinued at the end of 1987. The budgetary allocation for the second half of 1986 was 3.93 billion pesos, or about 0.6 per cent of GDP in that year. The aim was to create one million jobs of 60 days' duration. About two-thirds of the funds were under the control of the Ministry of Public Works and Highways to be used for feeder roads, schools and irrigation works. The rest were controlled by a variety of ministries and agencies including agriculture, agrarian reform and natural resources. An important feature of the programme was the involvement of non-governmental organizations in the monitoring of the projects. But in spite of the NGO involvement, the CEDP was subject to delays and it is not clear what proportion of the allocated funds were finally spent.

To sum up, the various labour-intensive public works programmes which were implemented in Indonesia, Thailand and the Philippines did play a useful role in generating employment and income in the agricultural slack season. But over the 1980s funding in both Thailand and Indonesia for these programmes was reduced in real terms, and more capital-intensive construction techniques were used. As a result, numbers employed fell, although it was not obvious that problems of rural unemployment and poverty in these countries had been solved. One problem with both the Thai RJCP and the Indonesian Inpres programmes was that neither was targeted towards the regions, and the people within those regions, where the problems of poverty and seasonal unemployment were most acute. In addition, as labour markets tightened over the 1980s, rural public works were increasingly viewed by government officials as irrelevant to the employment problems facing economies where pools of rural surplus labour were drying up, and where young people in particular wanted jobs which gave them skills which could then be used to secure more permanent employment in other parts of the economy.

Controlling Food Prices

By the 1980s, the proportion of the labour force employed in agriculture was falling in several countries in Southeast Asia, and the incomes of many rural households were becoming more diverse. In Thailand, it was estimated that almost 60 per cent of farm household income was derived from off-farm sources in 1982/83, which was almost as high as in Taiwan in 1980. The proportion for the Philippines was estimated to be 56 per cent in 1985, and 50 per cent in Indonesia in 1984 (Booth 2002b: Table 4). Given these trends, which accelerated over the 1990s, the focus of government policy in all three countries shifted from programmes specifically targeted to the agriculture sector to economy-wide measures. These included policies to stabilize food prices, and attempts to make government expenditures more pro-poor through cash transfers. In addition, several governments implemented fertility control policies and also began to experiment with various types of decentralization policies which were designed to give local communities more say in framing projects. In the remaining part of this chapter, the results of these policies are evaluated.

For well over a century, the countries of Southeast Asia have been divided into net foodgrain exporters and importers. Rice has been the key staple across the region, although corn, sweet potato and cassava have been widely consumed for many decades, and in recent years consumption of wheat-based foods has been growing rapidly. Some countries have switched from importing to exporting rice in particular years, but broadly speaking Thailand has always been the largest exporter, while Vietnam, Myanmar and Cambodia have all re-emerged as significant exporters since the early 1990s, as they were in the pre-1940 era. In 2016/17, these four countries exported over 20 million tons of rice, or about 45 per cent of global exports. The Philippines, Malaysia and Singapore are net importers while Indonesia has swung from being a large importer in the 1970s to a small exporter in the 1980s, and once again an importer in the 1990s and 2000s. Recent governments have pledged to achieve 'self-sufficiency' in rice, although imports have been permitted in years when dry weather affected domestic production. In 2018, imports exceeded two million tons. The Southeast Asian countries have also emerged as significant importers of wheat in recent years; Indonesia is now one of the top three wheat importers in the world. In 2016/17 wheat imports into Indonesia, the Philippines and Thailand and Vietnam amounted to 25.1 million tons, or 14 per cent of global imports (USDA 2018: 21). Southeast Asia as a region is also a net importer of corn and soybeans.

By the early twenty-first century, it had become clear that, with growing incomes and rapid urbanization, food consumption patterns were changing rapidly across Southeast Asia. Government responses to these changes have varied. Because rice has been the main staple, it has tended to be the focus of government intervention, but government policies have varied over time according to world market conditions, and fluctuations in domestic production and consumption. The proportion of total world rice production which is marketed internationally has always been quite small, and world market prices have been subject to considerable volatility. In both Indonesia and the Philippines, government agencies have been charged with regulating domestic markets to ensure 'remunerative' prices for farmers while at the same time keeping retail prices reasonably stable. In Indonesia, the National Logistics Board (Bulog) was given a monopoly over imports in the Suharto years, and did manage to keep domestic prices more stable than world prices for the years from 1969 to 1994 (Timmer 1996). Given the importance of rice in the Indonesian diet, and in household budgets over these years, this was a significant achievement. But after Suharto left office, the role of Bulog attracted considerable criticism, for reasons which will be discussed below.

In the Philippines, the National Food Authority (NFA) has been the key government agency charged with rice price policy and with food security. As with Bulog, its function is to ensure remunerative prices for farmers while at the same time stabilizing domestic wholesale and retail prices and protecting consumers from the volatility of world rice markets and also from fluctuations in domestic production due to climatic and other factors. Between 1990 and 2008, it achieved some success in stabilizing real prices of rice at the farm gate and in wholesale and retail markets (Intal, Cu and Illescas 2012: Table 1). But in most years from 1990 to 2002 domestic price stability was achieved at the cost of high nominal rates of protection. The wholesale price of rice within the Philippines was usually between twice and three times as high as the ex-Bangkok price of 35 per cent broken rice, adjusted for transport and handling costs (Intal, Cu and Illescas 2012: Table 2).

The high profits which the NFA made from buying cheap in international markets and selling dear in the domestic markets did reduce its need for budgetary subsidies, but that changed after 2004, when the ex-Bangkok price in peso terms rose sharply relative to the domestic price (Table 8.2). This greatly increased the budget support to the NFA, and led to a debate about the costs and benefits of its functions. Critics argued that the impact of NFA operations on farmgate prices was in fact quite small and varied across regions. Its dominant role in the import market did protect domestic consumers from fluctuations in the international market price, but the same result could have been achieved at less cost to the budget through a variable tariff. This would have the advantage that the profits accruing to the NFA in times of low world prices would instead accrue directly to the national budget (Intal, Cu and Illescas 2012: 41). These authors also argued that the private sector should be given a greater role in the internal rice market, which it could carry out more efficiently in most regions. To reduce storage and other costs, the size of the national stock should be reduced, and confined to low-quality rice.

Table 8.2: **Domestic prices of medium-quality rice as a ratio of ex-Bangkok prices (35 per cent broken), 2000-2007**

Year	Philippine Wholesale	Jakarta Wholesale
2000	2.13	1.64
2001	2.14	1.64
2002	1.81	1.82
2003	1.63	2.00
2004	1.26	1.59
2005	1.15	1.23
2006	1.15	1.81
2007	1.27	1.97

Sources: Ex-Bangkok 35 per cent broken and Philippine prices: Intal, Cu and Illescas (2012: Table 2); Jakarta wholesale prices from www.bps.go.id (accessed 20/11/2016).

Most studies of the NFA in the Philippines agree that the agency's operations have had little impact on poverty in the country and that the considerable budgetary outlays could have been better spent on other programmes, targeted more directly to the poor. Tigno (2012: 270) argued that 'the Philippine government appears to be highly sensitive to the political significance of its rice subsidy programme but insensitive to the financial and fiscal implications of such a programme and the fact that it fails to have a serious positive impact on overall poverty'. This raised the question of what other policies the government could implement which would have a greater impact. Would conditional cash transfers work better? Their role is examined in more detail below.

Over the 1990s and in the early 2000s, it was argued that Bulog in Indonesia played a more effective role in stabilizing rice prices without recourse to large budgetary subsidies, although it did receive assistance through subsidized loans from the state-owned banks. But by the early 2000s, it was clear that domestic rice prices were rising relative to ex-Bangkok prices; from 2003 to 2007 the differential was greater than in the Philippines (Table 8.2). Several studies pointed out that import restrictions which raised the domestic price of rice would have an adverse impact on poverty, as the poor in both rural and urban areas were in most cases net purchasers of rice (Warr 2005; McCulloch 2008). But since the spike in the world price in 2008/9, Indonesian policy has been directed towards using import controls to keep domestic prices above international levels. Rice self-sufficiency became official policy, although the policy has been modified under President Joko Widodo, with the result that domestic rice prices have risen sharply, even when international prices have been stable or falling. Between 2010 and 2016, the wholesale price of medium-grade rice increased by over 60 per cent, and in 2016 the average wholesale price in Indonesian markets was over twice the ex-Vietnam export price of 5 per cent broken grain, converted into rupiah.

The administration of Joko Widodo, which has frequently stated its commitment to reducing poverty, has permitted more rice imports since 2015, and the rate of increase in rice prices has slowed, although domestic prices are still well above world prices. But more sweeping reforms of food policy in Indonesia are difficult to implement. Many politicians still think that it is dangerous for Indonesia to rely on international markets for rice and other food staples, including corn and soybean, although the reasons for this concern are seldom clarified, and indeed imports of corn and soybean have been increasing. Several economists have pointed out that if the government wants to increase rice production, it would be preferable to focus on the rehabilitation of irrigation systems, both in Java and elsewhere, and on more investment in research (Simatupang and Timmer 2008). Others advocate a greater emphasis on crop insurance (Patunru and Respatiadi 2017). If the government wants to boost agricultural production more generally, it would be preferable to focus on crops where Indonesia continues to have a strong comparative advantage, such as rubber and oil palm, and allow more imports of foodgrains. In Java, many farmers are switching to horticulture, which is often more profitable than growing rice, especially for producers cultivating small plots close to large urban markets. It seems inevitable that, given continued population growth, Indonesia will have to rely more on food imports, and that attempts to curb imports through quantitative controls will only penalize the poor.

Concerns about the impact of rising rice prices on consumer welfare have not been confined to the two main rice-importing countries in Southeast Asia. In Vietnam, it has been argued that poorer households tend to be net buyers of rice and even 'among the 21% of households nationally that are net sellers of rice, only half (or 11.5% of all households) sell a fraction of their output large enough to ensure that their income gains outweigh their losses as consumers' (Coxhead, Linh and Tam 2012: 590). But the general equilibrium model results reported by these authors did show that the rural poor benefited in the longer run from the impact of higher rice prices on labour productivity and employment. Rice exports in Vietnam are dominated by state trading firms and they are required to use windfall gains from higher world prices to promote agricultural development. But in 2007/8 when world prices increased rapidly, there was little evidence, according to these authors, that the state trading companies did use their profits either to stabilize domestic prices or to promote productivity growth in the sector.

Making the Budget Pro-poor: What Can Governments Do?

The problem of the impact of the fiscal system on income distribution began to attract attention in Southeast Asia the 1970s, and several studies were published in that decade. Snodgrass (1975a: 283) argued that at independence the West Malaysian fiscal system 'was marked by regressivity in taxation of low-income groups and a highly unequal distribution of public services'. He pointed out that Malaysia was not a typical developing country in that budgetary revenues comprised 26-27 per cent of GDP, which was much higher than the Asian average. Even the poorer groups were taxed through export and import taxes and excises; export taxes fell to a disproportionate extent on the incomes of smallholder producers, which were often lower than those of urban wage earners who were below the income tax threshold (Booth 1980: 47-50). After independence, Snodgrass argued that the fiscal system became more progressive, but mainly because of changes in expenditures. In particular, he stressed the rise in expenditures aimed at low-income groups, especially Malays, through increased expenditure on agricultural development between 1958 and 1968. This was before the New Economic Policy placed even more emphasis on expenditures in agricultural development, land settlement and education. These findings were broadly confirmed by Meerman (1979: 324), who found that in 1974, after all budgetary effects had been considered, the share of the bottom four deciles in total income rose from 14 to 18 per cent.

In the Philippines, Tan (1975) examined the impact of the government budget for the early 1970s, and came to the conclusion that the government sector as a whole had virtually no impact on the distribution of income. On the tax side, she concluded that indirect taxes (in particular, taxes on alcohol, tobacco, and import duties) were inherently regressive and contributed to the overall regressivity of the tax system. On the expenditure side, she found that government expenditures on primary education and agricultural extension were progressive, but higher education expenditures largely benefited the higher income groups. Research in other parts of Southeast Asia tended to focus more on specific taxes: in Thailand a number of studies examined the impact of rice export taxes. It was argued that foreign demand elasticities and domestic supply elasticities were such that much of the tax was passed back to farmers in the form of lower prices. As farmers were on average earning lower incomes than many rice consumers, who benefited from lower prices in domestic markets, the tax had a significant adverse impact on the intersectoral distribution of income, although within both urban and rural areas, the rice export taxes improved the real incomes of the poor, as they were net purchasers of rice (Booth 1980: 50). Ingram (1971: 258) argued that Thai export taxes on rice were a tool for regulating the price of the economy's main wage good, and in effect became a means for keeping domestic wages lower than they might otherwise have been. This encouraged labour-intensive industrialization.

In Malaysia and Indonesia, export taxes on rubber also reduced the incomes of smallholder producers. Critics argued that their tax burden was higher than on urban workers earning incomes which fell below the threshold for the income tax (Booth 1980: 47-51). In Malaysia, smallholders received government assistance for replanting, which at least partially compensated for the higher tax burden, but this was not the case in Indonesia, where during the 1970s, smallholders were further penalized through the impact of the oil boom on the real exchange rate. These arguments ultimately led to the abolition of rice export taxes in Thailand, and changes in assessment procedures for rubber taxes in both Malaysia and Indonesia.

In the last two decades of the twentieth century, there was less interest on the part of international development agencies in the impact of government budgets on income distribution. The prevailing view was that governments in most middle- and low-income countries could do little to influence income distribution through the budget, and government expenditures should be confined to sectors where there was clear evidence of market failure, although there was often debate about which sectors these were. But in the early years of the new century, there was renewed interest in what governments could do to mitigate inequalities in the distribution of income and wealth in the developing world. What role could governments play in building social protection systems, which could help the disadvantaged to get access to government services such as health and education? In part, this focus on social protection was due to the impact which conditional cash transfers appeared to be having in several Latin American countries, which historically had had very skewed distributions of income and wealth, including both Brazil and Mexico. But it also reflected a renewed awareness on the part of politicians of the widespread popular concern about social and economic inequalities, and the growing expectation among electorates that governments must do something to correct these inequalities.

These concerns were especially apparent in Indonesia, where in the run-up to the 2014 election, inequality became an important issue. The National Medium-Term Development Plan explicitly included a target of reducing the Gini coefficient to 0.36 by 2019, although it was not clear how this was to be achieved. A survey commissioned by the World Bank found that a large majority of the respondents (92 per cent) felt that the distribution of income was quite unequal, or not equal at all (World Bank and Australian Aid 2015a: 9-10). There appeared to be a widespread conviction among those surveyed that inequality was increasing, that the rich were getting richer, and the poor, if not actually getting poorer, were falling behind in comparative terms. Another report published in 2015 found that, in 2012, the impact of the budget on income inequality was mildly progressive, mainly because of progressive social spending (World Bank and Australian Aid 2015b: 31). Perhaps surprisingly, the report found that energy subsidies were 'very slightly progressive and large enough in magnitude to roughly cancel out the indirect tax burdens created by Indonesia's VAT and excise tax regime'. The report also found that direct transfers more effectively targeted the poor than in-kind transfers, but the absolute amounts were also small, and they did not have broad coverage.

Other studies have agreed that government efforts to assist the poor in Southeast Asia have had limited impact. Warr and Sarntisart (2005: 217) found that Thailand's record of poverty reduction between the 1960s and 2000 was mainly due to rapid economic growth and that explicit government programmes to assist the poor were 'small in magnitude' and not well targeted. They argued that although the Thai government has claimed that pro-poor expenditures have increased as a proportion of total government expenditures in the 1990s, most programmes did not really focus on poor people. Their analysis showed that non-poor provinces in the early 2000s actually received somewhat higher per capita levels of poverty-related expenditures than poor provinces. Balisacan and Edillon (2005) in their analysis of the impact of government expenditures in the Philippines also found that up to the early 2000s, only very modest amounts had been spent on targeted schemes, and evaluations found that their impact was slight. These authors argued that sustained economic growth over decades was the key to the poverty problem in the Philippines, although they pointed out that the economic growth which had occurred in the 1990s appeared to have had only a weak impact on incomes of the poor. This point was also made by the Asian Development Bank. In a report published in 2009, it was argued that the economic growth which had occurred in recent years in the Philippines had not been translated into substantial poverty reduction, and that more targeted programmes were needed (Asian Development Bank 2009: 4).

Beginning in 2007, the Philippines launched a small pilot project called the Pantawid Pamilyang Pilipino Program (4Ps), which was modelled on conditional cash transfer programmes in Latin America. It offered 500 pesos per month to 6,000 households selected from the poorest municipalities, providing they agreed to six conditions regarding their children's school attendance, and participation in government-provided health programmes (Reyes and Tabuga 2012: 2-3). In the following years, the popularity of the 4Ps led to its rapid expansion under both President Arroyo and her successor, President N. Aquino. By 2014, it was estimated that 4.2 million families were participating (Kim and Yoo 2015: Figure 1). In its initial stages much of the funding came from the World Bank and the Asian Development Bank but by 2014 around two-thirds of the cost came from the national budget. The World Bank has claimed that it was one of the largest and best targeted conditional cash transfer programmes in the world.

Some evaluations of the programme have been carried out by independent researchers in the Philippines. Tutor (2014) found that it did have a significant impact on enrolments for children under twelve in the participating households but there was little impact on enrolments of children over twelve. She argued that the opportunity cost of a child's labour increased once they reached their teenage years, and very poor families needed their earnings. She also found that there was little impact on total household consumption of participating households, although they did increase their expenditures on carbohydrates and clothing. She suggested that it would be more efficient to target poor households in poor localities, although Reyes et al. (2015) argued that this could lead to exclusion of many poor households in other regions. Their analysis agreed that in its early years, the 4Ps had the greatest impact on primary enrolments; they argued that there was a need to boost transition from primary to secondary education for participating households.

Given the popularity of the 4Ps, it is likely that political support for it will continue in the Philippines. In Indonesia, the government has continued with the subsidized rice policy, first introduced in 1998. This accounted for around half of the household targeted social protection budget in 2010 (Alatas et al. 2013). In 2005 and 2008 a temporary unconditional cash transfer programme was introduced (Bantuan Langsung Tunai, or BLT), mainly to mitigate the impact of price shocks, including higher rice, gasoline and kerosene prices on poorer households. After that, a conditional cash transfer programme was introduced (Program Keluarga Harapan, or PKH), which reached 1.1 million households in 2010. By 2017, it had been expanded to reach 6.2 million households (TNP2K 2018: 19). The PKH was aimed at households where there were children below five, or children below 18 that have not finished the nine years of compulsory education. An evaluation of the targeted household programmes carried out in 2011 found little evidence of local elite capture, although those local elites who gained influence through informal institutions were found to be less prone to capture than those who held formal office (Alatas et al. 2013: 29).

Given the abundant evidence that poor families have higher infant and child mortality rates, and lower educational enrolments than those with higher incomes, a programme which makes government assistance to families conditional on both school attendance and attendance at health clinics could in principle help poorer households to close the gaps. But governments must be prepared to make resources available not just for the transfers, but also for increased health and education facilities. In both Indonesia and the Philippines, the main constraint on expanding provision of health and education facilities is limited budgetary resources. In both countries the ratio of budgetary revenues and expenditures to GDP was low compared with other ASEAN countries in 2015 (Table 8.3). In Indonesia, the Philippines and Vietnam, total budgetary expenditures per capita in 2015 were between $540 and $590 per capita, and only a small percentage of these expenditures were allocated to social protection policies. Ramesh (2014: 52) argued that in 2012, average per capita spending on social protection was only 1.1 per cent of per capita GDP in Indonesia, and 2.1 per cent in the Philippines, although a large part of expenditures in the Philippines went on social insurance which was mainly restricted to formal sector workers. The Indonesian system was more egalitarian, but in both countries the programmes in place were aimed at poor families with children, and did not cover the aged or the disabled. Ramesh also argued that more should be done to assist the transient poor, possibly through employment on public works projects.

Table 8.3: **Government revenues and expenditures as a percentage of GDP and expenditures per capita in ASEAN countries, 2015**

Country	Revenues (as % of GDP)	Expenditures* (as % of GDP)	Expenditures per capita (current 2015 dollars)
Brunei	20.3	34.3 (66.0)	13,212
Singapore	22.5	18.1 (15.6)	9,548
Malaysia	18.9	22.1 (22.1)	2,307
Thailand	19.2	20.5 (15.3)	1,166
Philippines	15.8	16.7 (18.2)	588
Vietnam	23.5	28.5 (23.8)	567
Indonesia	13.0	15.7 (14.7)	540
Lao PDR	15.5	23.5 (26.7)	470
Myanmar	21.7	26.0 (9.8)	309
Cambodia	16.8	19.4 (14.8)	208

* Figures in brackets refer to 1995.
Sources: Asian Development Bank (2015, Table 2.3: 2017: Tables 8.3 and 8.4).

Population Policies

As was pointed out in Chapter 1, population growth in the nineteenth and early twentieth centuries was considerably faster in Southeast Asia than in either China or India. By the 1930s, population was around 27 per cent of that in China, and 40 per cent of that in India. By 2015, these proportions had changed to 46 per cent and 37.5 per cent. In the roughly eight decades from the late 1930s to 2017, rates of population growth varied from 1.5 per cent per annum in Myanmar to over 3 per cent in Brunei (Table 8.4). International migration over these decades played only a limited role in population growth; the main reasons were high fertility and falling mortality. By the 1960s, several countries were concerned about what were seen as unsustainably high rates of population growth, and implemented national family planning programmes. In Singapore, Thailand, and Indonesia total fertility rates did fall through the decades from 1970 to 2010, and it is widely believed that the availability of modern contraceptive advice from both government and private clinics played a role in this fall. In the 1990s, fertility also began to decline in Vietnam. By 2017, total fertility rates were at or below replacement levels in Singapore, Brunei, Malaysia, Thailand and Vietnam (Table 8.4). But in other countries in the region they were still above replacement levels, and rates of population growth, although falling, were still above 1 per cent per annum.

The Philippine case is of particular interest as rates of population growth have been high over the past eight decades, although no higher than Malaysia. In both countries, government-financed family planning policies have been limited. In the Philippines, the Roman Catholic Church has opposed the use of most forms of contraception, while in Malaysia, governments have been reluctant to encourage the Malay majority to limit their fertility for reasons of population balance. But in both countries fertility has been falling in recent years, as more people access modern forms of contraception, especially in urban areas. An increase in the age of marriage has also occurred. In the Philippines, the evidence from the Demographic and Health Surveys shows that fertility declines steeply by wealth quintile. In the richest quintile, the total fertility rate in 2012 was below replacement at only 1.7, compared with 5.2 in the poorest quintile (Table 8.5).

Economists have argued that falling fertility affects economic growth as a result of the so-called demographic bonus, which results from a shift in the age structure of the population towards the 15-to-65 age group, who are assumed to be working. It is argued that children and the elderly are consumers rather than producers. A high percentage of the population

Table 8.4: Population in 2017 and estimated population growth rates, c. 1939 to 2017, total fertility rates (TFR) and dependency ratios, c.2017

Country	Population (millions) 2017	Annual growth rate (%)*	TFR 2017 **	Dependency ratio 2017 ***
Singapore (1939)	5.7	2.7	1.2	27
Brunei (1939)	0.4	3.1	1.9	28
Malaysia (1939)	31.6	2.5	2.0	31
Thailand (1937)	66.1	1.9	1.5	29
Philippines (1939)	105	2.4	2.8	37
Indonesia (1940)	264.0	1.7	2.4	33
Lao PDR (1940)	7.0	2.2	2.8	38
Vietnam (1939)	93.7	1.7	2.1	32
Myanmar (1941)	53.4	1.5	2.3	33
Cambodia (1940)	15.9	2.0	2.6	36

* Annual average growth rate of population from the years shown to 2017.
** Total fertility rates refer to the average number of children a women has from age 15 to 45.
*** Population under age 15 and over age 65 as a percentage of the population aged between 15 and 65.
Source: Population Reference Bureau (2017).

Table 8.5: Total fertility rates in the Philippines, by wealth quintiles, 2007 and 2012

Wealth Quintile	2007	2012
Poorest Quintile	5.2	5.2
Second Quintile	4.2	3.7
Third Quintile	3.3	3.1
Fourth Quintile	2.7	2.4
Richest Quintile	1.9	1.7
Average	3.3	3.0

Source: Mapa et al. (2017: Table 2); data from the Demographic and Health Surveys, Philippines.

under the age of fifteen, such as still occurs in parts of sub-Saharan Africa, implies that countries will struggle to provide adequate food, education and healthcare for all children. On the other hand, an increasing proportion of the population over 65 will place new strains on medical and care services. The demographic bonus is of limited duration; in much of Europe, and in Japan, Korea and Taiwan it lasted from the 1950s to 2000, but now these countries are facing higher costs of providing for the over-65 age group. Those who do not have occupational pensions and private healthcare provision become a charge on the state. But in those countries where around two-thirds of the population, or more, are in the 15-to-65 age groups, countries have the potential to achieve higher economic growth, because these people can be in productive employment rather than consuming resources.

It should be emphasized that the potential offered by the demographic bonus is not always realized. If rates of open unemployment are high, if many women are unwilling to work, or cannot find work, or if those in employment are trapped in low productivity occupations, the impact of the bonus created by falling fertility on economic growth may not be very great. Low productivity per worker translates into low incomes and persistent poverty. In the Southeast Asian context, Singapore, Malaysia and Thailand all managed to achieve rapid growth of output per worker in the decades after 1970 with low levels of open unemployment and high labour force participation rates. These countries have also seen a very sharp fall in poverty. This has also been the case in Vietnam since 1990, but because Vietnam started the transition later, the full impact of slowing population growth on incomes and poverty will take longer to materialize.

The Southeast Asian examples confirm that declining population growth can have a positive impact on incomes and the standard of living, providing governments also put in place other policies to achieve economic growth. Thailand has achieved faster poverty decline than the Philippines since the 1960s in part because of a reduction in fertility but, in addition, trade, exchange rate and foreign investment policies all allowed Thailand to realize the potential of the demographic bonus, at least until 1996. Myanmar has experienced low population growth for many decades, and fertility in 2017 was lower than in Indonesia, and not much higher than in Malaysia. Yet economic growth has been slow and poverty is probably higher than in many other Asian countries. Policies designed to slow population growth can certainly help in accelerating output per capita, and in reducing poverty, but they must be combined with other policies to promote sustained economic growth.

Decentralization Policies

In both Indonesia and the Philippines, the departure of Marcos in 1986 and Suharto in 1998 both led to policies aimed at decentralization of powers to subnational levels of government. In both countries, there is a large body of literature on the results of the various decentralization measures. In their survey of this literature, Malesky and Hutchinson (2016: 136) argued that many researchers found that 'decentralization had not fulfilled its economic and governance promises, even in the countries where it was implemented most earnestly'. This conclusion echoes research in other parts of the world, where reforms aimed at devolving more powers to sub-national levels of government have often failed to deliver the benefits which reformers hoped and expected of them. Explanations for this failure include the reluctance of central governments to devolve significant tax powers to the regions, the lack of administrative and technical competence at sub-national levels, and in some cases an increase in corruption, where sub-national governments lack even basic audit functions and local parliaments are either unable to control corrupt officials, or are complicit in their behaviour.

The reluctance to devolve taxation powers to the regions has inevitably made most sub-national levels of government across Southeast Asia dependent on central grants for many of their functions. This leads to what Tanzi (1996: 297) termed administrative rather than fiscal decentralization, where local government units (LGUs) account for a substantial proportion of total government expenditures (30 per cent or more in many cases) but collect a much lower proportion of total government revenues. In Indonesia, the reforms implemented after 2001 did lead to part of the revenues from natural resource exploitation being remitted back to the provinces and districts. This was intended to address the large imbalance between expenditures on consumption and investment within the province and total provincial GDP. But it was still the case that most taxation of mining companies is done at the central level, although some LGUs appear to have imposed extra levies.

There is also considerable evidence from Southeast Asia that many LGUs have struggled to cope with some of the spending responsibilities devolved to them. Typically, large infrastructure projects, such as main roads, remain the responsibility of the central government but the construction and maintenance of secondary roads are often the responsibility of LGUs. Even if they have the budgets to carry out this work (it appears that many do not), there are often coordination problems between the various levels of government, with the result that feeder roads are not built or maintained, and many rural communities cannot easily get produce to markets, or take advantage of employment opportunities in urban areas, while still living at home. Where health and education responsibilities have been devolved to provinces and sub-provincial governments, their efforts are hampered by a lack of qualified teachers, doctors and nurses. This problem has been made worse in Indonesia by the tendency to split provinces and districts outside Java into smaller units, which often cannot recruit or retain the staff needed to implement the spending functions allocated to them.

There is a large literature in Southeast Asia which argues that decentralization policies, especially when combined with elections of key officials in LGUs, have often led to elite capture of budgetary expenditures. The evidence for this is often based on fieldwork in a few regions, and it is often difficult to determine how widespread the problem is. A study based on statistical data for a large number of districts in Indonesia found that on balance 'decentralization seems to have improved service delivery and has made budgets more needs-oriented' (Schulze and Sjahrir 2014: 204). But the results were not uniform across all regions. Indeed, given that there are now more than 500 districts in Indonesia, it is to be expected that there would be considerable variation in outcomes. What is perhaps of concern is that these authors found that richer districts with larger revenues per capita tended to have better service delivery. Over time this may mean that existing disparities between districts in provision of health and education facilities, and certain types of infrastructure, may increase.

In the Philippines, where the decentralization reforms began in 1991, a literature has emerged which has tended to be critical of the results in terms of service delivery. Shair-Rosenfield (2016: 168) suggested that three factors, apart from lack of administrative capacity, explain the disappointing outcomes. First, there is often a lack of fiscal resources to carry out all the functions allocated to LGUs. Most of the important taxes including income, estate and inheritance taxes, the value added tax and customs duties have been retained at the centre, which appears reluctant to engage in even limited revenue sharing. Only the cities were able to cover more than half of their current operating income from their own revenues, while other LGUs remained very dependent on grants from the centre. Second, there is the problem of weak accountability, which is linked to the third factor, the persistence of patronage politics. Politicians at the national level continue to be beholden to local elites for electoral support, and have been reluctant to interfere with the ways in which the LGUs spent their budgets.

The problem of inadequate fiscal resources to fund local government activities appears to be universal throughout Southeast Asia. In Vietnam, Anh (2016: 204-205) pointed out that the central government has been reluctant to allow even limited decentralization for fear of undermining the uniformity of national policies. Fiscal resources have been inadequate even for those functions which have been devolved to LGUs, and there is still a lack of government accountability. Malesky and Hutchinson (2016: 136) argued that in Vietnam, along with Cambodia and Myanmar, government elites at the national level are still fearful of losing control over key sectors of policy. Thailand, which had been a highly centralized unitary state for over a century, appeared to be embarking on a new course with the 1997 constitution, which mandated a number of decentralization measures. But developments since 2006 have not supported either democracy or devolved government. Unger and Mahakanjana (2016: 185) found that inadequate fiscal resources and the 'meddlesome ways of central government officers' have impeded decentralization, but there have also been failings within LGUs, which have often failed to exploit the opportunities available to them. These opportunities in turn have been curtailed in the latest constitution, although there will probably be further changes in Thailand in the not too distant future.

It would be difficult to argue, on the evidence available in the second decade of the twenty-first century, that decentralization measures have by themselves played an important role in improving living standards across Southeast Asia, although in several cases they might have defused some tensions about the division of revenues, especially from natural resource exploitation, between the centre and the regions. For a variety of reasons most LGUs do not appear to have used whatever limited fiscal resources they have at their disposal on pro-poor expenditures. Although many donors have in recent decades become enthusiastic about community-driven development, it has been argued that the projects selected are often of limited value in empowering the poor (Sari and Widyaningrum 2012: 101).

Concluding Comments

Over the last six decades, most countries in Southeast Asia have experimented with a range of programmes, including land reform, land settlement projects, labour-intensive public works, interventions in the markets for basic staples, especially rice, and family planning policies. In almost all cases the results have been mixed, with only a limited impact on poverty alleviation. Part of the problem was that these policies often addressed several different goals, with poverty alleviation not always the most important. Labour-intensive public works were intended to provide employment for rural workers (mainly able-bodied males) during the agricultural slack season. It was expected that most of the beneficiaries would be poor, although many poor people were excluded from the programmes by reason of age, gender or physical disabilities. Land settlement policies were aimed at alleviating poverty in the sending regions, and might have achieved this goal, if only to a limited extent. But they were also intended to promote growth in those regions whose development potential was thought by government planners to be held back by small populations. In fact, large-scale in-migration of agricultural settlers often caused problems in the receiving regions. Many settlements were poorly planned and migrants were forced to take wage employment to make an adequate living. Where this was not available they often returned to their home regions, or to other locations. Had poverty alleviation considerations been paramount, the settlement programmes would probably have been implemented in different ways. Indeed, it might well have been more cost-effective to have implemented policies aimed at increasing the availability of non-agricultural employment in the sending regions, rather than moving people to new locations.

In recent years, cash transfers to the poor have gained favour, especially where these policies are made conditional on sending children to school, and attending health clinics. Given that there are still considerable differences across income groups in infant and child mortality, and in school attendance in most parts of Southeast Asia, there would seem to be considerable scope for extending these policies. But targeting is a problem. Dreze and Sen (2013: 191-192) have argued that the Bolsa Familia, the family welfare programme of the government of Brazil, has made an important contribution to poverty reduction in Brazil because there was a 'fairly well identified target group' mainly in urban areas. Around 85 per cent of the population in Brazil lives in towns and cities, which is a much higher proportion than in most parts of South and Southeast Asia. Dreze and Sen also found that Brazil had a fairly sophisticated administration in charge of screening applicants, and determining what sort of assistance they needed. The experience of India in targeting poverty assistance has been 'far from encouraging', for reasons which Dreze and Sen set out in considerable detail. Whether the Philippines, Indonesia and other countries in Southeast Asia who are contemplating conditional cash transfers will go down the Brazilian or the Indian route remains to be seen.[4]

Budgetary expenditures per capita are still low in most Southeast Asian countries; in six countries, total expenditures per capita were less than $600 in 2015 (Table 8.3). In the four countries where expenditures were higher, the headcount measure of poverty as measured by the World Bank was low. That does not mean that problems of relative deprivation have been solved in these countries; Singapore, Malaysia and Thailand continue to have high levels of income inequality, although there is evidence of decline in both

---

4   McCarthy and Sumarto (2018: 231) argued on the basis of surveys carried out in two villages in Aceh on the impact of a conditional cash transfer program that the targeting was very unsatisfactory. Only 14 per cent of households identified as poor using wealth rankings approved by the community actually received assistance, Half those receiving cash transfers were not poor using the community's standards.

Malaysia and Thailand in recent years. But their governments do have greater resources at their disposal to rectify at least some of the problems caused by these high inequalities, such as unequal access to education and healthcare. Elsewhere, government resources relative to population are much smaller. Limited budgetary resources do not necessarily imply that there is nothing governments can do to alleviate poverty. In the Indonesian case, a relaxation of controls on the import of food, especially rice, would certainly have an immediate impact on food prices and poverty, while not involving any direct budgetary outlay. In Vietnam, the government has apparently been able to provide most of the population with quite good basic healthcare in spite of limited budgetary expenditures. There seems much that the countries in Southeast Asia can learn from one another about what governments can do to improve living standards, and what policies should be avoided.

9   What Have We Learned?

A Century of Growth and Change

Perhaps the most important conclusion to be drawn from this survey of living standards across the ten countries of Southeast Asia is that, on most of the indicators widely used to measure living standards, there has been progress since the early years of the twentieth century. Although population growth has been rapid, national output and income have grown faster than population in all countries over the decades from the early twentieth to the early twenty-first century. Years of schooling have increased, and the great majority of people are now able to read and write in the national language. This is a considerable achievement given the low levels of literacy which prevailed in much of the region in 1950. Health indicators such as life expectancy have also improved, as have housing conditions. Increased provision of transport and communications infrastructure has led to better connectivity for many millions of people, who can travel both within and across national boundaries for employment and leisure activities.

But these improvements, while impressive, have not been uniform either within countries over time, or across countries and regions at a point in time. By the second decade of the twenty-first century, there were striking differences across the ten countries not just in per capita GDP but also in non-monetary indicators, including infant and child mortality, educational attainment, housing conditions and access to modern transport and communications infrastructure. There is also evidence that progress in reducing poverty, as measured by the proportion of the population below the poverty lines used by the World Bank, has differed across countries and between regions and socio-economic and ethnic groups within countries. Even those countries which have reduced extreme poverty to very low levels, such as Malaysia and Thailand, still exhibit quite high levels of income and wealth inequality. Indeed, one estimate shows that the Gini coefficient of wealth distribution in Thailand is the highest in the world (Credit Suisse 2018: Table 6-6). While economic growth in Thailand has been accompanied by a reduction in the headcount measure of poverty to low levels, it appears that a small number of Thais have been able to amass enormous wealth, while the great majority have only managed to accumulate far more modest holdings.

It has been argued in previous chapters that the ten countries of Southeast Asia have, in recent decades, shown considerable variation in a number of rankings of human development. According to the widely used Human Development Index, Singapore, Brunei, Malaysia and Thailand were all included in the very high or high human development categories in 2015, while the remaining countries were included in the medium human development group. Indonesia was ranked slightly higher than Vietnam and the Philippines, with Laos, Cambodia and Myanmar further down (Table 1.1). This contrasts with the situation in 1990, when the Philippines was included in the 'medium human development' category, while both Indonesia and Vietnam were still in the 'low human development' category (UNDP 1991: 120). The Inclusive Development Index published by the World Economic Forum used a broader range of indicators grouped under three headings: growth and development, inclusion and intergenerational equity, and sustainability. Of the 74 developing countries included in this index, Malaysia in 2018 was ranked 13, Thailand 17, Vietnam 33, Indonesia 36, the Philippines 38 and Laos 58 (World Economic Forum 2018: Table 1). Cambodia and Myanmar were excluded because of a lack of data.

The Human Development Index (HDI), and other composite indexes show that in recent years the Philippines has fallen behind, and Vietnam has forged ahead. While there have been absolute improvements in the components of the HDI in the Philippines, they have been slower than in both Indonesia and Vietnam. The relative decline of the Philippines is particularly striking given its high ranking in the latter part of the 1930s on both GDP per capita and a range of non-monetary indicators, including health and education. Both Indonesia and French Indochina by contrast were ranked much lower (Bennett 1951). The reasons for these reversals of fortune are examined further below. But first, it is important to look at the ongoing debate over the link between economic growth as conventionally measured using the System of National Accounts (SNA), and improvements in poverty.

Is Growth Enough?

At the turn of the millennium, a number of economists involved in research on international development argued that sustained economic growth over a period of decades was essential in order to achieve a broad-based improvement in living standards and a significant decline in income poverty. But was growth alone enough? Dollar and Kraay (2002: 218) argued that the evidence, derived from cross-country regressions from a sample of countries spanning four decades, showed that 'average incomes of the poorest fifth of a country on average rise or fall at the same rate as average incomes'. They also found that a variety of 'pro-growth' macroeconomic policies, such as low inflation, moderate size of government, sound financial development, respect for the rule of law, and openness to international trade, raise average incomes with little systematic effect on the distribution of income. They argued that their findings did not suggest a trickle-down effect whereby the rich got richer first and some of the benefits eventually trickled down to the poor. The conclusion they drew was that a sound macroeconomic environment encouraged a growth process which raised all incomes of rich and poor households alike.[1]

Dollar, Kleineberg and Kraay (2013) updated and expanded the results of Dollar and Kraay (2002) and confirmed the earlier results. They also claimed that the income shares of the bottom 20 per cent and the bottom 40 per cent of the distribution showed no systematic tendency to decline over time, although they did not deny that there were some changes in inequality in particular countries and time periods. They pointed out that in Asia in the 1990s and 2000s, the income growth of the bottom 40 per cent was only about 0.6 of mean growth, although they did not offer any explanation for this. In the Southeast Asian context, it has been argued, again on the basis of regression results, that poverty reduction across the region was 'overwhelmingly attributable to the high rate of growth of GDP per person' (Warr 2015: 325). Warr argued that the sectoral composition of the growth in Southeast Asia also had an impact; he found that poverty reduction outcomes were strongly related to the growth of both agriculture and services, but not to industrial growth.

These findings, which replicated earlier results for India by Ravallion and Datt (1996), contrasted with the Taiwan experience where Warr and Wang (1999) argued that the growth of the industrial sector was strongly associated with poverty reduction. The usual explanation for these differences is that Taiwan and the Republic of Korea adopted an export-oriented manufacturing strategy which, beginning in the 1960s, made use of abundant supplies of labour to increase exports of garments, textiles, shoes, toys and some electronic products. Although several countries in

1   The Dollar-Kraay work has attracted considerable criticism over the years. Perhaps the most serious is that relating to the accuracy of the data they used on income distribution and poverty. To the extent that the data are flawed for reasons discussed in previous chapters, their conclusions may not be robust. Pritchett and Kenny (2013: 24) drew attention to the problem in India of a large disparity between survey and national income data on household consumption. Chapter 7 has drawn attention to similar disparities in Indonesia and the Philippines.

Southeast Asia have also been successful in adopting this model, others relied to a greater extent on resource-based exports and used tariff
and non-tariff barriers to foster import-substituting industries for the
domestic market. Large investments were also made in the processing of
oil, gas and other mineral products. To the extent that these industries
were capital-intensive, they tended to absorb less labour, which either
stayed in the agricultural sector, or was absorbed into various service
sector occupations. In the case of the Philippines, Bautista (1990) argued
that in spite of the rapid agricultural growth which occurred in the years
from 1965 to 1980, the benefits accrued mainly to the more affluent segments of the rural population who controlled most of the arable land.
They tended to buy capital-intensive products which were produced in the
protected manufacturing sector, but their demand alone was insufficient
to sustain rapid growth of manufacturing industry. Labour absorption in
both agriculture and industry was low, and together with continued high
rates of population growth, many workers had no alternative to seeking
work in low-productivity service sector employment.

Bautista's analysis is confirmed by the evidence on the distribution of
the labour force by sector in various Southeast Asian countries, compared
with the figures for Japan, Taiwan and the Republic of Korea when those
countries had a roughly similar level of per capita GDP (Table 9.1). Several
countries in Southeast Asia had a higher proportion of the labour force in
agriculture than Japan and Taiwan, and also a higher proportion of the
non-agricultural labour force in services. In the Philippines in 1982, almost
78 per cent of the non-agricultural labour force was employed in services,
compared with 57 per cent in Taiwan in 1970. The service sector contains
a range of occupations, not all of which are of low productivity, but the
evidence indicates that in the Philippines only a small proportion of the
service sector labour force was employed in skilled, high-income occupations.
This was also the case in Indonesia, where the service sector accounted for
a much higher proportion of the non-agricultural labour force in 1990 than
was the case in Taiwan two decades earlier.

There are of course good economic reasons why service sector employment should be higher in Southeast Asia in recent decades than was the
case in Japan in the mid-1950s, or Taiwan in the 1970s. The tourist sector has
grown rapidly in most ASEAN countries in recent decades, and is oriented
to both foreign and domestic tourists. The evidence suggests that this does
create considerable employment in the hospitality sector and also in trade
and transport. In 2016 the ten ASEAN countries received 115.6 million
foreign tourists, of which 32.5 million went to Thailand, and 26.7 million

Table 9.1: Agricultural share of the labour force (ALF/TLF) and services as a share of the non-agricultural labour force (NALF)

Country/Year	ALF/TLF	Services/ NALF
Japan (1955)	42.9	59.8
Taiwan (1970)	36.7	55.8
RO Korea (1973)	50.0	60.6
Malaysia (1975)	49.3	68.8
Thailand (1978)	66.5	64.3
Philippines (1982)	51.7	77.6
Indonesia (1990)	49.9	64.7
Vietnam (2006)	54.7	59.6
Cambodia (2012)	33.2	62.2

Note: In the years shown per capita GDP (1990 International GK$) was between 2,400 and 2,600 for all the countries shown except Japan (2,771) and RO Korea (2,800). Data from Maddison Project Database, 2013.
Sources: Japan, RO Korea, Philippines, and Thailand: Booth (2002b: Table 6); Taiwan: Council for Economic Planning and Development (1992: 18); Malaysia: Government of Malaysia (1976: Table 8.1); Philippines: World Bank (1987: Table 1.3); Indonesia: Central Bureau of Statistics (1992: Table 41.9); Vietnam: ILO (2012: Table A2.2,); Cambodia: National Institute of Statistics (2013: Table 6.10).

to Malaysia.[2] Domestic tourism numbers are also growing rapidly in most parts of the region. Of course, not all the growth in service sector employment in the ASEAN countries was in the hospitality sector, but it has made a significant contribution.

The growing contribution of export-oriented services to foreign exchange earnings should also be borne in mind in interpreting the evidence on the share of the various Southeast Asian countries in total merchandise trade in the almost eight decades from 1937 to 2015 (Table 9.2). In the late 1930s, Indonesia accounted for around one-third of total exports from the region: by 2015, the proportion had fallen to a little under 13 per cent. The fall in Indonesia's share has been the result of a rapid increase in the share of the countries comprising the former Indochina, especially Vietnam, and also of the countries comprising what was British Malaya, although their share fell between 1995 and 2015. Thailand has steadily increased its share, while that of the Philippines increased between 1937 and 1965, but has fallen thereafter. Would the growing importance of service sector exports make any difference to the trends shown in Table 9.2? Probably not, as those countries which have experienced rapid growth of merchandise trade since the 1960s have also experienced fast growth in service sector exports, including tourism.

2 These figures are taken from ASEAN Secretariat (2018), Chapter 9.

Table 9.2:   Country shares of ASEAN merchandise exports, 1937-2015 (percentage
                       of ASEAN total)

Country	1937	1965	1995	2015
Myanmar	11.5	4.7	0.5	1.0
Indochina	6.5	3.0	4.9	14.8
Vietnam			4.4	13.8
Cambodia			0.5	0.7
Laos			n/a	0.3
Indonesia	33.6	15.1	13.2	12.8
British Malaya	34.3	48.1	58.1	48.0
Singapore			35.5	30.5
Malaysia			21.6	17.0
Brunei			1.0	0.5
Philippines	9.4	16.0	6.4	5.0
Thailand	4.7	13.1	16.9	18.3
Total	100	100	100	100

Sources: 1937 and 1965: Booth (2004: Table 4); 1995: ASEAN Secretariat (2010: Table V.3); 2015:
ASEAN Secretariat (2017: Table 5.2).

The evidence in Table 9.2 could be used to support the argument that open-
type policies supporting the rapid growth of both exports and national
income are all that is needed to bring about a rapid decline in poverty.
The various international comparisons published by both the World Bank
and the Asian Development Bank all agreed that by the early twenty-first
century, the headcount measure of poverty had declined to negligible levels
in Singapore, Malaysia and Thailand, all countries which have experienced
rapid growth of both merchandise and service exports. Vietnam, Laos and
Cambodia all experienced a rapid growth in exports since the mid-1990s,
together with a fall in poverty, although, as was argued in Chapter 7, the
official figures on the extent of the fall can be contested. But even if the
export growth benefited certain sections of the population more than
others, the trickle-down impact of the export growth appears to have been
impressive, while those countries with slower export growth and declining
export shares (especially the Philippines but also Indonesia) still appeared
to be struggling with higher levels of poverty in the second decade of the
new century.

But are other factors involved as well? What about access to land, or
access to off-farm employment in rural areas? If indeed growth in the
agricultural sector has had an important impact on declines in poverty
across Southeast Asia in recent decades, to what extent have government

policies facilitated such growth, through, for example, input subsidies or the dissemination of higher-yielding varieties of both food and non-food crops? Warr's regression analysis found that an increase in the real price of food reduces the rate at which poverty declines. This would suggest that governments should try to moderate the rate of growth of food prices in real terms through reducing those protectionist measures which increase domestic food prices relative to border prices, or even by subsidizing the price of key staples, such as rice. In fact, as was shown in Chapter 8, Indonesia has increased agricultural protection in recent years, especially in the food crop sector, and this has adversely affected the poorer households who are net consumers of rice. To compensate poor consumers for high rice prices, the Indonesian government has also introduced a policy of selling rice at subsidized prices to poor people.

It was argued in Chapter 8 that governments across Southeast Asia over the past six decades have experimented with a range of policies intended to reduce income poverty, and ensure a more equitable distribution of income and assets. The results have been at best mixed. Bold policy interventions have run out of steam, either for budgetary reasons or because of changes in the priorities of successive governments. Is this an argument for simply concentrating on those policies most likely to increase rates of economic growth, in the expectation that sooner or later the benefits of growth will trickle down to all sections of society? The problem with this argument is that, in the short and medium term, growth may be accompanied by increases in inequalities in the distribution of both income and wealth, which in turn can lead to social problems and the rise of new political forces which are less supportive of policies that are intended to promote rapid growth. In the next section, I try to summarize what we have learnt about the relationship between growth, poverty and inequality in Southeast Asia, before discussing future priorities for both government and civil society groups.

Growth, Poverty and Inequality: What the Evidence Shows

In spite of the ongoing debates about the reliability of the data, the following propositions about trends in poverty and inequality in Southeast Asia over the past five decades appear to be supported by the evidence:

(1) Rapid economic growth has over time reduced income poverty, using either the World Bank measure of extreme poverty or the various national

poverty lines. This has been true of Singapore, Malaysia, Thailand and Indonesia since the 1970s, and more recently of Vietnam, Laos and Myanmar.

(2) But the extent of the decline in poverty can be contested. National poverty lines have tended to be low relative to the estimates of per capita consumption expenditures from the national accounts estimates (Table 7.4). This reduces the credibility of the national poverty estimates among those civil society groups who are often distrustful of government claims about poverty reduction.

(3) When poverty lines are increased, as they have been by several statistical agencies in Southeast Asia in recent decades, there has often been a sharp increase in the headcount measure of poverty, which reflects the bunching of many households just above the poverty line.

(4) In the Philippines, the growth in per capita GDP which occurred in the years from 1950 to 1975 was not accompanied by falls in income poverty. Slow economic growth in the last two decades of the twentieth century meant that numbers in poverty remained stubbornly high, and indeed have fallen only modestly in the early twenty-first century, in spite of faster economic growth.

(5) Those countries and regions where fertility has fallen in recent decades, including Singapore, Malaysia, Thailand, Indonesia and Vietnam, appear to have reaped a demographic bonus in terms of faster growth and more rapid poverty decline.

(6) Periods of fast growth, including in Thailand (1970-1992), Indonesia (1984-1996) and Laos more recently have been accompanied by rising inequality in household income/expenditure. Slower growth in Thailand since 1997 appears to have been accompanied by a fall in inequality in household income and expenditure.

(7) The growth collapse in Indonesia in 1998, and the slow recovery caused the Gini of nominal household expenditures to fall very sharply. Since 2010 the Gini for household expenditures has been higher than in Vietnam and Thailand and about the same as in the Philippines (Table 7.11)

(8) Doubts have been raised about the accuracy of household surveys in both Indonesia and the Philippines, where there are large disparities

between the household survey data and those from the national accounts (Table 7.10). To the extent that these disparities are the result of under-reporting on the part of richer households, this suggests that the inequality estimates in both countries are underestimated. If some households are excluded from the sample altogether, this could affect the headcount measures of poverty.

(9) The estimates of wealth inequalities published by Credit Suisse are very high in global terms in both Thailand and Indonesia.

(10) Vietnam in recent years has a low headcount measure of poverty (using the World Bank estimates) given its low per capita GDP. It also has achieved quite high rankings in several recent estimates of human development using non-monetary estimates.

(11) As in many other countries, including those with high per capita GDP, there are sharp disparities in household access to health and education facilities by income or wealth status in most parts of Southeast Asia.

(12) Indonesia in recent rankings seems to have been a poor performer on health indicators, given its relatively high per capita GDP. This is especially the case for indicators relating to child health and maternal mortality.

(13) In most countries in Southeast Asia where headcount measures of poverty are available at the sub-national level, there appear to be marked differences by region. These differences are not always highly correlated with estimates of regional GDP, especially in the resource-rich regions of Indonesia, where at least until the 1990s, there were significant export surpluses, which funded an outward flow of funds to the centre and abroad.

(14) Until recently, it was argued that no country in Southeast Asia was following the 'Northeast Asian' model of rapid export-led growth with equity, although recent evidence indicates that Vietnam may be doing so to a greater extent than its neighbours.

If these propositions can be accepted as broadly accurate, they raise some important questions about why some countries, and regions within countries, have apparently performed better than others in terms of both poverty alleviation and inequality, not just since the 1990s, but over the longer term. The Philippines appears to have experienced the most dramatic relative decline since the 1950s, while Vietnam since the 1990s seems to have experienced rapid growth with equity, and remarkable progress in human development, given its relatively low per capita GDP. The following section examines the reasons for these outcomes.

Reversals of Fortune: What Went Wrong in the Philippines and Right in Vietnam?

By the early years of the twenty-first century, it was widely argued that the Philippines had fallen behind other countries in the region in terms of both monetary and non-monetary indicators although as was shown in Chapter 7, the country scored better on some indicators than others. In particular, the country still scored well on a number of educational indicators, especially for women, compared with Thailand, Indonesia and Vietnam. It was also ranked very high on the Global Gender Gap Index, prepared by the World Economic Forum. But on other indicators, including the extent of undernourishment and poverty, the Philippines appeared to be doing less well than either Indonesia or Vietnam. Economists studying the Philippines often seemed to be convinced that the country has been plagued by very high levels of inequality, and that 'deeply entrenched and high levels of inequality impede reform' (Balisacan and Hill 2003: 20). These authors pointed out that the Philippines never experienced a Taiwan-style land reform, and claimed that the poor rural constituency was neglected compared with post-1970 policies in Indonesia and Malaysia. Elsewhere, Balisacan, Fuwa and Debuque (2004: 234) argued that 'the Philippines has a higher incidence of rural landlessness than its Southeast Asian neighbours, due to a combination of a plantation sector growing tropical cash crops and a high incidence of tenancy within the peasant sector'.

These authors did not attempt any detailed comparisons of inequality or land tenure systems in other Asian countries to substantiate their claims. As far as income inequality is concerned, the evidence does suggest that inequality has been high in the Philippines for a number of decades, but not necessarily higher than in other countries in the region, including Thailand, Indonesia and Malaysia, which at least until 1997, performed better than the Philippines in terms of economic growth. Discussions of inequality in the Philippines have often been based on comparisons using household survey data which are not always comparable.[3] Neither is it easy to substantiate claims that rural landlessness and tenancy are greater problems in the Philippines than in other parts of Asia. It was argued in Chapter 5 that the concept of landlessness is not easy to quantify, although evidence from Java indicated that by the late colonial era many rural households were cultivating very small holdings, and a considerable number had no access to land at all. The problems became more acute after 1950, as the rural population continued to grow, and government attempts at land reform, and land settlement in other islands were frustrated by lack of budgetary resources.

The Philippines was hardly unique in having a large estates sector. In both Indonesia and Malaysia large estates were also developed during the colonial era. In most cases they were owned by foreign companies and were the target of nationalist resentment after independence. In the late 1950s, the Dutch-owned estates in Indonesia were nationalized, and became state enterprises, which they have remained. There was no attempt at the time or subsequently to distribute the estate land to smallholders. Land under smallholder cultivation of crops such as rubber, coffee and spices did increase in many parts of Southeast Asia, but mainly through extending the cultivation frontier. The amount of land controlled by large estates in Indonesia declined until the 1980s, when the palm oil boom led to a rapid resurgence of plantation agriculture, controlled by both Indonesian and foreign firms (Booth 2012; Table 4.3). In the Philippines, the large estate sector was mainly owned by indigenous Filipinos, often of mixed Chinese and Spanish descent. These were the families who played a dominant role in post-1946 politics, and formed the backbone of what has been termed *cacique* democracy (Anderson 1988).

Building on the work of Anderson and others, Hutchcroft (1998) made a distinction between the patrimonial administrative state (Thailand since the 1960s, and Indonesia under Suharto) and the patrimonial oligarchic state (the Philippines since 1946). There was an assumption that the Philippine oligarchic state produced a more skewed distribution of income and wealth, although this was not rigorously demonstrated. There was also an assumption that landed elites dominated the congress, and this prevented land reform. But as was argued in Chapter 8, the Philippines has had some success in implementing agrarian reform policies, at least compared with

3   An example of this is a survey of poverty in the Philippines, published by the Asian Development Bank (2009). The author appeared determined to show that inequality was higher in the Philippines than in other parts of Asia, and in Table 20 presented estimates of Gini coefficients drawn from different, and non-comparable, sources.

Indonesia and Thailand. It has been argued that the large estates (hacienda) have been abolished in many parts of the country, with the exception of the sugar-producing regions in Negros Occidental (Ballesteros 2019). The combination of land reform programmes and population growth has led to a continual reduction in average holding size to a little over one hectare. In Indonesia during the Suharto era, the emphasis was on moving families owning little or no land from densely settled regions to Sumatra, Kalimantan and Eastern Indonesia. These programmes were, at best, mixed in their results. In Thailand, land reform initiatives did not receive much political support after the 1970s, and by the 1990s, the proportion of land in holdings over ten hectares in Thailand was not much different from the Philippines (Table 6.7). In all three countries, the proportion of land in holdings over five hectares was much higher than in Taiwan in 1975.

Thus, while it is true that the Philippines has not followed the Taiwan path of growth with equity, the evidence indicates that Indonesia and Thailand have not done so either. In both countries, rural non-farm incomes grew more slowly than in Taiwan, and the proportion of land in holdings over five hectares was much higher in all three countries in the last decades of the twentieth century than in Taiwan. The argument that the Philippines had a higher proportion of landlessness than other countries in Southeast Asia has not been substantiated by any rigorous appraisal of the evidence. Tenancy was certainly high in the Philippines in the 1930s, although there were striking regional variations (Spencer 1952: Table 8). The various land reform programmes carried out since the 1950s have redistributed land from landlords to cultivators, but there appears to have been less success in dealing with the growing numbers of rural people who owned no land at all, or only very small plots which could not support a family of five or six. These households were forced to rely on self-employment in the non-agricultural sectors, and wage labour for most of their income, as was the case in the more densely settled parts of Indonesia.

A crucial difference between the Philippines and other Southeast Asia countries in the decades since the 1960s has been the slow decline in fertility and the faster growth of population in both urban and rural areas. As was argued in Chapter 8, there are striking differences between wealth classes in fertility, with the poorest 40 per cent of the population having the largest families (Table 8.5). Whether this reflects a deliberate strategy on the part of the poor to have larger families to provide security, or an inability to access modern family planning facilities, remains unclear. But the combination of low-income and larger families makes it difficult for many households to break out of the poverty trap; children drop out of education early and cannot obtain secure employment. It is striking that a very high percentage of the non-agricultural labour force in the Philippines is absorbed in services rather than industrial occupations compared with Taiwan and South Korea when they had roughly similar levels of per capita GDP (Table 9.1). While some service jobs are well-paid and secure, many are not. One explanation for the continuing high levels of poverty in the Philippines could be that a high percentage of the labour force, especially those with less education, continue to be trapped in unproductive service sector work.

If the slow progress in alleviating poverty in the Philippines can be attributed to rapid population growth, and a failure to generate sufficient employment in the more productive sectors of the economy, what explains the apparently better performance of the Vietnamese economy since the 1990s? The poverty data published by the World Bank, which show a much lower proportion of the population under the $1.90 and $3.10 lines in Vietnam than in either the Philippines or Indonesia, are probably distorted by problems with the survey data in all three countries. But it is likely that poverty is lower in Vietnam than would be expected given low per capita GDP and low average household consumption because of the rather unusual conditions prevailing in the country when the reform process began, and the successful mix of economic policies which have been pursued over the past three decades. The reform process began when many Vietnamese were very poor and the distribution of household income rather egalitarian. Glewwe (2004b: Tables 1.1 and 1.2) estimated that 58 per cent of the population was below the official poverty line in 1994, and the Gini coefficient was a relatively low at 0.33.[4] Land reform policies had led to the elimination of large landholdings, and only about 8 per cent of the rural population was estimated to be landless in 1993. Many of these would have had access to some non-agricultural incomes (Ravallion and Van de Walle 2008: Table 3.3).

A second factor was the strong commitment of government to assist those who were seen as casualties of the long war against both the French and the Americans, which led to an unusually comprehensive health system for a poor country. To the extent that many people in both urban and rural areas were able to access free or low-cost healthcare, an illness might not have had the same serious impact on household budgets compared with other countries where income per capita was higher, but where the provision of free or subsidized healthcare was restricted to a limited number of households who were often quite well-off. A third factor relates to the export-led industrialization which has been an important feature of the

---

4   It is not clear whether this was estimated from household income or expenditure data.

Vietnamese economy since the 1990s. This strategy generated employment in the manufacturing sector and also in construction and utilities. The share of non-agricultural employment in the service sector in 2006 was quite close to that in Taiwan and South Korea when these countries had similar levels of per capita GDP, and much lower than in the Philippines (Table 9.1). In addition, fertility has been falling rapidly in Vietnam over the past three decades, and as a result the growth of the labour force is slowing and open unemployment is quite low.

As was pointed out in Chapter 8, the government of Vietnam had implemented land reform in the north after 1955, and the south after 1975. But the distribution of land, although very egalitarian compared to most other parts of Southeast Asia, was not always very efficient. The government adopted a more liberal approach to land market reform in the early 1990s, which permitted land to be reallocated to those households able and willing to cultivate it. Ravallion and Van de Walle (2008: Table 3.4) found evidence of rising landlessness after 1993, especially in the Southeast and Mekong Delta regions. But they argued that the rising landlessness did not lead to greater poverty. Even in the Mekong Delta the headcount measure of poverty among the landless households was falling, although it was higher in 2004 than for those households cultivating land. It appears that the rapid growth of non-agricultural employment opportunities absorbed many of those in the southern districts who gave up their rights to agricultural land.

The evidence does suggest that the Vietnamese government has been very successful in providing healthcare, including family planning services, to both urban and rural populations. Chapter 7 reviewed the evidence that by the early years of the twenty-first century, Vietnam had low levels of infant and under-five mortality compared with other Asian countries at similar or higher levels of per capita GDP. In addition, Vietnam achieved quite equal outcomes in under-five mortality across wealth quintiles, compared to other low- and middle-income countries. It also had lower levels of stunting and wasting in children than most other countries in Southeast Asia, including both the Philippines and Indonesia, although the percentage of the total population considered undernourished was slightly higher than the Southeast Asian average (Table 7.12). On the composite index of human capital compiled by Lim et al. (2018), Vietnam was already higher than either the Philippines or Indonesia in 1990, and was much higher by 2016 (Table 7.13). It appears that the delivery of basic health services has been unusually successful for a lower-middle-income country, and this has helped to increase confidence among the population that the accelerated economic growth of the past three decades has brought benefits to most parts of the country.

But it needs to be emphasized that the favourable national picture in Vietnam does mask considerable differences in the headcount measure of poverty between the majority Kinh-Hoa group and ethnic minorities, especially those concentrated in the northern uplands and central highlands. Furthermore, the differences appear to have been increasing over time (Baulch et al. 2012: 104). Distance from the main urban centres, low educational levels, and poor Vietnamese language skills are usually given as the main reasons why these groups face difficulties in accessing jobs in the urban sector. The same problems seem to occur in those parts of the Philippines where Muslims comprise most of the population. The headcount measure of poverty in the Autonomous Region of Muslim Mindanao (ARMM) was 40 per cent in 2015, compared with the national average of 16.5 per cent (Philippine Statistics Authority 2016: Table 3). While the headcount measure had declined for the country as a whole between 2006 and 2015, it had increased in the ARMM.

What Statistical Indicators Are Most Useful?

The last three decades have seen a proliferation of indictors intended to rank countries according to human development. Some of these ranking devices combine both monetary and non-monetary indicators, while others focus exclusively on non-monetary indicators. It was pointed out in Chapter 7 that there has in recent years been some criticism of 'mash-up' indices, and an appeal for a dashboard of discrete measures relating to specific development goals (Ravallion 2016: 279-289). But what development goals should be given priority? All the countries in Southeast Asia are members of the United Nations and are presumably committed to pursuing the Sustainable Development Goals, adopted in 2014. They comprise seventeen goals which countries are supposed to work towards in the years from 2015 to 2030. The seventeen goals are related to alleviating poverty and hunger, and achieving good health, literacy, and gender equality. Environmental goals include provision of clean water and affordable clean energy, and protection of both land and the oceans. Economic goals include economic growth, the provision of decent work, and reduced inequality. Both governments and the private sector are also supposed to commit to the goals of responsible production and consumption, industrial innovation and the provision of infrastructure. The only political goal is a general commitment to peace, justice and strong institutions, plus international partnership in achieving these goals.

The various indicators which have been discussed already in the context of Southeast Asia, including the Human Development Index (HDI) and its offshoots, the Multidimensional Poverty Index (MPI) and the Inclusive Development Index, as well as recent attempts to rank countries according to human capital, together provide a large body of information on all these goals. But they are not necessarily packaged in ways which are useful to policymakers, or to those parts of civil society with an interest in specific development goals. As we have seen, the countries of Southeast Asia have in fact had a very mixed record on particular indicators; some have done well on some goals and less well on others. Those countries which have been included in the very high and high human development categories (Singapore, Brunei, Malaysia and Thailand) have not just reduced the proportion of their populations below the $1.90 threshold to virtually zero; they have also done well on educational achievement and on child health indicators (Tables 7.12 and 7.14). The Philippines continues to do well on educational outcomes, in spite of a higher proportion of the population under the $1.90 threshold and a lower overall ranking on the HDI, and on the Inclusive Development Index (World Economic Forum 2018). Indonesia, by contrast, ranks slightly above the Philippines and Vietnam using the HDI, but lower than either of these countries using the MPI (Tables 1.1 and 1.7). Indonesia's achievement on some health outcomes has been especially disappointing, given its relatively high per capita GDP. It has rates of stunting and wasting in children that are well below the average for Southeast Asia (Table 7.12). Indonesia also has high rates of maternal mortality in comparison with other Southeast Asian countries. In 2010, only Laos and Cambodia had higher rates (National Academy of Sciences 2013: Table 2-10). These results help to explain Indonesia's rather low score on the World Bank Human Capital Index for 2018, as well as on the composite human capital indicators compiled by Lim et al. (2018).

Indonesia also does not score very highly on the various indicators of gender inequality reviewed in Chapter 7, although it does better than most Muslim-majority countries. On the other hand, the Philippines ranks very high in the Global Gender Gap Index (GGGI), although less well on the Gender Inequality Index. But it has been argued that the strong performance of the Philippines on the GGGI reflects the fact that women from urban middle- and upper-class families have for many decades had good access to secondary and tertiary education, and thus to professional careers. Both boys and girls from poorer, rural backgrounds have much less chance of completing high school and going on to college. These differentials in access to education by income group and region still persist in Indonesia and Thailand, and probably in other parts of Southeast Asia as well.

To the extent that most countries in Southeast Asia are committed to attaining the sustainable development goals, they will need to monitor carefully a range of both monetary and non-monetary indicators. Under pressure from both national governments and international agencies as well as from a range of non-governmental organizations, statistical agencies across the region will continue to carry out household surveys, which will be used to estimate both poverty and inequality. In addition, both census and survey data will be used to monitor progress on other goals including health, literacy, gender equality and environmental protection. Where there are obvious problems of data quality, especially regarding household survey data, it is crucial that statistical agencies try to remedy the deficiencies. The problems of the social surveys across Southeast Asia were extensively discussed in Chapter 7; especially in Indonesia and the Philippines there would seem to be, as Srinivasan (2010: 150) argued, 'an urgent need for a serious research programme for reconciliation' between survey and national accounts data. It may be that the problems go well beyond a tendency on the part of the richest households to under-report their incomes and expenditures. In other parts of the world, it appears that households at different levels of income are reluctant to participate in surveys, and that is probably true in Southeast Asia as well.[5]

Another problem which has attracted scholarly attention in recent years concerns the estimation of the poverty line. Some analysts have been very critical of the World Bank's poverty lines, which are considered to be too low to sustain even a very basic level of living, even in low- and middle-income countries (Pritchett and Kenny 2013; Hickel 2017: 48-51). The World Bank has defended its low poverty line (now $1.90 a day) on the grounds that it is important to measure extreme poverty. But Pritchett and Kenny (2013: 3) point out that while tracking the numbers below a very low poverty line may be useful for some purposes in some countries, it should not be the only measure used. In the Southeast Asian context, where by the second decade of the twenty-first century it appeared that only Laos had more than 10 per cent of the population below the $1.90 poverty line, and where national poverty lines are also low relative to average household expenditures, there would seem to be a strong argument for using higher poverty lines which would sustain a higher quality of living. Where low poverty lines are used, whether set by international or national agencies, which result in low headcount measures of poverty, there is a danger that governments may

5   See *Economist*, 26 May to 1 June 1 2018, p. 61 for a discussion of the problems with implementing social surveys in the United Kingdom and other high-income countries.

think that the poverty problem has been solved and that policies intended to assist the poor are no longer needed.

If a higher poverty line is used in Southeast Asia, it is clear that the headcount and other measures of poverty would increase sharply. Even using the rather low international and national poverty lines currently adopted, a number of studies in various parts of Southeast Asia have argued that many households whose incomes are just above the poverty threshold are at risk of becoming poor if the income of one or more household members falls. This was an important explanation for the sharp increase in the headcount measure of poverty in Indonesia in the wake of the 1998 collapse in GDP. In Thailand, the impact of the crisis on poverty was less dramatic; it appeared that those people who lost jobs in the formal sector had savings to draw on, or were able to find other employment which kept them above the official poverty threshold, although it is likely that a higher poverty line would have shown a greater increase in numbers of poor. In Vietnam, an analysis of poverty dynamics using panel data from the Household Living Standard Surveys from 2002 to 2006 found that while large numbers of households moved out of poverty over these years, many did not move far above the poverty line, so that they remained vulnerable to further downturns (Baulch and Dat 2012: 38).

While many households tend to move in or out of poverty according to family circumstances, or to macroeconomic fluctuations, others remain chronically poor. These are often households living in remote regions, where households are poorly served by transport infrastructure, and access to health and educational facilities is very limited. Even in areas which are better connected to markets, when household members are old, or infirm and poorly educated, they have few opportunities for productive employment, and often depend on remittances from family members working away from home, or on charity from neighbours or religious institutions. Better government provision of healthcare would certainly help these people, but it may not by itself be sufficient to keep them above the poverty line. The problem of poverty among the aged will become more obvious as populations age, and will have to be addressed through more comprehensive pension provision, at least part of which will come from the government budget.

A related problem concerns the measurement of income distribution. With the exception of Singapore, all countries in Southeast Asia rely on household surveys to estimate inequality, and to the extent that the survey data underestimate the incomes and expenditures of the better-off, most measures, including those based on decile shares, as well as the Gini coefficient, will underestimate the true extent of inequality. The lack of solid evidence on underestimation of income and expenditures across the income range means that the use of household surveys to estimate any distributional indicator is fraught with problems. If the extent of underestimation varies across countries (or even across regions within countries) or varies over time, then comparisons of inequality indicators across countries and regions are likely to be problematic. This is also true of comparisons over time. This reinforces the need for more open discussions about the quality of household survey data in Southeast Asia. National statistical agencies and planning agencies have a crucial role to play in such discussions.

Concluding Comments

In concluding, it will be useful to return to the questions raised in the first chapter. As was argued at the beginning of this chapter, there is strong evidence that, according to most of the indicators widely used to measure living standards, there has been progress across Southeast Asia since the early years of the twentieth century. It is true that in both the colonial and postcolonial eras, many governments could have done more to improve the living standards of the peoples under their control, given the resources which they had at their disposal. In most cases they could have mobilized more from both domestic and foreign sources. But there has been progress on a range of monetary and non-monetary indicators, and this progress has often been widely shared. With the possible exception of the Philippines at some periods after 1950, there is little support for the argument that economic growth, where it has occurred, has been 'immiserizing' in the sense that it has left large sections of the population no better off, or even poorer than they had been before economic growth began. Where there have been periods when income poverty, or living standards more broadly defined, stagnated or fell, they have usually been periods when per capita economic growth was low or negative, such as the 1940s in many parts of the region, in Indochina in the 1970s, or in Indonesia in the decade from 1957 to 1967, or at the end of the twentieth century.

But the benefits of growth, as conventionally measured, have not been evenly spread, and this has often caused resentment in those regions, or among particular groups of people who feel they have been left behind. While there can be little doubt that most regions, and the great majority of people, in Thailand have experienced an improvement in living standards since the 1960s, many Thais living in the north and south of the country resent the fact that the central part of the country, especially the Greater

Bangkok region, has forged ahead more rapidly. Similar resentment is felt
by many Indonesians at the rapid growth of the Greater Jakarta region, by
Filipinos about Metro Manila, and by Malaysians about the booming region
around Kuala Lumpur. In all these regions, poverty is much lower than
the national average, and non-monetary indicators relating to health and
education are often higher. While there are good reasons for the emergence
of these dynamic growth poles, it is inevitable that those left behind in
slower growing regions, often with poorer infrastructure, schools and health
facilities, feel a sense of relative deprivation, if not actual impoverishment.
High and in some cases increasing inequality has strengthened the perception that rising GDP will not necessarily lead to broad-based improvements
in living standards for all. This perception is likely to be strengthened by
the evidence that the distribution of wealth in countries such as Thailand
and Indonesia is very skewed, with the top 1 per cent owning about half of
total wealth. To the extent that much of this wealth is untaxed and can be
passed on in its entirety to children and grandchildren, it is probable that
inequalities in income and wealth will persist over generations.

Opinions vary about the impact of high inequality on economic growth
over the longer term. Some have argued that high levels of inequality cause
waste of talent if able students from poor backgrounds are forced to drop out
of school, while more affluent but less gifted students continue, even though
society might not benefit much from their education. Poor dropouts from
the education system are sometimes tempted into criminal activities as a
way of increasing their incomes; this in turn leads to higher expenditures
by the wealthy on security (Bourguignon 2015: 132-134). To the extent that
the wealthy use private schools and hospitals, as well as private security
services, this makes them less willing to pay taxes to governments whose
services they consider inadequate and do not use.

While some degree of inequality in income and wealth might create
incentives for poorer groups to work harder to improve their own incomes,
it will also lead to greater frustration if they feel that no amount of effort
can lead to a significant improvement in their living standards, or those of
their children. How these various forces will play out in Southeast Asia in
coming decades is far from clear. Even in those countries such as Thailand
and Malaysia, where sustained economic growth over decades has largely
eliminated severe poverty, pronounced inequalities among both people and
regions still exist, and have led to support for politicians, such as Thaksin
in Thailand, who have promised to remedy these inequalities. To the extent
that those who feel they have been left behind are able to express their
frustrations through the electoral process, it is likely that politicians who

claim to represent their interests will attract considerable support, even if they are not very specific on policies. In the countries where the electoral process works less well, or not at all, those who feel they have not benefited from economic growth may turn to more violent forms of protest. As long as inequalities remain high, and governments are either unwilling or unable to assist those left behind, they are likely to pose a continuing threat to political and social stability.

Given that high levels of income inequality are likely to persist in Southeast Asia in coming decades, what can governments do to improve the living standards of the people and the regions which have been left behind? In recent years, there have been quite striking differences across the ten Southeast Asian countries in government expenditures as a percentage of GDP, ranging from 28.5 per cent in Vietnam to 15.7 per cent in Indonesia (Table 8.3). But government expenditures per capita only exceeded $600 per capita in four Southeast Asian countries in 2015. Even if 20 per cent of total expenditures were devoted to policies designed to assist the poor, this would amount to at most $120 per capita, and much less in Myanmar and Cambodia. Even allowing for the fact that the cost of providing assistance would tend to be lower in the poorest countries where labour costs and prices of basic needs are lower, it is doubtful that governments could achieve much with these amounts. In the poorest countries in the region, budgetary funds for poverty alleviation policies will have to be supplemented by external assistance.

In middle-income countries, particularly Indonesia and the Philippines, increased expenditures on poverty alleviation strategies will have to come from increased government revenues. As was argued in Chapter 8, both these countries have implemented a range of policies over the past five decades which have been intended to alleviate poverty. The results have been at best mixed. Following the Latin American model, the Philippines and Indonesia are now implementing conditional cash transfer (CCT) programmes, with most of the funding coming from budgetary sources. Whether these funds will be adequate for nationwide programmes remains to be seen. CCT programmes focus on families with children, and so often exclude the elderly poor, and those families who do not have children but are vulnerable to poverty for other reasons.

Given the limited government budgets available, there appears to be a consensus among governments in Asia that some form of targeting is essential in order to maximize the impact of government anti-poverty policies. But the problem of identifying the poor is far from easy to solve, especially when official poverty lines are often low relative to average household expenditures, and many households classified as above the poverty line in one year may fall below it in the next. In the Indian context, some scholars have argued for universal provision of at least some welfare policies (Dreze and Sen 2013: 194-195). In states such as Kerala and Tamil Nadu, which have much higher HDI scores than the national average for India, health, education and other assistance policies have been provided on a universal rather than targeted basis. On the other hand, it seems clear that governments with limited resources could achieve more in terms of assisting poor families if accurate targeting of the available budget funds was feasible.

But even if targeting could be improved, most governments in Southeast Asia will still face budget constraints, so difficult decisions will have to be made about allocating limited funds among competing policies. Which policies are most likely to be effective in combating poverty? To the extent that many families with incomes above the poverty threshold will face a sharp decline in income if a family member falls ill, there would seem to be a strong case for subsidized or even free provision of healthcare. Education is already heavily subsidized in most parts of the region, particularly at the primary and lower secondary levels, although there is plenty of evidence that teachers often demand extra payments from parents, and penalize those students whose parents are unable or unwilling to pay. Subsidized provision of basic foods, especially rice, have in some cases been an effective means of assisting the poor, especially in those countries such as Indonesia, where domestic rice prices are well above world market levels. But the first-best solution would probably be to eliminate agricultural protection.

More research is certainly needed on the most effective way of assisting the poor across the Southeast Asian region. There has been a distinguished tradition of research on poverty and inequality in Southeast Asia since the 1960s in the Philippines, Malaysia, Indonesia and Thailand by both domestic and foreign scholars. More recently, researchers in Vietnam, Laos and Myanmar have also published studies, often in conjunction with foreign scholars. This research has complemented work by international agencies, especially the World Bank and the Asian Development Bank. The evidence suggests that, at the end of the second decade of the twenty-first century, problems of poverty and relative deprivation are still serious in many parts of Southeast Asia. Debates will continue about measurement of poverty, and better statistics, published in a timely and open way, will certainly assist these debates and hopefully lead to more effective policy interventions.

Bibliography

Abaya-Ulindang, Faina C. (2015) 'Land Resettlement Policies in Colonial and Post-colonial Philippines: Key to Current Insurgencies and Climate Disasters in its Southern Mindanao Island', paper presented at the conference 'Land Grabbing, Conflict and Agrarian-Environmental Transformation: Perspectives from East and Southeast Asia', Chiangmai University, June

Abrera, Ma. Alcestis S. (1976) 'Philippine Poverty Thresholds', in Mahar Mangahas (ed.), *Measuring Philippine Development: Report of the Social Indicators Project*, Manila: The Development Academy of the Philippines

Adas, Michael (1974) *The Burma Delta: Economic Development and Social Change on an Asian Rice Frontier, 1852-1941*, Madison: University of Wisconsin Press

Adas, Michael (1998) 'Improving on the Civilising Mission? Assumptions of United States Exceptionalism in the Colonisation of the Philippines', *Itinerario* 22 (4): 44-66

Adhiati, M. Adriana Sri, and Armin Bobsien (2001) *Indonesia's Transmigration Programme: An Update*. Report prepared for Down to Earth, Thornton Heath, UK

Ahluwalia, Montek S. (1974) 'Income Inequality: Some Dimensions of the Problem', in H. Chenery et al. (1974) *Redistribution with Growth: Policies to Improve Income Distribution in Developing Countries in the Context of Economic Growth: A Joint Study*, ed. Ian Bowen and Brian J. Svikhart, London: Oxford University Press, published for the World Bank and the Institute of Development Studies, University of Sussex

Alatas, Vivi, Abhijit Banerjee, Remma Hanna, Benjamin A. Olken, Ririn Purnamasari and Mathew Wai-Poi (2013) 'Does Elite Capture Matter? Local Elites and Targeted Welfare Programs in Indonesia', Working Paper 18798, Cambridge, MA: National Bureau of Economic Research

Albert, Jose Ramon G., Jesus C. Dumagan and Arturo Martinez, Jr (2015) 'Inequalities in Income, Labor and Education: The Challenge of Inclusive Growth', Discussion Paper Series, no. 2015-01, Quezon City: Philippines Institute of Development Studies,

Alburo, Florian, and E.L. Roberto (1980) 'An Analysis and Synthesis of Poverty Research in the Philippines', in *Survey of Philippine Development Research I*, Manila: Philippine Institute for Development Studies

Alkire, Sabina, and Gisela Robles (2017a) *Global Multidimensional Poverty Index 2017*, Oxford: Oxford Poverty and Human Development Initiative, www.ophi.org.uk, accessed 27 May 2019

Alkire, Sabina, and Gisela Robles (2017b) 'Multidimensional Poverty Index Summer 2017: Brief Methodological Role and Results', *OPHI Methodological Notes 45*, Oxford: Oxford Poverty and Human Development Initiative, www.ophi.org.uk, accessed 27 May 2019

Alkire, Sabina, and P. Santos (2014) 'Measuring Acute Poverty in the Developing World: Robustness and Scope of the Multidimensional Poverty Index', *World Development* 59: 251-274

Allen, Robert C. (2005) 'Real Wages in Europe and Asia: A First Look at the Long-Term Patterns', in Robert C. Allen, Tommy Bengtsson and Martin Dribe (eds), *Living Standards in the Past: New Perspectives on Well-being in Asia and Europe*, Oxford: Oxford University Press

Allen, Robert C., Jean-Pascal Bassino, Debin Ma, Christine Moll-Murata and Jan Luiten van Zanden (2005) 'Wages, Prices, and Living Standards in China, Japan, and Europe, 1738-1925', paper presented at the Departmental Seminar, Department of Economic History, London School of Economics

Allen, Robert C., Tommy Bengtsson and Martin Dribe (2005) 'Introduction', in Robert C. Allen, Tommy Bengtsson and Martin Dribe (eds), *Living Standards in the Past: New Perspectives on Well-being in Asia and Europe*, Oxford: Oxford University Press

Amendola, Nicola, Giacomo Gabbuti and Giovanni Vecchi (2018) 'On the Use of Composite Indices in Economic History: Lessons from Italy, 1861-2017', HHB Working Papers, Series 11, Oxford: Historical Household Budgets Project

Anand, Sudhir (1983) *Inequality and Poverty in Malaysia: Measurement and Decomposition*, New York: Oxford University Press for the World Bank

Anand, Sudhir, Paul Segal and Joseph E. Stiglitz (eds) (2010) *Debates on the Measurement of Global Poverty*, Oxford: Oxford University Press

Anderson, Benedict (1988) 'Cacique Democracy in the Philippines: Origins and Dreams', *New Left Review* 169, 1-24

Andersson, Magnus, Anders Engvall and Ari Kokko (2006) 'Determinants of Poverty in Lao PDR', SIDA Country Economic Report 2005:10, Stockholm: Swedish International Development Agency

Andrews, James M. (1935) *Siam: Second Rural Survey 1934-1935*, Bangkok: Bangkok Times Press Ltd

Andrus, J.R. (1948) *Burmese Economic Life*, Stanford: Stanford University Press

Anh, Vu Thanh Tu (2016) 'Vietnam: Decentralization amidst Fragmentation', *Journal of Southeast Asian Economies* 33 (2): 188-208

Aquino, Eustaquio G. (1931) *Land Utilization in the Philippines*, Manila: Institute of Pacific Relations

ASEAN Secretariat (2010) *ASEAN Statistical Yearbook 2010*, Jakarta: ASEAN Secretariat

ASEAN Secretariat (2017) *ASEAN Statistical Yearbook 2016/17* Jakarta: ASEAN Secretariat

ASEAN Secretariat (2018) *ASEAN Statistical Yearbook 2018* Jakarta: ASEAN Secretariat

Asher, Mukul G., and Anne Booth (1992) 'Fiscal Policy', in Anne Booth (ed.), *The Oil Boom and After: Indonesian Economic Policy and Performance in the Soeharto Era*, Singapore: Oxford University Press

Asian Development Bank (2008) *Key Indicators for Asia and the Pacific 2008*, Mandaluyong City: Asian Development Bank

Asian Development Bank (2009) *Poverty in the Philippines: Causes, Constraints, and Opportunities*, Mandaluyong City: Asian Development Bank

Asian Development Bank (2012) *Cambodia: Country Poverty Analysis: December 2011*, Mandaluyong City: Asian Development Bank

Asian Development Bank (2014a) *ADB Basic Statistics*, Mandaluyong City: Asian Development Bank

Asian Development Bank (2014b) *Cambodia: Country Poverty Analysis, 2014*, Mandaluyong City: Asian Development Bank

Asian Development Bank (2014c) 'Poverty in Asia: A Deeper Look', in *Key Indicators for Asia and the Pacific 2014*, Mandaluyong City: Asian Development Bank

Asian Development Bank (2015) *Key Indicators for Asia and the Pacific 2015*, Mandaluyong City: Asian Development Bank

Asian Development Bank (2017) *Key Indicators for Asia and the Pacific 2017*, Mandaluyong City: Asian Development Bank

Asian Development Bank (2018) *Basic 2018 Statistics*, Mandaluyong City: Asian Development Bank, Economic Research and Regional Cooperation Department

Asra, Abuzar (1989a) 'Inequality Trends in Indonesia, 1969-1981: A Re-examination', *Bulletin of Indonesian Economic Studies* 25 (2): 100-111

Asra, Abuzar (1989b) 'Poverty Trend in Indonesia, 1970-1987', *Ekonomi dan Keuangan Indonesia* 37 (3): 379-392

Asra, Abuzar (2000) 'Poverty and Inequality in Indonesia: Estimates, Decomposition and Key Issues', *Journal of the Asia Pacific Economy* 5 (1 and 2): 91-111

Asra, Abuzar (2014) *Cerdas Menggunakan Statistik* [Accurate use of statistics], Bogor: In Media

Asra, Abuzar, and Vivian Santos-Francisco (2003) 'Poverty Lines: Eight Countries' Experiences and the Issue of Specificity and Consistency', in Christopher M. Edmonds (ed.), *Reducing Poverty in Asia: Emerging Issues in Growth, Targeting and Measurement*, Cheltenham: Edward Elgar

Asra, Abuzar, Isidro P. David and Romulo A. Virola (1997) 'Poverty Assessment in the Philippines and Indonesia: A Methodological Comparison', *Journal of Philippines Development* XXIV (2): 257-274

Aten, Bettina, and Alan Heston (2010) 'Use of Country Purchasing Power Parities for International Comparisons of Poverty Levels: Potential and Limitations', in Sudhir Anand, Paul Segal and Joseph E. Stiglitz (eds), *Debates on the Measurement of Global Poverty*, Oxford: Oxford University Press

Atkinson, A.B. (2010) 'Top Incomes in a Rapidly Growing Economy: Singapore', in A.B. Atkinson, Thomas Piketty and Emmanuel Saez (eds), *Top Incomes: A Global Perspective*, Oxford: Oxford University Press

Baker, Chris, and Pasuk Phongpaichit (1995) *Thailand: Economy and Politics*, Kuala Lumpur: Oxford University Press

Balisacan, Arsenio, and Rosemarie Edillon (2005) 'Poverty Targeting in the Philippines', in John Weiss (ed.), *Poverty Targeting in Asia*, Cheltenham: Edward Elgar

Balisacan, Arsenio, Sharon Piza, Dennis Mapa, Carlos Abad Santos and Donna Odra (2010) 'The Philippine Economy and Poverty during the Global Economic Crisis', *The Philippine Review of Economics* XLVII (1): 1-37

Balisacan, Arsenio M. (1990) 'Why Do Governments Do What They Do? Agrarian Reform in the Philippines', in D.B. Canlas and H. Sakai (eds), *Studies in Economic Policy and Institutions: The Philippines*, Tokyo: Institute of Developing Economies

Balisacan, Arsenio M. (1994) *Poverty, Urbanization and Development Policy: A Philippine Perspective*, Diliman: University of the Philippines Press

Balisacan, Arsenio M. (1997) 'Getting the Story Right: Redistribution and Poverty Alleviation in the Philippines', *Philippine Review of Economics and Business* XXXIV (1): 1-37

Balisacan, Arsenio M. (1999) 'What Do We Really Know – or Don't Know – about Economic Inequality and Poverty in the Philippines?', in Arsenio M. Balisacan and S. Fujisaki (eds), *Causes of Poverty: Myths, Facts and Policies: A Philippine Study*, Diliman: University of the Philippines Press

Balisacan, Arsenio M. (2000) 'Growth, Redistribution and Poverty: Is the Philippines an Exception to the Standard Asian Story?', *Journal of the Asia Pacific Economy* 5 (1 and 2): 125-140

Balisacan, Arsenio M. (2003) 'Poverty and Inequality', in Arsenio M. Balisacan and Hal Hill (eds), *The Philippine Economy: Development, Policies and Challenges*, Oxford: Oxford University Press

Balisacan, Arsenio M., and Hal Hill, 'An Introduction to the Key Issues', in Arsenio M. Balisacan and Hal Hill (eds) (2003) *The Philippine Economy: Development, Policies and Challenges*, Oxford: Oxford University Press

Balisacan, Arsenio M., and Nobuhiko Fuwa (2004) 'Going beyond Crosscountry Averages: Growth, Inequality and Poverty Reduction in the Philippines', *World Development* 32 (11): 1891-1907

Balisacan, Arsenio M., Nobuhiko Fuwa and Margarita H. Debuque (2004) 'The Political Economy of Philippine Rural Development since the 1960s', in Takamasa Akiyama and Donald F. Larson (eds), *Rural Development and Agricultural Growth in Indonesia, the Philippines and Thailand*, Canberra: Asia Pacific Press

Ballesteros, Marife (2019) 'The Philippines Needs to Rethink Its Agricultural Policy', *East Asia Form*, 15 March

Ballesteros, Marife, Jenica Ancheta and Tatum Ramos (2017) 'The Comprehensive Agrarian Reform Program after 30 Years: Accomplishments and Forward Options', Discussion Paper Series, 2017-34, Quezon City: Philippine Institute of Development Studies

Banens, Maks (2000) 'Vietnam: A Reconstruction of Its 20th Century Population History', in Jean-Pascal Bassino, Jean-Dominique Giacometti and K. Odaka (eds), *Quantitative Economic History of Vietnam 1900-1990*, Tokyo: Hitotsubashi University, Institute of Economic Research

Bank Indonesia (1955) *Annual Report 1955*, Jakarta: Bank Indonesia

Bank Indonesia (1956) *Annual Report 1956*, Jakarta: Bank Indonesia

Bank Negara Malaysia (1961) *Annual Report, 1961*, Kuala Lumpur: Bank Negara Malaysia

Bank Negara Malaysia (2006) *Annual Report and Statement of Accounts, 2006,* Kuala Lumpur: Bank Negara Malaysia

Barclay, George (1954) *Colonial Development and Population in Taiwan*, Princeton: Princeton University Press

Barker, Randolph, and Robert W. Herdt, with Beth Rose (1985) *The Rice Economy of Asia*, Washington, DC: Resources for the Future Inc.

Barnett, H.L. (1947) *Malayan Agricultural Statistics*, Kuala Lumpur: Department of Agriculture

Bassino, Jean-Pascal (2000) 'Public Finance in Vietnam under French Rule 1895-1954', in Jean-Pascal Bassino, Jean-Dominique Giacometti and K. Odaka (eds), *Quantitative Economic History of Vietnam 1900-1990*, Tokyo: Hitotsubashi University, Institute of Economic Research

Bassino, Jean-Pascal, Marion Dovis and John Komlos (2018) 'Biological Well-being in the Late Nineteenth Century Philippines', *Cliometrica* 12: 33-60

Batalla, Eric Vincent C. (2016) 'Divided Politics and Economic Growth in the Philippines', *Journal of Current Southeast Asian Affairs* 3: 161-186

Baten, Joerg, Mojgen Stegl and Pierre van der Eng (2013) 'The Biological Standard of Living and Body Height in Colonial Indonesia: 1770-2000', *Journal of Bionomics* 15 (2): 103-122

Batson, Benjamin A. (1984) *The End of the Absolute Monarchy in Siam*, Singapore: Oxford University Press

Baulch, Bob, and Vu Huong Dat (2012) 'Poverty Dynamics in Vietnam, 2002-2006', in Nguyen Thang (ed.), *Poverty, Vulnerability and Social Protection in Vietnam: Selected Issues*, Hanoi: The Goi Publishers

Baulch, Bob, Hoa Thi Minh Nguyen, Hung Thai Pham and Phuong Thu Thi Phuong (2012) 'Ethnic Minority Poverty in Vietnam', in Nguyen Thang (ed.), *Poverty, Vulnerability and Social Protection in Vietnam: Selected Issues*, Hanoi: The Goi Publishers

Bautista, Romeo (1990) 'Rapid Agricultural Growth Is Not Enough: The Philippines, 1965-80', paper presented at the conference 'Agriculture on the Road to Industrialization', Council of Agriculture, Taipei, September

Bautista, Romeo (1994) 'Dynamics of Rural Development: Analytical and Policy Aspects', *Journal of Philippine Development* XXI (1 and 2): 93-134

Baxter, James (1941) *Report on Indian Migration*, Rangoon: Government Printing and Stationery

Bayly, Christopher, and Tim Harper (2004) *Forgotten Armies: Britain's Asian Empire and the War with Japan*, London: Penguin Books

Bayly, Christopher, and Tim Harper (2007) *Forgotten Wars: The End of Britain's Asian Empire*, London: Penguin Books

Beegle, Kathleen, Joachim De Weerdt, Jed Friedman and John Gibson (2012) 'Methods of Household Consumption Measurement through Surveys: Experimental Results from Tanzania', *Journal of Development Economics* 98: 3-18

Beenstock, Michael (1980) 'The Cost of Nutrition in Indonesia and the Poverty Line', in *Health, Migration and Development*, Westmead: Gower Publishing

Bengstsson, Tommy (2004) 'Living Standards and Economic Stress', in Tommy Bengtsson, Cameron Campbell and James Z. Lee (eds), *Life under Pressure: Mortality and Living Standards in Europe and Asia, 1700-1900*, Cambridge, MA: MIT Press

Benjamin, Dwayne, Loren Brandt and Brian McCaig (2016) 'Growth with Equity: Income Inequality in Vietnam 2002-14', Discussion Paper no. 10392, Bonn: IZA

Bennett, M.K. (1951) 'International Disparities in Consumption Levels', *American Economic Review* 41: 632-649

Bennison, J.J. (1928) *Report of an Enquiry into the Standard and Cost of Living of the Working Classes in Rangoon*, Rangoon: Superintendent, Government Printing and Stationery

Beresford, Melanie, Nguon Sokha, Rathin Roy, Sau Sisovanna and Ceema Namazie (2004) *The Macroeconomics of Poverty Reduction in Cambodia*, Report Submitted to the Ministry of Economics and Finance, Phnom Penh: UNDP

Berreman, Gerald D. (1956) 'The Philippines: A Survey of Current Social, Economic and Political Conditions', Data Paper no. 19, Ithaca: Cornell University Southeast Asia Program

Berry, Albert (1978) 'Income and Consumption Distribution Trends in the Philippines 1950-70', *Review of Income and Wealth* 24 (3): 313-331

Bhalla, Surjit S. (2010) 'Raising the Standard: The War on Global Poverty', in Sudhir Anand, Paul Segal and Joseph E. Stiglitz (eds), *Debates on the Measurement of Global Poverty*, Oxford: Oxford University Press

Bidwell, R.L. (1970) *Currency Conversion Tables: A Hundred Years of Change*, London: Rex Collings

Birnberg, Thomas B., and Stephen A. Resnick (1975) *Colonial Development: An Econometric Study*, New Haven: Yale University Press

Bolt, Jutta, and Jan Luiten van Zanden (2014) 'The Maddison Project: Collaborative Research on Historical National Accounts', *Economic History Review* 67 (3): 627-651

Bolt, Jutta, Robert Inklaar, Herman de Jong and Jan Luiten van Zanden (2018) *Maddison Project Database, 2018*, https://www.rug.nl/ggdc/historicaldevelopment/maddison/releases/maddison-project-database-2018, accessed 27 May 2019

Boomgaard, Peter (1991) 'The Non-agricultural Side of an Agricultural Economy: Java, 1500-1900', in Paul Alexander, Peter Boomgaard and Ben White (eds), *In the Shadow of Agriculture: Non-farm Activities in the Javanese Economy, Past and Present*, Amsterdam: Royal Tropical Institute

Boomgaard, Peter (2003) 'Smallpox, Vaccination, and the Pax Neerlandica Indonesia, 1550-1930', *Bijdragen tot de Taal-, Land en Volkenkunde* 159: 590-617

Boomgaard, Peter (2014) 'Population Growth and Environmental Change: A Two-Track Model', in Norman G. Owen (ed.), *Routledge Handbook of Southeast Asian History*, Abingdon: Routledge

Boomgaard, Peter, and A.J. Gooszen (1991) *Population Trends, 1795-1942*, Amsterdam: Royal Tropical Institute

Boomgaard, Peter, and J.L. van Zanden (1990) *Food Crops and Arable Lands: Java 1815-1942*, Amsterdam: Royal Tropical Institute

Boonyamanond, Sawarai, and Sureeporn Punpuing (2012) 'Impact of the 1997-98 Financial Crisis on Employment, Migration and Poverty: Lessons Learnt from Thailand', in Aris Ananta and Richard Barichello (eds), *Poverty and Global Recession in Southeast Asia*, Singapore: ISEAS

Booth, Anne (1974) 'Land Ownership in Klaten', *Bulletin of Indonesian Economic Studies* 10 (3): 135-140

Booth, Anne (1980) 'The Economic Impact of Export Taxes in ASEAN', *Malayan Economic Review* 25 (1): 36-61

Booth, Anne (1988) *Agricultural Development in Indonesia*, Sydney: Allen and Unwin for the Asian Studies Association of Australia

Booth, Anne (1990) 'The Evolution of Fiscal Policy and the Role of Government in the Colonial Economy', in Anne Booth, W.J. O'Malley and Anna Weidemann (eds), *Indonesian Economic History in the Dutch Colonial Era*, New Haven: Yale University Southeast Asia Studies

Booth, Anne (1993) 'Counting the Poor in Indonesia', *Bulletin of Indonesian Economic Studies* 29 (1): 53-84

Booth, Anne (1997a) 'Poverty in South East Asia: Some Comparative Estimates', in Chris Dixon and David Drakakis-Smith (eds), *Uneven Development in South East Asia*, Aldershot: Ashgate

Booth, Anne (1997b) 'Rapid Economic Growth and Poverty Decline: A Comparison of Indonesia and Thailand 1981-1990', *Journal of International Development* 9 (2): 169-187

Booth, Anne (1998) *The Indonesian Economy in the Nineteenth and Twentieth Centuries*, Basingstoke: Macmillan Press

Booth, Anne (1999) 'Initial Conditions and Miraculous Growth: Why Is South East Asia Different from Taiwan and South Korea?', *World Development* 27 (2): 301-321

Booth, Anne (2001a) 'The Causes of South East Asia's Economic Crisis: A Sceptical Review of the Debate', *Asia Pacific Business Review* 8 (2): 19-48

Booth, Anne (2001b) 'Initial Conditions and Miraculous Growth: Why Is Southeast Asia Different from Taiwan and South Korea?', in K.S. Jomo (ed.), *Southeast Asia's Industrialization: Industrial Policy, Capabilities and Sustainability*, Basingstoke: Palgrave

Booth, Anne (2002a) 'The Changing Role of Non-farm Activities in Agricultural Households in Indonesia: Some Insights from the Agricultural Censuses', *Bulletin of Indonesian Economic Studies* 38 (2): 179-200

Booth, Anne (2002b) 'Rethinking the Role of Agriculture in the "East Asian" Model: Why Is Southeast Asia Different from Northeast Asia?', *ASEAN Economic Bulletin* 19 (1): 40-51

Booth, Anne (2003) 'The Burma Development Disaster in Comparative Historical Perspective', *South East Asia Research* 11 (2): 141-171

Booth, Anne (2004) 'Linking, De-linking and Re-linking: South East Asia in the Global Economy in the 20th Century', *Australian Economic History Review* 44 (1): 35-51

Booth, Anne E. (2007a) *Colonial Legacies: Economic and Social Development in East and Southeast Asia*, Honolulu: University of Hawaii Press

Booth, Anne (2007b) 'Night Watchman, Extractive, or Developmental States? Some Evidence from Late Colonial South-east Asia', *Economic History Review* 60: 241-266

Booth, Anne (2012) 'Measuring Living Standards in Different Colonial Systems: Some Evidence from South East Asia, 1900-42', *Modern Asian Studies* 46 (5): 1145-1181

Booth, Anne (2013) 'Colonial Revenue Policies and The Impact of the Transition to Independence in Southeast Asia', *Bijdragen tot de taal-, land- en Volkenkunde* 169: 1-31

Booth, Anne (2014a) 'Before the "Big Bang": Decentralization Debates and Practice in Indonesia, 1949-99', in Hal Hill (ed.), *Regional Dynamics in a Decentralized Indonesia*, Singapore: ISEAS

Booth, Anne (2014b) 'Land Taxation in Asia: An Overview of the 19th and 20th Centuries', *Oxford Development Studies* 42 (1): 1-18

Booth, Anne (2015) 'Trade and Growth in the Colonial and Post-colonial Periods', in J. Touwen and Alice Schrikker (eds), *Promises and Predicaments: Trade and Entrepreneurship in Colonial and Independent Indonesia in the 19th and 20th Centuries: Essays in Honour of Thomas Lindblad*, Singapore: NUS Press

Booth, Anne (2016) *Economic Change in Modern Indonesia: Colonial and Post-colonial Comparisons*, Cambridge: Cambridge University Press

Booth, Anne, and Kent Deng (2017) 'Japanese Colonialism in Comparative Perspective', *Journal of World History* 28 (1): 61-98

Booth, Anne, and R.M. Sundrum (1981) 'Income Distribution', in Anne Booth and Peter McCawley (eds), *The Indonesian Economy during the Soeharto Era*, Kuala Lumpur: Oxford University Press

Bourguignon, François (2015) *The Globalization of Inequality*, Princeton: Princeton University Press

Boyce, James K. (1993) *The Philippines: The Political Economy of Growth and Impoverishment in the Marcos Era*, Basingstoke: The Macmillan Press for the OECD Development Centre

Brand, W. (1958) 'Differential mortality in the town of Bandung' in *The Indonesian Town*, The Hague: W. van Hoeve Ltd.

Branisa, Boris, Stephan Klasen, Maria Ziegler, Denis Drechsler and J. Jutting (2014) 'The Institutional Basis of Gender Inequality: The Social Institutions and Gender Index (SIGI)', *Feminist Economics* 20 (2): 29-64

Breman, Jan (2002) 'New Thoughts on Colonial Labour in Indonesia', *Journal of Southeast Asian Studies* 33 (2): 333-339

Bresciani, Fabrizio, Gershon Feder, David O. Gilligan, Hanan G. Jacoby, Tongroj Onchan and Jamie Quizon (2002) 'Weathering the Storm', *World Bank Research Observer* 17 (1): 1-20

Broadberry, Stephen, and Bishnupriya Gupta (2006) 'The Early Modern Great Divergence: Wages, Prices and Economic Development in Europe and Asia, 1500-1800', *Economic History Review* LIX (1): 2-31

Brocheux, Pierre (1995) *The Mekong Delta: Ecology, Economy and Revolution, 1860-1960*, Madison: University of Wisconsin Press

Brocheux, Pierre, and Daniel Hemery (2009) *Indochina: An Ambiguous Colonization, 1858-1954*, Berkeley: University of California Press

Brown, Colin (1987) 'The Influenza Pandemic of 1918 in Indonesia', in Norman G. Owen (ed.), *Death and Disease in Southeast Asia: Explorations in Social, Medical and Demographic History*, Singapore: Oxford University Press

Brown, Ian (1988) *The Elite and the Economy in Siam c. 1890-1920*, Singapore: Oxford University Press

Brown, Ian (2005) *A Colonial Economy in Crisis: Burma's Rice Cultivators and the World Depression of the 1930s*, London: Routledge Curzon

Brown, Ian (2013) *Burma's Economy in the Twentieth Century*, Cambridge: Cambridge University Press

Bureau of Census and Statistics (1947) *Yearbook of Philippine Statistics, 1946*, Manila: Bureau of Census and Statistics

Bureau of Census and Statistics (1960) *Handbook of Philippine Statistics, 1903-1959*, Manila: Bureau of Census and Statistics

Bureau of Census and Statistics (1971) *Yearbook of Philippine Statistics, 1969*, Manila: Bureau of Census and Statistics

Butcher, John (1993) 'Revenue Farming and the Changing State in Southeast Asia', in John Butcher and Howard Dick (eds), *The Rise and Fall of Revenue Farming*, Basingstoke: Macmillan Press

Centraal Kantoor voor de Statistiek (1932-1940) *Indische Verlag II, Statistisch Jaaroverzicht van Nederlandsch-Indie over het Jaar 1932-1940*, Batavia: Landsdrukkerij

Central Bank of the Philippines (1956) *Seventh Annual Report 1955*, Manila: Central Bank of the Philippines

Central Bank of the Philippines (1960) *Eleventh Annual Report 1959*, Manila: Central Bank of the Philippines

Central Board of Statistics (2009) *Statistical Yearbook of Indonesia 2009*, Jakarta: Central Bureau of Statistics

Central Board of Statistics (2012) *Statistical Yearbook of Indonesia 2012*, Jakarta: Central Bureau of Statistics

Central Board of Statistics (2015a) *Ringkasan Eksekutif Pengeluaran dan Konsumsi Penduduk Indonesia* [Executive summary of consumption and expenditure of Indonesia], Jakarta: Central Board of Statistics

Central Board of Statistics (2015b) *Statistical Yearbook of Indonesia 2015*, Jakarta: Central Bureau of Statistics

Central Bureau of Statistics (1947) *Statistical Pocketbook of Indonesia 1941*, Batavia: G. Kolff

Central Bureau of Statistics (1959) *Statistical Pocketbook of Indonesia, 1959*, Jakarta: Biro Pusat Statistik

Central Bureau of Statistics (1961) *Statistical Pocketbook of Indonesia, 1961*, Jakarta: Biro Pusat Statistik

Central Bureau of Statistics (1971) *Statistical Pocketbook of Indonesia, 1968 and 1969*, Jakarta: Biro Pusat Statistik

Central Bureau of Statistics (1975) *1971 Population Census, Population of Indonesia, Series D*, Jakarta: Central Bureau of Statistics

Central Bureau of Statistics (1983) *Results of the 1980 Population Census, Series S.2*, Jakarta: Central Bureau of Statistics

Central Bureau of Statistics (1992) *Results of the 1990 Population Census, Series S.2*, Jakarta: Central Bureau of Statistics

Central Bureau of Statistics (1995) *Sensus Pertanian 1993, Sampel Rumahtangga Pertanian Pengguna Lahan*, Jakarta: Central Bureau of Statistics

Central Bureau of Statistics (1997) *Statistical Yearbook of Indonesia 1996*, Jakarta: Central Bureau of Statistics

Central Service of Statistics (c. 1946) *Statistical Yearbook of Thailand, No 21, 1939-40 to 1944*, Bangkok: Central Service of Statistics

Central Statistical and Economics Department (1963) *Statistical Year Book 1961*, Rangoon: The Revolutionary Government of the Union of Burma

Chander, Datuk R., and B. Welsh, 2015, 'Malaysia's 2020 missed opportunity: Najib Tun Razak's 11th Malaysia Plan', *New Mandala Inquirer* 1, http://asiapacific.anu.edu.au/newmandala, accessed 18 January 2016

Chander, Ramesh (1980) 'Recent Experience in Household Surveys in Malaysia and the Philippines', in Christopher Scott, Paulo de Andre and Ramesh Chander, 'Conducting Surveys in Developing Countries: Practical Problems and Experience in Brazil, Malaysia and the Philippines', LSMS Working Paper, no. 5, Washington, DC: World Bank

Chandra, Siddharth (2008) 'Economic Histories of the Opium Trade', in Robert Whaples (ed.), *EH.Net Encyclopedia*, 10 February, http://eh.net/?s=Economic+Histories+of+the+Opium+, accessed 18 July 2019

Chang, Yunshik (1966) *Population in Early Modernization: Korea*, PhD dissertation, Princeton University

Cheetham, Russell J., and Edward K. Hawkins (1976) *The Philippines: Priorities and Prospects for Development: Report of a Mission Sent to the Philippines by the World Bank*, Washington, DC: World Bank

Chenery, H., et al. (1974) *Redistribution with Growth: Policies to Improve Income Distribution in Developing Countries in the Context of Economic Growth: A Joint Study*, ed. Ian Bowen and Brian J. Svikhart, London: Oxford University Press, published for the World Bank and the Institute of Development Studies, University of Sussex

Chernichovsky, Dov, and Oey Astra Meesook (1984a) 'Patterns of Food Consumption and Nutrition in Indonesia: An Analysis of the National Socioeconomic Survey, 1978', World Bank Staff Working Papers, no. 670, Washington, DC: World Bank

Chernichovsky, Dov, and Oey Astra Meesook (1984b) 'Poverty in Indonesia: A Profile', World Bank Staff Working Papers, no. 671, Washington, DC: World Bank

Choy, Keen Meng, and Ichiro Sugimoto (2018) 'Staple Trade, Real Wages and Living Standards in Singapore, 1870-1939', *Economic History of Developing Regions* 33 (1): 18-50

Chiba, Yoshihiro (2010) 'The 1919 and 1935 Rice Crises in the Philippines: The Rice Market and Starvation in American Colonial Times', *Philippine Studies* 58 (4): 523-556

Cleary, Mark C. (1992) 'Plantation Agriculture and the Development of Native Land Rights in British North Borneo, c. 1880-1930', *Geographical Journal* 158 (2): 170-181

Collier, William L., Soentoro, Gunawan Wiradi, Effendi Pasandaram, Kabul Santoso and Joseph L. Stepanek (1982) 'Acceleration of Rural Development in Java', *Bulletin of Indonesian Economic Studies* 18 (3): 84-101

Colonial Office (1955) *An Economic Survey of the Colonial Territories, Vol. V: The Far Eastern Territories*, London: Her Majesty's Stationery Office

Commission of the Census (1941) *Volume II: Summary for the Philippines and General Report of Population and Agriculture 1939*, Manila: Bureau of Printing

Commonwealth of the Philippines (1941) *Yearbook of Philippine Statistics 1940*, Manila: Bureau of Census and Statistics

Concepcion, Isabelo (1933) *The Physical Growth of Filipinos*, Manila: Institute of Pacific Relations

Corpuz, O.D. (1989) *The Roots of the Filipino Nation*, 2 vols., Quezon City: Aklahi Foundation

Corpuz, O.D. (1997) *An Economic History of the Philippines*, Quezon City: University of the Philippines Press

Costello, Michael (1992) 'The Demography of Mindanao', in Mark Turner, R.J. May and Lulu R. Turner (eds), *Mindanao: Land of Unfulfilled Promise*, Quezon City: New Day Publishers

Council for Economic Planning and Development (1992) *Taiwan Statistical Data Book 1992*, Taipei: Council for Economic Planning and Development

Coxhead, Ian, Vu Hoang Linh and Le Dong Tam (2012) 'Global Market Shocks and Poverty in Vietnam: The Case of Rice', *Agricultural Economics* 43: 575-592

Crafts, N.F.R. (1997) 'Some Dimensions of the "Quality of Life" during the British Industrial Revolution', *Economic History Review* 50 (4): 617-639

Crafts, Nicholas (2002) 'The Human Development Index, 1870-1999: Some Revised Estimates', *European Review of Economic History* 6: 395-340

Credit Suisse (2017) *Global Wealth Databook, 2017*, Zurich: Credit Suisse AG Research Institute

Credit Suisse (2018) *Global Wealth Databook, 2018*, Zurich: Credit Suisse AG Research Institute

Creutzberg, P. (1975) *Changing Economy in Indonesia: Vol. 1, Export Crops 1816-1940*, The Hague: Martinus Nijhoff

Creutzberg, P. (1976) *Changing Economy in Indonesia: Vol. 2, Public Finance 1816-1939*, The Hague: Martinus Nijhoff

Dandekar, V.M., and N. Rath (1971) *Poverty in India*, Pune: Indian School of Political Economy

Dapice, David (1980) 'Trends in Income Distribution and Levels of Living, 1970-75', in Gustav Papanek (ed.), *The Indonesian Economy*, New York: Praeger Special Studies

Das Gupta, Ajit (1979) 'Underdevelopment, Past and Present: Some Comparisons of Pre-industrial Levels of Living-II', *The Indian Economic and Social History Review* 16 (1): 33-52

Dasgupta, Partha (1993) *An Inquiry into Well-being and Destitution*, Oxford: Clarendon Press

Deaton, Angus (2010) 'Measuring Poverty in a Growing World (or Measuring Growth in a Poor World)', in Sudhir Anand, Paul Segal and Joseph E. Stiglitz (eds), *Debates on the Measurement of Global Poverty*, Oxford: Oxford University Press

Deaton, Angus, and Bettina Aten (2017) 'Trying to Understand the PPPs in ICP 2011: Why are the Results so Different?', *American Economic Journal: Macroeconomics* 9 (1): 243-264

Deaton, Angus, and Olivier Dupriez (2011) 'Purchasing Power Parity Exchange Rates for the Global Poor', *American Economic Journal: Applied Economics* 3: 137-166

Deaton, Angus, and Valerie Kozel (eds) (2005) *The Great Indian Poverty Debate*, Delhi: Macmillan India Ltd

De Bevoise, Ken (1995) *Agents of Apocalypse: Epidemic Disease in Colonial Philippines*, Princeton: Princeton University Press

De Haas, J.H. (1939) 'Mortality According to Age Groups in Batavia, Especially among Children', *Indian Journal of Pediatrics* VI (26): 231-249

De Jong, Frida, and Wim Ravesteijn (2008) 'Technology and Administration: The Rise and Development of Public Works in the East Indies', in Wim Ravesteijn and Jan Kop (eds), *For Profit and Prosperity: The Contribution Made by Dutch Engineers to Public Works in Indonesia, 1800-2000*, Zaltbommel/Leiden: Aprilis/KITLV Press

De Jong, L. (2002) *The Collapse of a Colonial Society: The Dutch in Indonesia during the Second World War*, Leiden: KITLV Press

De Langen, C.D. (1934) 'The General State of Health of the Inhabitants', in Department of Economic Affairs, *Geld- en Producten-Huishouding, Volksvoeding en -Gezondheid in Koetowinangoen*, Buitenzorg: Archipel Drukkerij

Demombynes, Gabriel, and Linh Hoang Vu (2015) *Demystifying Poverty Measurement in Vietnam*, Hanoi: World Bank Country Office

Department of Economic Affairs (1934) *Geld- en Producten-Huishouding, Volksvoeding en -Gezondheid in Koetowinangoen*, Buitenzorg: Archipel Drukkerij

Department of Information (1993) *Lampiran Pidato Pertanggungjawaban Presiden/Mandataris Majelis Permusyawaratan Rakyat Republik Indonesia* [Appendix to the accountability speech delivered to the People's Deliberation Council], Jakarta: Department of Information

Department of Information (1994) *Lampiran Pidato Kenegaraan Presiden Republic Indonesia*, Jakarta: Department of Information

Department of Information (1998) *Lampiran Pidato Kenegaraan Presiden Republic Indonesia*, Jakarta: Department of Information

Department of Statistics (1936) *Malayan Year Book 1936*, Singapore: Government Printing Office

Department of Statistics (1939) *Malayan Year Book 1939*, Singapore: Government Printing Office

Department of Statistics (2015) *Yearbook of Statistics: Singapore 2015*, Singapore: Department of Statistics

Department of Statistics: Malaysia (1997) *Yearbook of Statistics: Malaysia 1996*, Kuala Lumpur: Department of Statistics

Department of Statistics: Sabah (1996) *Yearbook of Statistics: Sabah 1996*, Kota Kinabalu: Department of Statistics, Malaysia (Sabah Branch)

Department of Statistics: Sarawak (1998) *Yearbook of Statistics: Sarawak 1998*, Kuching: Department of Statistics, Malaysia (Sarawak Branch)

Department van Landbouw, Nijverheid en Handel (1922-1930) *Statistisch Jaaroverzicht van Nederlandsch-Indie*, Batavia: Department van Landbouw, Nijverheid en Handel

Desbarats, Jacqueline (1987) 'Population Redistribution in the Socialist Republic of Vietnam', *Population and Development Review* 13 (1): 43-77

De Vries, Jan (2008) *The Industrious Revolution: Consumer Behavior and the Household Economy, 1650 to the Present*, Cambridge: Cambridge University Press

De Zwart, Pim, and Jan Luiten van Zanden (2015) 'Labour, Wages and Living Standards in Java, 1680-1914', *European Review of Economic History* 19 (3): 215-234

Direction des Services Economiques (1947) *Annuaire Statistique de l'Indochine, 1943-46*, Hanoi: Direction des Services Economiques

Dixon, John A. (1984) 'Consumption', in Walter P. Falcon, W.O. Jones and S.R. Pearson (eds), *The Cassava Economy of Java*, Stanford: Stanford University Press

Dollar, David (2004) 'Reform, Growth and Poverty', in Paul Glewwe, Nisha Agrawal and David Dollar (eds), *Economic Growth, Poverty and Household Welfare in Vietnam*, Washington, DC: The World Bank

Dollar, David, and Aart Kraay (2002) 'Growth in Good for the Poor', *Journal of Economic Growth* 7: 195-225

Dollar, David, Tatjana Kleineberg and Aart Kraay (2013) 'Growth Is Still Good for the Poor', World Bank Policy Working Paper, WPS 6568

Drabble, John (1991) *Malayan Rubber: The Inter-war Years*, London: Macmillan

Drake, P.J. (2004) *Currency, Credit and Commerce: Early Growth in Southeast Asia*, Aldershot: Ashgate

Dreze, Jean, and Amartya Sen (2013) *An Uncertain Glory: India and Its Contradictions*, London: Allen Lane

Ducanes, Geoffrey (2010) 'The Case of the Missing Remittances in the FIES: Could It Be Causing Us to Mismeasure Welfare Changes?', Discussion Paper no. 2010-04, Quezon City: University of the Philippines School of Economics

Ducanes, Geoffrey M., and Edita Abella Tan (2014) 'Who Are the Poor and Do They Remain Poor?', Discussion Paper, 2014-08, Quezon City: University of the Philippines School of Economics

Dumont, Rene (1957) *Types of Rural Economy: Studies in World Agriculture*, London: Methuen and Co.

Dung, Bui Minh (1995) 'Japan's Role in the Vietnamese Starvation of 1944-45', *Modern Asian Studies* 29 (3): 573-618

Dykstra, Sarah, Charles Kenny and Justin Sandefur (2014) 'Global Absolute Poverty Fell by Almost Half on Tuesday', CGD Policy Blogs, 2 May, Center for Global Development, https://www.cgdev.org/blog/global-absolute-poverty-fell-almost-half-tuesday, accessed 30 May 2014

ECAFE (1964) 'Review of Long-term Economic Projections for Selected Countries in the ECAFE Region', Development Programming Techniques Series, no. 5, Bangkok: United Nations Economic Commission for Asia and the Far East

Elson, R.E. (1997) *The End of the Peasantry in Southeast Asia*, Basingstoke: Macmillan Press Ltd

Escosura, Leandro Prados de la (2018) 'Well-being Inequality in the Long Run', EHES Working Papers in Economic History, no. 131, May

Esmara, Hendra (1986) *Perencanaan dan Pembangunan di Indonesia* [Planning and development in Indonesia], Jakarta: Gramedia

Estudillo, Jonna P. (1997) 'Income Inequality in the Philippines, 1961-91', *Developing Economies* XXXV (1): 68-95

Estudillo, Jonna P., Kinnalone Phimmavong and Francis Mark A. Quimba (2017) 'Moving out of Poverty: A Brief Review of the Process of Inclusive Growth in the Lao People's Democratic Republic', *The Philippine Review of Economics* LIV (1): 32-46

Evans, L.W. (1939) *Federated Malay States, Report of the Registrar-General of Births, and Deaths for the Year 1938*, Kuala Lumpur: FMS Government Press

Fabella, Raul V. (2014) 'Comprehensive Agrarian Reform Program (CARP): Time to Let Go', Discussion Paper no. 2014-02, Quezon City: University of the Philippines School of Economics

FAO, IFAD, UNICEF, WFP and WHO (2017) *The State of Food Security and Nutrition in the World: Building Resilience for Peace and Food Security*, Rome: FAO

Fearnside, Philip M. (1997) 'Transmigration in Indonesia: Lessons from Its Environmental and Social Impacts', *Environmental Management* 21 (4): 553-570

Feeny, David (1982) *The Political Economy of Productivity: Thai Agricultural Development 1880-1975*, Vancouver: University of British Columbia Press

Feinstein, Charles H. (1998) 'Pessimism Perpetuated: Real Wages and the Standard of Living in Britain during and after the Industrial Revolution', *Journal of Economic History* 58 (3): 625-658

Fernando, M.R. (1989) 'Javanese Peasants and By-employment at the Turn of the Century', in
    R.J. May and William J. O'Malley (eds), *Observing Change in Asia: Essays in Honour of J.A.C.
    Mackie*, Bathurst: Crawford House Press

Findlay, Ronald, and Nats Lundahl (1994) 'Natural Resources, "Vent for Surplus" and the Staples
    Theory', in G.M. Meier (ed.), *From Classical Economics to Development Economics*, Basingstoke:
    Macmillan Press

Fujita, Koichi (2009) 'Agricultural Labourers in Myanmar during the Economic Transition: Views
    from the Study of Selected Villages', in Koichi Fujita, Fumiharu Mieno and Ikuko Okamoto
    (eds), *The Economic Transition in Myanmar after 1988: Market Economy versus State Control*,
    Singapore: NUS Press

Furnivall, J.S. (1943) *Educational Progress in Southeast Asia*, New York: Institute of Pacific Relations

Furnivall, J.S. (1944) *Netherlands India: A Study of Plural Economy*, Cambridge: Cambridge
    University Press

Furnivall, J.S. (1957) *An Introduction to the Political Economy of Burma*, 3rd ed., Rangoon: Peoples'
    Literature Committee and House

Fuwa, Nobuhiko (2000) 'Politics and Economics of Land Reform in the Philippines: A Survey',
    Washington, DC: The World Bank

General Statistics Office (2013) *Statistical Yearbook of Vietnam 2013*, Hanoi: Statistical Publishing
    House

Ghai, D. (1999) 'The World Employment Programme at the International Labour Organization',
    Geneva: ILO

Giacometti, Jean-Dominique (2000a) 'Sources and Estimations for Economic Rural History
    of Vietnam in the First Half of the 20th Century', in Jean-Pascal Bassino, Jean-Dominique
    Giacometti and K. Odaka (eds), *Quantitative Economic History of Vietnam 1900-1990*, Tokyo:
    Hitotsubashi University, Institute of Economic Research

Giacometti, Jean-Dominique (2000b) 'Wages and Consumer Price for Urban and Industrial
    Workers in Vietnam under French Rule (1910-1954)', in Jean-Pascal Bassino, Jean-Dominique
    Giacometti and K. Odaka (eds), *Quantitative Economic History of Vietnam 1900-1990*, Tokyo:
    Hitotsubashi University, Institute of Economic Research

Gibson, John (2005) 'Statistical Tools and Estimation Methods for Poverty Measures Based on
    Cross-Sectional Household Surveys', in *Handbook on Poverty Statistics: Concepts, Methods
    and Policy Use*, New York: United Nations Statistics Division

Glewwe, Paul (2004a) 'An Investigation of the Determinants of School Progress and Academic
    Achievement in Vietnam', in Paul Glewwe, Nisha Agrawal and David Dollar (eds), *Economic
    Growth, Poverty and Household Welfare in Vietnam*, Washington, DC: The World Bank

Glewwe, Paul (2004b) 'An Overview of Economic Growth and Household Welfare in Vietnam in
    the 1990s', in Paul Glewwe, Nisha Agrawal and David Dollar (eds), *Economic Growth, Poverty
    and Household Welfare in Vietnam*, Washington, DC: The World Bank

Glewwe, Paul, Michele Gragnolati and Hassan Zaman (2002) 'Who Gained from Vietnam's Boom
    in the 1990s?', *Economic Development and Cultural Change* 50 (4): 773-792

Goh, Keng-Swee (1956) *Urban Incomes and Housing: A Report on the Social Survey of Singapore,
    1953-54*, Singapore: Government Printing Office

Goh, Keng-Swee (1976) 'A Socialist Economy That Works', in C.V. Devan Nair (ed.), *Socialism That
    Works: The Singapore Way*, Singapore: Federal Publications

Gomez, Edmund Terence, and Jomo K.S. (1997) *Malaysia's Political Economy: Politics, Patronage
    and Profits*, Cambridge: Cambridge University Press

Gooszen, Hans (1999) *A Demographic History of the Indonesian Archipelago, 1880-1942*, Singapore:
    Institute of Southeast Asian Studies

Goudal, Jean (1938) 'Labour Conditions in Indo-china', Studies and Reports Series B (Economic Conditions) no. 26, Geneva: International Labour Office

Gourou, Pierre (1945) *Land Utilization in French Indochina*, New York: Institute of Pacific Relations

Govaars, Ming (2005) *Dutch Colonial Education: The Chinese Experience in Indonesia, 1900-42*, Singapore: Chinese Heritage Centre

Government of Malaysia (1976) *Third Malaysia Plan, 1976-80*, Kuala Lumpur: Ibrahim Bin Johari

Government of Malaysia (1989) *Mid-term Review of the Fifth Malaysia Plan 1986-90*, Kuala Lumpur: National Printing Department

Grajdanzev, Andrew J. (1944) *Modern Korea*, New York: Institute of Pacific Relations

Gran, Guy (1975) *Vietnam and the Capitalist Route to Modernity: Village Cochinchina, 1880-1940*, PhD dissertation, University of Wisconsin

Grimm, Michael, et al. (2010) 'Inequality in Human Development: An Empirical Assessment of 32 Countries', *Social Indicators Research* 97: 191-211

Grist, D.H. (1941) *Malayan Agricultural Statistics, 1940*, Kuala Lumpur: Department of Agriculture, Straits Settlements and Federated Malay States

Hardjono, Joan (1977) *Transmigration in Indonesia*, Kuala Lumpur: Oxford University Press

Haughton, J.H., and Dominique Haughton (1997) 'Explaining Child Nutrition in Vietnam', *Economic Development and Cultural Change* 45 (3): 541-556

Haughton, J.H., and S. Khandker (2009) *Handbook on Poverty and Inequality*, Washington, DC: World Bank

Haughton, J.H., and S. Khandker (2014) 'The Surprising Effects of the Great Recession: Losers and Winners in Thailand in 2008-09', *World Development* 56: 77-92

Hayami, Yujiro, Ma. Agnes R. Quisumbing and Lourdes S. Adriano (1990) *Toward an Alternative Land Reform Paradigm*, Manila: Ateneo de Manila Press

Henley, David (2004) 'Rizification Revisited: Re-examining the Rise of Rice in Indonesia with Special Reference to Sulawesi', in Peter Boomgaard and David Henley (eds), *Smallholders and Stockbreeders: A History of Foodcrop and Livestock Farming in Southeast Asia*, Leiden: KITLV Press

Henry, Yves (1932) *Economie Agricole de L'Indochine*, Hanoi: Gouvernement General de l'Indochine

Herrin, Alejandro, and Ernesto M. Pernia (2003) 'Population, Human Resources and Employment', in Arsenio M. Balisacan and Hal Hill (eds), *The Philippine Economy: Development, Policies and Challenges*, Oxford: Oxford University Press

Hickel, Jason (2017) *The Divide: A Brief Guide to Global Inequality and Its Solutions*, London: Windmill Books

Hill, Hal (1996), *The Indonesian Economy since 1966*, Cambridge: Cambridge University Press

Hlaing, Aye (1965) *An Economic and Statistical Analysis of Economic Development of Burma under British Rule*, PhD dissertation, University of London

Hobsbawm, E.J. (1975) 'The Standard of Living Debate', in A.J. Taylor (ed.), *The Standard of Living in Britain in the Industrial Revolution*, London: Methuen

Hodge, Andrew, Sonja Firth, Tiara Marthias and Eliana Jimenez-Soto (2014) 'Location Matters: Trends in Inequalities in Child Mortality in Indonesia. Evidence from Repeated Cross-Sectional Surveys', *PLoS ONE* 9 (7): e103597, https://doi.org/10.1371/journal.pone.0103597, accessed 8 January 2016

Hooley, Richard (2005) 'American Economic Policy in the Philippines, 1902-1940: Exploring a Dark Age in Colonial Statistics', *Journal of Asian Economics* 16: 464-488

Horrell, Sara, and Jane Humphries (1992) 'Old Questions, New Data, and Alternative Perspectives: Families' Living Standards in the Industrial Revolution', *Journal of Economic History* 52 (4): 849-880

Horrell, Sara, and Jane Humphries (1995) 'Women's Labour Force Participation and the Transition to the Male-Breadwinner Family, 1790-1865', *Economic History Review* 48 (1): 89-117

Houweling, Tanja A.J., and Anton E. Kunst (2010) 'Socio-economic Inequalities in Childhood Mortality in Low- and Middle-Income Countries: A Review of the Evidence', *British Medical Bulletin* 93 (1): 7-26

Houweling, Tanja A.J., Anton E. Kunst, Gerard Borsboom and Johan P. Mackenbach (2006) 'Mortality Inequalities in Times of Economic Growth: Time Trends in Socioeconomic and Regional Inequalities in Under 5 Mortality in Indonesia, 1982-1997', *Journal of Epidemiology and Community Health* 60: 62-68

Huck, Paul (1995) 'Infant Mortality and Living Standards of English Workers during the Industrial Revolution', *Journal of Economic History* 55 (3): 528-55

Huff, Gregg (2001) 'Entitlements, Destitution and Emigration in the 1930s Singapore Great Depression', *Economic History Review* 54: 290-323

Huff, Gregg (2012) 'Export-led Growth, Gateway Cities and Urban Systems Development in Pre-World War II Southeast Asia', *Journal of Development Studies* 48 (10): 1431-1452

Huff, Gregg (2019) 'Causes and Consequences of the Great Vietnam Famine, 1944-1945', *Economic History Review* 72 (1): 286-318

Huff, Gregg, and Giovanni Caggiano (2007) 'Globalization, Immigration, and Lewisian Elastic Labor in Pre-World War II Southeast Asia', *Journal of Economic History* 67 (1): 33-67

Hugo, Graeme, T.H. Hull, Valerie Hull and Gavin Jones (1987) *The Demographic Dimension in Indonesian Development*, Singapore: Oxford University Press

Hull, Terence H. (1995) 'Looking Back to the Hygiene Study Ward: A Brief Guide to the Literature', Working Papers in Demography, no. 54, Canberra: Research School of Social Sciences, Australian National University

Hutchcroft, Paul (1998) *Booty Capitalism: The Politics of Banking in the Philippines*, Ithaca: Cornell University Press

Hutchcroft, Paul (2000) 'Colonial Masters, National Politicos, and Provincial Lords: Central Authority and Local Autonomy in the American Philippines, 1900-1913', *Journal of Asian Studies* 52 (2): 277-306

ILO (1974) *Sharing in Development: A Programme of Employment, Equity and Growth for the Philippines*, Geneva: International Labour Office

ILO (2012) *Labour and Social Trends in Viet Nam 2009/10*, Geneva: International Labour Organization

Ingleson, John (1988) 'Urban Java during the Depression', *Journal of Southeast Asian Studies* XIX (2): 292-309

Ingram, J. (1964) 'Thailand's Rice Trade and the Allocation of Resources', in C.D. Cowan (ed.), *The Economic Development of South-East Asia*, London: George Allen and Unwin

Ingram, J. (1971) *Economic Change in Thailand, 1850-1970*, Kuala Lumpur: Oxford University Press

Intal, Ponciano S., Jr, Leah Francine Cu and Jo Anne Illescas (2012) 'Rice Prices and the National Food Authority', Discussion Paper Series, no. 2012-27, Makati: Philippine Institute of Development Studies

Jitsuchon, Somchai (1990) 'Alleviation of Rural Poverty in Thailand', ARTEP Working Paper, New Delhi: ILO-ARTEP

Johnston, B.F. (1953) *Japanese Food Management in World War II*, Stanford: Stanford University Press

Jomo, K.S. (1990) *Growth and Structural Change in the Malaysian Economy*, London: Macmillan

Jones, L.W. (1966) *The Population of Borneo: A Study of the Peoples of Sarawak, Sabah and Brunei*, London: Athlone Press

Kakwani, Nanak, and E.M. Pernia (2000) 'What Is Pro-poor Growth?', *Asian Development Review* 18 (1): 1-16

Kakwani, Nanak, and Medhi Krongkaew (2000) 'Analysing Poverty in Thailand', *Journal of the Asia Pacific Economy* 5 (1 and 2): 141-160

Khor, Kok-Peng (1983) *The Malaysian Economy: Structures and Dependence*, Kuala Lumpur: Marican and Sons

Kim, Eunju, and Jayoung Yoo (2015) 'Conditional Cash Transfers in the Philippines: How to Overcome Institutional Constraints for Implementing Social Protection', *Asia and the Pacific Policy Studies* 2 (1): 75-89

King, Dwight Y., and Peter D. Weldon (1977) 'Income Distribution and Levels of Living in Java, 1963-1970', *Economic Development and Cultural Change* 25 (4): 699-711

King, Victor (1986) 'Land Settlement Schemes and the Alleviation of Rural Poverty in Sarawak, East Malaysia: A Critical Commentary', *Southeast Asia Journal of Social Science* 14 (1): 71-99

Kloosterboer, J. (1960) *Involuntary Labour since the Abolition of Slavery: A Survey of Compulsory Labour throughout the World*, Leiden: E.J. Brill

Konkel, Rob (2014) 'The Monetization of Global Poverty: The Concept of Poverty in World Bank History, 1944-90', *Journal of Global History* 9: 276-300

Kozel, Valerie (ed.) (2014) *Well Begun but Not Yet Done: Progress and Emerging Challenges for Poverty Reduction in Vietnam*, Washington, DC: World Bank

Kraft, Aleli D., Kim-Huong Nguyen, Elina Jiminez-Soto and Andrew Hodge (2013) 'Stagnant Neonatal Mortality and Persistent Health Inequality in Middle-Income Countries: A Case Study of the Philippines'. *PLoS ONE* 8 (1): e53696, https://doi.org/10.1371/journal.pone.0053696, accessed 18 July 2019

Kravis, Irving B., Alan Heston and Robert Summers (1978) *International Comparisons of Real Product and Purchasing Power*, Baltimore and London: Johns Hopkins University Press for the World Bank

Krongkaew, Medhi (1979) 'The Determination of Poverty Band in Thailand', *Philippine Economic Journal* XVIII (4): 396-417

Krongkaew, Medhi (1987) 'The Economic and Social Impact of Thailand's Rural Job Creation Programs', *Philippine Review of Economics and Business* 14 (3 and 4): 237-272

Krongkaew, Medhi (1990) 'Poverty and Public Policy in Thailand', paper presented at the 'Symposium on Poverty Alleviation in the 1990s', Sasakawa Peace Foundation, Tokyo

Krongkaew, Medhi (1993) 'Poverty and Income Distribution', in Peter G. Warr (ed.), *The Thai Economy in Transition*, Cambridge: Cambridge University Press

Krongkaew, Medhi, and N. Kakwani (2003) 'The Growth-Equity Trade-off in Modern Economic Development: The Case of Thailand', *Journal of Asian Economics* 14: 735-757

Kurihara, Kenneth (1945) *Labor in the Philippine Economy*, Stanford: Stanford University Press

Kuznets, Simon (1966) *Modern Economic Growth: Rate, Structure and Spread*, New Haven: Yale University Press

Laovakul, Duangmanee (2016) 'Concentration of Land and Other Wealth in Thailand', in Phongpaichit, Pasuk, and Chris Baker (eds), *Unequal Thailand: Aspects of Income, Wealth and Power*, Singapore: NUS Press

Larkin, John A. (1993) *Sugar and the Origins of Modern Philippine Society*, Berkeley: University of California Press

Lasker, Bruno (1950) *Human Bondage in Southeast Asia*, Chapel Hill: University of North Carolina Press

Lasker, Bruno, and W.L. Holland (eds) (1934) *Problems of the Pacific, 1933: Economic Conflict and Control*, London: Oxford University Press

Lathapipat, Dilaka (2016) 'Inequality in Education and Wages', in Pasuk Phongpaichit and Chris Baker (eds), *Unequal Thailand: Aspects of Income, Wealth and Power*, Singapore: NUS Press

Lava, Horacio (1938) 'Levels of Living in the Ilocos Region', Study no. 1, Philippine Council of the Institute of Pacific Relations, Manila: College of Business Administration, University of the Philippines

Lecaillon, Jacques, Felix Paukert, Christian Morrisson and Dimitri Germidis (1984) *Income Distribution and Economic Development: An Analytical Survey*, Geneva: International Labour Office

Legarda, Benito J. (1999) *After the Galleons: Foreign Trade, Economic Change and Entrepreneurship in the Nineteenth-Century Philippines*, Madison: University of Wisconsin, Center for Southeast Asian Studies in cooperation with Ateneo de Manila University Press

Leigh, Andrew, and Pierre van der Eng (2009) 'Inequality in Indonesia: What Can We Learn from Top Incomes?', *Journal of Public Economics* 93: 209-212

Lieberman, Samuel, Joseph J. Capuno and Hoang Van Minh (2004) 'Health Decentralization in East Asia: Some Lessons from Indonesia, the Philippines and Vietnam', Discussion Paper 0408, Quezon City: University of the Philippines School of Economics

Lim, Lin Lean (1975) 'Income Distribution in West Malaysia, 1967-68', in *Income Distribution, Employment and Economic Development in Southeast and East Asia: Papers and Proceedings of the Seminar Sponsored Jointly by the Japan Economic Research Center and the Council for Asian Manpower Studies*, Tokyo: The Japan Economic Research Center and the Council for Asian Manpower Studies

Lim, Stephen S., et al. (2018) 'Measuring Human Capital: A Systematic Analysis of 105 Countries and Territories 1990-2016', *Lancet* 392: 1217-1734

Lindblad, J. Thomas (2008) *Bridges to New Business: The Economic Decolonization of Indonesia*, Leiden: KITLV Press

Lindert, Peter (2004) *Growing Public*, Cambridge: Cambridge University Press

Lindert, Peter, and J. Williamson (1983) 'English Workers' Living Standards during the Industrial Revolution: A New Look', *Economic History Review* 36 (1): 1-25

Lipton, Michael (1983) 'Poverty, Undernutrition and Hunger', World Bank Staff Working Paper, no. 597, Washington, DC: World Bank

Little, I.M.D. (1976) 'Review', *Journal of Development Economics* 3: 99-106

Locher-Scholten, Elsbeth (2000) 'Female Labour in Twentieth-Century Colonial Java: European Notions-Indonesian Practices', in *Women and the Colonial State: Essays on Gender and Modernity in the Netherlands Indies 1900-1942*, Amsterdam: Amsterdam University Press

López Jerez, M. (2014) *Deltas Apart: Factor Endowments, Colonial Extraction and Pathways of Agricultural Development in Vietnam*, PhD dissertation, University of Lund

MacAndrews, Colin (1977) *Mobility and Modernisation: The Federal Land Development Authority and Its Role in Modernising the Rural Malay*, Yogyakarta: Gadjah Mada University Press

Maddison, Angus (2003) *The World Economy: Historical Statistics*, Paris: OECD Development Centre Studies

Maddison, Angus (2005) 'Measuring and Interpreting World Economic Performance 1500-2001', *Review of Income and Wealth* 51 (1): 1-35

Maddison, Angus (2007) *Contours of the World Economy, 1-2030 AD: Essays in Macro-economic History*, Oxford: Oxford University Press

Malesky, Edmund J., and Frances E. Hutchinson (2016) 'Varieties of Disappointment: Why Has Decentralization Not Delivered on Its Promises in Southeast Asia?', *Journal of Southeast Asian Economies* 33 (2): 125-138

Manderson, Lenore (1996) *Sickness and the State: Health and Illness in Colonial Malaya, 1870-1940*, Cambridge: Cambridge University Press

Mangahas, M. (1975) 'Income Inequality in the Philippines: A Decomposition Analysis', in *Income Distribution, Employment and Economic Development in Southeast and East Asia*, Tokyo: The Japan Economic Research Center

Mangahas, Mahar (1979) 'Poverty in the Philippines: Some Measurement Problems', *Philippine Economic Journal* XVIII (4): 630-640

Mangahas, Mahar (1982) 'What Happened to the Poor on the Way to the Next Development Plan?', *Philippine Economic Journal* XXI (3 and 4): 126-146

Mangahas, Mahar (1983) 'Measurement of Poverty and Equity: Some ASEAN Social Indicators Experience', *Social Indicators Research* 13: 253-279

Mangahas, Mahar (1985) 'Rural Poverty and Operation Land Transfer', in R. Islam (ed.), *Strategies for Alleviating Poverty in Rural Asia*, Bangkok: ILO-ARTEP

Mangahas, Mahar (1987a) 'The Political Economy of Land Reform and Distribution in the Philippines', in *Agrarian Reform: Experiences and Expectations*, Manila: Center for Research and Communication

Mangahas, Mahar (1987b) 'Rural Employment Creation in the Philippines and Thailand', in *Rural Employment Creation in Asia and the Pacific*, Manila: Asian Development Bank

Mangahas, Mahar (ed.) (1976) *Measuring Philippine Development: Report of the Social Indicators Project*, Manila: The Development Academy of the Philippines

Mangahas, Mahar, and Bruno Barros (1979) 'The Distribution of Income and Wealth: A Survey of Philippine Research', Discussion Paper 7916, Quezon City: Institute of Economic Development and Research, School of Economics, University of the Philippines,

Manurungsan, Sompop (1989) *Economic Development of Thailand, 1850-1950*, PhD dissertation, State University of Groningen

Mapa, Dennis S., Manuel Leonard F. Albis, Michael Dominic del Mondo and John Carlo P. Daquis (2017) 'High Fertility Rate and High Youth Unemployment: Twin Challenges to the Demographic Dividend for the Philippines', Working Paper Series 2017-02, Quezon City: University of the Philippines School of Statistics

McCarthy, John, and Mulyadi Sumarto (2018) 'Distributional Politics and Social Protection in Indonesia: Dilemma of Layering, Nesting and Social Fit in Jokowi's Poverty Policy', *Journal of Southeast Asian Economies* 35 (2): 223-236

McCulloch, Neil (2008) 'Rice Prices and Poverty in Indonesia', *Bulletin of Indonesian Economic Studies* 44 (1): 45-63

McLennan, Marshall S. (1969) 'Land and Tenancy in the Central Luzon Plain', *Philippine Studies* 17 (4): 651-82

Mears, Leon A. (1961) *Rice Marketing in the Republic of Indonesia*, Jakarta: Institute for Economic and Social Research, University of Indonesia

Mears, Leon A., M. Agabin, T.L. Anden and R.C. Marquez (1974) *The Rice Economy of the Philippines*, Manila: University of the Philippines Press

Meerkerk, Elise van Nederveen (2017) 'Challenging the De-industrialization Thesis: Gender, and Indigenous Textile Production in Java under Dutch Colonial Rule, c. 1830-1920', *Economic History Review* 70 (4): 1219-1943

Meerman, Jacob (1979) *Public Expenditure in Malaysia: Who Benefits and Why?*, New York: Oxford University Press for the World Bank

Meesook, Oey Astra (1975) 'Income Inequality in Thailand, 1962/63 and 1968/9', in *Income Distribution, Employment and Economic Development in Southeast and East Asia: Papers and Proceedings of the Seminar Sponsored Jointly by the Japan Economic Research Center and the Council for Asian Manpower Studies*, Tokyo: The Japan Economic Research Center and the Council for Asian Manpower Studies

Meesook, Oey Astra (1979) 'Income Consumption and Poverty in Thailand, 1962/63 to 1975/76', World Bank Staff Working Paper, no. 364, Washington, DC: The World Bank

Mertens, Walter (1978) 'Population Census Data on Agricultural Activities in Indonesia', *Majalah Demografi Indonesia* 9: 9-53

Mesters, Hans (1996) 'J.L. Hydrick in the Netherlands Indies: An American View on Dutch Public Health Policy', in Peter Boomgaard, Rosalio Sciortino and Ines Smyth (eds), *Health Care in Java: Past and Present*, Leiden: KITLV Press

Metzer, Jacob (1998) *The Divided Economy of Mandatory Palestine*, Cambridge: Cambridge University Press

Milanovic, Branko (2006) 'Inequality and Determinants of Earnings in Malaysia, 1984-1997', *Asian Economic Journal* 20 (2): 191-216

Milanovic, Branko (2016) *Global Inequality: A New Approach for the Age of Globalization*, Cambridge, MA: Belknap Press

Miller, Hugo H. (1920) *Economic Conditions in the Philippines*, rev. ed., Boston: Ginn and Company

Ministry of National Planning (1960) *The National Income of Burma*, Rangoon: Government Printing and Stationery, Union of Burma

Ministry of Planning and Finance and World Bank Group (2017) *An Analysis of Poverty in Myanmar*, Yangon: Ministry of Planning and Finance

Miranda, Evelyn A. (1991) 'American Economic Imperialism and the Development of the Philippine Oligarchy: The Filipino Legislative Elite, 1900-35', *Kabar Sebarang* 21: 55-68

Mokyr, Joel (1988) 'Is There Still Life in the Pessimist Case? Consumption during the Industrial Revolution, 1790-1850', *Journal of Economic History* XLVIII (1): 69-92

Morimoto, Kokichi (1931) 'Rising Standards of Living in Japan', in Bruno Lasker (ed.), *Problems of the Pacific 1931*, Chicago: University of Chicago Press

Mortimer, Rex (1974) *Indonesian Communism under Sukarno: Ideology and Politics*, Kuala Lumpur: Oxford University Press

Mukhopadhaya, Pundarik (2014) *Income Inequality in Singapore*, Abingdon: Routledge

Murray, Martin J. (1980) *The Development of Capitalism in Colonial Indochina*, Berkeley: University of California Press

Myers, Ramon H., and S. Yamada (1984) 'Agriculture Development in the Empire', in Ramon H. Myers and Mark Peattie (eds), *The Japanese Colonial Empire, 1895-1945*, Princeton: Princeton University Press

Myint, Hla (1958) 'The "Classical Theory" of International Trade and the Underdeveloped Countries', *Economic Journal* 68: 317-37

Myint, Hla (1971) 'The Inward and Outward-Looking Countries of Southeast Asia', in *Economic Theory and the Underdeveloped Countries*, New York: Oxford University Press

National Academy of Sciences (2013) *Reducing Maternal and Neonatal Mortality in Indonesia: Saving Lives, Saving the Future*, Washington, DC: The National Academies Press

National Census and Statistical Office (1976) *Labor Force August 1975*, National Sample Survey of Households Bulletin, Series no. 46, Manila: National Census and Statistical Office

National Economic and Development Authority (1976) *NEDA Statistical Yearbook of the Philippines 1976*, Manila: National Economic and Development Authority

National Institute of Statistics (2013) *Labour Force and Child Labour Survey 2012*, Phnom Penh: National Institute of Statistics and Ministry of Planning

National Institute of Statistics (2014) *Statistical Yearbook of Cambodia 2013*, Phnom Penh: National Institute of Statistics

National Statistical Coordination Board (2000) *Statistical Yearbook of the Philippines, 2000*, Manila: National Statistical Coordination Board

National Statistical Office (1971) *Report of the Labour Force Survey*, Bangkok: Office of the Prime Minister

National Statistical Office (1976) *Statistical Yearbook Thailand, Number 31, 1974-1975*, Bangkok: National Statistical Office, Office of the Prime Minister

National Statistical Office (2015) *Statistical Yearbook Thailand 2015*, Bangkok: National Statistical Office

NEDA (1975) *The Philippine Food Balance Sheets, CY 1953 to CY 1972*, Manila: National Economic and Development Authority

NEDA (1978) *The National Income Accounts, CY 1946-1975 (Link Series)*, Manila: National Economic and Development Authority

Nicol, Bruce M. (1974) *Food and Nutrition in the Agricultural Development Plan for Indonesia*, Jakarta: FAO Planning Team

Nitisastro, Widjojo (1970) *Population Trends in Indonesia*, Ithaca: Cornell University Press

Norlund, Irene (1991) 'The French Empire, the Colonial State in Vietnam and Economic Policy: 1885-1940', *Australian Economic History Review* 31 (1): 72-89

Nugroho (1967) *Indonesia: Facts and Figures*, Jakarta: Central Bureau of Statistics

Ochse, J.J., and G.J.A. Terra (1934) 'The Function of Money and Products in Relation to Native Diet and Physical Condition in Koetowinangoen (Java)', in Department of Economic Affairs, *Geld- en Producten-Huishouding, Volksvoeding en -Gezondheid in Koetowinangoen*, Buitenzorg: Archipel Drukkerij

Osman-Rani, H. (1987) 'Employment and Poverty Eradication Projects: Malaysia's Experience 25 Years after Independence', *Philippine Review of Economics and Business* 14 (3 and 4): 273-322

Owen, Norman G. (1972) 'Philippine Economic Development and American Policy: A Reappraisal', *Solidarity* 7 (9): 49-64

Owen, Norman G. (1984) *Prosperity without Progress: Manila Hemp and Material Life in the Colonial Philippines*, Berkeley: University of California Press

Ozmucur, Suleyman, and Sevet Pamuk (2002) 'Real Wages and Standards of Living in the Ottoman Empire, 1489-1914', *Journal of Economic History* 62 (2): 293-321

Paderanga, C.W., Jr (1987) 'A Review of Land Settlements in the Philippines, 1900-1975', *Philippine Review of Business and Economics* 24 (1 and 2): 1-54

Palmore, James A., Ramesh Chander and Dorothy Fernandez (1975) 'The Demographic Situation in Malaysia', East-West Population Institute, Reprint Series 70, Honolulu: University of Hawaii

Pannarunothai, Supasit, and Anne Mills (1997) 'The Poor Pay More: Health-Related Inequality in Thailand', *Social Science and Medicine* 44 (12): 1781-1790

Papanek, Gustav (1980) 'The Effect of Economic Growth and Inflation on Workers' Incomes', in Gustav Papanek (ed.), *The Indonesian Economy*, New York: Praeger Special Studies

Parthasarathi, Prasannan (1998) 'Rethinking Wages and Competitiveness in the Eighteenth Century: Britain and South India', *Past and Present* 158: 79-109

Patten, Richard, Belinda Dapice and Walter Falcon (1980) 'An Experiment in Rural Employment Creation: The Early History of Indonesia's Kabupaten Development Program', in G.F. Papanek (ed.), *The Indonesian Economy*, New York: Praeger Special Studies

Patunru, Arianto, and Hizkia Respatiadi (2017) *Protecting the Farmers: Improving the Quality of Social Protection Schemes for Agricultural Workers in Indonesia*, Jakarta: Center for Indonesian Policy Studies

Peattie, Mark (1984) 'Introduction', in Ramon H. Myers and Mark Peattie (eds), *The Japanese Colonial Empire, 1895-1945*, Princeton: Princeton University Press

Peebles, Gavin, and Peter Wilson (2002) *Economic Growth and Development in Singapore, Past and Present*, Cheltenham: Edward Elgar

Pelzer, Karl (1945) *Pioneer Settlement in the Asiatic Tropics*, New York: American Geographical Society

Penders, C.L.M. (1984) *Bojonegoro 1900-1942: A Study of Endemic Poverty in North-east Java, Indonesia*, Singapore: Gunung Agung

Penders, C.L.M. (ed. and trans.) (1977) *Indonesia: Selected Documents on Colonialism and Nationalism 1830-1942*, St Lucia: University of Queensland Press

Penny, David, and Masri Singarimbun (1973) 'Population and Poverty in Rural Java: Some Economic Arithmetic from Sriharjo', Cornell International Agricultural Development Monograph 41, Ithaca: Department of Agricultural Economics, Cornell University

Perdana, Ari A., and John Maxwell (2005) 'Poverty Targeting in Indonesia: Programs, Problems and Lessons Learned', in John Weiss (ed.), *Poverty Targeting in Asia*, Cheltenham: Edward Elgar

Pfanner, M. Ruth (1969) 'Burma', in Frank Golay, Ralph Anspach, M. Ruth Pfanner and E.B. Ayal, *Underdevelopment and Economic Nationalism in Southeast Asia*, Ithaca: Cornell University Press

Philippine Statistics Authority (2014) *Philippine Statistical Yearbook 2014*, Manila: Philippine Statistics Authority

Philippine Statistics Authority (2016) 'Poverty Incidence among Filipinos Registered at 21.6% in 2015', PHDSD 1610-04, Manila: Philippine Statistics Authority

Phongpaichit, Pasuk, and Chris Baker (1995) *Thailand: Economy and Politics*, Kuala Lumpur: Oxford University Press

Phongpaichit, Pasuk, and Chris Baker (2016) 'Introduction: Inequality and Oligarchy', in Pasuk Phongpaichit and Chris Baker (eds), *Unequal Thailand: Aspects of Income, Wealth and Power*, Singapore: NUS Press

Pincus, Jonathan, and John Sender (2008) 'Quantifying Poverty in Viet Nam: Who Counts?', *Journal of Vietnamese Studies* 3 (1): 108-150

Polak, J.J. (1943) 'The National Income of the Netherlands Indies, 1921-39', in P. Creutzberg (ed.), *Changing Economy of Indonesia, Vol. 5: National Income*, The Hague: M. Nijhoff

Pomeranz, Kenneth (2000) *The Great Divergence: China, Europe, and the Making of the Modern World Economy*, Princeton: Princeton University Press

Pomeranz, Kenneth (2003) 'Women's Work, Family and Economic Development in Europe and East Asia: Long-term Trajectories and Contemporary Comparisons', in G. Arrighi, H. Takeshi and M. Seldon (eds), *The Rise of East Asia: Perspectives of 50, 150 and 500 Years*, London: Routledge

Pomeranz, Kenneth (2005) 'Standards of Living in Eighteenth-Century China: Regional Differences, Temporal Trends and Incomplete Evidence', in Robert C. Allen, Tommy Bengtsson and Martin Dribe (eds), *Living Standards in the Past: New Perspectives on Well-being in Asia and Europe*, Oxford: Oxford University Press

Poot, Huib (1979) *Evaluation of the Tambon Development Programme in Thailand*, Bangkok: ILO-ARTEP

Popkin, Samuel L. (1979) *The Rational Peasant: The Political Economy of Rural Society in Vietnam*, Berkeley: University of California Press

Population Reference Bureau (2017) *2017 World Population Data Sheet*, Washington, DC: Population Reference Bureau

Population Reference Bureau (2018) *2018 World Population Data Sheet*, Washington, DC: Population Reference Bureau

Pradhan, Menno (2009) 'Welfare Analysis with a Proxy Consumption Measure: Evidence from a Repeated Experiment in Indonesia', *Fiscal Studies* 30 (3/4): 391-417

Pradhan, Menno, Asep Suryahadi, Sudarno Sumarto and Lant Pritchett (2000) 'Measurement of Poverty in Indonesia: 1996, 1999 and Beyond', Policy Research Working Paper 2438, Washington, DC: World Bank

Prescott, Nicholas (1997) 'Poverty, Social Services, and Safety Nets in Vietnam', World Bank Discussion Paper no. 376, Washington, DC: World Bank

Prescott, Nicholas, and Menno Pradhan (1997) 'A Poverty Profile of Cambodia', World Bank Discussion Paper no. 373, Washington, DC: World Bank

Priebe, Jan (2014) 'Official Poverty Measurement in Indonesia since 1984: A Methodological Review', *Bulletin of Indonesian Economic Studies* 50 (2): 185-205

Pritchett, Lant (1997) 'Divergence, Big Time', *Journal of Economic Perspectives* 11 (3): 3-17

Pritchett, Lant, and Charles Kenny (2013) 'Promoting Millennium Development Ideals: The Risks of Defining Development Down', CGD Working Paper 338, Washington, DC: Center for Global Development

Putzel, James (1992) *A Captive Land: The Politics of Agrarian Reform in the Philippines*, New York: Monthly Review Press

Pyatt, Graham (2003) 'Development and the Distribution of Living Standards: A Critique of the Evolving Data Base', *Review of Income and Wealth* 49 (3): 333-358

Raffles, Thomas Stamford (1978) *The History of Java*, 2 vols., Oxford: Oxford University Press

Ragayah Haji Mat Zin (2012) 'Poverty Eradication and Income Distribution', in Hal Hill, Tham Siew Yean and Ragayah Haji Mat Zin (eds), *Malaysia's Development Challenges: Graduating from the Middle*, Abingdon: Routledge

Ramesh, M. (2014) 'Social Protection in Indonesia and the Philippines: Work in Progress', *Journal of Southeast Asian Economies* 31 (1): 1-17

Ranis, Gustav, and Frances Stewart (1993) 'Rural Non-agricultural Activities in Development: Theory and Application', *Journal of Development Economics* 40: 75-101

Ranis, Gustav, Frances Stewart and Emma Samman (2006) 'Human Development: Beyond the Human Development Index', *Journal of Human Development* 7 (3): 323-358

Rao, V.V.B. (1990) 'Income Distribution in Singapore: Trends and Issues', *Singapore Economic Review* XXXV (1): 143-160

Rao, V.V.B., and M.K. Ramakrishnan (1976) 'Economic Growth, Structural Change and Income Inequality, Singapore, 1966-1975', *Malayan Economic Review* XXI (2): 92-122

Ravallion, Martin (2003) 'Measuring Aggregate Welfare in Developing Countries: How Well Do National Accounts and Surveys Agree?', *Review of Economics and Statistics* 85 (3): 645-652

Ravallion, Martin (2015) 'Towards Better Global Poverty Measures', Working Paper 417, Washington, DC: Center for Global Development

Ravallion, Martin (2016) *The Economic of Poverty: History, Measurement and Policy*, New York: Oxford University Press

Ravallion, Martin, and Dominique van de Walle (2008) *Land in Transition: Reform and Poverty in Rural Vietnam*, Basingstoke: Palgrave Macmillan

Ravallion, Martin, and Gaurav Datt (1996) 'How Important to India's Poor Is the Sectoral Composition of Economic Growth?', *World Bank Economic Review* 33 (4): 667-702

Ravallion, Martin, and Michael Lokshin (2007) 'Lasting Impacts of Indonesia's Financial Crisis', *Economic Development and Cultural Change* 56 (1): 27-56

Ravallion, Martin, S. Chen and P. Sangraula (2009) 'Dollar a Day Revisited', *World Bank Economic Review* 23 (2): 163-184

Reid, Anthony (1988) *Southeast Asia in the Age of Commerce, 1450-1680, Vol. 1: The Lands below the Wind,* New Haven: Yale University Press

Reid, Anthony (2001) 'Southeast Asian Population History and the Colonial Impact', in Ts'ui-jung Liu, James Lee, David Sven Reher, Osamu Saito and Wang Feng (eds), *Asian Population History*, Oxford: Oxford University Press

Reid, Anthony (2015) *A History of Southeast Asia: Critical Crossroads*, Chichester: Wiley Blackwell

Reyes, Celia M., and Aubrey D. Tabuga (2012) 'Conditional Cash Transfer Program in the Philippines: Is it Reaching the Extremely Poor?', Discussion Paper Series, no. 2012-42, Makati: Philippine Institute for Development Studies

Reyes, Celia M., Aubrey D. Tabuga, Christian D. Mina and Ronina D. Asis (2015) 'Promoting Inclusive Growth through the 4Ps', Research Paper Series no. 2015-01, Makati: Philippine Institute for Development Studies

Rose, Beth (1985) *Appendix to the Rice Economy of Asia*, Washington, DC: Resources for the Future

Rudra, Ashok (1974) 'Minimum Level of Living: A Statistical Examination', in T.N. Srinivasan and P.K. Bardhan, *Poverty and Income Distribution in India*, Calcutta: Statistical Publishing Society

Rueff, Gaston (1945) 'Post-war Social and Economic Problems of French Indo-China', paper presented at the ninth conference of the Institute of Pacific Relations, Hot Springs, Virginia, 6-17 January

Runes, I.T. (1939) *General Standards of Living and Wages of Workers in the Philippine Sugar Industry*, Manila: Philippine Council, Institute of Pacific Relations

Saito, T., and Kin Kiong Lee (1999) *Statistics on the Burmese Economy: The Nineteenth and Twentieth Centuries*, Singapore: Institute of Southeast Asian Studies

Sajogyo (1975) *Usaha Perbaikan Gizi Keluarga* [ANP evaluation study, 1973], Bogor: Institut Pertanian Bogor

Sari, Yulia Indrawati, and Nurul Widyaningrum (2012) 'Community-Driven Development and Empowerment of the Poor in Indonesia', in Anne Booth, Chris Manning and Thee Kian Wie (eds), *Land, Livelihood, the Economy and the Environment in Indonesia: Essays in Honour of Joan Hardjono*, Jakarta: Yayasan Pustaka Obor Indonesia

Sarntisart, Isra (2005) 'Socio-economic Consequences of the Crisis', in Peter Warr (ed.), *Thailand beyond the Crisis*, Abingdon: RoutledgeCurzon

Scheltema, A.M.P.A. (1936) *The Food Consumption of the Native Inhabitants of Java and Madura*, Batavia: Ruygrok and Co. for the Institute of Pacific Relations

Schulze, Gunther G., and Bambang Suharnoko Sjahrir (2014) 'Decentralization, Governance and Public Service Delivery', in Hal Hill (ed.), *Regional Dynamics in a Decentralized Indonesia*, Singapore: ISEAS

Schwulst, E.B. (1932) 'Report on the Budget and Financial Policies of French Indo-China, Siam, Federated Malay States and the Netherlands East Indies', in *Report of the Governor General of the Philippine Islands 1931*, Washington, DC: United States Government Printing Office

Sen, Amartya (1987) 'The Standard of Living: Lecture II, Lives and Capabilities', in Geoffrey Hawthorn (ed.), *The Standard of Living*, Cambridge: Cambridge University Press

Sen, Amartya (1999) *Development as Freedom*, New York: Anchor Books

Shair-Rosenfield, Sarah (2016) 'The Causes and Effects of the Local Government Code in the Philippines: Locked in a Status Quo of Weakly Decentralized Authority?', *Journal of Southeast Asian Economies* 33 (2): 172-187

Shah, Sultan Nazrin (2017) *Charting the Economy: Early 20th Century Malaya and Contemporary Malaysian Contrasts*, Oxford: Oxford University Press

Shammas, Carole (1983) 'Food Expenditure and Economic Well-Being in Early Modern England', *Journal of Economic History* XLIII (1) 89-100

Shari, Ishak (1979) 'Estimation of Poverty Lines and the Incidence of Poverty in Peninsular Malaysia, 1973', *Philippine Economic Journal* XVIII (4): 418-449

Shari, Ishak (2000) 'Economic Growth and Income Inequality in Malaysia, 1971-95', *Journal of the Asia Pacific Economy* 5 (1 and 2): 112-124

Shari, Ishak, and Ragayah Haji Mat Zin (1990) 'The Patterns and Trends of Income Distribution in Malaysia, 1970-1987', *Singapore Economic Review* XXXV (1): 102-123

Shepherd, Jack (1941) *Industry in Southeast Asia*, New York: Institute of Pacific Relations

Siamwalla, Ammar (1972) 'Land, Labour and Capital in Three Rice-Growing Deltas of Southeast Asia, 1800-1940', Center Discussion Paper no. 150, New Haven: Yale University Economic Growth Center

Simatupang, Pantjar, and C. Peter Timmer (2008) 'Indonesian Rice Production: Policies and Realities', *Bulletin of Indonesian Economic Studies* 44 (1): 65-80

Skoufias, Emmanual, Asep Suryahadi and Sudarno Sumarto (2000) 'Changes in Household Welfare, Poverty and Inequality during the Crisis', *Bulletin of Indonesian Economic Studies* 36 (2): 97-114

Slocomb, Margaret (2010) *An Economic History of Cambodia in the Twentieth Century*, Singapore: NUS Press

Smith, T.E. (1952) *Population Growth in Malaya: An Analysis of Recent Trends*, London: Royal Institute of International Affairs

Snodgrass, D.R. (1975a) 'The Fiscal System as an Income Distributor in West Malaysia', in David Lim (ed.), *Readings on Malaysian Economic Development*, Kuala Lumpur: Oxford University Press

Snodgrass, D.R. (1975b) 'Trends and Patterns in Malaysian Income Distribution', in David Lim (ed.), *Readings on Malaysian Economic Development*, Kuala Lumpur: Oxford University Press

Snodgrass, D.R. (1980) *Inequality and Economic Development in Malaysia*, Kuala Lumpur: Oxford University Press

Spencer, J.E. (1952) *Land and People in the Philippines: Geographic Problems in Rural Economy*, Berkeley: University of California Press

Srinivasan, T.N. (2010) 'Irrelevance of the $1-a-Day Poverty Line', in Sudhir Anand, Paul Segal and Joseph E. Stiglitz (eds), *Debates on the Measurement of Global Poverty*, Oxford: Oxford University Press

Statistique General de l'Indochine (1937) 'Naissances et deces dans la region de Saigon-Cholon en 1936', *Bulletin Economique de l'Indochine* 40: 823-834

Steinberg, David (1981) *Burma's Road toward Development: Growth and Ideology under Military Rule*, Boulder: Westview Press

Stewart, John R. (1949) *Japan's Textile Industry: A Report for the United Nations Economic Commission for Asia and the Far East*, New York: Institute of Pacific Relations

Suehiro, Akira (1981) 'Land Reform in Thailand: The Concept and Background of the Agricultural Land Reform Act of 1975', *Developing Economies* XIX (4): 314-347

Sugimoto, Ichiro (2011) *Economic Growth of Singapore in the Twentieth Century: Historical GDP Estimates and Empirical Investigations*, Singapore: World Scientific Publishing Co.

Summers, Robert, and Alan Heston (1991) 'The Penn World Table (Mark 5): An Expanded Set of International Comparisons, 1950-88', *Quarterly Journal of Economics* 106 (2): 327-366

Sundaram, Jomo Kwame (1988) *A Question of Class: Capital the State and Uneven Development in Malaya*, New York: Monthly Review Press

Sundrum, R.M. (1957) 'Population Statistics of Burma', Economics Research Project, Statistical Paper no. 3, Rangoon: Economics, Statistics and Commerce Departments, University of Rangoon

Sundrum, R.M., and Anne Booth (1980) 'Income Distribution in Indonesia: Trends and Determinants', in Ross Garnaut and Peter McCawley (eds), *Indonesia: Dualism, Growth and Poverty*, Canberra: Research School of Pacific Studies, Australian National University

Suratman and Patrick Guinness (1977) 'The Changing Focus of Transmigration', *Bulletin of Indonesian Economic Studies* 13 (2): 78-101

Szreter, Simon, and Graham Mooney (1998) 'Urbanization, Mortality, and the Standard of Living Debate: New Estimates of the Expectation of Life at Birth in Nineteenth-Century British Cities', *Economic History Review* 51 (1): 84-112

Tadem, Eduardo C. (2015) 'Philippine Agrarian Reform in the 21ˢᵗ Century', Discussion Note no. 2, Conference on Land Grabbing, Conflict and Agrarian-Environmental Transformation: Perspectives from East and Southeast Asia, Chiangmai University, June

Tan, E.A. (1975) 'Taxation, Government Spending and Income Distribution in the Philippines', in *Income Distribution, Employment and Economic Development in Southeast and East Asia: Papers and Proceedings of the Seminar Sponsored Jointly by the Japan Economic Research Center and the Council for Asian Manpower Studies*, Tokyo: The Japan Economic Research Center and the Council for Asian Manpower Studies

Tan, Edita, and Virginia Holazo (1979) 'Measuring Poverty Incidence in a Segmented Market: The Philippine Case', *Philippine Economic Journal* XVIII (4): 450-491

Tanzi, Vito (1996) 'Fiscal Federalism and Decentralization: A Review of Some Efficiency and Macroeconomic Aspects', in *Annual World Bank Conference on Development Economics 1995*, Washington, DC: World Bank

Tao, L.K. (1931) 'Food Consumption in the Chinese Standard of Living', in Bruno Lasker (ed.), *Problems of the Pacific 1931*, Chicago: University of Chicago Press

Taylor, A.J. (ed.) (1975) *The Standard of Living in Britain in the Industrial Revolution*, London: Methuen

Terwiel, B.J. (2011) *Thailand's Political History: From the 13ᵗʰ Century to Recent Times*, Bangkok: Riverside Books

Than, Mya, and Nobuyoshi Nishizawa (1990) 'Agricultural Policy Reforms and Agricultural Development in Myanmar', in Mya Than and Joseph L.H. Tan (eds), *Myanmar: Dilemmas and Options*, Singapore: ISEAS

Therborn, Göran (2013) *The Killing Fields of Inequality*, Cambridge: Polity Press

Thompson, E.P. (1968) *The Making of the English Working Class*, Harmondsworth: Penguin Books

Thompson, Virginia (1947) *Labor Problems in Southeast Asia*, New Haven: Yale University Press

Thompson, Virginia (1967) *Thailand: The New Siam* 2ⁿᵈ ed., New York: Paragon Book Reprint Corporation

Tigno, Jorge V. (2012) 'The Price of Rice and Politics of Poverty in the Philippines', in Aris Ananta and Richard Barichello (eds), *Poverty and Global Recession in Southeast Asia*, Singapore: ISEAS

Timmer, C. Peter (1996) 'Does Bulog Stabilise Rice Prices in Indonesia? Should It Try?', *Bulletin of Indonesian Economic Studies* 32 (2): 45-74

Timmer, C. Peter (2004) 'The Road to Pro-Poor Growth: Indonesia's Experience in Regional Perspective', *Bulletin of Indonesian Economic Studies* 40 (2): 177-207

Timmer, C. Peter (2015) 'The Dynamics of Agricultural Development and Food Security in Southeast Asia: Historical Continuity and Rapid Change', in Ian Coxhead (ed.), *Routledge Handbook of Southeast Asian Economics*, Abingdon: Routledge

Tinakorn, Prahee (1995) 'Industrialization and Welfare: How Poverty and Income Distribution Are Affected', in Medhi Krongkaew (ed.), *Thailand's Industrialization and Its Consequences*, London: Macmillan

TNP2K (2018) *Program Bantuan Pemerintah untuk Individu, Keluarga, dan Kelompok Tidak Mampu: Menuju Bantuan Sosial Terintegrasi* [The government program for individuals, families and backward groups: Towards integrated social protection: Executive summary], Jakarta: National Tean for the Acceleration of Poverty Reduction

Touzet, Andre (1939) *Le Probleme Colonial et La Paix du Monde, Vol. 1*, Paris: Librairie du Recueil Sirey

Tutor, Melba V. (2014) 'The Impact of Philippines' Conditional Cash Transfer Program on Consumption', Discussion Paper no. 2014-05, Quezon City: University of the Philippines School of Economics

UNDP (1991) *Human Development Report 1991*, New York: Oxford University Press for the United Nations Development Program

UNDP (1998) *Human Development in Myanmar: An Internal Report*, Yangon: United Nations Development Program

UNDP (2003) *Human Development Report*, New York: Oxford University Press for the United Nations Development Program

UNDP (2010) *Human Development Report 2010: The Real Wealth of Nations: Pathways to Human Development*, Basingstoke: Palgrave Macmillan for the UNDP

UNDP (2016) *Human Development Report 2016: Human Development for Everyone*, New York, United Nations

UNESCO (1957) *World Illiteracy at Mid-Century: A Statistical Study*, Paris: UNESCO

Unger, Danny, and Chandra Mahakanjana (2016) 'Decentralization in Thailand', *Journal of Southeast Asian Economies* 33 (2): 172-187

UNU-WIDER (2018) *World Income Inequality Database (WIID)*, December, Helsinki: UNU WIDER, https://www.wider.unu.edu/project/wiid-world-income-inequality-database, accessed 19 July 2019

USDA (2018) *Grain: World Markets and Trade* October, Washington, DC: United States Department of Agriculture, Foreign Agricultural Service

Utrecht, E. (1969) 'Land Reform in Indonesia', *Bulletin of Indonesian Economic Studies* 5 (3): 71-88

Van der Eng, Pierre (1995) 'An Inventory of Secular Changes in Human Growth in Indonesia', in J. Komlos (ed.), *The Biological Standard of Living in Three Continents: Further Explorations in Anthropometric History*, Boulder: Westview Press

Van der Eng, Pierre (1996) *Agricultural Growth in Indonesia*, Basingstoke: Macmillan Press

Van der Eng, Pierre (1998) 'Cassava in Indonesia: A Historical Re-appraisal of an Enigmatic Crop', *Tonan Ajia Kenkyu* [Southeast Asian studies] 36 (1): 3-31

Van der Eng, Pierre (2000) 'Food for Growth: Trends in Indonesia's Food Supply, 1880-1995', *Journal of Interdisciplinary History* 30 (4): 591-616

Van der Eng, Pierre (2002) 'Indonesia's Growth Performance in the Twentieth Century', in Angus Maddison, D.S. Prasada Rao and William Shepherd (eds), *The Asian Economies in the Twentieth Century*, Cheltenham: Edward Elgar

Van der Eng, Pierre (2010) 'The Sources of Long-term Growth in Indonesia, 1880-2008', *Explorations in Economic History* 47: 294-309

Van der Eng, Pierre (2013a) 'Historical National Accounts Data for Indonesia, 1880-2012', mimeo, Australian National University

Van der Eng, Pierre (2013b) 'Why Didn't Colonial Indonesia Have a Competitive Cotton Textile Industry?', *Modern Asian Studies* 47 (3): 1019-1054

Van Ginneken, Wouter (1976) *Rural and Urban Income Inequalities in Indonesia, Mexico, Pakistan, Tanzania and Tunisia*, Geneva: International Labour Office

Van Ginneken, Wouter, and Jong-goo Park (eds) (1984) *Generating Internationally Comparable Income Distribution Estimates*, Geneva: International Labour Office

Van Laanen, Jan T.M. (1990) 'Between the Java Bank and the Chinese Moneylender: Banking and Credit in Colonial Indonesia', in Anne Booth, W.J. O'Malley and Anna Weidemann (eds), *Indonesian Economic History in the Dutch Colonial Era*, New Haven: Yale University Southeast Asia Studies

Van Leeuwen, Bas, and Peter Foldvari (2016), 'The Development of Inequality and Poverty in Indonesia, 1932-2008', *Bulletin of Indonesian Economic Studies* 52 (3): 379-402

Van Leeuwen, Robert (1975) 'Central Government Subsidies for Regional Development', *Bulletin of Indonesian Economic Studies* 11 (1): 66-75

Van Niel, Robert (trans.) (1956) *Living Conditions of Plantation Workers in 1939-40: Final Report of the Coolie Budget Commission*, Ithaca: Department of Far Eastern Studies, Cornell University

Van Zanden, Jan L. (1999) 'Wages and the Standard of Living in Europe, 1500-1800', *European Review of Economic History* 2: 175-197

Van Zanden, Jan L. (2003) 'Rich and Poor before the Industrial Revolution: A Comparison between Java and the Netherlands at the Beginning of the 19th Century', *Explorations in Economic History* 40: 1-23

Van Zanden, Jan L., Joerg Baten, Marco Mira D'Ercole, Anke Rijpma, Conal Smith and Marcel Timmer (eds) (2014) *How Was Life? Global Well-being since 1820*, Paris: OECD Development Centre

Virola, Romulo A., Virginia N. Ganac and Christopher Ivo S. Bacani (2000) 'Poverty Assessment in the Philippines', NSCB Technical Papers no. 2000-002, Manila: National Statistical Coordination Board

Visaria, Leela, and Pravin Visaria (1983) 'Population (1757-1947)', in Dharma Kumar and Meghnad Desai (eds), *The Cambridge Economic History of India, Vol. 2: c. 1757-1970*, Cambridge: Cambridge University Press

Visaria, P. (1980) 'Poverty and Living Standards in Asia: An Overview of the Main Results and Lessons of Selected Household Surveys', Living Standards Measurement Study, Working Paper no. 2, Washington, DC: World Bank

Visman, F.H., et al. (1941) *Verslag van de Commissie tot Bestudeering van Staatrechtelijke Hervormingen*, Batavia: N.p.

Vlieland, C.A. (1932) *British Malaya: A Report on the 1931 Census and on Certain Problems of Vital Statistics*, London: Crown Agents

Wagstaff, Adam, and Nga Nguyet Nguyen (2004) 'Poverty and Survival Prospects of Vietnamese Children under Doi Moi', in Paul Glewwe, Nisha Agrawal and David Dollar (eds), *Economic Growth, Poverty and Household Welfare in Vietnam*, Washington, DC: The World Bank

Walinsky, Louis J. (1962) *Economic Development in Burma, 1951-60*, New York: Twentieth Century Fund

Warr, Peter (2005) 'Food Policy and Poverty in Indonesia: A General Equilibrium Analysis', *Australian Journal of Agricultural and Resource Economics* 49 (4): 429-451

Warr, Peter (2009) 'Poverty Reduction through Long-term Growth: The Thai Experience', *Asian Economic Papers* 8 (2): 51-76

Warr, Peter (2015) 'The Drivers of Poverty Reduction', in Ian Coxhead (ed.), *Routledge Handbook of Southeast Asian Economics*, Abingdon: Routledge

Warr, Peter, and Isra Sarntisart (2005) 'Poverty Targeting in Thailand', in John Weiss (ed.), *Poverty Targeting in Asia*, Cheltenham: Edward Elgar

Warr, Peter, and Wen-Thuen Wang (1999) 'Poverty, Inequality and Economic Growth in Taiwan', in Gustav Ranis and Hu Sheng-Cheng (eds), *The Political Economy of Development in Taiwan: Essays in Memory of John C.H. Fei*, Cheltenham: Edward Elgar

Warr, Peter, Sitthiroth Rasaphone and Jayant Menon (2015) 'Two Decades of Declining Poverty despite Rising Inequality in Laos', Working Papers in Trade and Development 2015/13, Canberra: ANU College of Asia and the Pacific, Australian National University

Wertheim, W.F. (1964) *East-West Parallels: Sociological Approaches to Modern Asia*, The Hague: W. van Hoeve Ltd

White, Benjamin (1991) 'Economic Diversification and Agrarian Change in Rural Java, 1900-1990', in Paul Alexander, Peter Boomgaard and Ben White (eds), *In the Shadow of Agriculture: Non-farm Activities in the Javanese Economy, Past and Present*, Amsterdam: Royal Tropical Institute

Wiegersma, Nancy (1988) *Vietnam, Peasant Land, Peasant Revolution; Patriarchy and Collectivity in the Rural Economy*, Basingstoke: Macmillan Press

Williamson, Jeffrey G. (1998) 'Real Wages and Relative Factor Prices in the Third World, 1820-1940: Asia', Discussion Paper no. 1844, Harvard Institute of Economic Research

Williamson, Jeffrey G. (2000) 'Globalization, Factor Prices and Living Standards in Asia before 1940', in A.J.H. Latham and Heita Kawakatsu (eds), *Asia Pacific Dynamism, 1550-2000*, London: Routledge

Williamson, Jeffrey G. (2011) *Trade and Poverty: When the Third World Fell Behind*, Cambridge, MA: MIT Press

Williamson, Jeffrey G. (2015) 'Trade, Growth and Distribution in Southeast Asia, 1500-1940', in Ian Coxhead (ed.), *Routledge Handbook of Southeast Asian Economics*, Abingdon: Routledge

Wood, Leonard (1926) *Report of the Governor General of the Philippine Islands 1924*, Washington, DC: Government Printing Office

World Bank (1980a) *Indonesia: Employment and Income Distribution in Indonesia: A World Bank Country Study*, Washington, DC: The World Bank

World Bank (1980b) *World Development Report, 1980*, Washington, DC: The World Bank

World Bank (1987) *Philippines: A Framework for Economic Recovery: A World Bank Country Study*, Washington, DC: The World Bank

World Bank (1988) *Indonesia: The Transmigration Program in Perspective*, Washington, DC: The World Bank

World Bank (1990) *World Development Report, 1990: Poverty*, Washington, DC: The World Bank

World Bank (1993) *The East Asian Miracle: Economic Growth and Public Policy*, Oxford: Oxford University Press

World Bank (1995) *Vietnam: Poverty Assessment and Strategy*, Washington, DC: World Bank East Asia and Pacific Region

World Bank (2001) *World Development Report, 2001*, Washington, DC: The World Bank

World Bank (2014a) *Purchasing Power Parities and Real Expenditures of World Economies: Summary of Results and Findings of the 2011 International Comparison Program*, Washington, DC: World Bank

World Bank (2014b) *Where Have All the Poor Gone? Cambodia Poverty Assessment, 2013: A World Bank Country Study*, Washington, DC: World Bank

World Bank (2017) *Monitoring Global Poverty: Report of the Commission on Global Poverty*, Washington, DC: World Bank Group

World Bank (2018) *The Human Capital Project*, Washington, DC: The World Bank

World Bank and Australian Aid (2015a) *A Perceived Divide: How Indonesians Perceive Inequality and What They Want Done about It*, Jakarta: World Bank Office

World Bank and Australian Aid (2015b) *Taxes and Public Spending in Indonesia: Who Pays and Who Benefits?*, Jakarta: World Bank Office

World Bank and Australian Aid (2016) *Indonesia's Rising Divide*, Jakarta: World Bank Office

World Economic Forum (2017a) *The Global Gender Gap Report 2017*, Geneva: World Economic Forum

World Economic Forum (2017b) *The Global Human Capital Report 2017*, Geneva: World Economic Forum

World Economic Forum (2018) *The Inclusive Development Index 2018*, Geneva: World Economic Forum

Yoshihara, Kunio (1988) *The Rise of Ersatz Capitalism in South-east Asia*, Singapore: Oxford University Press

Yusuf, Arief Anshory, and Peter Warr (2018) 'Anti-globalisation, Poverty and Inequality in Indonesia', in Arianto A., Mari Pangestu and M. Chatib Basri (eds), *Indonesia in the New World: Globalisation, Nationalism and Sovereignty*, Singapore: ISEAS Yusof Ishak Institute

Zablan, Z.C. (1978) 'Trends and Differential in Mortality', in *Population of the Philippines*, Bangkok, United Nations Economic Commission for Asia and the Pacific

Zeldin, Theodore (1981) *France 1848-1945: Anxiety and Hypocrisy*, Oxford: Oxford University Press

Zimmerman, Carle (1936) *Consumption and Standards of Living*, New York: Van Nostrand and Co.

Zimmerman, Carle C. (1999) *Siam Rural Economic Survey 1930-31*, Bangkok: White Lotus

Index